DATE DUE

BRODART, CO.   Cat. No. 23-221

Categorizing Cognition

Toward Conceptual Coherence in the Foundations of Psychology

Graeme S. Halford, William H. Wilson, Glenda Andrews,
and Steven Phillips

The MIT Press
Cambridge, Massachusetts
London, England

MIT Press books may be purchased at special quantity discounts for business or sales promotional use. For information, please email special_sales@mitpress.mit.

This book was set in Stone Sans and Stone Serif by Toppan Best-set Premedia Limited. Printed and bound in the United States of America.

Library of Congress Cataloging-in-Publication Data

Halford, Graeme S.
 Categorizing cognition : toward conceptual coherence in the foundations of psychology / Graeme S. Halford, William H. Wilson, Glenda Andrews, and Steven Phillips.
     pages cm
 Includes bibliographical references and index.
 ISBN 978-0-262-02807-3 (hardcover : alk. paper)
 1. Cognition. 2. Categorization (Psychology) 3. Concepts. I. Title.
 BF311.H288 2014
 153.01—dc23
                        2014013236

10 9 8 7 6 5 4 3 2 1

For Kylie Chellew-Halford, Odette Chellew-Halford,
and Amelia Chellew-Halford
For Debbie Street
For George and Millie Hohl
For Dalva Phillips

Contents

Plan of Chapters

Chapters are intended to follow the logical development of the argument, but they can be read in a different order. For example, some readers might prefer to read chapters 4 and 5 before chapters 2 and 3, and since chapter 10 presents the "takeaway" message, some readers might prefer to read that first. For all readers' reference, there is a road map for the book at the end of chapter 1.

Preface

Conceptual coherence is of great value in all sciences—a fact illustrated by the importance of the periodic table in chemistry and the classification system in biology. Such conceptual coherence has proved elusive in psychology so far, but several important lines of progress in the last few decades have made it more possible. These include relational knowledge, a cognitive complexity metric that has a high degree of generality, new conceptions of working memory, detailed and penetrating conceptions of human reasoning, and identification of the properties of the major categories of cognitive processes. In this book, we utilize these advances to propose a categorization of cognition based on core properties of the constituent processes. Our formulation is based on numerous demonstrated correspondences between cognitive processes with similar underlying structures but different surface properties. We also have shown that there is a mathematical basis for these correspondences that are therefore not coincidental.

Coherence depends on finding the right criteria for assigning phenomena to categories, which in turn depends on discovering the fundamental properties of key phenomena. Higher cognition is distinguished by the representation of the structure of tasks and situations. These representations have to be accessible to a wide range of processes, including some that are applicable beyond the situation where the representation was learned, and they must do more than compute outputs. For example, higher cognitive representations enable mappings between representations based on common structure, permitting content-independent transfer and providing a means to adapt to as-yet-unforeseen situations. We proposed a long time ago that the structure of representations could form the basis of a system for categorizing cognitive processes, and experience has shown that the categorizations hold up over a wide range of paradigms and domains. Categories based on common sense or traditional distinctions such as abstract versus concrete are inadequate for the purpose of achieving coherence.

While conducting a very extensive reading of the literature covering a wide range of topics, going back several decades, we have thought carefully about the possibilities for achieving coherence, and now we are convinced that at least the beginning of a coherent formulation is feasible. Our reading of the literature has provided multiple examples of contradictions and inconsistencies, and we have found that they can be resolved by our categorization. The relational knowledge literature that has developed over the last three decades has been important for providing the means to a coherent formulation. From this literature, we have identified dynamic structural alignment as the foundational property of higher cognition, as discussed in chapter 2.

We have found that bringing areas of advancing knowledge together has led to unexpected solutions to some fundamental issues. For example, by integrating relational knowledge, a contemporary theory of working memory, and longstanding findings in infant cognition, we have been able to devise a new approach to the origin of symbolic processes. As a result, some performances in infancy can be seen to reflect symbolic processes, albeit of a simple kind. In addition, we have seen links between processes observed in infant cognition and fundamental language processes. Thus, the dynamic creation of bindings in working memory between objects and locations can be seen as essentially the same process as the assignment of words to roles in sentence comprehension. This has been proposed in chapters 2 and 6.

Many advances have made a coherent categorization of cognition feasible. Working memory now can be measured with greater precision using latent variable techniques, and it has been shown to be a major factor in reasoning and intelligence. It has been shown to play a major role in reasoning and higher cognition generally and is essential to the establishment of representations used in symbolic processes. In addition, working memory provides a new way of handling the question of individual and developmental differences in capacity. The nature of symbolic processes is also better understood. Attempts to avoid postulating symbolic processes in the past have tended to obscure fundamental differences in cognitive processes. A task performed symbolically can be very different from one performed by subsymbolic processes, and reluctance to recognize this fact can lead to confusion, inconsistency, and proliferation of exceptions.

Extensive research has shown that it is not possible to define a cognitive process solely by the behavior that it manifests. Using the classical conditional discrimination task, we show that an instance of the task can be performed by any of three distinct cognitive processes, each with a unique set of properties. These processes are discriminable by established, objective methodologies. Each category of cognition corresponds to processes that are performed in many other tasks and paradigms. Thus, a cognitive process in the conditional discrimination paradigm might relate to a process in another possibly very different paradigm, more than to another process performed in conditional discrimination. Therefore, a single set of observed behaviors does not permit categorization of the relevant cognitive process.

There has been resistance to attempts to achieve coherence for a number of reasons. Explanation of all cognition by a single set of processes sometimes has been seen as more desirable, or more parsimonious, than categorization of cognitive processes. However, parsimony is not achieved by theories that produce inconsistencies and exceptions, and we propose that a categorization based on foundational properties yields both coherence and parsimony. There also has been a tendency to avoid foundational issues, and concentration on exciting findings of previously unknown capabilities has discouraged the investigation of species differences and developmental progressions. We do not deny the achievements in animal cognition and cognitive development, but we have shown that their significance is actually increased by defining their place in a coherent conception of cognition. Large accumulated databases on infant and animal cognition entail both the need and the opportunity to identify the core properties that distinguish different levels of cognition. Cognitive complexity and processing capacity have been eschewed in much of the research conducted in recent decades because they are seen as conflicting with efforts to demonstrate cognitive precocity in infants and young children and/or to attribute humanlike cognitions in other animal species. However, this has often led to fragmentation and inconsistency, as when higher cognitions are attributed on the basis of very restricted criteria.

Cognitive complexity and its corollary, cognitive capacity, also have been neglected in applied cognition. Complexity is a major issue in 21st-century life as well as in cognitive psychology, and we propose to give it at least some of the attention that it deserves. In chapter 4, we show how the usual objections to these concepts are without validity. In chapter 9, we provide a brief sketch of how our theory can be applied to practical issues in human factors, based on our own experience of consultation in that field.

The purpose of this book is to provide at least a beginning of a categorization system that will yield the coherence that often has been advocated for psychology, but never achieved.

Acknowledgments

There are many collaborators and mentors who deserve credit for their contributions to research in this work. These include Antonio Ciampi, John Bain, Roderick McDonald, John Keats, Michael Humphreys, Alan Baddeley, Cathy Brown, Paul Bakker, Keith Holyoak, Michael Chapman, Donald Broadbent, Julie McCredden, Geoffrey Goodwin, Rosemary Baker, Mavis Kelly, Janet Wiles, John Flavell, Nelson Cowan, Mark Chappell, Deanna Kuhn, Gillian Boulton-Lewis, Ross Gayler, Henry Markovits, Janie Busby, Toni Jones, Lyn English, Elizabeth Leitch, Damian Birney, Kerry Chalmers, Brett Gray, Christine Boag, Kevin Collis, John Sheppard, Robbie Case, Pierre Barrouillet, Philip Johnson-Laird, Usha Goswami, Robert Siegler, James Dixon, Peter Bryant, Brentyn Ramm, Murray Maybery, Dianne Bennett, Susan Smith, Tracey Zielinski, Candida Peterson, Henry Wellman, Philip Zelazo, Jason Mattingley, Kalina Christoff, Luca Cocchi, Tim Cutmore, Tony Simon, Klaus Oberauer, Campbell Dickson, Paul Stanley, and Bonnie Ingram.

We also would like to mention our family and friends for their patience, support, and forbearance.

1 Introduction and Statement of the Problem

All sciences need ways to classify the phenomena that they investigate. Consider, for example, what chemistry would be like without the periodic table, or biology without the taxonomic system for classifying life forms. Scientific classifications are based on core properties of phenomena that are most strongly related to other properties. Thus, chemical elements are classified in the periodic table by their atomic weight, which is linked to many fundamental properties such as valence (see, e.g., Luder, 1943; Mayr & Bock, 2008). Biological classifications are based on evolutionary history and structural features such as the type of skeleton or nervous system (Atran, 1993). Classifications are often counterintuitive. For example, whereas the layperson might categorize the European hedgehog, the North American porcupine, and the Australian echidna together because they all possess spines, in biology, they belong to three different families of mammals. The hedgehog belongs to an order of insectivorous mammals, which classifies it with the shrews and moles, while the porcupine is classified with rodents, along with rats, squirrels, rabbits, and capybaras. The echidna, an egg-laying mammal, is classified with the only other monotreme, the platypus. Thus, reliance on superficial properties, such as having spines, would be misleading.

Here, we will not try to imitate other sciences in developing a classificatory system, but we will take one point from the work of people like Dmitri Mendeleev with the periodic table, or the work of such legendary figures as Carl Linnaeus, Alfred Russel Wallace, and Charles Darwin in biology: that coherence requires a very wide-ranging examination of the scientific phenomena studied in the field. It is unlikely to be achieved by examining specific paradigms, nor will it result solely from applying the scientific method (Edelman, 2012). Detailed reviews of the literature are essential to ensure consistency with the database, but there is also a need to focus on properties that transcend individual paradigms and phenomena. As Meiser

(2011) notes: "As a consequence of the focus on single paradigms, commonalities of research questions and findings across different paradigms are easily overlooked, and theoretical accounts are closely tied to the features of the experimental paradigm rather than to unifying theoretical frameworks" (p. 186). This does not diminish the importance of empirical science, and cross-paradigm assessment needs to be balanced with a commitment to well-established empirical findings. We agree with Garcia-Marques and Ferreira (2011) when they point out that good experiments have a life of their own and are "one of the most important sources of scientific progress" (p. 197). Therefore, each category of cognitive process must be identified by empirical procedures.

In this book, we will present evidence of important underlying similarities between seemingly different tasks, and conversely, there are cases of apparent similarity that entail very different core processes. We will attempt to define a system that facilitates the discovery of general principles, thereby taking a step toward overcoming the isolation and fragmentation of theory that has plagued psychology. We recognize that a classificatory system can be valid only with respect to certain purposes of a science, and no perfect system is possible (Dupré, 2006). Nevertheless, cognitive science and psychology have clear purposes that are sufficient to make an attempt at scientific classification worthwhile. The periodic table classifies elements rather than compounds, and the system that we shall describe classifies relatively basic versions of cognitive tasks but also allows compound processes, such as the combination of heuristic and analytic processes in the model of Evans (2006), discussed later in this chapter (and shown in figure 1.1). As with many other scientific classifications, exceptions are probably inevitable, but we have found that a number of apparent exceptions turn out to be quite consistent with our formulation when examined more closely. Thus, true exceptions are rare.

One potential benefit of a coherent theory of cognitive processes is that it would lead to fruitful hypotheses for the acquisition of higher cognitive functions. We will demonstrate that symbolic processes, which are often a source of difficulty in mathematics and science education (Smith, 2007), depend on structural alignment, which has considerable potential to provide improved educational methods.

Perhaps most important, a coherent conceptual structure will assist with the interpretation of empirical results, as it does in other sciences. In psychology, however, there is no such coherent framework, and interpretations often depend on the presuppositions and even the ambitions of the researchers concerned with the paradigm. For example, if infants

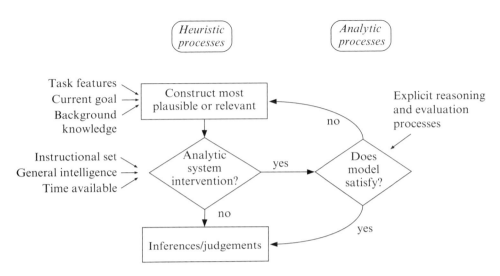

Figure 1.1
Proposed interaction between heuristic and analytic processes. Adapted from Evans (2006, figure 3), by permission of Springer Science and Business Media.

are observed to perform in a way that matches the abilities of older children or adults in certain (often very limited) respects, or if other species exhibit abilities that would be a challenge to humans, does this argue against age or species differences? At present, there is no systematic way to deal with such issues because we lack definitions of the core properties of higher cognition, with no clear or generally valid way to differentiate them from other levels of cognitive performance. Given that even the best-controlled experiments yield results that are compatible with a large (theoretically infinite) array of interpretations, selection of the most valid interpretation can be a major challenge. A more coherent theory of cognition can provide at least some worthwhile indicators to overcome the limitations that are inherent in empirical investigation.

We find common ground with Stenning and van Lambalgen (2008) when they say: "A corollary of the lack of background abstract theories in psychology is the use of direct operationalization of abstract concepts in experimental procedures: data categories are assumed to be very closely related to their theoretical categories. As a consequence, the data observed are supposed to have a direct bearing on the theoretical hypotheses. In mature sciences this doesn't happen. There are always 'bridging' inferences required between observation and theory, and an apparent falsification may direct attention to unwarranted auxiliary assumptions." (p. 17). We will consider Stenning and van Lambalgen's proposals in relation to our own, together with other contemporary conceptions of reasoning, in chapter 8. We also have common ground with Mausfeld (2012), who argues that interpretation of neuroscience findings based on tacit common sense or on prevailing vogues can be misleading and detrimental. He also states that we take for granted, and therefore fail to notice, "those mental aspects ... that pertain to the most fundamental principles of our mental make-up ... these aspects will pass unnoticed exactly *because* of their foundational nature." (p. 7; italics in original). We propose that interpretation of empirical findings on the basis of foundational or core properties is essential to both behavioral and neuroscience research. We recognize that achieving this goal is not easy, but we are confident that the science has progressed to the point where it is realistic to move in the direction that Mausfeld suggests.

Classification of cognitive tasks must be based on core properties, which raises the question whether we have sufficient foundational knowledge to develop a worthwhile classificatory system in psychology. From many years of careful consideration of thousands of scientific publications and reviews, ranging over many domains in cognitive science, cognitive development, and animal cognition, we believe that the required knowledge exists. There is now a huge empirical database, as well as associated models, of cognitive processes in human and other animal species, and a similarly rich store of information about development of cognition across the human lifespan. A critically important consideration is the existence of ingenious methodologies for studying underlying cognitive processes as being distinct from their surface manifestations. Great progress has been made in the study of specific processes, such as concept acquisition, reasoning strategies, working memory, and the nature of intelligence, which enables insights that would not have been possible in previous decades.

There are also highly successful unified theories of cognition, most notably the Soar cognitive architecture (Newell, 1990; Simon, Newell, & Klahr, 1991) and Adaptive Control of Thought—Rational (ACT-R; Anderson, 1993, 2005; Anderson et al., 2004). These theories have been enormously influential and have been considerable help to us in a number of ways. We utilized them in developing the Transitive Inference Mapping Model (TRIMM; Halford et al., 1995) which is a self-modifying production system model of the development of transitive inference strategies that is discussed in chapter 6. More important, they show how higher cognitive processes can emerge from basic functions such as spreading activation, representation of goal hierarchies, and the interaction of semantic networks and production rules (Anderson et al., 2004). The integrated memory model of Humphreys, Wiles, and Dennis (1994) also contributes to coherence in the field by showing that human memory processes can be categorized by the properties of data structures and operations, independent of specific implementations. They define their aim thus: "We try to identify a finite set of functions (computational primitives) out of which all other functions can be composed" (Humphreys, Wiles, & Dennis, 1994, p. 656). Marsh and Boag (2013) propose an integration of evolutionary adaptive processes with the study of individual differences as a way of increasing conceptual coherence and explanatory power in the discipline. These formulations share a concern for greater theoretical depth and breadth. The now rapidly growing field of cognitive neuroscience also provides an important additional source of data that facilitates the interpretation of behavioral research findings.

It might be asked why we are proposing a new theory when so much excellent theorizing already exists. Part of the answer is that we still see a need for more coherence in the discipline, as illustrated by the many examples that we examine. More important, we have found that complexity of the information required to recognize correspondence between cognitive representations is a consistent discriminator of cognitive levels across widely differing paradigms. Therefore, we propose that cognitive psychology and cognitive science have progressed to the point where we can make at least a first attempt to define the type of classification system that psychology seriously needs, but so conspicuously lacks. This admittedly ambitious goal is the subject of this book.

Box 1.1
De Neys's experiment

De Neys (2006) tested adults with three levels of working memory spans on syllogistic reasoning tasks that varied in logical validity and believability. For example, they might be given, "All fruits can be eaten *and* hamburgers can be eaten," and asked whether the conclusion "Hamburgers are fruits" logically follows from the premises. He also used three levels of a conflicting working memory load. The results are shown in figure 1.2 (Fig. 2, de Neys 2006).

Box 1.1
(continued)

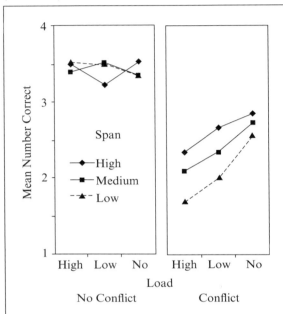

Figure 1.2
Results of the study by de Neys (2006). Adapted from de Neys (2006), figure 2, copyright © 2006 by Sage Publications. Reproduced by permission of Sage Publications.

The subjects needed analytic reasoning when logical validity and believability were in conflict, and in this condition, reasoning performance was related to both working memory span and size of conflicting load. Where there was no conflict between validity and believability, heuristics would produce correct answers. In this condition, there was no effect of span or conflicting load. This experiment neatly demonstrates that people can operate on a heuristic level or on an analytic level, and that the latter depends more on working memory. This study also provides a neat illustration of *converging operations* in cognitive science research. Three factors, comprising logical validity versus believability, working memory span, and conflicting working memory load, converge on the study of heuristic and analytic processes.

First, some caveats. Acceptance of some of our proposals might entail rethinking some well-accepted interpretations of the literature, but we aim to show how findings in areas as diverse as infancy and animal intelligence can be interpreted more systematically using the proposed theory. We suggest that this is worthwhile because it results in greater conceptual coherence, which in turn can increase parsimony by providing more powerful principles that integrate a large number of otherwise disparate phenomena. Another proviso is that we cannot classify cognitive processes solely by their observable behaviors, even though much of our data comes from behavioral measures, because the same cognitive process might be manifest in a number of distinct behaviors, while distinct cognitive processes might be manifest in the same behavior in some contexts. This is not a major obstacle because the methodologies developed in psychology and cognitive science provide ways of identifying underlying processes using converging operations, such as those used by Paivio (1971) to investigate imagery, or by Just and Carpenter (1992) to identify some of the underlying cognitive processes in language. A good example of converging operations in cognitive science is De Neys (2006), discussed in box 1.1. We cannot categorize cognitive processes by paradigms because, as we will soon illustrate, the same or similar paradigms might relate to very different cognitions. There is no alternative to seeking the core processes that underlie our phenomena of interest, and the accumulated contributions in the field make this an achievable goal.

Some of the phenomena that we discuss might also seem rather unfashionable, even passé. This occurs because we have gone back into the history of the discipline in an effort to create a coherent system. Thus, we include elemental association as a cognitive process in our schema (Humphrey, 1951, 1963). This is necessary because these phenomena have a place in the spectrum of cognitive processes regardless of their current status. Furthermore, some longstanding findings are more "settled" and less subject to controversy, which makes it easier to discern properties and relationships that are fundamental to coherence. Another reason for considering long-established findings is that we propose reinterpretations that *increase* the significance of some phenomena. An example would be the learning set, or learning-to-learn paradigm, which originated with Harlow (1949). This has traditionally been interpreted as discrimination learning by reinforcement (Medin, 1972; Reese, 1963), but in chapter 6, we argue that some versions of it can be a means by which structured, symbolic processes emerge from experience with isomorphs. Another example is that some of the findings arising from the work of Piaget (1950) become much more consistent with other literature if interpreted in terms of our formulation (Halford & Andrews, 2006). The age differences that Piaget and his collaborators observed can largely be attributed to development of the ability to process greater complexity (Andrews & Halford, 2011), and to structured knowledge acquisition processes that are not yet well known, but that we discuss further in chapter 4.

Finally, perhaps the most important proviso of all is that reinterpretation in no way implies denigration. In our efforts to formulate a more coherent account of cognition, we have studied the highest-quality research contributions in many paradigms, and we believe that their significance increases rather than decreases from integration into a coherent system. For brevity, we cite reviews wherever possible, but our conclusions are based on an intensive and wide-ranging analysis of the literature.

Types of cognition

We begin with a brief review of the numerous distinctions that have been made between types or levels of cognitive processes. Thus, Norman (1986) notes "two modes of operation, one rapid, efficient, subconscious, the other slow, serial, and conscious" (p. 542). Other distinctions include automatic versus controlled cognition (Logan, 1979; Schneider & Shiffrin, 1977), implicit versus explicit (Clark & Karmiloff-Smith, 1993; Karmiloff-Smith, 1990), associative versus rule-based (Sloman, 1996, 2002), and associative versus analytic (Oberauer, 2009).

In a different genre, Piaget (1950) proposed four major stages: the sensorimotor, preoperational, concrete operational, and formal operational, each of which features a number of substages. The preoperational stage comprises two major substages, the preconceptual and intuitive, which correspond to different levels in our categorization. Each stage is characterized by a different type of cognitive process, which Piaget attempted to capture by distinct psychologics (Piaget, 1957). The number of attempts to define distinct levels attests to the widespread perception that some kind of distinction is necessary. However, an important reservation is that a single system can operate at more than one level (alternatively, one reasoner can operate at two levels of system, with distinct processing demands, as posited by De Neys [2006]; see box 1.1). Regardless of terminology, the important point is that distinct processes do not necessarily imply different systems. It is also possible that distinct processes might reflect an underlying continuum (Bonner & Newell, 2010). However, defining component levels would be an important step to defining this continuum, and some of our proposals, such as those relating to development of working memory, provide insights into a possible continuum of cognitive capacity.

There have been several important attempts to systematize the distinctions that have been defined by other authors. Evans (2003) proposed that the distinction between System 1 and System 2 cognition, adopted from Stanovich & West (2000), captures the essential differences between levels of cognitive processes. System 1 is rapid, parallel, automatic, and relatively effortless, and only the products are posted in consciousness. System 1 includes both associative and innate (or modular) processes; it is evolutionarily and developmentally early and is less likely to be impaired by brain damage than System 2. System 2 is slow and sequential, is limited in capacity, and is more highly correlated with intelligence than System 1 (Stanovich & West, 2000). There is a continuing controversy about this formulation (see Evans & Stanovich [2013a,b]). We will propose our own categories for cognition that are motivated by the need for conceptual coherence and do not presuppose distinct systems.

The System 1/System 2 distinction can be linked to a number of other discussions of similar issues. System 2 is more analytic, whereas System 1 processes depend more on heuristics and retrieval from memory. System 1 is modifiable by (usually incremental) adjustments as a function of experience, whereas System 2 knowledge is strategically modifiable by other cognitive processes, such as hypothesis testing and switching between strategies. System 2 depends on brain structures that evolved more recently (Penn et al., 2012), and are slower to develop in humans. System 1 and System 2 are not mutually exclusive in humans (De Neys, 2006); in reasoning and language, they are mutually supportive. Explicit computational models can account for the selection of different systems depending on reinforcement history (Frank, Cohen, & Sanfey, 2009), and they can be integrated, as in the CLARION model (Sun & Zhang, 2004). System 2 processes are typically applied to knowledge acquired through System 1.

Evans (2006) developed this position further with an extension of his earlier (Evans, 1984) heuristic-analytic theory. The essence of Evans's position here is that the most plausible or relevant mental model is constructed based on heuristic processes that take account of task features, current goal, and background knowledge. The model is assessed by the analytic system based on instructional set, general intelligence (strongly identified with working memory capacity), and time available. If the model is accepted, it is used to generate inferences or judgments. An important feature of this theory is that it contains a plausible blend of heuristic and analytic processes, both of which have been shown to be important in reasoning, as discussed in chapter 2. The power of the theory is increased further by the proposal that mental models include beliefs as well as knowledge and can incorporate hypothetical and suppositional information. Evans also distinguishes between dual-process and dual-system accounts of cognition. We accept this distinction because dual processes refer to distinct types of cognitive processes, but they do not necessarily imply qualitative differences. We will propose several levels of cognitive process, but all can exist within the same cognitive system. They operate in interdependent fashion, with higher systems superimposed on lower ones.

However, Evans (2008) has developed the level distinction even further by postulating Type 1 and Type 2 processes operating within one system. This expresses the consensus that fast, automatic, and unconscious (Type 1) processes are distinct from those that are slow, effortful, and conscious (Type 2), while avoiding the implication of distinct systems. Evans (2008) suggests that "Type 2 processes are those that require access to a single, capacity-limited central working memory resource, while Type 1 processes do not require such access" (p. 270). Evans also notes that Type 1 processes are more diverse and less unified than Type 2 processes. To avoid unnecessary complications, we will include associative and modular processes under Type 1. Because working memory is highly correlated with fluid intelligence (Kane et al., 2004; Oberauer, 2009), Type 2 processes are more highly correlated with intelligence than Type 1, as noted previously by Stanovich and West (2000). Other properties of System 1 and System 2 are retained. Type 2 processes include the kinds of operations that are needed to support symbolic processes, such as constructing mental models used in deductive inference (Johnson-Laird & Byrne, 2002; Johnson-Laird, 2010). The distinction between Type 1 and Type 2 processes provides a starting point for the categorization that we will propose. This distinction is corroborated by findings that Type 1 and Type 2 cognitive tasks activate different neural networks (Goel & Dolan, 2003) but this does not necessarily imply distinct systems. Oberauer (2009) has integrated the distinction with an innovative conception of working memory, to be reviewed in chapter 3, and proposes that associative and analytic systems are end points of a continuum, arising from interacting subsystems of working memory. The demands made by analytic reasoning on working memory resources are demonstrated by De Neys (2006; see box 1.1).

Phillips, Halford, and Wilson (1995) have proposed that the distinction between implicit and explicit knowledge is captured by a distinction between associative and relational knowledge. This is consistent with the proposal of Morewedge and Kahneman (2010), who identify System 1 with associative processes. We will elaborate on this in chapter 2. We propose that relational knowledge is the basis of higher cognition (Halford et al., 2010) and that it is the essence of Type 2 cognition as defined by Evans (2008). Relational knowledge plays a role in reasoning processes such as mental models (Goodwin & Johnson-Laird, 2005; Johnson-Laird & Byrne, 1991; Johnson-Laird, 2010) and analogy (Gentner, 1983, 2010; Halford, 1992; Hofstadter, 2001; Holyoak & Thagard, 1995; Holyoak, 2012). Mapping between relational representations also has been proposed to distinguish human cognition from that of other animals (Penn, Holyoak, & Povinelli, 2008a,b). If animals are taught to choose a pair of items that are the same (AA), then, if tested on other pairs that are the same (BB) or different (BC), they should choose the pair (BB) that matches the relation they have been taught to recognize. The question is whether they can do this by purely perceptual judgments, or whether they actually represent a relation of sameness that goes beyond perception (Penn, Holyoak & Povinelli, 2008a §2.2). Consideration of this issue depends on defining the properties of relational representations and devising procedures for identifying them empirically.

Higher cognition has often been characterized as rule-based, and relations and rules are similar to the extent that any rule can be expressed as a relation, as both rules and relations can be represented as sets of ordered n-tuples [e.g., {(red, stop), (green, go), ...}]. Relations also accommodate both rule-based and probabilistic inferences (Halford, Wilson, & Phillips, 2010). However, relations have properties that are not explicitly identified with rules (e.g., see table 1 in Sloman, 1996). Relations also have been more prominent in reasoning processes such as analogy and mental models, which are not necessarily rule-based, and in transfers across different domains of knowledge. In chapter 6, we will consider how the properties of relational knowledge contribute to the symbolic transition.

However, Type 1 and Type 2 processes have distinct properties that must be taken into account in any systematic theory that integrates across paradigms. Quite a lot of the discussions in this book will be devoted to procedures by which these types can be distinguished empirically, including both behavioral and neuroscience measures. In chapter 2, we will propose a new classification of cognitive processes that incorporates the distinction between Type 1 and Type 2 processes and subsumes the distinction between subsymbolic and symbolic processes. In the next section, we will consider transitivity as an example of tasks that require a new classificatory system to remove inconsistencies and anomalies.

Transitivity: Two paradigms for one task

Transitive inference is fundamental to much of the reasoning process (James, 1890), and it relates closely to processes that have even wider relevance, such as premise integration (Halford, 1984; Andrews & Halford, 2002; Maybery, Bain, & Halford, 1986). Given premises *aRb* and *bRc*, where *R* is a transitive relation, then *aRc* can be inferred (e.g., if $a > b$ and $b > c$, then $a > b > c$ and $a > c$). One way to make this inference is to integrate the premises into an ordered triple, *aRbRc* (e.g., $a > b > c$). Integration of premises in this way also occurs in other forms of reasoning, such as categorical syllogisms (which will be discussed in chapter 8), and is arguably a fundamental process in deductive inference. We make frequent reference to these processes in developing our argument.

In this section, we will consider two very different paradigms, both of which have been used to assess transitivity. These have been classified by Goel (2007) as implicit and explicit transitivity, but for reasons that will become apparent, we will refer to them as the *transitivity of choice paradigm* and the *transitive inference paradigm,* respectively.

The transitivity of choice paradigm

The transitivity of choice paradigm was developed from a study of transitivity in young children by Bryant and Trabasso (1971). It has the advantage that it permits a wide range of species and procedures to be compared within the same paradigm. As we will show in chapter 5, it illustrates how distinct levels of cognitive processes can be produced with only minor differences in procedure, and it also shows how the levels can be distinguished by theoretical analysis. A seminal study was that of McGonigle and Chalmers (1977), who trained squirrel monkeys to choose one member of each pair in a series (*A+B−*, *B+C−*, *C+D−*, *D+E−*, where + indicates a rewarded choice and − indicates nonrewarded choice). To assess transitivity of choice, they were tested on untrained nonadjacent pairs, with the most interest focused on *B* and *D*, because *B+* and *B−* had occurred equally often in training, as had *D+* and *D−*. Monkeys showed a 90 percent preference for *B* over *D*, and basically similar data have been found with species ranging from pigeons (von Fersen et al., 1991) to chimpanzees (Boysen et al., 1993) and human children (Chalmers & McGonigle, 1984; see also Bryant and Trabasso, 1971). The basis on which these discriminations can be made will be a major consideration in the rest of this work.

Transitive inference

Transitive inference, although superficially similar to transitivity of choice, has important differences, one of which is that there is considerably more evidence that it is typically performed with a representation of structure. Consider this problem: John is taller than Peter, and Michael is taller than John; who is tallest? This can be processed by ordering the elements according to size in working memory: i.e., (Michael, John, Peter). From this, we can state that "Michael is taller than Peter", implying that Michael is the tallest (Halford, 1993; Halford et al., 2010; Riley & Trabasso, 1974; Sternberg, 1980). This representation can be constructed by integrating the premises, as shown in figure 1.3. An ordering schema, such as top-bottom or left-right, can serve as a template for construction of the integrated representation. However, the representation is validated by correspondence to the premises, a matter to which we will devote considerable discussion (see also Goodwin & Johnson-Laird, 2005). This type of transitive inference is typically mastered at a median age of approximately five years (Andrews & Halford, 1998, 2002; Pears & Bryant, 1990).

This transitive inference differs from transitivity of choice in several ways:

1. In transitive inference, there is a representation of the elements (Michael, John, Peter) ordered according to the relation in the premise. The representation is explicit in that the elements retain their identity in the integrated representation, and the relation is represented in the sense that participants are aware at some level that the elements are ordered with respect to that relation. By contrast, in transitivity of choice, there is no scale underlying the relationship (Markovits & Dumas, 1992), and the ordering is sometimes attributable to the relative strength of association

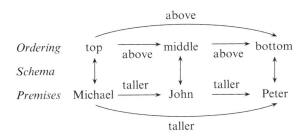

Figure 1.3
Premises mapped into an ordering schema in a transitive inference task.

between elements and responses e.g., the choice response is most strongly associated with A and most weakly with E (Wynne, 1995), as discussed further in chapter 2. There is also a limited ability to recover components of the relationship, as we will see when we consider theoretical models in more detail in chapter 2.

2. In transitive inference, there is a valid transitive inference because if we know aRb and bRc, where R is a transitive relation, then aRc necessarily follows. By contrast, transitivity of choice tasks contain implicit inferences of the form: A is rewarded and B is not, B is rewarded and C is not; therefore, A is rewarded and C is not. In a logical sense, this is an invalid inference because "rewarded/nonrewarded" is not a transitive relation. The task can be performed because the association between B and $R+$ is stronger than between D and $R+$ (Wynne, 1995). The lack of structure in transitivity of choice makes it natural for it to be performed by means other than logical reasoning.

The representation in transitive inference can be constructed in working memory, which can (at least sometimes) be done after a single presentation of the premises, whereas transitivity of choice typically requires hundreds of trials that result in gradations in associative strength from A to E.

3. Transitive inference is typically limited to children of approximately 4 years or older and adults, whereas transitivity of choice can be performed by younger children and by many other species.

4. Premise integration in transitive inference imposes a processing load on working memory (Maybery, Bain, & Halford, 1986; Halford, 1993), whereas there is no evidence of a working memory load that is specifically associated with premise integration in transitivity of choice.

We recognize that many variations on this set of processes are possible, including fuzzy representations (Brainerd & Kingma, 1984; Brainerd & Gordon, 1994). Transitivity of choice can be performed by analytic processes similar to those used in transitive inference, in which case participants tend to be aware of the order of elements, and performance is associated with working memory (Libben & Titone, 2008). However, these issues do not detract from our claim that there is a need to categorize such performances in a way that recognizes differences in procedure, process, and performance.

It might be considered that transitivity of choice is preferable as a cognitive measure because it yields higher rates of success. However, we think the important consideration is that they differ markedly in procedures, processes, and performances, and it is quite inappropriate to regard them as alternative measures of the same construct. This is not to deny the importance of transitivity of choice, but it is in no way equivalent to transitive inference, and performance of the former does not imply competence in the latter. This example starkly illustrates the need for a systematic way of classifying tasks such as this according to deep, or nontrivial, properties. Such a classification would indicate additional criteria that should be met before attributing transitive reasoning to any class of participants.

We are also happy to acknowledge that these categories of tasks require more explicit definition, and we will address this question in chapter 2. The core of the differences between the tasks is that transitive inference entails an internal and accessible representation of structure, whereas transitivity of choice entails internal processes that compute an output, but no accessible representation of structure. We will expand considerably on this distinction in subsequent chapters.

Definitions based on structural correspondence

We will proceed now to discuss some relatively new aspects of the distinction between types of cognitive processes. Our proposals encompass seven levels of process, and we also envisage an underlying continuum, for which our levels can be seen as an approximation. We will present proposals for the factors that underlie the continuum.

The essence of our proposal is that recognition of structural correspondence between cognitive representations is a crucial ability that discriminates levels of cognitive functions, and that it is the basis of cognitive capacity. Halford and Wilson (1980) showed that levels of cognitive processes can be defined by the amount of information that is required to establish a correspondence between representations. Children were trained on a series of isomorphic tasks, each of which entailed movements around a geometric array. The movements were determined by nonword "secret codes." Having learned the structure, they were required to transfer it to unfamiliar materials based solely on relations among the elements in the task. The study assessed the emergence of symbolic relational knowledge, including variables, from experience with isomorphic structures. The amount of information required to establish a valid mapping from the learned structure to an isomorphic, unfamiliar structure was manipulated.

A group of 4- to 6-year-old children learned the task and showed successful transfer, indicating the emergence of relational knowledge from experience with isomorphic concrete instances. Their acquisition was limited by their information-processing capacities, the 4-year-olds successfully performing only tasks that required less complex (binary) relations, whereas 6-year-olds were also successful at isomorphic transfer with more complex (ternary) relational tasks. This is a limited demonstration of how levels of cognitive tasks can be distinguished by the amount of information required for transfer between representations on the basis of structure. We will elaborate on this idea extensively in the pages and chapters that follow.

The study by Halford and Wilson (1980) was an early demonstration of the idea that levels of cognitive processes can be identified by the information required to map from one representation to another, but this principle now has been elaborated as a theory that has found wide application. The study was published back to back with a study of analogical reasoning by Gick and Holyoak (1980) that marked the start of a major movement into the study of relational knowledge. They investigated the transfer between reasoning tasks based on the concept of convergence. One was a military problem, in which a commander attacked a fortress by sending forces along roads that converged at the fortress. The other was a radiology problem, in which a tumor had to be destroyed by converging radiation from separate sources. Both scenarios required analogical reasoning based on the structural similarity between the first (source) and subsequent (target) tasks. The study of relational knowledge has been one of the most successful areas of cognitive science (Holyoak, 2012) and has widespread application, to which we will make frequent reference.

All of this indicated that levels of cognitive process could be defined by the amount of information required for a valid mapping between representations. Halford, Wilson, and Phillips (1998) elaborated this dependency into the relational complexity metric.

Relational Complexity of Cognitive Tasks

The relational complexity (RC) metric is defined in detail by Halford et al. (1998) and is considered in more detail in chapter 2, but we will review it here briefly to show how it fits into the current formulation. Relations can have varying numbers of arguments, sometimes referred to as *roles* or *slots*. The number of arguments determines the relational complexity. Thus, the binary relation "larger than" has two roles or slots, one for a larger entity and another for a smaller one, each of which can be filled in a variety of ways. We can write this as *larger* = {(*horse, cat*), (*dog, mouse*),...}. *Between* is a ternary relation because an entity is related to entities on each side of it:

e.g., 5 is between 3 and 8. Therefore *between* relates three elements. We can write this as *between*(3, 5, 8). Each argument of a relation is a source of variation, or a dimension. An *n*-ary relation can be thought of as a set of points in *n*-dimensional space, so a unary relation is a set of points in a one-dimensional space, a binary relation is a set of points in a two-dimensional space, and so on. Dimensionality of relations is associated with processing load, which forms the basis of a conceptual complexity metric. Halford et al. (2005) presented evidence that adult human processing capacity is limited to one quaternary relation in parallel, though this is a soft limit, and some individuals might process quinary relations under optimal conditions. There is evidence that the complexity of relations that can be processed in parallel increases with age (Andrews & Halford, 2002; Halford, 1993; Halford, Wilson & Phillips, 1998, sections 6.2 and 6.3). The relational complexity metric has been applied to reasoning, including the knights and knaves problem (Birney & Halford, 2002) and categorical syllogisms (Zielinski, Goodwin, & Halford, 2010); to language comprehension (Andrews, Birney, & Halford, 2006); mathematics education (English & Halford, 1995); cognitive development (Andrews & Halford, 2002; Andrews, Halford, & Boyce, 2012; Halford, 1993; Halford & Andrews, 2006); and industrial contexts (as discussed in chapter 9). These will be described in subsequent chapters.

Concepts too complex to be processed in parallel are handled by *segmentation* (decomposition into smaller segments that can be processed serially) and *conceptual chunking* (recoding representations into lower rank, but at the cost of making some relations inaccessible). For example, $v = st^{-1}$ (velocity = distance/time) is instrinsically a ternary relation, but it can be recoded as a binding between a variable (velocity) and a constant (the value of the velocity), which effectively reduces (chunks) it to a binary relation such as *value*(*v*, 50). However, this makes relations between velocity, distance, and time inaccessible (e.g., we cannot answer questions such as "How is speed affected if the distance is doubled and time held constant?" without using the information in the original ternary relation). This means that there are limits to the use of conceptual chunking, which we will consider in detail.

Complex tasks are normally segmented into steps, each of which is of sufficiently low relational complexity to be processed in parallel. The steps are processed serially. Where a task is segmented into steps that are performed serially, the steps typically differ in relational complexity. The complexity of the task as a whole is determined by the most complex relation that has to be processed in parallel in any step. Expertise is important for devising strategies that reduce the complexity of relations that have to be processed in parallel, though the structure of the task sometimes imposes a limit on complexity reduction strategies. Thus, the *effective relational complexity* of a task is the most complex relation that has to be processed in parallel, using the most efficient strategy available. Procedures for determining effective relational complexity have been defined (see Halford, Wilson and Phillips, 1998, section 3.4.3; see also Halford, Cowan, and Andrews, 2007). The essential principle is that a relation cannot be decomposed if the variables interact, because interacting variables must be interpreted jointly. This is analogous to analysis of variance, where variables that interact must be interpreted jointly. Even where relations are theoretically decomposable, some participants might be unable to take advantage of decomposition because the required strategies might be unavailable to them. Where it is desired to test processing load effects, strategies for segmentation or chunking sometimes can be inhibited by experimental procedures, so that processing load effects can be observed. Furthermore, spontaneous development of strategies can impose a processing load. Testing processing load theory, of course, requires that these factors be determined independently. This is best done by developing models of the cognitive processes used in performing the task (Halford, Wilson and Phillips, 1998, section 6).

Two propositions entailed by our thesis are that tasks of equal cognitive complexity form an equivalence class in a realistic psychological sense, and that tasks can be distinguished by the complexity of information that is required to be processed. Andrews and Halford (2002) demonstrated both of these, using closely matched tasks with two different levels of relational complexity in six different domains. Because all cognitive tasks are influenced by many factors besides complexity, careful experimental control was required. The devised tasks required ternary relations in the domains of transitivity, hierarchical classification, class inclusion, cardinality, relative-clause sentence comprehension, and hypothesis testing. The study also included simpler binary-relation (two-variable) items for each domain (except hypothesis testing because no binary relational equivalent could be devised), with procedures and task variables held constant. This ensured that participants had relevant domain knowledge and understanding of task demands. Thus, relational complexity was manipulated with other factors tightly controlled.

Andrews and Halford (1998, 2002) explain this in detail for the tasks that they used, but for illustrative purposes, we will consider how it was done for transitive inference, using the task in figure 1.4. The task was

Transitive Inference Task

Premises

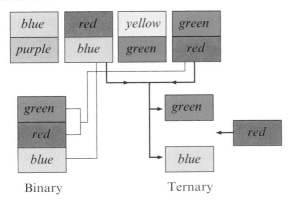

Binary   Ternary

Figure 1.4
Transitive inference task used by Andrews and Halford (2002). Adapted from Andrews and Halford (2002), figure 3, p. 173. Copyright © Elsevier 2002, with permission from Elsevier.

adapted from one devised by Pears and Bryant (1990). Children were required to place colored blocks in top-down order consistent with premises, presented as pairs of colored blocks. In figure 1.4, the premises are blue above purple, red above blue, yellow above green, green above red, implying the following top-down order: yellow, green, red, blue, purple. Children were required to order the middle three blocks to avoid nontransitive inferences that are possible with end blocks (e.g., yellow only appears as high, and this enables it to be placed on top without considering the relations outlined later in this discussion). The four premise pairs remained visible throughout the task and participants were trained to use them when ordering the problem blocks. In the ternary relational task illustrated in figure 1.4, participants were shown a green and a blue block. These can be ordered by reasoning that green is above red and red is above blue, so the blocks should be ordered green, red, blue; therefore, green is above blue. As a check on this strategy, they were then asked to place red, and would be expected to realize that it should be inserted between green and blue. This provides a further check that the task has been performed by ordering elements according to the premises. To place the first two blocks, both premises have to be processed in a single decision, which is analogous to the transitive inference relating to people ordered by height, as discussed previously. In the binary relational task, participants had to first place green and red, and then add blue. In this task, pairs can be ordered serially, so that no more than one premise has to be considered in a single decision. Notice, however, that the tasks are closely matched in that the same three blocks have to be ordered in two steps using the same premises. The essential difference is that in the ternary task, two binary relational premises have to be integrated into a ternary relation in a single decision, and in the binary relational task, the premises can be considered serially, never processing more than one binary relation in a single decision. That is, they can be segmented in accordance with relational complexity theory.

Andrews and Halford (2002) administered their tasks with items at both levels to children aged 3 to 8 years. Ternary-relation items were more difficult than comparable binary-relation items, but the difference was greater for the younger children. There was also a difference in the age of mastery, with ternary relations being processed at a median age of 5 years, while the corresponding binary relational tasks were processed by 3- to 4-year-olds. Rasch analysis, which measures task and person differences (Andrich et al., 1998) showed support for the hypothesis that binary- and ternary-relation items formed separate complexity classes. As shown in figure 1.5, there is a huge complexity effect with 3- to 4-year-old children, but performances converged toward the age of 8 years. Procedures were designed to ensure adequate knowledge of task demands and strategies, such as integration of premises. Furthermore, the hypothesis that the differences reflected knowledge would have to contend with similar effects across several domains, as well as with findings that premise integration yields processing load effects in transitive inference (even with university students), and the effects persisted over hundreds of trials (Maybery, Bain, & Halford, 1986). We always acknowledge the significance of knowledge, but no variable should be given priority, so neither knowledge nor complexity explanations should be accepted as default hypotheses.

Cross-task correlations were positive between tasks in the six domains mentioned previously and tasks loaded on a single factor that accounted for 80 percent of age-related variance in fluid intelligence. The six tasks, therefore, appear to have some structural commonalities, despite their very different materials and procedures. An example of this is shown in figure 1.6. Transitive inference and class inclusion are very different tasks, yet they have a similar underlying structure, comprising links among three variables. Capturing this structural commonality is a major function of the relational complexity metric, and of the more extended *representational rank* metric that we will consider in chapter 2.

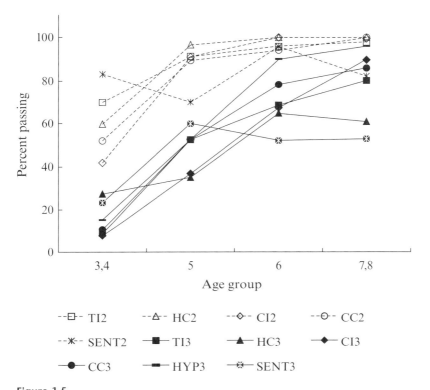

Figure 1.5
Performance on ternary relational and corresponding binary relational tasks as a function of age. The codes are as follows: TI, transitive inference; HC, hierarchical classification; CI, class inclusion; CC, cardinality; SENT, sentence comprehension; HYP, hypothesis testing; 2, binary relational; and 3, ternary relational. Reproduced from figure 7 of Andrews and Halford (2002), p. 202. Copyright © Elsevier 2002, with permission from Elsevier.

The relational complexity metric of Halford et al. (1998) is limited to unary to quinary relations. In chapter 2, we extend the metric to include subsymbolic processes, which impose lower processing loads. This is why they tend to be effortless and parallel (Norman, 1986), but they are also less accessible to other cognitive processes. Higher cognitive tasks tend to be serial because they entail relational representations, which impose high processing loads that must be reduced by segmentation or conceptual chunking. In chapter 2, we will propose that the core of higher cognition is relational processing, a distinguishing feature of which is assignment to roles (i.e., *structural alignment*). Thus, the proposition "John loves Mary"

Transitivity and class inclusion are superficially different, yet both entail ternary relations:

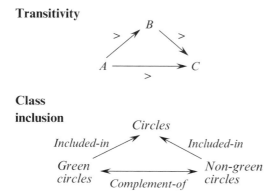

Transitivity

Class inclusion

Figure 1.6
Proposed underlying structure for transitivity and class inclusion. The structure is defined by relations rather than entities, and relations can be represented by arrows, which foreshadows the category definition of structure considered later in this chapter. Adapted from Andrews and Halford (2002), figure 1, p. 166. Copyright © Elsevier 2002, with permission from Elsevier.

entails assignment of John to the lover role and Mary to the loved role. To put this in more general terms, structural alignment is arguably the core difference between relational knowledge and association.

Mathematical basis for equivalence classes of concepts

We have shown that transitive inference and class inclusion, although very different in terms of materials and procedures, have a similar underlying structure that could be a possible explanation for similar ages of attainment, and also predicts other properties such as processing load. We also reviewed research by Andrews and Halford (2002), who identified a correspondence between concepts from six different domains. By contrast, implicit and explicit transitivity, though notionally the same concept, have very different attainment profiles, reflecting different underlying processes. So the question is: How do we account for these apparently inconsistent findings? We propose to find an explanation based on the principle, first enunciated by Halford and Wilson (1980), that we can categorize cognitive processes by the information required to map between an internal representation of the task and task stimuli. The mathematical basis for this principle was *category theory* (Arbib & Manes, 1975; Mac Lane, 1971, 2000), which has the potential to increase the precision of the formulation and link it to a body of theory that has wider scientific relevance. The axioms of category theory constructions provide constraints on what constitutes structural relations, and these are beneficial to a system for categorizing cognitive processes. We will show that many correspondences that have been observed, but not appreciated, reflect profound structural similarities that deserve to be investigated more intensively and in a formally precise way. This was the original motivation for inventing category theory with respect to mathematics (Eilenberg & Mac Lane, 1945).

Category theory was also used by Phillips, Wilson, & Halford (2009) to show, formally, the underlying structural relationship between reasoning tasks such as transitive inference and class inclusion. Transitive inference and class inclusion involve closely related (technically, *dual*) underlying structures. Hence, their developmental profile is similar because the same amount of information is needed to map between task representation and stimuli. The following is an outline of the structural relationship between transitive inference and class inclusion from a category theory perspective. Formal details are found in Phillips, Wilson, and Halford (2009). This treatment will be expanded in chapter 4.

Cognitive processes are typically conceived as transitions (or *functions*) between sets of cognitive states. The flavor of the category theory account can be captured by defining transitive inference and class inclusion in terms of the more familiar formalisms of Cartesian products and disjoint unions. In the transitive inference task in figure 1.4, a red block sitting on top of a blue block can be represented as the pair of states (*red, blue*). The set of pairs {(*blue, purple*), (*red, blue*), (*yellow, green*), (*green, red*)} represents the premises; *red* (block) is above *blue* (block); *green* is above *red*; *blue* is above *purple*; and *yellow* is above *green*. We will refer only to those pairs that would be used to assess transitive inference [i.e., (*green, red*) and (*red, blue*)] because the rest are controls for nontransitive inferences.

The Cartesian product of these premises with themselves includes ((*green, red*), (*green, red*)) and ((*green, red*), (*red, blue*)), among others. Retaining only those premise pairs whose second component in the first pair is the same as the first component in the second pair, we have ((*green, red,*), (*red, blue*)) and two others. Removing one of the redundant middle elements (and inner brackets) leaves instances such as (*green, red, blue*), corresponding to the transitive inference that *green* is above *blue*. In category theory terms further explained in chapter 4, this treats transitive inference as a *pullback*, in this case a special kind of subset of a Cartesian product.

A class inclusion task consists of a set of items (e.g., apples, *A*), a complementary set (i.e., nonapple fruit, *B*) and their union (i.e., fruit). The disjoint union of two sets *A* and *B* is the set *A* + *B*, which corresponds to the set of fruit. Disjoint union and Cartesian product are *dual*—their mathematical structures are closely related in a category theory sense (see chapter 4, and Phillips, Wilson, & Halford, 2009). Whereas the correspondence in figure 1.6 is intuitive and approximate, the correspondence in terms of Cartesian products and disjoint unions is formal and precise. This means that the correspondences that we observed are not accidental; they have a mathematical basis that relates to a wide-ranging body of theory and lays a foundation for more extensive inferences.

We will return to these issues in subsequent chapters, but for now, we note that a mathematical basis exists for the structural correspondences between some tasks that differ markedly in their surface properties. The categorization of cognitive processes based on mappings between representations offers an account of the *deep structure* underlying cognition.

Conclusion

All sciences need to categorize the phenomena that they study based on core properties or deep structure. We propose that cognitive science has matured to the point where cognitions can be categorized by the information that is required to form mappings between representations. The proposals cross the boundaries between research paradigms and provide a formulation that covers human and nonhuman cognition, as well as the full range of ages in human cognition. Information required for mappings can be defined by the relational complexity metric based on the number of variables that are related in a single cognitive representation. The effects of knowledge and task factors are fully considered, but no factor is given priority to explain phenomena.

Concepts at the same level of complexity form equivalence classes that have been demonstrated empirically for some significant cognitive domains. The relational complexity metric, elaborated in chapter 2, not only defines the complexity of cognitive tasks performed by human adults and older children, but enables it to be distinguished from the undoubtedly impressive performances of other species, and of human infants. Some animal cognitions, including many in areas such as communication and navigation, raise doubts as to the superiority of human cognition.

However, we lack a systematic way of classifying these phenomena. The categorization that we propose groups them into equivalence classes that have both an empirical and a mathematical basis.

We propose that a more integrated, coherent account of cognition is now possible and would have many benefits. The conceptual fragmentation of psychology tends to result in confusion, inconsistency, and a proliferation of exceptions, all of which hamper some aspects of progress. A coherent account of the science would assist with interpretation of empirical results, for example, by providing definitions of the core properties of higher cognition. Thus, when new phenomena are discovered, they could be categorized according to defined criteria that would suggest appropriate control experiments as well as other research hypotheses (Halford et al., 2012).

An integrated conception of cognition would also lead to fruitful hypotheses for acquisition of higher cognitive functions. We will demonstrate that symbolic processes, which are often a source of difficulty in mathematics and science education, depend on structural alignment, which has considerable potential to provide improved educational methods.

Road map for the book

There are three major categories of cognitive processes, which we characterize as Representational Ranks 0, 1, 2+, and which are explained in chapter 2 and summarized in table 2.1. The most basic processes are associative, of which there are two levels: (1) nonstructured (Rank 0), which is equivalent to elemental association, $(a_1 \rightarrow a_2)$, with no intervening processes and no transformation of inputs; and (2) functionally structured (Rank 1), in which there are one or more intervening states, and representations can be transformed or recoded (e.g., $a_1 \rightarrow a_h \rightarrow a_2$). Then there is a symbolic level (Rank 2+, identified with analytic cognition), in which a

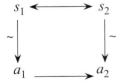

Figure 1.7
Structural alignment (~) of symbols $s_1 - s_2$ with another representation $a_1 - a_2$.

structured representation is superimposed on the lower levels and interacts adaptively with them. Probabilistic versions of these levels are obtained by considering a_i and s_j as sets of possible states instead of single states.

Symbols require an operating system that is best conceptualized in terms of relational knowledge, as defined in box 2.1. This level enables symbolization ($s_1 \leftrightarrow s_2$), the validity of which is established by structural alignment (vertical links in figure 1.7) between the two kinds of representations. The process of structural alignment necessitates a capacity for dynamically rebinding representations and depends on working memory. The three major levels are all illustrated with a common paradigm, conditional discrimination (shown in figure 2.1).

The basic properties that distinguish relational from associative levels are given in chapters 2 and 3. Structural alignment is the core property of relational (and therefore symbolic) cognition, and it depends on working memory. Consequently, relational levels are more effortful than associative levels, and effort depends on cognitive complexity. A further consequence is that capacity limitations lead to the serial processing of complex relational tasks. The substantial variance shared by working memory and fluid intelligence is attributed, at least partly, to the role of working memory in forming symbolic representations. The complexity of relational knowledge and its connection to task difficulty is developed in chapter 4. Assignment of tasks to representational rank categories is considered in detail in chapter 5 and is summarized in table 5.1.

The major categories of cognition can be identified with types of neural net architectures, which provide existence proofs for the relevant processes. Ranks 0 and 1 correspond to two- and three-layered feedforward networks, respectively, as detailed in chapter 2. Rank 2+ corresponds to properties of symbolic-connectionist models [e.g., the Structured Tensor Analogical Reasoning (STAR) and Discovery of Relations by Analogy (DORA) models], discussed in chapter 3, together with neuroscience evidence of brain regions characteristically activated by this level of cognition.

Acquisition of relational knowledge is partly self-supervised because it depends on structural alignment, and it is central to the development of higher cognition (chapter 6). Neural net models of acquisition processes are discussed in chapter 7. The theory of relational knowledge is applied to contemporary reasoning models in chapter 8. Applications of categories of cognition are considered in chapter 9, and conclusions are presented in chapter 10.

2 Properties of Cognitive Processes

In this chapter, we define the major types of cognitive processes that we have identified in the existing empirical research base. These cognitions are distinguished by the type of representation and by the processes that operate on them (i.e., the operating system). Representations and processes in turn influence observable cognitive performances. Cognitive representations, symbols, and structure are important to our approach, so they are defined first.

Cognitive representations are internal states containing information that can be used by an animal, whether human or nonhuman, to interact with the environment in an adaptive manner. We distinguish cognitive representations from those that occur for other reasons, such as maps or diagrams, or from correspondences that have no representational function, such as houses with a similar structure but that cannot be said to represent each other. Adaptation has been shown by many authors to be a core property of cognition. Piaget (1950) held that intelligence was an extension of biological adaptation, and similar points have been made by many other researchers. Anderson (1991) developed the Adaptive Control of Thought—Rational (ACT-R) model of cognition, in which adaptation plays a major part. See also Halford (1993) for similar proposals about cognitive development. An important feature of this adaptation is optimization of information acquisition and use. This factor plays a major role in the Bayesian rationality theory of Oaksford and Chater (2007). In this formulation, heuristics that optimize information gain can account for phenomena including conditional reasoning, syllogistic inference, and the Wason Selection Task (discussed in chapter 8).

Acceptance of adaptation means that action-related prediction of the environment is a core function of cognition (Clark, 2013; Moore, 2012). In their most basic form, this prediction takes the following form: Given a situation, if action X is performed, the outcome will be Y (with some approximately estimated probability). However, current conceptions of prediction entail considerable top-down processing, which Clark (2013) characterizes as "hierarchical predictive coding." The essential idea is that perception is not based solely on sensory input but entails progressive reduction of prediction error using stored knowledge. This would include knowledge of Bayesian "hyperpriors," such as "there is only one object (one cause of sensory input) in one place, at a given scale, at a given moment. Another ... might be that the world is usually in one determinate state or another." (Clark, 2013, p. 196). Another aspect of this conception is provided by Raichle (2010), who proposes that intrinsic processes (i.e., those that do not respond to external input) constitute a much larger proportion of brain activity than previously recognized.

Hierarchical predictive encoding entails considerable knowledge that is common to perception and cognition. Thus, Clark (2013) states: "The process of perception is thus inseparable from rational (broadly Bayesian) processes of belief fixation, and context (top-down) effects are felt at every intermediate level of processing. As thought, sensing, and movement here unfold, we discover no stable or well-specified interface ... between cognition and perception." (p. 190). Hierarchical predictive coding is an exciting development in the field, but it has a long way to go before its implications are fully determined. Meanwhile, we see no reason to doubt that perception and conception share some profoundly important processes, but the kinds of distinctions that are mandated by the accumulated cognitive literature are not precluded by those common processes; in fact, they are likely to be superimposed on them. Our function is to define the essential categories of cognition, and we propose that structural alignment is a major discriminating property and has a role in higher cognition beyond the binding process that is entailed in perception. The reason is that perception binding is subject to built-in structural constraints that discriminate between features such as color and orientation. Binding in higher cognitive processes is more dynamic and flexible, so there is no prior structural constraint that assigns elements to roles. To illustrate, in the representation of a transitive inference shown in figure 1.3 in chapter 1 of this book, the elements are assigned to roles in the structure solely by the relations in the premises, and there is no prior structural constraint.

Halford and Wilson (1980) made the point that the formal definition of representations in cognition is essentially the same as the definition proposed by Coombs, Dawes, and Tversky (1970) and Suppes and Zinnes (1963) for measurement theory. The structure of any aspect of the world is represented by a relational system comprising a set of elements and relations. The validity of the representation is defined by structural correspondence between the representation and the represented structure. A more detailed account is given in appendix 2.1.

Accepting that prediction is a core function of cognition does not necessarily support heuristic theories against analytic or symbolic theories because analytic and symbolic cognitions extend the scope and power of predictions by constructing internal models of situations. Heuristic theories tend to yield predictions based on experience, whereas a mental model generates inferences, such as the transitive inference discussed in chapter 1, that go beyond experience.

A *symbol* is one building block of cognitive representation and is "processor relative" (Clark, 1992, p. 193), so the meaning of symbols depends on interpretation by a symbol processing system. According to the Physical Symbol System hypothesis (Newell, 1980), symbols depend on a system of operations for recursively composing them into more complex symbols, which can be further composed, and so on (see also Fodor & Pylyshyn, 1988). However, symbols that serve the functions of human cognition are typically more graded, less categorical, and less "all-or-nothing" than those that serve the functions of artificial intelligence or information technology. Consequently, Penn, Holyoak, and Povinelli (2008, §10.1) have proposed the *Symbolic Approximation hypothesis*, meaning that cognitive symbols share important properties with physical symbols, including the ability to support rulelike cognition, but they also entail partial matches.

Box 2.1

> **Relational representations** are defined by Halford, Wilson, and Phillips (2010) as "a binding between a relation symbol and a set of ordered tuples of elements." (p. 497). An example of a *tuple* is an ordered pair (2-tuple) like (*elephant, mouse*). Thus, representation of the binary relation *largerThan* includes the symbol *largerThan*, the roles *larger-object* and *smaller-object*, and a set of ordered pairs such as{(*elephant, mouse*), (*pig, cat*)}. The symbols *larger-object, smaller-object* show the roles or slots that comprise the structure of the relation. The roles are not always represented explicitly but may be indicated by position in the expression; e.g., in *largerThan(elephant, mouse)*, the first role is for the larger entity and the second for the smaller entity. Computational models differ in the way roles are represented, as we show in chapter 7. The relation symbol signifies the *intension* of the relation and specifies which relation is represented, so the symbol *larger* indicates that the elements are ordered by size. The ordered *n*-tuples represent the *extension* of the relation

Box 2.1
(continued)

and indicate the elements that are related. Furthermore, they can embody statistical knowledge. For example, the relation *largerThan*={(*horse1*, *dog1*), (*horse2*, *dog2*), (*dog3,horse3*), ...} represents the relative frequency of pairs where the horse is larger than the dog, thereby capturing the probabilistic nature of representations.

A *relational instance* comprises the relation symbol and one ordered *n*-tuple. Thus *largerThan(horse,dog)* is an instance of the *largerThan* relation. Of course, *largerThan(horse,dog)* is also a *proposition*. The difference between a relational instance and a proposition is that the proposition may be false, whereas the relational instance is asserted to be true (at least in the situation being discussed).

In formal mathematical terms, an *n-ary* *relation R* is a subset of the Cartesian product of *n* sets: $R \subseteq A_1 \times A_2 \times ... \times A_n$, such that its defining property *P* holds for those elements. Such a relation is said to have *arity n*. Relations of arities 1, 2, and 3 are referred to as *unary, binary,* and *ternary,* respectively. If the tuple $(a_1, a_2, ..., a_n) \in R$, then $P(a_1, a_2, ..., a_n)$ is true. For example, *(cat, mouse)* $\in P_{largerThan}$ signifies that $P_{largerThan}(cat, mouse)$ is true. We shall refer to *R* and *largerThan* as relation-symbols and $a_1, a_2, ..., a_n$ as arguments. A relation named *R* may be referred to as $R(A_1, A_2, ..., A_n)$ when we want to explicitly refer to the name (role) that each argument plays in the relation. Therefore, we can say that *(cat, mouse)* is an instance of the relation *largerThan(Object1, Object2)*.

Relational knowledge (Goodwin & Johnson-Laird, 2005; Phillips, Halford, & Wilson, 1995; Halford, Wilson and Phillips, 1998) captures the properties of higher cognition, including syntax and semantics (Halford, Wilson, & Phillips, 2010), and arguably provides the most psychologically realistic account of a symbol processing system. *Relational representations* are defined in box 2.1. To illustrate our argument, the meaning of symbols for natural numbers, such as 1, 2, 3, etc., depends on set quantification, including counting (Carey, 2009), and on operations such as arithmetic addition (e.g., 3 = 2 + 1). Counting can be conceptualized as relational knowledge (Andrews & Halford, 2002), and addition and multiplication are ternary relations.

Symbol systems are sets of symbols with relations and operations defined on them. Despite early recognition of the importance of relations to cognition (Spearman, 1923), for some decades, there was less development of relational theory in psychology than there was in some other fields such as database theory (Codd, 1990). We will define higher cognitive processes in terms of relations, functions, and operations, but since functions and operations are special cases of relations, our argument embraces them too (see box 2.6).

Structure is a concept that has an important role in our argument, and this term has been given many meanings in psychology (e.g., Piaget, 1950; Wertheimer, 1945; Spearman, 1923); but our usage is consistent with the mathematical definition. It is defined mathematically as a set or sets on which one or more operations or relations are defined, and category theory (discussed in chapters 1 and 4) is a theory of structure. We use operations and relations in the conventional mathematical sense, so that functions include mathematical operations [e.g., the binary operation of arithmetical addition is a function of two variables, so the sum of a and b can be expressed as $f(a,b) = a + b$]. We use the terms *nonstructured* and *structured* to refer to whether there is an internal representation. A task might have structure, but the crucial question is whether there is an internal representation of the structure. It is important that, as we will show, structured tasks sometimes can be performed without an internal representation of structure.

Distinguishing the levels

The three major levels of cognition are shown in table 2.1 and entail distinct types of representation and distinct processes. The levels are ordered so that higher levels retain the computational advantages of lower levels, but not vice versa. The functionally structured level incorporates the properties of the nonstructured level, and the symbolically structured level incorporates the properties of both lower levels but also has certain unique properties. Before elaborating on the levels, we will consider modular cognitive processes.

Modularity

Evidence exists for modular processes that are highly specialized for dealing with particular activities. A *module* (M. Anderson, 1992; Fodor, 1983; Just & Carpenter, 1992) is a fast, domain-specific set of processes that are informationally encapsulated, impose only very low processing loads, are not strategically modifiable, and show little or no relationship to individual differences in intelligence. Modular processes entail specific mechanisms that are specialized for particular functions. Processes that are arguably modular include detection of causal links (Leslie & Keeble, 1987), perceptual processes (Pylyshyn 1999), and enumeration of sets of up to four elements (Gelman & Gallistel, 1978; Wynn, 1992, 1995), though the interpretation of some findings has been challenged by Simon, Hespos, and Rochat (1995). We propose, consistent with Halford, Wilson, & Phillips (1998), that many modular processes are not symbolic and do not entail explicit, accessible representations of relations. Consequently, they belong in the category of Type 1 processes described by Evans (2008). Anderson et al. (2004) propose that the perceptual-motor module, goal module, declarative module, and procedural module are informationally encapsulated, but they post their outputs into buffers that are accessible to a central production system that coordinates the various inputs and produces outcomes that are linked to the external world.

We are conservative when postulating that a cognitive task is modular. We assume that the early stages of visual processes are modular, in that top-down processes that affect them are not greatly penetrated by nonvisual information (Pylyshyn, 1999). However, we believe that as yet, there is insufficient evidence to conclude that syntactic processing is entirely modular, as proposed by Fodor (1983), because it is influenced by capacity limitations under certain conditions (Just & Carpenter, 1992). Similarly, we would not yet adopt the proposal by Leslie (1987) that concept of mind is modular, because it too is influenced by capacity limitations (Davis & Pratt, 1995; Frye, Zelazo, & Palfai, 1995), although components such as attention to social signals that indicate mental states might be modular (Andrews et al., 2003). We will argue in chapter 8 that the case for modular theories of tasks, such as the Wason Selection Task (Wason 1968), gains some of its plausibility because insufficient attention has been paid to the role of cognitive complexity (Cocchi et al., 2013; see also Stenning & Van Lambalgen, 2008).

Tasks that are automatic are also known not to impose processing loads (Hasher & Zachs, 1979; Logan, 1979; Schneider & Shiffrin, 1977). Automaticity develops due to practice under constant mapping conditions; that is, where the input–output functions of a task remain constant. This can result in associations between entities forming chunks that reduce processing loads.

Chapter 3 will review evidence that relational processing activates regions of the frontal lobes with links to the parietal lobe (e.g., Christoff et al., 2001; Knowlton & Holyoak, 2009; Waltz et al. 1999), and also possibly involves a cingulo-opercular system (Cocchi et al., 2013). It may turn out that one of these systems functions as a module, albeit one that differs in significant ways from the types of modules mentioned previously. The important point is that the question of how symbolically structured processes operate will also address the question of whether these processes constitute some kind of module. Our purpose has been to define the properties of symbolically structured processes and show how they can be distinguished from other major classes of processes that involve a wide range of phenomena. Our formulation admits the possibility of modular symbolic processes without being symbolically structured and hence capacity limited (i.e., horizontal without vertical arrows in figure 1.7).

There are modular processes of great sophistication, two of the most important being animal communication and animal navigation systems (Giurfa et al., 2001; Srinivasan, 2011). There must be cognitive processes that generate these behaviors, but there might not be an internal representation of the structures underlying the performances. This distinction is of fundamental importance and will be addressed extensively in this and later chapters, including theoretical models and empirical criteria for different levels of cognitive structure. Thus, while these performances might be impressive, they might not entail cognitive representations of structure, so they do not meet our definition of cognitive complexity based on the number of entities bound into a cognitive representation.

The classificatory system that we have developed can discriminate between these undeniably impressive sets of processes and the processes of higher cognition. One feature that distinguishes higher cognition from these modular systems is accessibility, not only to other processes within the same system, but to other systems, including some with which they might have little informational overlap. The ability to make structure-consistent mappings between representations is a major component of higher cognitive processes in this respect. We will address the factors that lie at the core of these processes and propose that binding fillers and roles (i.e., structural alignment) is the foundational process for symbolically structured cognition.

We can illustrate the issue by contrasting feature binding in early vision and object-location binding in reasoning. Both can be interpreted as relational processing, but they have differences with implications for the underlying implementations. Relations in vision are defined over small sets of possible elements (e.g., orientation, color). Structural alignment is not required because the features themselves define what role/position they belong to (e.g., an orientation feature cannot also be a color feature). By contrast, relations in reasoning are defined over larger sets for which it is not feasible to have a feature detector at every location. The same element may appear in more than one position (role or slot), so structural alignment is required to bind elements to roles, which imposes a processing load.

Table 2.1
Properties of ranks

Rank	Architecture	Processing Characteristics	Modification Processes	Information Used to Establish Correspondence	Sensitivity to Complexity
Nonstructured (Rank 0)	A link between a mental state representing input and a mental state representing output, without intervening mental states.	Links can be chained; can converge or diverge. Links are all of the same kind and are unlabeled. Link is strengthened in accordance with an associative growth function whenever represented entities co-occur. There is no internal representation of structure.	Strengthening links; formation of new links	Element similarity	Low; mainly affects rate of acquisition; no upper limit
Functionally structured (Rank 1)	The link between mental state representing input and the mental state representing output is mediated by an internal representation that recodes the input.	Representations are determined by input-output functions. Representations can reflect the statistical structure of the input–output functions that are learned. Similarities of representations tend to reflect similarities of functional relations processed. Content independent transfer is possible, but this is restricted by the input–output functions learned. Can represent degrees of similarity within / between categories. Inputs are composed into compound representations, but components do not retain their identity in the composition. There is no relational representation. There is no symbol system. Difficulty of recoding input can inhibit learning.	Modifying internal representation; modifying strength of links; can be simulated by learning algorithm (e.g., back-propagation, autoencoding)	Internal representation	Quadratic function of number of inputs, but strongly influenced by need to find an appropriate recoding of the input

| Symbolically structured (Ranks 2+) | Explicit, accessible, internal representation of relations; each relation has a symbol, which is bound to the arguments (fillers) assigned to roles. Representations validated by structural correspondence. | Structural alignment. There are bindings between roles and fillers. Can process propositions. Compositionality. Accessibility of components. Systematicity. Higher-order relations can be represented. Analogy, transfer to isomorphs. Generativity. Variables and structural correspondence. | Formation of representation of structure (mental model) in working memory; modifiability online | Structure-consistent mapping between representations | Exponential in the number of variables bound in a representation; limit is defined by number of bound entities (arity of the relation) rather than the information coded in each component. |

Box 2.2

Representational rank can be defined as the number of identifiable components bound into a structured representation, such that the components satisfy the constraints imposed by the structure. An example would be a cognitive representation of the binary relations *more-than* and *less-than* defined on a finite set of positive integers, such as >(3, 2), >(5, 4) and <(2, 5), <(3, 7). There are constraints between the components so that, for the relation >, the integer in the first position (first slot) of each pair must be greater than the integer in the second position (with the opposite constraint for <). There is a further constraint as well; for example, given (3,2), the relation must be >. Each instance of a binary relation, such as >(3,2), has three components, >, 3, and 2, so this representation would be Rank 3. The complexity of a cognitive process depends on representational rank, and higher ranks impose higher processing loads. We hypothesize that cognitive performances have similar properties within ranks and differ between ranks, and supporting evidence will be presented in later chapters.

Psychological properties of ranks

In this section, we will consider the properties of the three main levels of cognitive tasks shown in table 2.1: nonstructured, functionally structured, and symbolically structured, corresponding to Ranks 0–2+. For definition of ranks, see box 2.2.

We will illustrate the basic properties of the levels in table 2.1 by reference to a single task, conditional discrimination, an example of which is shown in figure 2.1A. Conditional discrimination can be performed at three distinct levels, and these levels are discriminable by empirical techniques that are applicable to articulate and inarticulate participants. This enables abilities at different ages, or of different species, to be discriminated without extraneous demands, such as the requirement to state a rule verbally. Conditional discrimination has been historically important (Lashley, 1938), has been the subject of extensive empirical investigation with nonhuman animals and children (Gollin & Schadler, 1972; Rudy, 1991), and is isomorphic to the Dimensional Change Card Sort task (Zelazo et al., 2003), which is important in the contemporary literature.

The example in figure 2.1 is a shape discrimination such that triangle is positive (i.e., should be selected) when the background is black (black, triangle → $R+$; black, square → $R-$), and the discrimination is reversed when the background is white (white, triangle → $R-$; white, square → $R+$). We will consider the learning and transfer functions for this task to provide a

A original task

black   triangle $\longrightarrow$ $R+$
black   square $\longrightarrow$ $R-$
white   triangle $\longrightarrow$ $R-$
white   square $\longrightarrow$ $R+$

B isomorphic task

green   circle $\longrightarrow$ $R+$
blue   cross $\longrightarrow$?
green   cross $\longrightarrow$?
blue   circle $\longrightarrow$?

C mapping between isomorphs

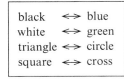

E

black, triangle, $R+$
black, square, $R-$
white, triangle, $R-$
white, square, $R+$

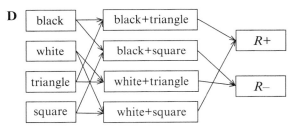

Figure 2.1
Conditional discrimination. A, original task; B, a task that is isomorphic to the original, in which all responses after the first can be predicted by structure-mapping and generating inferences; C, the mapping between isomorphs; D, basic structure of a three-layered net that could learn the conditional discrimination; E, the task shown as ordered 3-tuples.

constant reference for the properties belonging to each level of cognitive process. The levels also will be distinguished by referring to more complex structured learning tasks (Halford, Bain et al., 1998; Halford & Busby, 2007; Phillips & Halford, 1997; Phillips, 1998, 1999) and to a wide range of other tasks to be considered later in this book.

We consider neural net models that provide plausible implementations of mechanisms that could underlie each level. This is done to provide an existence proof of mechanisms that can operate at each of the specified levels. This chapter does not present a general review of neural net models; those are reviewed elsewhere (Shultz, 2012; Thomas & McClelland, 2008).

Box 2.3

> Formally, a **nonstructured** process P_0 is a mapping *assoc* from a mental state m_i in the set M_i to a mental state m_o in the set M_o. The most usual psychological interpretation of nonstructured processes is elemental association. The mapping *assoc* (associate) can be written as *assoc*: $M_i \rightarrow M_o$.

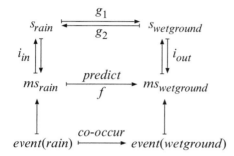

Figure 2.2
Association between rain and wet ground: the mental state representing rain is associated with the mental state representing wet ground (i.e., rain predicts wet ground). The functions g_1 and g_2 are symbolic and are in structural correspondence with the mental states. Thus, the symbolic level can be integrated with associative links. The symbol $\mapsto$ indicates individual element mappings.

Nonstructured processes

Architecture

A nonstructured process has no internal representation other than input and output, so it is Rank 0 (see box 2.3). It corresponds to what is normally understood as elemental association, mentioned in chapter 1.

An example of a nonstructured process is the association between rain and wet ground, as shown in figure 2.2. Perception of the external event, rain, produces a mental state ms_{rain}, representing rain, and perception of wet ground produces a mental state $ms_{wetground}$, representing wet ground. There is an associative link between ms_{rain} and $ms_{wetground}$, which is strengthened by contiguity of rain and wet ground and represents the statistical links in the environment, viz., that rain is likely to make the ground wet. The strength is incremented in accordance with an associative learning model (Rescorla & Wagner, 1972), though other factors such as informativeness play a part as well.

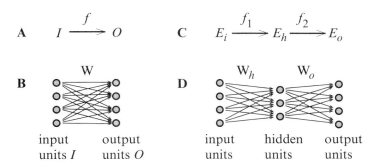

Figure 2.3
Panel (A) shows a schematic representation of a nonstructured process, and Panel (B) shows the corresponding neural net architecture. Panel (C) shows a schematic representation of a functionally structured process, and Panel (D) shows the architecture of a corresponding feedforward net model. The number of input, hidden, and output units varies, and typically would be larger than in the examples shown here.

Nonstructured processes can be chained, so that the output of one association is the input to another: $m_1 \rightarrow m_2 \rightarrow m_3 \rightarrow \ldots \rightarrow m_n$, as in mediating response theories (e.g., Kendler & Kendler, 1962). They may converge, so that m_1 and m_2 elicit m_3, or diverge, so that m_1 elicits m_2 and m_3. The associative link is part of the process that creates the representation but is not itself a mental state. It is part of our formal definition of nonstructured processes that an associative link per se cannot be a component of another association: For example, we cannot have $(m_1 \rightarrow m_2) \rightarrow m_3$. By contrast, symbolically structured processes can be formed into recursive, hierarchical structures using higher-order relations (Phillips, Halford, & Wilson, 1995).

The mental states m_i and m_o may represent ideas (Locke, 1690/1924), things or objects (James, 1890), stimuli and responses (Hull, 1943), or events (Lieberman, 1993). Nonstructured associations are *elemental,* in the sense that they are formed between entities that are not transformed in the process of forming the association (Humphrey, 1951). The term *elemental* should not be confused with the everyday meaning of the word *elementary,* and elemental associations can form the basis of some very complex performances. Gallistel (1990) has proposed that association might involve symbols. There can be associations between symbols, but we define symbolic functions in terms of the criteria that are specified later in this chapter, and we would classify associative learning as symbolic only if it were demonstrated to have these properties.

The conditional discrimination task cannot be learned in its entirety by elemental association, without special procedures as outlined next, because each cue element is equally associated with each response, which causes associative interference. In figure 2.1A, for instance, notice that "black" is equally associated with R+ and R–, and the same is true for "white," "triangle," and "square." It would be possible to learn the shape discrimination while holding the background constant, so it would be possible to learn black, triangle → R+ and black, square → R–. Alternatively, the two background conditions could be distinguished in a way that avoids associative interference, such as by isolating them in subtasks. However, associative interference would occur if the full set of four items were learned by elemental association. At this nonstructured level, transfer to the isomorphic task in figure 2.1A requires that every associative link be relearned. There is no recognition of the structure that is common to the two tasks. See box 2.4, which defines the essential properties of a network at this level.

Box 2.4

> **Two-layer feedforward networks** are in a general class of networks that we define as consisting of (1) a group of input units, represented by an activation vector **I**; (2) a group of output units represented by an activation vector **O**; (3) connections propagating inputs to outputs, with weights represented by a matrix **W**; and (4) output activations governed by the equation $\mathbf{O} = F(\mathbf{IW})$, where F is some function, typically sigmoid, which takes as its argument the weighted sum **IW** of the input unit activations (**I**). The values of the components of **W** depends on past co-occurrence of inputs and outputs (e.g., Hebbian learning).

Possible neural net implementation of nonstructured processes: two-layered, feedforward nets

Elemental associations can be implemented by two-layered nets, such as the simple pattern associator of McClelland, Rumelhart, and Hinton (1986); see figures 2.3A, B. A number of models have captured detailed properties of associative learning by using input or stimulus nodes with modifiable connections to output or motor nodes (Gluck & Thompson, 1987; Sutton & Barto, 1981). See box 2.4 for further details of these networks. There are no intragroup connections and no reverse directed connections. This class of networks is nonstructured in the sense that the only internal representation is the connection weights, which are not accessible to other network processes. Weights are parameters, rather than inputs, to a process, and we do not interpret them as mental states.

Functionally structured processes

Functionally structured processes correspond closely to the class of three-layered nets that have been used to model a wide range of cognitive functions. For reviews, see Thomas and McClelland (2008) and Shultz (2012). Further specifications are given in box 2.5. The multilayered net models (including feedforward net models) that we consider here are presented as existence proofs of processes that can operate according to our specifications for this level. This does not preclude neural net models of higher rank cognition, and in chapter 4, we will consider some advanced models that might be claimed to operate in accordance with Rank 3, 4, or 5.

Architecture
At the functionally structured level, a computational process leads to an internal representation that is a transformation of the input and which in turn produces the output.

Properties of functionally structured processes

Some properties of functionally structured processes can be derived from the definition, without simulation. We will illustrate this fact using conditional discrimination, which is the best-known task that conforms to the formal definition of a functionally structured process.

Box 2.5

Functionally structured processes (P) can be defined formally as follows:

A functionally structured process P consists of three state spaces, E_i, E_h, E_o (input, hidden, output), and a pair of mappings, $f_1: E_i \rightarrow E_h$, $f_2: E_h \rightarrow E_o$. An input state, $e_i \in E_i$, is taken to an output state, $e_o \in E_o$, via an internal or hidden state, $e_h \in E_h$, as follows (see figure 2.3C): $f(e_i) = f_2(f_1(e_i)) = e_o$. Thus, the action of the process is the composition mapping $f = f_2 \cdot f_1: E_i \rightarrow E_o$.

Box 2.5

(continued)

> Functionally structured processes have an internal representation (in E_h), but they are rank 1 because it functions in a wholistic fashion. Even if there is more than one mental state representation, Rank 1 representations are not composed into a structure of the kind that characterize Rank 2+ cognitions, considered later.
>
> As noted in the main text and figure 2.3D, functionally structured processes are frequently modeled using three-layer feedforward neural networks, whose structure is as follows: (1) input and output groups of units; (2) a group of hidden units; (3) weights ($\mathbf{W}_h$) propagating activation from input to hidden units, and weights ($\mathbf{W}_o$) propagating activation from hidden to output units; and (4) an output activation (O) governed by this equation: $\mathbf{O} = F(\mathbf{W}_o \bullet G(\mathbf{W}_h \bullet \mathbf{I}))$, where F and G are the activation functions for output and hidden units, respectively. The hidden units are dynamic representations. The operator $\bullet$ denotes matrix-vector multiplication.

Conditional discrimination cannot be acquired through elemental association without special procedures because of associative interference, as noted previously, but it can be learned by fusing or "chunking" element and background into a configuration such as "black/triangle," as shown in figure 2.1D. The configurations are computed representations, and the process conforms to the definition of functionally structured processes. Associative interference is avoided because each instance is learned independently of the others (e.g., black/triangle → R+ is learned apart from the other three items of the original task in figure 2.1B). The cues in each instance become distinct, so the representation of "triangle" is not the same in "black/triangle" as in "white/triangle." In the configural representation, the entities do not retain their identity. The relation between the components is not represented, and no function is defined that would enable retrieval of "shape, given color," or retrieval of "color, given shape."

This example of conditional discrimination illustrates that functionally structured processes can perform tasks that could not be performed by lower-level processes such as elemental association. They are also predicted to have more powerful transfer properties. This occurs because the representations computed by the function f_1: $E_i \rightarrow E_h$ are a form of abstraction that is independent of some properties of the input. It is possible to compute the similarity or difference between the input elements, and these representations are significant for the interpretation of a number of performances that we will examine (see, for example, figure 5.3 and the associated discussion in chapter 5). However, the generality of the properties represented will be limited by the input–output functions that have been learned.

The conditional discrimination task illustrates some limitations of functionally structured processes. Although the internal representations are composed of combined inputs (such as "black/triangle"), the components do not retain their identity, and there is no function that would recover the components from the composition. For example, there is no function that recovers "black" from "black/triangle" in figure 2.1D. We refer to this property as *compositionality*, to be defined when we discuss symbolic cognition. The internal state $e_h \in E_h$ is a representation that is required to compute the output, but it is not accessible except through E_i, and no function $E_o \rightarrow E_h$ is defined. There is no symbol system, such as those that are defined for symbolically structured processes. Properties of functionally structured processes have been demonstrated by neural net modeling in a wide range of contexts, including models by Rumelhart, Hinton, and Williams (1986), Pearce (1994), and Schmajuk and DiCarlo (1992).

Modification

Rank 1 processes can be modified by relearning the links between input and the internal representation, and between the representation and output. This will result in changes to the internal representation. In neural net models, this entails a learning algorithm such as backpropagation or autoencoding.

Difficulty of learning

Conditional discrimination is an example of configural learning, in which discriminations between cues are conditional on other cues. Another configural learning task is oddity, which requires choosing the element that is different from all the others. Using A, B, C to represent cues and +, – for positive and negative responses, respectively, this can be represented as follows:

Oddity (A A $B+$ but B B $A+$).

The other configural learning tasks are transverse patterning ($A+$ versus $B–$, $B+$ versus $C–$, $C+$ versus $A–$), and negative patterning ($A+$, $B+$, $AB–$).

The interaction between cues means that the correct response cannot be determined by the additive combination of associative strengths. The cues have to be recoded into a configuration. Configural learning tasks belong to a larger category that Clark and Thornton (1997) call "Type-2" problems, in which learning depends on computing a representation that recodes the input but does not represent structure (Halford, 1997). All configural learning and Type-2 tasks are difficult to learn (Gollin & Schadler, 1972; Rudy, 1991), and Clark & Thornton (1997) attribute this to the difficulty of recoding the inputs. An example of this is finding the configural representation such as "black/triangle" in the conditional discrimination task in figure 2.1D. Because the possible recodings are unlimited, some constraints are needed to determine an appropriate code. This is a likely explanation (at least partly) of the well-known difficulty of acquiring conditional discrimination (Gollin & Schadler, 1972). The space of possible recodings of Type-2 problems is the space of computable functions, and some constraints are required to reduce this space to manageable size, thereby making the recodings possible (Clark & Thornton, 1997).

Correspondence

Transferring to other tasks depends on compatibility of the codes in the internal representation. Transfers are more efficient with functionally structured processes, but still fall short of the best human capabilities. If we were to switch $R+$ and $R-$ in the conditional discrimination task in figure 2.1A (e.g., black, triangle $\rightarrow R-$, black, square $\rightarrow R+$, etc.) there would be less relearning than with elemental association because links between inputs and configural representations can be retained. Transferring to an isomorphic task has been explored by neural net modeling. The simulation of transfer between instances of the structured tasks used by Halford, Bain et al. (1998) has shown that feedforward neural net models, which are functionally structured and which do not have explicit representation of relations, cannot match human transfer capabilities (Phillips & Halford, 1997; Phillips, 1999).

Sensitivity to complexity is higher than for Rank 0 processes, but is considerably less than for Rank 2+ processes. Processing is by parallel-acting constraints, whereas in higher-rank tasks, the processing of complex tasks tends to be serial because of the high processing loads. In multilayered feedforward nets, the number of weights normally has a quadratic dependence on the number of inputs, so sensitivity to processing load is greater than with two-layered nets but less than with nets used to simulate symbolically structured processes, discussed next. Thus, neural net models of different levels of cognitive processes may explain why higher cognitive processes are more effortful or impose higher processing loads.

To summarize, functionally structured processes entail a computed internal representation that recodes the input and mediates input–output functions, and the internal representation reflects aspects of the environment. However, these representations are restricted by the input–output functions computed and, at least in their most basic form, they do not have all the properties of symbolically structured processes. The next step is to define a new family of systems that do have these properties.

Symbolically structured processes

In this section, we will argue that the properties of higher cognitive processes can be derived from representations that are based on relations and that are in structural alignment with the functions that characterize the organism–environment interaction. This provides an alternative criterion for validity of representations. Whereas functionally structured processes are valid if they enable input–output functions to be computed, symbolically structured processes are valid if they represent the structure of situations and events in the environment. Validation by structure, rather than elements or features, gives greater flexibility, enables a higher level of abstraction, and corresponds to what is usually called "explicit" representation; that is, "information in the system," as well as "information to the system" (Clark & Karmiloff-Smith, 1993). Another important property is that symbolic representations are constructed in working memory, and working memory measures account for a high proportion of the performance variance in symbolic processes (Kane et al., 2004; Oberauer, 2009).

Because relations are at the core of the formulation, we will consider them in some mathematical detail, as shown in boxes 2.1 and 2.6. Then we will consider properties of symbolically structured processes that do not occur at lower levels. We are concerned with the minimum requirements for representation of this level of cognitive process, and for the sake of brevity, we will not deal with all the complexities of symbolic representation in this discussion.

Box 2.6

A **function** is a relation in which mappings exist and are unique—that is, a binary relation $R \subseteq X \times Y$ is a function if and only if (a) for every $x \in X$, there is a $y \in Y$ such that xRy, and also (b) if xRy and xRz, then $y = z$. Thus, in the relation *motherOf(Person, Mother)*, the *Mother* role is a function of the *Person* role, since every person has a unique mother, while *childOf(Mother, Child)* does not determine a function, since a person can have more than one child (or no children). Functional relationships are more usually expressed as, e.g., *motherOf(Person) = Mother*, and a functional instance as e.g., *motherOf(george) = catherine*.

An **operation** is a function (and hence a relation). A unary operation such as negation (where x is converted to $-x$) is a function of one variable; a binary operation is a function of two variables; and so on. For example, the binary addition operation on the natural numbers N can be viewed as a function +: $N \times N \rightarrow N$: e.g., $+(2, 3) = 5$, although it is more usual to write this as $2 + 3 = 5$. In relation notation, addition is a ternary relation, and $+(2, 3, 5)$ is an instance of the relation +.

Relational algebra defines operations on relations, such as the union, intersection, and difference of two relations with the same attributes. There are also operations to transform attributes, and to combine relations that have different attribute sets. We introduce some of these in chapter 3.

Relational representations

We will define higher cognitive processes in terms of relations, functions, and operations, but since functions and operations are special cases of relations, as mentioned previously, our arguments in terms of relations often embrace functions and operations as well. The essence of a relational representation is shown in box 2.1 as a set of ordered tuples of elements, and we will elaborate on this here. Functions and operations are outlined in box 2.6.

Structural alignment

Structural alignment is the foundational property of relational representations. There is a binding of fillers to roles, as well as a binding between roles. For example, the *largerThan* relation includes roles for a larger and a smaller entity, each of which can be instantiated in a variety of ways. Thus, in the *largerThan* relation, the ordered pairs {(*elephant, mouse*), (*pig, cat*), ...}

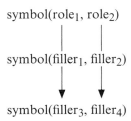

Figure 2.4
Aligning roles and fillers

are assigned so that *elephant* and *mouse* in the first pair are aligned with *pig* and *cat*, respectively, in the second pair. Alignment of *n*-tuples to form roles is a core process in the construction of relational representations (Goodwin & Johnson-Laird, 2005; Halford, Wilson, & Phillips, 1998, 2010). It arguably enables the transition to relational knowledge, and many important properties flow from it, as we will see shortly. Possible mechanisms for structural alignment have been developed in computational models of analogy and relational knowledge, as discussed in chapter 3. (See figure 2.4.)

The assignment is dynamic and engages working memory, a concept that is considered in more detail in chapter 4. However, we want to note two critically important points here. The first is to notice the information that is required to align instances. To align (*elephant, mouse*), with (*pig, cat*), we have to process both elements in each relational instance. There is nothing inherent in *elephant* or *pig* that assigns them to the larger role in every instance. *Elephant* is assigned to the larger slot because it is compared with *mouse*, but it would not be so assigned if compared with *whale*. The other point is that it is not possible to decompose these instances into subproblems because we must have the concept before we can perform the decomposition. The correspondence has to be processed intact in the first instance, and the relational representation has to be constructed based on unsupervised experience with instances. This imposes a load on working memory that depends on the number of related entities, a matter to which we will pay a lot of attention in this book, especially in chapter 4.

A *relational symbol* is an important facet of the representation of a relation, as it documents the *intension* of the relation, whereas the *tuples* of the relation express the *extension* of the relation, as mentioned in box 2.1. The binding between the symbol and the roles must be such that the truth of the relation is maintained (e.g., *elephant* must be larger than *mouse*, rather than vice versa).

In many contexts, it is appropriate to speak of a *relational schema*. For example, *loves(Lover, Beloved)* would be a suitable schema for a version of the *loves* relation, but it would be connected to semantic memory in a way that would enable semantic information (e.g., the emotional features of the relation) to be retrieved. The schema consists of symbols (the three symbols *loves*, *Lover*, and *Beloved* in our example), and it designates the roles that occur in this relation. Without the fillers in roles, the symbol is meaningless, while without the schema and its symbols, the relation is inscrutable. Consequently, symbolic structural alignment is crucial to the formation of relational representations. Although it is unconventional to view it in this way, there is a role for symbols in relational representations, which can be seen as intrinsic parts of role-filler bindings.

Next, we will define structural correspondence, including a mathematical treatment in box 2.7, and then we will derive the properties that follow from the definitions.

Structural correspondence

Symbolic processes must have some independence of the causal or statistical links to the environment that determine functionally structured processes, and it must be possible for symbols to be arbitrary (e.g., so we can use *dog* to represent a certain domestic quadruped, or even to represent other objects, such as *hot dogs*). However, symbols must be mapped to their referents with some degree of consistency. The requirement for consistency can be met by structural correspondence of the representation with the segment of the world that is represented (Halford & Wilson, 1980; Holland et al., 1986; Suppes & Zinnes, 1963). Reasoning heuristics, such as judging the frequency of events by their availability in memory (Tversky & Kahneman, 1973), work because cognitive representations are approximations to the structure of the environment. Holland et al. (1986) have proposed a condition–action rule implementation of structural correspondence that provides varying degrees of generality and accuracy and can handle misrepresentations and cognitive illusions. In both representations (Holland et al., 1986) and analogies (Holyoak & Thagard, 1989), structural correspondence is a soft constraint that may be violated for specific elements if there is good correspondence overall.

Clark (2013, §1.2) suggests that hierarchical predictive coding is not just a matter of finding a mapping between environment and cognitive representations, but also entails error correction and inference. On the other hand, the position that he details does not entail explicitly symbolic processes, such as constructing mental models to represent premises, as with the transitive inference discussed in chapter 1. Our formulation is designed to handle symbolic processes, and it includes error correction and inference processes, such as those that have been investigated in the analogical reasoning literature.

Box 2.7

At the symbolically structured level, there is a symbolic function, $g: S_1 \rightarrow S_2$, that represents the input–output function $f: M_{in} \rightarrow M_{out}$. Symbolic mapping between s_{rain} and $s_{wetground}$ [i.e., $g_1(s_{rain}) = s_{wetground}$ and $g_2(s_{wetground}) = s_{rain}$)] is shown in figure 2.2. $g_2: s_{wetground} \rightarrow s_{rain}$ is a symbol system that is mapped to $f: ms_{wetground} \rightarrow ms_{rain}$ by the functions i_{in} and i_{out}. The symbolic mapping $g_1: s_{rain} \rightarrow s_{wetground}$ represents the mapping $f: ms_{wetground} \rightarrow ms_{rain}$ if it is in structural correspondence with it. In essence, the functions are in structural correspondence if the diagram is commutative or closed. For example, if we start at $s_1 \in S_1$ and apply g_1 followed by the interpretation function i_{out}, the result is the same as if we apply i_{in}, then f. Formally, $i_{out}(g_1(s_1)) = f(i_{in}(s_1))$.

Another illustration of commutativity is given in figure 2.5. Notice that it does not matter what the elements are, so long as the mappings are consistent. This means the representation is content-independent.

Properties of symbolic structures

Symbolically structured representations are distinct from functionally structured representations in several ways. First, symbolic structures serve other functions besides computing an output. The representation in figure 2.2 includes functions g_1 and g_2, which are in structural correspondence with the input–output functions and represent them. One consequence of this is that a symbolically structured representation can be mapped into another representation, forming an analogy, which is the key to many higher cognitive processes (Holyoak, 2012). By contrast, the process in figure 2.1D has a representation that only serves to compute an input–output function. Second, the functions g_1 and g_2 are in structural correspondence with the input–output functions and represent them. Second, the functions g_1 and g_2 give access in both directions, so the activation of $s_{wetground}$ permits the retrieval of s_{rain}. This permits abduction as well as prediction, so if we see that the ground is wet, we can infer that it has rained. Structural correspondence provides a basis for bidirectional access that is not entailed in computing input–output functions. Third, the mappings i_{in}: $ms_{rain} \rightarrow s_{rain}$ and i_{out}: $ms_{wetground} \rightarrow s_{wetground}$ are bidirectional and reflect a cognitive process of symbol binding. A mental state that is not a symbol can elicit a symbol and vice versa. By contrast, the mappings between the *event(rain)* and ms_{rain}, or between *event(wetground)* and $ms_{wetground}$, are unidirectional and causal. This is consistent with perceptual functions because it is possible for *event(rain)* to produce a mental state representing *rain*, but not the reverse (i.e., thinking "rain" does not make it rain).

Fourth, the fact that symbols in symbolically structured representational processes are freed from the causal links between inputs and mental states and are constrained only by structural correspondence means that alternative representations can be maintained. It also means that representations at the symbolically structured level are arbitrary, in the way that symbols are arbitrary, and no assumptions are made about the resemblance between symbols S and mental states M representing environmental entities E. This flexibility means that symbolically structured representations are *dynamic*. A dynamic binding is one that is formed in one trial or few trials, is held in active memory, and decays with time (Halford, Bain et al., 1988; Halford, Wilson, & Phillips, 1998). Fifth, symbols enter into symbol systems.

However, structural correspondence by itself would not be enough because of the symbol grounding problem (Harnad, 1990), and the links between mental states and external entities shown in the lower half of figure 2.2 are necessary to keep representations anchored in reality. Thus, the symbolically structured level complements, rather than displaces, the functionally structured level of processing.

Complexity of symbolic structures

The number of symbols bound in a representation exerts a constraint on the properties of symbolically structured processes.

Two-symbol structures

The representation just considered (figure 2.2) is an example of the simplest symbolically structured level because just two symbols are bound into a structured representation. An example of a simple symbolically structured process would be a dynamic binding between two symbols, one representing an object and the other representing a location. Suppose that we see an object (O) hidden at location (L) and form a binding between these symbols that would enable us to answer the questions: Where was O hidden? (at L), and what is hidden at L? (object O). We can represent this as a binding between symbols $s_O \leftrightarrow s_L$.

A representation based on a binding of two symbols can represent a binary relation $r(X, Y)$ if there is no symbol representing r as a variable, or a unary relation $r(X)$ if r is a symbol representing a variable. It also can represent a univariate function. Compositionality requires that represented symbols retain their identities in the composed object. In this case, while s_O and s_L retain their identities, no new symbol is formed. That requires a structure with more symbols. We will consider this in the next section and show how, in theory, the formulation generalizes to symbolically structured representations of arbitrary complexity, but for information processing reasons (Halford et al., 1998; Halford et al., 2005), a binding of six symbols is the most complex that is attainable psychologically.

Three-symbol structures

Figure 2.5 shows an example of a three-symbol structure, in which the symbols s_{black} and s_{dog} are combined to create the symbol $s_{blackdog}$. That is, $s_{black}, s_{dog} \rightarrow s_{blackdog}$. This corresponds with mental states arising from experience of the world (i.e., if something is black and a dog, then it is a black dog), so the composition of the symbols corresponds to the symbol for the composition. In the three-symbol structure, the components s_{black} and s_{dog}

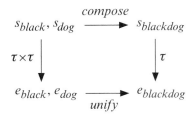

Figure 2.5
The composition of the symbols s_{black} and s_{dog} is in structural correspondence to the composition of environmental entities e_{black} and e_{dog} if the diagram commutes. This means that if we start with s_{black}, s_{dog} and apply the *compose* operator followed by the interpretation operator τ, the result is the same as if we first apply $\tau\times\tau$, and then apply the *unify* operator. The interpretation operator τ maps the symbols s to the environmental entities e that they represent.

retain their identities in the composite representation $s_{blackdog}$, and they are retrievable from it.

The structural correspondence constraint is critical to compositionality. For example, the meaning of the compound symbol *blackdog* must correspond to the entities that are formed by combining the entities represented by *black* and *dog*.

Symbolic structure and higher cognitive processes

In this section, we describe properties of higher cognitive processes based on the definition of symbolically structured processes given previously. This includes demonstrating that symbolically structured processes embody the structural properties that have been important for higher cognitive processes historically (Humphrey, 1951; Mandler & Mandler, 1964) and in twentieth-century movements including Gestaltists (Wertheimer, 1945), Piagetians (Piaget, 1950), information-processing theorists (Anderson, 1983; Hunt, 1962; Miller, Galanter, & Pribram, 1960; Newell, 1990), and linguists (Chomsky, 1980; Fodor, 1975, 2000).

Rules have been a convenient basis for modeling higher cognitive processes and for distinguishing them from more basic processes such as association (Hinton, 1990; Sloman, 1996; Smith, Langston, & Nisbett, 1992). Explicit representation of a rule can be captured by relations, as noted in chapter 1, and relations provide a mathematical and psychological underpinning for rules. The properties of productivity, compositionality, and systematicity, which Sloman (1996; see also Smith et al., 1992) proposed as being important for rules, can be captured by relations. A distinguishing characteristic of rules is that they relate variables. However, our definition of symbolically structured processes, based on functions and relations, handles variables.

A number of cognitive performances now have been observed in which it is difficult to determine whether rules are being followed. For example, the criterion of abstractness used by Sloman (1996) and Smith et al. (1992) is difficult to apply, and it is not clear what it means if we say that the cognitive performances of infants or nonlinguistic species are abstract. Throughout this work, we find that abstract—concrete is not an adequate basis for categorizing cognitive processes. Furthermore, in this formulation, we will define empirical criteria for all three levels of function that are applicable to both linguistic and nonlinguistic participants.

Perhaps the most cogent reasons for preferring relations to rules as a basis for conceptualization of higher cognition is that much human reasoning is essentially analogical, and analogy is based on representation of relations rather than rules.

Similarity

Similarity provides a good illustration of the fundamental properties of relational representations. In relational representations, similarity is specific to roles (Gentner, 2010). Consider the following sentences:

Jane feeds cat. (1)

Bob feeds dog. (2)

Cat feeds Jane. (3)

The meanings of these sentences can be expressed by relational representations:

feeds(Jane, cat)

feeds(Bob, dog)

feeds(cat, Jane)

In these representations, sentences 1 and 2 are more similar than 1 and 3, despite identical elements in the latter pair. The reason is that similarity is assessed within roles, so in 1 and 2, the *feeder* role is bound to a human agent and the *fed* role is bound to an animal recipient. However, in 1 and 3, the roles are bound to different agents, *human* and *cat*. By contrast, if we consider a nonstructured representation in which similarity is determined simply by the proportion of matching features regardless of roles, then sentences 1 and 3 would be more similar. This point is of fundamental importance, and in chapter 6, we will consider ways that it could be used to determine, for example, whether cognition is relational, and therefore symbolic, in some inarticulate participants, such as infants in their first few months.

Box 2.8

> **Compositionality** can be defined formally in terms of symbolically structured representations, as shown in figure 2.6.
>
> Assume a set of symbols S and an environment E, a collection of partial operations o_j of arity a_j which operate both on S and on E, and an interpretation map $\iota:S \rightarrow E$. The operation o_j combines a sequence of symbols from S,

Box 2.8
(continued)

of length a_j, to produce another symbol from S: $o_j(s_1, ..., s_{aj}) = s$. Then the operation o_j is *compositional* if $\iota(o_j(s_1, ..., s_{aj})) = o_j(\iota(s_1), ..., \iota(s_{aj}))$.

Thus, compositionality is based on the structural correspondence principle used to define representations in symbolically structured processes. The mapping $\iota:S \to E$ may be thought of as finding the interpretation or *meaning* of a symbol.

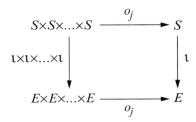

Figure 2.6
Compositionality expressed as a commutative diagram

Propositions

Propositions, which are the core of some models of higher cognitive processes, are defined as the smallest unit of knowledge that can have a truth value. Propositions are like relational instances in that they have the same syntactic structure:

relationsymbol/predicate(argument₁, argument₂, ..., argumentₙ)

For example, *eats(mouse, cheese)* is both a relational instance and a proposition. However, the technical restriction that a relation must be true does not apply to propositions (Halford, Wilson, & Phillips 1998, §2.2.2).

Compositionality

Not all meanings are compositional. In English, for example, the phrase *kick the bucket* has at least two meanings—one compositional (or literal) and one idiomatic ("die"). However, compositionality is an important principle for deriving the meanings of structures (see box 2.8).

Because the constituent states retain their identity, there is an operation that permits those constituents to be retrieved. This leads to the next property, *accessibility*.

Accessibility of components

Accessibility of components of symbolically structured processes follows from the fact that components of relations can be retrieved. Thus, given the propositions *likes(Jane, pizza)* and *likes(Fred, pizza)*,, and given *likes(?, pizza)*, a representation containing *Jane + Fred* will be retrieved. An *n*-ary relational instance $r(a_1, ..., a_n)$ contains $n + 1$ objects: the relation symbol and the *n* arguments. Given *n* components, we can retrieve one or more candidates for the $n + 1$st component. However, in theory, accessibility is more general than this. Given *x* components ($0 < x < n + 1$), we can retrieve a structure representing the remaining $[(n + 1) - x]$ components.

Where more than one relational instance is represented, the answers obtained will not always be unique. For example, given the relation *motherOf*, the query *motherOf(woman, ?)* may yield *child, toddler, infant, baby, teenager*, etc. Access may not be equally efficient in each direction. For example, arithmetic addition corresponds to a ternary relation + that contains triples like (3,2,5), (5,4,9). It might be *easier* to access a sum given two addends [i.e., +(3,2,?)] than to access an addend given the sum and the other addend [i.e., +(3, ?, 5)], but access in both directions is possible. Having learned the addition table, we can perform subtraction, but perhaps not as efficiently as addition. Another limitation is that accessibility refers to retrieval of information that is represented, not to retrieval of any information whatsoever. Thus, a child who does not know what *eagles* prey on, and who is given the query *preysOn(eagle, ?)*, will provide no answer simply because no proposition such as *preysOn(eagle, rabbit)* is represented in memory.

Accessibility may develop progressively in a cognitive representation. It is conceivable for a child to know, in the early stages of learning addition, that 2 plus 3 gives 5, but recognition that 2 is the number that you add to 3 to get 5 may develop gradually. It might reflect retrieval efficiency. That is, children are taught to retrieve 5, given 2 + 3, but are given less practice at retrieving 2, given 5 – 3. Nevertheless, we implicitly take advantage of accessibility when we teach children a table for addition but not for subtraction, and for multiplication but not for division.

Consciousness and awareness

Awareness or consciousness is a property of relational knowledge, and the distinction made by Evans (2003) between System 1 and System 2 is based partly on awareness, as noted in chapter 1. Awareness sometimes can be used as an indicator of higher cognitive process, and Andrews et al. (2012) assessed conditional discrimination by awareness of components of the task. This is tantamount to assessing awareness by accessibility, which is more directly measurable. In our efforts to define the core properties of higher cognition, we have found that consciousness is better regarded as a correlated rather than a defining property of relational knowledge.

Box 2.9
Modifiability example

Suppose that we have multiple two-symbol mappings g and h, such that $g: S \rightarrow T$ and $h: S \rightarrow T$. An example would be a switch from $g(s) = t_1$ to $h(s) = t_2$, where $s \in S$, $t_1, t_2 \in T$. By objectifying g and h as additional symbolic states, a three-symbol mapping F is created, such that $F:\{g, h\} \times S \rightarrow T$. By providing the first argument to F, the mapping between symbolic states in S and T is modified accordingly, $F(g): S \rightarrow T$ and $F(h): S \rightarrow T$.

Strategic modifiability

Input–output functions can be modified strategically by substituting relation symbols. For example, we can switch from the mappings $3,2 \rightarrow 5$ and $4,5 \rightarrow 9$ to $3,2 \rightarrow 6$ and $4,5 \rightarrow 20$ by switching from the addition operation symbol to the multiplication symbol. That is, we can switch from $+: 3,2 \rightarrow 5; 4,5 \rightarrow 9$ to $\times: 3,2 \rightarrow 6; 4,5 \rightarrow 20$, and so on. The reason for this is that each relation symbol is bound to a specific set of mappings, so $+$ is bound to mappings that include $3,2 \rightarrow 5; 4,5 \rightarrow 9$ while $\times$ is bound to mappings that include $3,2 \rightarrow 6; 4,5 \rightarrow 20$. Thus, a child who hypothesizes that *area* is defined as *length + breadth* can switch to *length* $\times$ *breadth* by substituting relation symbols, thereby obtaining more accurate estimates (N. H. Anderson, 1980); see box 2.9.

Modifiability online can be achieved by adding an operation symbol as a variable in the representation, thereby increasing its complexity. This means that more complex structures can be created to take account of additional sources of variation in an environment. Thus, a person who experiences inconsistencies because different mappings are required in different contexts can create a more complex structure in which two sets of mappings are bound to different context symbols. Doing this removes conflict in the task. Task switching in executive functions (Logan, 2003; Monsell, 2003) could entail online modifiability because a switch can be made by substituting relation symbols, thereby activating a new set of mappings. This is consistent with the proposal by Halford, Andrews et al. (2010) and Andrews, Halford et al. (2013) that executive functions depend on relational processing.

Systematicity

Systematicity is a property of cognition that concerns the distribution of cognitive capacities. One of the most cited examples that illustrates the property is the "John loves Mary" example, provided by Fodor & Pylyshyn (1988) in their introduction of the concept and its implications for a theory of cognitive architecture. That is, if one has the capacity to understand the expression "John loves Mary," then one also has the capacity to understand the related expression "Mary loves John." As this example suggests, cognition is not simply an arbitrary collection of capacities; rather, cognition comes in clumps of structurally related capacities. So, one has both the capacity to understand "John loves Mary" *and* the capacity to understand "Mary loves John," or neither capacity. There is no situation of having one without the other.

The concept of systematicity has been characterized further by McLaughlin (2009), who described five schemata for classes of examples of systematicity, all of which take the form:

Ceteris paribus, a cognizer is able to mentally represent *that P* if and only if the cognizer is able to mentally represent *that $\tau(P)$*, where τ is some transformation of propositions P.

In McLaughlin's first collection of systematic schemata (which he calls *SG1*), P is *aRb*, where R is a relational predicate, and $\tau(P)$ is *bRa*. McLaughlin's SG1 includes Fodor and Pylyshyn's "John loves Mary" example.

Systematicity has implications for the nature of cognitive architecture. Fodor & Pylyshyn argued that thought, like language, generally has a grammatical structure (classical cognitive system). With the right configuration of grammatical rules, a classical cognitive system can be constructed to realize both "John loves Mary" and "Mary loves John" capacities, because they are composed from a common grammatical rule: e.g., *Sentence → Agent loves Patient*, where *Agent* and *Patient* are to be replaced by their instances, *John* and *Mary*, thus affording all four possible combinations. The separation of capacity-common (e.g., *Sentence → Agent loves Patient*) and capacity-specific (e.g., *Agent → John | Mary*) components affords the kind of generalization that is characteristic of systematic capacities, where inferences are made available on the basis of the roles (e.g., *Agent, Patient*) that fillers (e.g., *John, Mary*) play, independent of the value of those fillers. Thus, we can generally infer who is the lover from an expression of the form *a loves b* regardless of the value of *a*, simply from the syntactic (relational) knowledge that the lover fills the position prior to the symbol signifying the *loves* relation. Connectionist (neural network) systems also can support systematicity analogously via shared neural resources (e.g., weighted connections) for capacity-common components and separated neural resources for capacity-specific components.

Although classical and connectionist systems can be configured to support systematicity, they also can be configured to support some, but not all systematically related capacities (Aizawa, 2003). Hence, systematicity does not necessarily follow from the principle of shared grammatical rules or weighted connections. In this sense, classical and connectionist principles are too general, or insufficiently constrained, in that they admit nonsystematic models of cognition, where systematicity is supposed to be a property. So, systematicity is not fully explained by classical or connectionist theory (Aizawa, 2003).

A mathematical basis that provides a principled theory-constraining model, whether classical symbolic/logic-based, connectionist, or the more recent Bayesian approaches, was provided by Phillips and Wilson (2010, 2011, 2012) and Wilson and Phillips (2012) for various kinds of systematic capacities using mathematical category theory. Category theory provides an additional ingredient, called a *universal construction,* which is not found in other theoretical frameworks. In one sense, the categorical approach is similar to the classical or connectionist approach in that systematically related capacities share a common component. However, the category-theoretic approach is more specific, in that a universal construction precludes the cases of shared components that do not support systematicity.

The concept of systematicity proposed by Gentner (1983) is distinct from the one outlined previously and pertains to analogical mapping in that people prefer mappings based on collections of higher-order relations to mappings based on lower-order relations in isolation. We agree that higher-order relations are important to analogy, and indeed are fundamental to many higher cognitive processes. Indeed, recent work shows that these two apparently distinct conceptions of systematicity are related by the formal, category theory notion of universal construction: intuitively, they are both a kind of optimization of cognitive resources (Phillips, 2014).

Higher-order relations

A *higher-order relation* is one where the elements in one or more arguments are themselves relations. Higher-order relations enable propositions to be composed into complex propositions such as *knows(John, contains(cup, drink))*; i.e., "John knows that cup contains drink." In this case, *knows* is a higher-order relation, the arguments of which are *John* and *contains(cup, drink)*. The second argument can be represented as the chunk *contains(cup, drink)*, and its components are inaccessible while the higher-order relational instance is being processed. It can be unchunked for processing in a subsequent step of the task.

The formulation in the previous section, which applies to first-order relations, can be applied to higher-order relations by replacing the elements with symbols for corresponding relational instances. These symbols are reduced or chunked representations of the relational instances (Wilson et al., 2001). For example, $a > b \Rightarrow b < a$. *Implies* can be expressed as a higher-order relation in the prefix form that we have been using as follows: $\Rightarrow(> (a,b), < (b,a))$. Replacements can be applied recursively to permit *m*-order relations. Higher-order relations can represent constraints between relations, such that certain relations imply or cause other relations.

Recursion

In a higher-order relation, it is possible that the relation name at the outer level may be the same as a relation name at an inner level: this is the case in a higher-order relation instance such as "Jack knows that Jill knows that Jack likes Jill" [or, in prefix notation, *knows(Jack, knows(Jill, likes(Jack, Jill)))*]. Such a relational instance is said to be *recursive*. Recursive nesting can be arbitrarily deep: another example would be *knows(Jill, knows(Steve, knows(Jack, knows(Jill, likes(Jack, Jill)))))*. Capacity limits have been observed in recursive processing of sentences with embedded clauses (Andrews, Birney, & Halford, 2006). This research is discussed in chapter 4. An upper limit can occur where propositions refer to mental states (Kinderman, Dunbar, & Bentall, 1998), but this is probably because they are resistant to decomposition by conceptual chunking and segmentation. That is, it is hard to decompose a sentence such as "Jack knows that Jill knows that Jack likes Jill" because it is hard to find a semantic meaning for a component such as "*Steve knows (Jack knows)*" without processing the remainder of the sentence. Thus, the limit arguably reflects complexity effects that apply to relational processing as outlined in this book, rather than a phenomenon that is intrinsic to the representation of mental states per se.

Fitch, Hauser, and Chomsky (2005) have proposed that recursion is an essential foundation for language, and we accept a role for it in relational knowledge. Higher-order relational representations, with lower levels embedded within higher levels and the same operation being performed at each level, forms a basis for recursion (Phillips et al., 1995).

Conclusion and criteria for symbolic processes

Using the classic conditional discrimination task as our reference example, we have shown that an instantiation of the task can be performed by any of three distinct levels of cognitive processes. Nonstructured processing has limitations in this context, but it is still well exemplified in the conditional discrimination task, while functionally structured and symbolically structured processing are also implemented. These levels have been defined formally, and empirical indicators have been specified. Possible implementations by neural nets have been considered for the first two levels, and the more complex implementation of symbolically structured processes is considered in chapter 3. Conditional discrimination is one of many examples of how the same behavioral performance can reflect sets of very different cognitive processes, so cognition cannot be defined solely by observed behaviors, but requires processes to be specified and objective indicators to be employed. We will elaborate on this point in subsequent chapters. For example, in chapter 5, we show how it is possible to switch between nonstructured and functionally structured processes using procedures that seem insignificant but produce major changes in processes.

We have defined symbolic cognition in terms of representations, knowledge, and processes that are well established in the cognition literature, but which are consistent with physical symbol systems and combinatorial syntax and semantics. We identified structural alignment as the foundational property of symbolically structured processes. The criterion for symbolic processes is dynamic mapping between relational representations, validated by structural correspondence, and yielding ability to predict unknown components, as in the transfer to the isomorphic conditional discrimination task in figure 2.1B. The criteria for the three levels of cognitive processes, elaborated upon in subsequent chapters, can be applied consistently to behavioral data, neural net models, and neuroscience evidence of brain activations.

Furthermore, we propose that dynamic mapping between relational representations is the main driver for development of symbolic processes, and in chapter 6, we will consider evidence for it in human infants.

Appendix 2.1

Structural correspondence

In their important early theoretical contribution, Coombs et al. (1970, p.11) defined representation (in the context of cognitive systems and models of cognitive systems) as follows:

A system $\alpha = (A, R)$ is said to be *represented* by another system $\beta = (B, S)$ if there exists a function f from A into B [which assigns to each x in A a unique $f(x)$ in B] such that for all x, y in A,

   $x \, R \, y$ implies $f(x) \, S \, f(y)$.

   Thus, α is represented by β if there exists a correspondence f that maps A into B in such a way that if the relation R holds between some x and y in A then the relation S holds between $f(x)$ *and* $f(y)$ in B, *where* $f(x)$ *and* $f(y)$ are the images of x and y, respectively.

They add: "If both β represents α and α represents β, the two systems are called *isomorphic*." This is in fact not always correct because, for example, it is possible to have a map $f: A \rightarrow B$ that maps everything in A to the same point in B, and then if S is reflexive, then the implication is trivially satisfied, so β represents α, and similarly for a map $g: B \rightarrow A$ that maps everything in B to a single point in A, with R reflexive. The correct definition of isomorphism here requires f to be a bijection; that is, that f be a one-to-one correspondence. Coombs et al. (1970) note that they are aware that their definition of isomorphism differs from that of Suppes and Zinnes (1963), which we examine below.

Another problem with this definition is that the map f goes from A to B, and Coombs et al. phrase the definition so that in this case, "α is represented by β" rather than "β is represented by α." In the case where we are talking about a model and an environment, we would normally expect that the model would represent the environment. So A is the environment, B is the model, and f goes from environment to model. Normally, however, the environment is richer than the model—there are bits of the environment that are not represented in the model [e.g., irrelevant bits or bits that have detail that is unnecessary to model (and would complicate the model unnecessarily, or even make it intractable)], so it is not possible to define a function from environment to model—only a partial function. However, it *is* possible to define a function from model to environment. Thus, it is preferable to say that, along with Coombs et al., β is represented by α. The same considerations apply if A/α is a model of a mind, and B/β is the mind being modeled.

Either way, such a representation is called a *structural correspondence* because the correspondence (or function) f is such that the structure, in the form of the relation R in α and the relation β in S, is preserved by f.

Suppes and Zinnes (1963, pp. 5–6), in their seminal contribution in this area, give a different definition. This also has difficulties because it builds isomorphism into the definition, and isomorphism between model and environment does not normally occur, as the model is simpler than the environment, as noted previously. Suppes and Zinnes say (replacing their Gothic symbols with Greek ones):

Let $\alpha = <A, R_1, \ldots, R_n>$ and $\beta = <B, S_1, \ldots, S_n>$ be similar relational systems. Then β is an *isomorphic* image of α if there is a one-one function f from A onto B such that, for each $i = 1, \ldots, n$ and for each sequence $<a_1, \ldots, a_n>$ of elements of A, $R_i(a_1, \ldots, a_n)$ if and only if $S_i(f(a_1), \ldots, f(a_n))$.

A better definition, for the purpose of defining relational representations, incorporates elements of both of these, as follows:

Let $\alpha = <A, R_1, \ldots, R_n>$ and $\beta = <B, S_1, \ldots, S_n>$ be similar relational systems. The system β is said to be *represented* by the system α if there exists a function f from A into B [which assigns to each x in A a unique $f(x)$ in B)] such that for all $a_1, \ldots, a_n$ in A and all $i = 1, \ldots, n$, $R_i(a_1, \ldots, a_n)$ implies $S_i(f(a_1), \ldots, f(a_n))$. The representing map f is said to be a *morphism* (or *homomorphism*) of relational systems. The morphism is said to be an *isomorphism* if f is also bijective (i.e., a one-to-one correspondence).

With this definition, let us consider the situation where we have two representations of an environment, as shown in figure 2.7.

Clearly, in this situation there is no structural correspondence (morphism) from α to γ or vice versa. Let us define the *range* of a function f, ran f, to be $\{f(x) \mid x \in \text{dom } f\}$, where dom f refers to the domain of f; that is, the set on which f is defined. In order for there to be a chance of a

α and γ are in structural correspondence with the environment β, via the maps f and g, but α and γ are not in structural correspondence with each other.

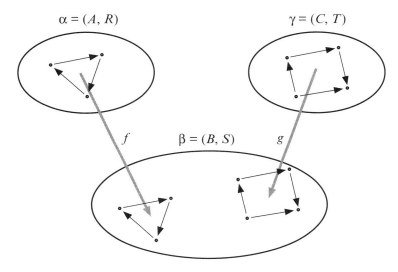

Figure 2.7
Interactions between structural correspondences

structural correspondence, we would want either ran $f \subseteq$ ran g, or maybe ran $g \subseteq$ ran f. In the simple case where ran f = ran g, the maps f and g are then "onto" the same subset of the environment B, and part of the problem goes away. Even in this case, though, there is the problem of finding, say, a left inverse for g; that is, a structure-preserving map $g^*: B \rightarrow C$ such that $g^* {\circ} g = 1_C$. In other words, it preserves the same relation(s) that g preserves, but in the opposite direction. Note that such a map might exist even if g is not a bijection—a function can have a left inverse without having the right inverse property as well. If such a function g^* does exist, then $g^* {\circ} f$: $A \rightarrow C$ can be constructed and is a morphism of relational systems from α to γ. But it is not *guaranteed* to exist.

3 Relational Knowledge in Higher Cognition

In this chapter, we give a more detailed account of the role of relational knowledge in higher cognition and make further comparisons of symbolically structured processes with lower levels.

Relations versus associations

Our formulation of symbolic structure is based on relations, and relational representations differ from associations in five main ways. These are structural alignment, symbolization, higher-order representation, accessibility, and generalization.

Structural alignment
Structural alignment was defined in chapter 2 as the foundational property of relational knowledge. In essence, entities are assigned to roles, so that *loves(John, Sally)* is represented by assigning *John* to the *Lover* role and *Sally* to the *Loved* role. Similarity depends on role assignment, so *feeds(Jane, cat)* is not similar to *feeds(cat, Jane)* because the elements are assigned to different roles. Role assignment is not part of the definition of associations, and structural alignment is a major difference between relations and associations.

Symbolization
Representations of symbolically structured processes are based on functions and relations, and the symbols for these can form part of the representation (Phillips, Halford, & Wilson, 1995). This contrasts with associations, where the link between entities is not symbolized. Consider two commonplace associations; cup is associated with drink, and cup is also associated with saucer. These associations may vary in strength, but they are of the same kind and are not distinguished by labels, whereas the

corresponding relations are distinct and are labeled. The relation between cup and drink is one of containment: a cup *contains* a drink. However, the relation between cup and saucer is one of relative position: A cup is *placed on* a saucer. This distinction appears to have been realized first by Selz (cited in Humphrey, 1951), who argued that a relational fact, or *wissen,* is defined by the objects that stand in the relation and by the relation itself. This statement is consistent with propositional network models that entail labeled links between entities (e.g., Anderson, 1983, 1993). It is also consistent with the memory model of Humphreys, Wiles, and Dennis (1994, §2.2), which distinguishes between associative processes consisting of a binding linking two items and relational processes comprised of a binding between a relation and two items. Our conception of relational knowledge is much broader than this, but the existence of this conceptual link implies the potential for integration of the memory model of Humphreys, Wiles, and Dennis (1994) with representational rank theory.

Higher-order representations

Symbolization enables relational representations to be arguments to other representations, yielding higher-order relations (Halford, Wilson, & Phillips, 1998; Wilson, Halford et al. 2001). An association cannot be an argument to another association in this way, as noted with respect to nonstructured processes.

Accessibility

Accessibility, in the technical sense defined in chapter 2, is intrinsic to relational representations but does not appear to be inherent in association because it is not absurd to say that there exists an association $E_1 \rightarrow E_2$, but no association $E_2 \rightarrow E_1$. This means that E_1 is not necessarily accessible, given E_2.

Generalization

Generalization of relations is based on mechanisms that include structural correspondence, using the processes of analogy, but generalization of associations is based on element similarity.

Symbolically structured processes depend on relations. One of the most important consequences of this is that they enable analogical reasoning.

Analogy and transfer to isomorphs

Analogy has long been recognized as an important component of intelligence (Binet & Simon, 1980; Piaget, 1950) and is arguably fundamental to higher cognitive processes (Halford, 1993; Hofstadter, 2001). It plays a significant role in mathematics (English & Halford, 1995; Polya, 1954), science (Dunbar, 2001; Dunbar & Klahr, 1989; Gentner et al., 1997; Holyoak & Thagard, 1995; Tweney, 1998), politics, art, religion, pedagogy, communication, humor, and law (see review by Holyoak & Thagard, 1995). Its basic role in reasoning is indicated by the fact that mental models, which are important to some theories of human reasoning (Johnson-Laird, 1983; Johnson-Laird & Byrne, 1991; Polk & Newell, 1995) and of cognitive development (Halford, 1993), are essentially analogs. See box 3.1. Analogy is used to effect transfer between isomorphic tasks (Halford, Bain, et al., 1998; Novick, 1988; Reed, Ackinclose, & Voss, 1990; Reed, 1987), and is particularly important to transfer between domains (Gentner & Gentner, 1983; Gick & Holyoak, 1983).

Box 3.1

A *mental model* comprises a display of entities that represent relations that are essential to the structure of the task and that permit inferences to be made (Goodwin & Johnson-Laird, 2005). There has to be structural correspondence between the mental model and what it represents (e.g., the structure of a reasoning task). Mental model theory is consistent with logical schemas (Rips, 2001) to some extent, the essential difference being that a logical schema comprises a formal principle (e.g., modus ponens), whereas a mental model comprises arrays of entities, the principle being implicit rather than explicit. However, the logical schema still has to be mapped onto a problem, and since this mapping is the essential operation of relational knowledge, mental models and logical schemas do not differ in ways that materially affect our argument. See also Johnson-Laird (2010).

An *analogy* is a structural correspondence between two cognitive representations, one called a *base* or *source,* the other a *target* (Gentner, 1983, Holyoak, 2012; Holland et al., 1986).

Contemporary models of analogy (Doumas, Hummel, & Sandhofer, 2008; Falkenhainer, Forbus, & Gentner, 1989; Halford et al., 1994; Holyoak

& Thagard, 1989; Hummel & Holyoak, 1997, Holyoak & Hummel, 2001; Keane, Ledgeway, & Duff, 1994; Mitchell & Hofstadter, 1990; Wilson, Marcus, & Halford, 2001) appear to have reached a consensus that the following two principles are basic to analogy: *uniqueness of mapping*, so that each element in one structure is mapped to one and only one element in the other structure; and *symbol–argument consistency*, so that if a relational instance $r(a_1, ..., a_n)$ in one structure is mapped to a relational instance $s(b_1, ..., b_n)$ in the other structure, then r is mapped to s, and the arguments $a_1, ..., a_n$ are mapped to the arguments $b_1, ..., b_n$, respectively, and vice versa. These are essentially structural correspondence criteria.

Box 3.2

ACME: An early model that successfully implemented mapping by parallel constraint satisfaction was the Analogical Constraint Mapping Engine (ACME; Holyoak & Thagard, 1989). The model implemented the principles of structural correspondence by forming connections between units. Uniqueness was implemented by inhibitory connections, which tended to preclude mapping to more than one element, while symbol-argument consistency was implemented by excitatory connections that tended to ensure that arguments of a relation are mapped in a way that is consistent with the mapping of the corresponding symbols. One test of the model entailed matching the performance of a sample of adults on the *boy-dog* analogy, with the source and target propositions as shown in table 3.1. The correct mappings are shown in the third column.

Five of the eight participants produced the same six mappings generated by ACME (as shown in the right column), and two produced four of the six, while one participant produced no mappings. This study provides an existence proof that corresponds to our intuition that it is possible to map representations without benefit of semantic cues (e.g., there is no semantic information indicating that *smart* should be mapped to *hungry*). The mapping is justified solely by structural correspondence, as embodied in the principles of analogical mapping.

One important point is that, while there is no doubt that semantic and pragmatic (e.g., motivational) information can influence mapping, structural correspondence remains the criterion that determines the validity of a mapping. For example, suppose that *hungry(Rover)* had been *smart(Rover)*. Then it would have been easy to map *smart(Rover)* to *smart(Bill)*. However, structural correspondence still would apply, semantic information simply making it easier to implement. Another point is that, according to relational complexity theory, this analogy is too complex for the whole set of

---

Box 3.2
(continued)

propositions to be mapped in a single step, and the task would have to be segmented into subtasks. For example, I find it useful to map *smart* to *hungry* first because both occur twice, and then *Bill* (which occurs twice) is mapped to *Rover* (which occurs twice). Then the remaining mappings can be performed, thereby verifying the initial partial mapping. A smaller set of propositions could be mapped in parallel, without segmenting the task in this way.

Table 3.1
Mappings for the *boy-dog* analogy

Source	Target	Correct Mapping
smart(Bill)	*hungry(Rover)*	*smart—hungry*
tall(Bill)	*friendly(Rover)*	*tall—friendly*
smart(Steve)	*hungry(Fido)*	*timid—frisky*
timid(Tom)	*frisky(Blackie)*	*Tom—Blackie*
tall(Tom)	*friendly(Blackie)*	*Steve—Fido*
		Bill—Rover

The similarity in this respect between representations and analogy was recognized by Holland et al. (1986), who showed that representations are morphisms between a mental model and the environment, and analogy is a second-order morphism between two mental models. For discussion of morphisms, see the glossary and the appendix in chapter 2. The important point for our purposes is that the ability to form analogies follows naturally from our theory of representations because structural correspondence is transitive.

Analogical reasoning is influenced by similarity of the elements and relations in the mapped representations (Holyoak, 2012), and also is influenced by knowledge of the domain (Goswami, 1992). Thus, the mapping of the premises *John is taller than Peter* and *Michael is taller than John* into the ordering schema *top-middle-bottom* (see chapter 1, figure 1.3) would be easier if, for example, we knew that Michael was very tall, as Michael could be mapped to the *top* position, and less structural information would need to be processed to make this assignment. Nevertheless, structural correspondence is crucial (Blanchette & Dunbar, 2000), and analogies can be formed without similarity or semantic knowledge. For example, with the transitive inference example in figure 1.3, and in the analogy used by Holyoak and Thagard (1989), semantic knowledge plays no part. Thus, structural correspondence enables reasoning that transcends similarity and domain knowledge.

The mapping criteria are soft, in the sense that some inconsistencies can be tolerated if the overall match is good. These criteria are incorporated in computational models such as that of Holyoak and Thagard (1989), detailed in box 3.2; and Doumas, Hummel, and Sandhofer (2008), discussed in chapter 7.

Variables and structural correspondence

One of the basic properties of symbolic processes is that they use representations that include variables and have some independence of content. Analogical mappings that meet the criteria for structural correspondence, as defined previously, align entities in corresponding roles, so the roles effectively function as variables. Relations have roles that range over the set of elements, which can be instantiated in a variety of ways. Therefore, representing relational instances and putting them in structural correspondence by analogical mapping create representations in which the slots function as variables. This is a form of abstraction. For example, the relation *olderThan* has two arguments or roles, one for an older entity and one for a younger entity. These can be instantiated in a variety of ways, such as *olderThan(Tom, John)*, *olderThan(John, Peter)*, and *olderThan(Tom, Peter)*. The slot for the older entity and the slot for the younger entity both function as variables.

Transfer between isomorphs and the generativity test

Analogical mapping can effect transfer between isomorphic tasks, and it provides a useful test for symbolically structured processes, as Halford, Bain, et al. (1998) have shown. It can be illustrated with conditional discrimination, which has a well-defined structure (see figure 2.1 in chapter 2). The task can be learned by a functionally structured process called *configural association,* by Rudy (1991), without representation of the components of the structure, as noted in chapter 2. However, this would not permit transfer to isomorphs. With symbolically structured representations, transfer to isomorphs is possible and, importantly, it is possible to generate items that have not been presented thus far. This can be illustrated with the isomorphic task shown in figure 2.1B. Once one item in the isomorphic task is known (e.g., *green, circle → R+*), it is possible to generate the remaining three items, regardless of the order of presentation. The item *green, circle* → *R+* is an *information item* because it enables the isomorphic task to be mapped to the original task, permitting the remaining items of the isomorphic task to be generated. Figure 2.1C shows the correct mappings between elements of the original and isomorphic conditional discrimination tasks. We refer to this as the *generativity test,* and it is an important empirical criterion for symbolically structured processes. As we will show in chapter 6, the generativity test can be used with inarticulate participants in very simple tasks, such as the two-object discrimination learning set task, and provides a powerful way of distinguishing symbolic from subsymbolic performance.

It is possible to construct an extended version of conditional discrimination, in which subjects are required to demonstrate *accessibility* of components as a test for symbolically structured processing. In the task in figure 2.1, subjects might be given a shape (e.g., *triangle*) and a response (e.g., *R+*) and asked to determine which color is required to satisfy that response (*black*). This accessibility test was used by Andrews et al. (2012), and also by Halford, Bain, et al. (1998) with a different structure but the same principles.

Notice that both functionally structured and symbolically structured processes can be studied with the same procedure, conditional discrimination. The levels are distinguished by performance on isomorphic tasks, with the generativity test. This is important because no extraneous demands, such as verbal protocols, explanations, or statements of rules, are required. It is therefore usable with pre-articulate or inarticulate participants. We will argue that is an important technique for determining whether symbolic processes are being used.

Transfer to isomorphs with generation of unknown items is a form of analogy because it entails mapping the structure of the original task into the transfer task (Gentner, 1983; Halford, Bain et al., 1998). However, this requires the relations in the task to be represented. Analogical mapping to isomorphs is not possible with configurations because the elements lose their identity, and the structure is not represented (e.g., in figure 2.1B, the configuration "black/triangle" does not provide a basis for transfer to "green/circle"). While a three-layered net such as that shown in figure 2.1D could learn conditional discrimination, transfer to isomorphs would not match that of symbolically structured processes (Phillips, 2000). However, symbolic connectionist models of analogy, such as that of Holyoak and Hummel (2001) or Wilson, Halford et al. (2001), could do so in principle.

Database operations

A collection of facts in a memory system is a collection of relational instances. Hence, it can be analyzed by mathematical and computational tools applicable to relations. The relevant field of knowledge has been investigated by computer scientists studying relational databases (e.g., Codd, 1990). Here, we summarize the ideas from relational database theory that are relevant to cognitive modeling.

We begin our description of database theory with some definitions. A relational instance or proposition has a number of *attributes*. For example, *hasRead(Jane, Iliad)* has two attributes, one for each position in the template *hasRead(–,–)*; that is, one for *Jane* and one for *Iliad*. The two attributes in our example might be termed *Reader* and *Book*. Then we would say that {*Reader, Book*} is the *schema* of the relation. Another example, representing part of the relation *between*, is shown in table 3.2 in the tabular form favored in database theory. The top row of the table is the schema, and each subsequent row is a *tuple* of the relation.

The familiar operations on relations include *union* and *intersection*, which can be applied to sets of tuples. Further operations of significance to us include *project, select, natural join,* and *attribute renaming,* which we shall now describe.

Projection
The *project* operator discards some of the columns of the table. So if S = {*Hazard1, Hazard2*} in the example in table 3.2, then the projection $\pi_S(r)$ is as shown in table 3.3. We can talk about projecting the whole relation, or just individual tuples.

Table 3.2
A table as a representation of four tuples in a relation r on the schema {*Hazard1, Person, Hazard2*}

Hazard1	Person	Hazard2
Devil	Joe	Deep blue sea
Rock	Mary	Hard place
Stool 1	Chris	Stool 2
Stool 1	Jane	Stool 2

Table 3.3

The relation obtained by projecting the relation *r* in table 3.2 onto {*Hazard1, Hazard2*}

Hazard1	Hazard2
Devil	Deep blue sea
Rock	Hard place
Stool 1	Stool 2

Note: The last two rows of *r* become a single row in the projection.

Table 3.4

The relation here is the selection from the relation *r* in table 3.3 using the restriction expressed in the relation in table 3.2
schema:

Hazard1	Person
Devil	Joe
Rock	Joe
Stool1	Joe

Selection from *r* for this schema:

Hazard1	Person	Hazard2
Devil	Joe	Deep blue sea

Selection

The *select* operator produces a new relation that contains only those rows of a relation that satisfy some specified condition. Common applications in computer databases might use a condition like Age $\geq$ 55. In our applications, we shall be interested in a specific type of restriction, which we now describe. If *r* and *s* are relations on the relational schemas *R* and *S*, then we define the selection from *r* for schema *s* to be the tuples *t* from *r* that have a "compatible" tuple $u \in s$, in the sense that the components of *t* agree with those of *u* on their common attributes. Table 3.4 has an example.

Join

The *natural join* operator combines relations based on a common value in a shared attribute. If *r* and *s* are relations whose schemata have a common element, like *Wife* in table 3.5, then the *natural join of r and s* is obtained

Table 3.5
The relation on the right is the *join* of *r* and *s* along the shared field *Wife*

r		s		Join of *r* and *s*		
Husband	Wife	Wife	Parent	Husband	Wife	Parent
Tom	Tania	Tania	Ursula	Tom	Tania	Ursula
Dick	Dora	Tania	Vernon	Tom	Tania	Vernon
Harry	Helen	Dora	Frank	Dick	Dora	Frank
		Helen	Irma	Harry	Helen	Irma

by "gluing together" all the tuples in *r* and all the tuples in *s* that have the same *Wife* value. See table 3.5 for an example.

Renaming

Sometimes the attribute on which the join is to be made doesn't have the same name in the two relations to be joined: In the relation *s* in table 3.5, it is surprising that the attributes are called *Wife* and *Parent*—presumably they started out as *Daughter* and *Parent*, but then *Daughter* was renamed as *Wife*. *Renaming* just changes the name of an attribute/column.

Existence of the *select, project,* and natural *join* operations extends the accessibility of relational representations; thus, the *select* and *project* operators enable specific components of relations to be retrieved. Another property is that relations can be transformed in various ways. The natural *join* operator corresponds to the important function of integration of cognitive representations. In transitive inference, considered in chapter 1, premises are integrated into an ordered set of three elements from which a transitive inference can be derived. Another operator is *inverse*, which allows *larger(elephant, mouse)* to be transformed to *smaller(mouse, elephant)*.

The transformations *select, project, natural join,* and *inverse* mean that our conception of relational knowledge is relevant to linguistic processes, such as grammatical transformations. Thus, *John loves Mary* can be transformed to the passive voice as *Mary is loved by John* by utilizing the inverse operation; i.e., *loves(John,Mary)* becomes *is_loved_by(Mary,John)*. The change in the relation symbol from *loves* to *is_loved_by* serves as a marker of the change from the active to the passive voice.

To summarize, we have expanded our conception of relational knowledge, first by a more detailed comparison with subsymbolic processes, then by considering the role that it plays in some higher cognitive processes, including analogy and transfer to isomorphs. We have also outlined relational database theory as used in computer science to indicate some of the further potential for relational knowledge in cognitive theory. Now we consider how the distinctions between the three levels of cognition that we have defined correspond to the architectures and processes of distinct neural networks.

Symbolic structure and functional structure: Neural net models

The properties of functionally structured processes are well captured by certain neural net models that we considered in chapter 2. Now we want to look at some neural nets that capture the essential properties of symbolically structured processes.

As noted in chapter 2, structural alignment is the core property of symbolically structured cognition, so we will consider two approaches to this problem. The first is based on synchronous oscillation (Doumas, Hummel, & Sandhofer, 2008; Hummel & Holyoak, 1997; Shastri & Ajjanagadde, 1993). Units representing a role oscillate in phase with units representing the filler bound to that role, and out of phase with units representing other roles and fillers (see figures 3.1 A and B). This has been modified in the Discovery of Relations by Analogy (DORA) model (Doumas, Hummel, & Sandhofer, 2008), where the roles and fillers oscillate in close temporal proximity (though not synchronously), but the principle is essentially the same. The relational instance *loves*(*John*,*Mary*) would be represented by units representing the agent role of *loves* oscillating in synchrony with units representing *John*, while units representing the patient role of *loves* oscillated in synchrony with units representing *Mary*. Units representing the agent oscillate out of synchrony with units representing the patient. The DORA model implements the properties of relational knowledge listed by Halford, Wilson, and Phillips, (1998, §4.2). However, the most important property for our purposes is that more complex relations require more distinct phases, so a binary relation requires three phases (including one for the relation symbol), and a ternary relation needs four phases, as shown in figures 3.1A and 3.1B. Quaternary relations require five phases, and this is one possible explanation for the upper limit of relational complexity, to be discussed in chapter 4.

The other approach to binding is based on a product operation, such as tensor product (Halford, Wilson & Phillips, 1998; Smolensky, 1990) or circular convolution (Plate, 1995). In the Structured Tensor Analogical Reasoning (STAR) model (Halford, Wilson & Phillips, 1998; Wilson, Halford, et al., 2001), the relation-symbol and roles (arguments) are each

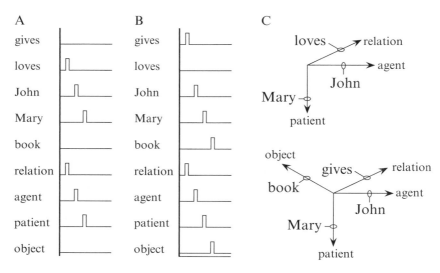

Figure 3.1

A, B. Synchronous oscillation representation of role bindings in two propositions: *loves(John, Mary)* and *gives(John, Mary, book)*. C. tensor representations of the same bindings, shown schematically. Here, *loves(John, Mary)* is represented by a three-dimensional structure in which vectors representing *loves*, *John*, and *Mary* each occupy one rank of the tensor. Similarly, *gives(John, Mary, book)* is represented by a four-dimensional structure in which vectors *gives*, *John*, *Mary*, *book* each occupy one rank of the tensor. Relation symbols and fillers are linked by binding units, as shown in figure 3.2.

Box 3.3

In the STAR model, the relational instance $r(a_1, a_2, ..., a_n)$ is represented in a tensor product space $V_R \otimes V_1 \otimes V_2 \otimes ... \otimes V_n$. The representations of relational instances can be superimposed, the resulting structure being called a tensor product. For example, *loves(John, Mary)* and *loves(Cathy, Tom)* would be represented as $v_{loves} \otimes v_{John} \otimes v_{Mary} + v_{loves} \otimes v_{Cathy} \otimes v_{Tom}$. In general, the *n*-ary relational instance $r(a_1, a_2, ..., a_n)$ is represented by a rank $n + 1$ tensor $v_r \otimes v_{a1} \otimes v_{a2} \otimes ... \otimes v_{an}$. A set of relational instances is represented by the sum of such tensors. Operations resembling vector-matrix products are used to access the content of tensor representations, so

$$v_{loves} \bullet (v_{loves} \otimes v_{John} \otimes v_{Mary} + v_{loves} \otimes v_{Cathy} \otimes v_{Tom}) = v_{John} \otimes v_{Mary} + v_{Cathy} \otimes v_{Tom}.$$

Here, • represents the vector-tensor product. It is common to use orthonormal sets of representation vectors, although near-orthonormal representations (e.g., sparse random vectors) are a possibility too (Wilson, Street, & Halford, 1995).

represented by the vectors, and the binding is represented by the outer product of these vectors, as shown in figures 3.1C and 3.2. For mathematical details, see box 3.3. STAR also has features in common with an integrative memory model (Humphreys, Bain, & Pike, 1989) and a role-filler binding model put forth by Smolensky (1990).

In the STAR model, there is a natural correspondence between the mathematical properties of a relation and its representation in neural nets. Order is significant in a tensor, just as it is in a relation. Thus, one axis of the tensor represents the relation-symbol, and each of the remaining axes corresponds to a role (argument) of the relation. At the neural net level, there is a group of units for each tensor axis (relation symbol or role) connected to a group of binding units, one for each tensor element, representing relational instances. Thus, units are connected by binding units, as shown in figure 3.2.

Symbol-argument-argument Representation

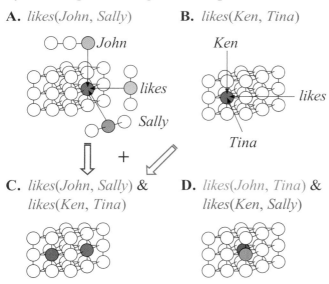

A. *likes(John, Sally)*

John

likes

Sally

B. *likes(Ken, Tina)*

Ken

likes

Tina

+

C. *likes(John, Sally)* &
likes(Ken, Tina)

D. *likes(John, Tina)* &
likes(Ken, Sally)

Figure 3.2
The STAR model representation of binary relations. The input units, representing the relation symbol (*likes*) and fillers (*John* and *Sally*), are shown in panel A. Each input unit is connected to 3 × 3 = 9 binding units; for example, the pink unit in the *John* input vector provides input to all nine binding units on the rightmost face of the 3 × 3 × 3 array. For simplification, the input units are omitted from panels B, C and D. Reproduced from Halford, Wilson, & Phillips (2010), figure 3, panels c–f. Copyright © Elsevier, 2010. Reproduced with permission from Elsevier.

The STAR model implements the accessibility property because components can be retrieved from the tensor representation of one or more relational instances. Thus, given the representation in figure 3.2A, the following queries yield the outputs indicated: *likes(John, ?)* yields *Sally*; likes(?, *Sally*) yields *John* and ?(*John, Sally*) yields *likes*.

The similarity of two relational representations also can be determined from structures of this type, provided that the representation is extended to include a similarity metric. The important thing is that components are aligned with roles in the representation. Thus, *feeds(Jane, cat)* and *feeds(cat, Jane)* would derive most of their similarity from the common relation *feeds*, since *Jane* and *cat* do not align between the two representations. The similarity of these representations would be low because elements are aligned with different roles, whereas *feeds(Bob, dog)* would be observed to have higher similarity to *feeds(Jane, cat)* than to *feeds(cat, Jane)* because of the similarity between *Bob* and *Jane* and between *dog* and *cat*. Retrieval processes as used in proportional analogy are shown in box 3.4 and figure 3.3.

In this representation, the components, symbol, and arguments retain their identities since each is represented by a single vector, and the same vector can be used to represent a component in any role. For example, *loves(John, Mary)* and *loves(Mary, John)* are represented by the same vectors representing each component in the two very different propositions. Therefore, *Mary* is represented by v_{Mary} and *John* by v_{John} in both roles. Any component can be retrieved from this representation, thus fulfilling the accessibility property (Halford, Wilson, & Phillips, 1998). The accessibility property is applied to proportional analogy problems in box 3.4 and figure 3.3.

Box 3.4

> **STAR:** The STAR model (Halford et al. 1994) achieved the binding and retrieval of facts in a system that solved proportional analogy problems. A collection of facts like *motherOf(woman, baby)*, *largerThan(woman, baby)*, *loves(woman, baby)*, and corresponding facts for *mare* and *foal* where applicable, plus some irrelevant facts like *largerThan(mare, cat)*, were bound to the system's tensor product network memory using the outer product binding technique adopted from Smolensky (1990). Then, vectors representing the concepts *woman* and *baby* were provided as cues to the tensor, resulting in the retrieval of the bundle of relation symbols bound to that pair of concepts, as shown in figure 3.3.

Box 3.4
(continued)

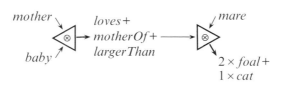

Figure 3.3
STAR model processing of a proportional analogy.

The unanalyzed bundle of relation symbols was then input on the same side of the tensor, while *mare* was input as the first argument, resulting in retrieval from the second argument position of a salience-weighted set of vectors representing concepts, with the most salient concept—in this case *foal*—corresponding to the solution of the proportional analogy task.

It is important to note that role-filler bindings alone are insufficient to define propositions or relational instances. If we represent *likes(John, Sally)* and *likes(Ken,Tina)* solely by binding John and Ken to the "liker" role and Sally and Tina to the "liked" role, the result would be identical to *likes(John,Tina)* and *likes(Ken,Sally)*. The role assignments do not represent the *n*-tuples that comprise the relational instances (in this example, they do not show who is the liker of whom). By contrast, these representations are distinguished in STAR, as shown in figures 3.2C and 3.2D. In DORA, this problem is obviated because propositions are represented by four hierarchical levels of units (as shown in figure 7.3), and the binding of the P unit at the top of the hierarchy to the RB, PO, and semantic units serves to identify specific propositions. This problem is serious, however, for relations that entail many instances, as Halford, Wilson, & Phillips (1998, §§4.1.1.1 and 4.1.3) point out. For example, in the ternary relation *arithmetical addition*, every number is bound to every role (e.g., the number 3 is bound to the first "addend" role in 3 + 2 = 5, to the second "addend" role in 4 + 3 = 7, and to the "sum" role in 1 + 2 = 3). The effect is that role-filler bindings alone do not identify relational instances. DORA and similar models get around this by representing relational instances as tree structures whose root corresponds to the whole relational instance, thereby linking together all the bindings associated with the instance.

The merits of competing models, including those that employ role-filler and symbol-argument-argument bindings and product versus synchronous oscillation, are likely to be debated for some time. For our purposes, the properties that are common to these methods are more important because they indicate the properties that are required for symbolic-relational processes. Specifically, each component is preserved in the binding. In the tensor product model (figure 3.1C), the *rank* of the tensor product is one more than the *arity* of the relation. In the synchronous oscillation model (figure 3.1, A, B), the phases correspond to the components of the relation, including the *relation* symbol. Thus, rank equals number of phases of oscillation plus one. We can see that even models as different as synchronous oscillation and tensor products agree that the relation-symbol and each argument or slot must retain its identity in the composite representation. This means that the concept of rank is relevant to both. A model that represents an n-ary relation necessarily has $n + 1$ components that retain their identity in the representation.

One take-home message from the tensor product model is that core properties of relational knowledge can be implemented by the comparatively simple procedure of linking structurally aligned components of a relational representation in such a way that all are accessible, as shown in figures 3.1C and 3.2. Structural alignment is the essential property of relational representations, as noted in chapter 2, but once that is achieved, the rest depends on interconnection between components (specifically, between symbol and arguments and between arguments). These interconnections are conveniently implemented by computing the tensor product of the vectors representing the components, or by DORA-style relational instance trees. The important implication is that this very complex set of interconnections provides the basis of relational, and therefore symbolic, representations. Those brain regions that are activated in representation of relations, therefore, should be able to provide this rich set of interconnections.

However, a critical feature of relational knowledge is that inference and prediction of outcomes will depend on assignment to roles (i.e., on structural alignment). In the reference example in figure 1.2, prediction and inference clearly would be impaired if the taller element (*John*) were assigned to the shorter role and the shorter element (*Peter*) were assigned to the taller role. It is clear, therefore, that accuracy of inference and prediction is a strong driver of role assignment. However, there is a deeper issue here as to how this role assignment is achieved. In the current example, it would mean that taller elements must be assigned consistently to the same role and shorter elements to a different role. These then become representations of the taller and shorter roles, respectively, by virtue of consistent alignment.

The demands of prediction will tend to drive consistent role assignment. That is, it will ensure that in a series of instances such as *taller(John, Peter)*, ..., *taller(Michael, John)*, the taller element will be assigned to the appropriate slot, otherwise the representation will become fuzzy and prediction will be impaired. We will consider this issue further in chapter 6.

To summarize, representational ranks are shown in figure 3.4 together with the cognitive process represented, the representation in the tensor product-based neural net models, and typical cognitive tasks.

Cognitive neuroscience evidence for symbolically structured processes

The link between relational knowledge and neuroscience has been illustrated by Andrews et al. (2013) in their reinterpretation of a classic study by Luria (1980, p. 581). Luria examined the performance of frontally impaired patients on problems such as, "A son is 5 years old; in 15 years, his father will be twice as old as he. How old is his father now?" As interpreted by Andrews et al., (2013):

A successful strategy needs to be guided by a sequence of operations, for example: $(5 + 15) = 20; 2 \times 20 = 40; 40 - 15 = 25$. According to Relational Complexity theory planning such a sequence entails a composition of ternary relations and this would impose a high processing load (Andrews & Halford, 2002). Frontally-impaired patients appeared unable to represent such a complex relation, and they defaulted to simpler relations such as $15 \times 5 = 75$ or $3 \times 15 = 45$ which did not match the structure of the problem. Their ineffective problem solving attempts might reflect reduced capacity for relational processing. (p. 45)

The functions of the prefrontal cortex (PFC) correspond in many ways to symbolic cognition. The PFC has a high degree of interconnectivity and appears to be specialized for activation-based processing, with the corresponding properties of speed, flexibility or modifiability, and accessibility (O'Reilly & Munakata, 2000, pp. 380–381). Representations are more likely to be arbitrary, language-based, and discrete, and the components, such as vocabulary, need to have been learned previously. The PFC appears to be suitable for representing relations (Robin & Holyoak, 1995). This is consistent with evidence that the PFC is associated with differentially large growth during human evolution (Preuss, 2000), and with the large gaps between human and ape reasoning (Penn et al., 2008a). In the last decade,

Cognitive Process	Neural Net Specification	Representational Rank	Typical Cognitive Tasks
no internal representation (elemental association)	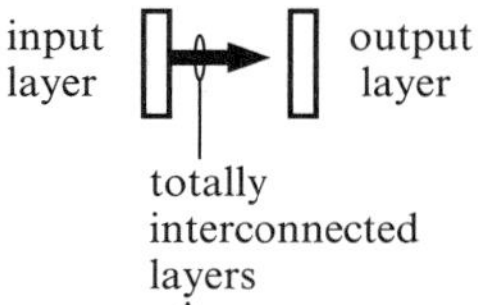 input layer → output layer; totally interconnected layers	0	conditioning; linear transitivity of choice
computed internal representation (configural association)	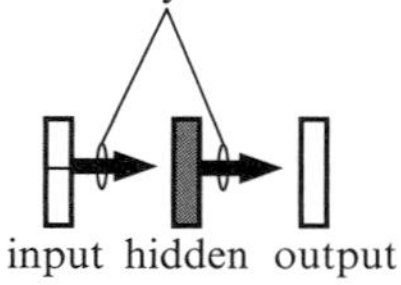 input hidden output	1	conditional discrimination; prototype; circular transitivity of choice
unary relation	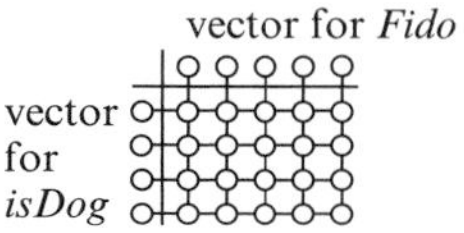 vector for *Fido*; vector for *isDog*	2	match-to-sample; identity-position integration; category label distinct from category
binary relation	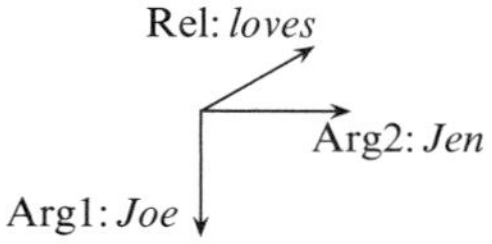 Rel: *loves*; Arg2: *Jen*; Arg1: *Joe*	3	relational match-to-sample; mastery of A-not-B; complementary categories
ternary relation	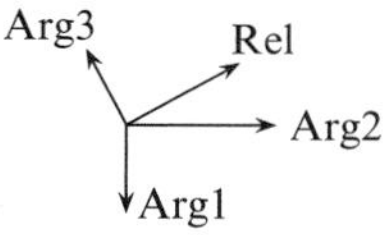 Arg3; Rel; Arg2; Arg1	4	transitive inference; hierarchical categories; concept of mind
quaternary relation	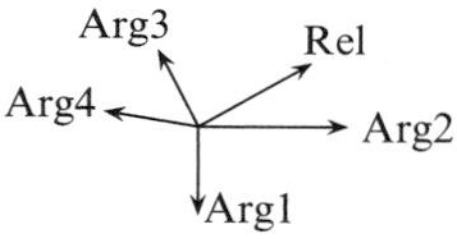 Arg3; Rel; Arg4; Arg2; Arg1	5	proportion; balance scale
quinary relation	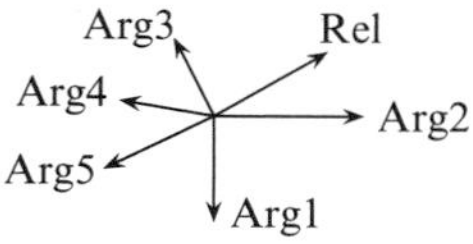 Arg3; Rel; Arg4; Arg2; Arg5; Arg1	6	certain cases of: • double centre-embedded sentences • Tower of Hanoi

Figure 3.4
Representational ranks with cognitive processes, schematics for corresponding neural nets, and typical cognitive tasks. Adapted from figure 16.6 of Halford et al. (2007) by permission of Oxford University Press.

both brain imaging and impairment studies have yielded more detailed knowledge of regions of the PFC that are involved in symbolic processes (Burgess, Dumontheil, & Gilbert, 2007; Ramnani & Owen, 2004). Smith, Keramatian, and Christoff (2007) show in a direct and elegant manner that the rostrolateral prefrontal cortex (RLPFC) is activated when processing relations. A task that required the comparison of relations (e.g., whether shapes differ by color or texture) was compared to a control task that required the comparison of a single feature (e.g., shape or texture). Functional magnetic resonance imaging (fMRI) records showed that relational comparison activated the RLPFC (lateral BA10) in all ten participants. It also has been suggested that the PFC might account for relational processing in executive functions (Halford et al., 2010; Waltz et al., 1999, 2004).

In this section, we consider brain regions that are activated when adults construct representations in working memory, and establish correspondences between cognitive representations. In a subsequent section titled "Developmental cognitive neuroscience evidence", we will consider the development of these regions and the implications for symbolic processes in infancy.

Working memory

Maintenance of a dynamic binding between verbal and spatial information in working memory produced greater activation in the right middle and superior frontal gyri , as compared with separate retention of verbal and spatial information (Prabhakaran et al. 2000). Other involvements of the PFC in memory appear to reflect the control of information (Postle, 2006) or strategic processes (Stuss & Alexander, 2005), but since these are symbolic, they actually may reflect the processing of relations. The PFC appears to be responsible for the maintenance of prospective (i.e., goal-related) memory, whereas the parietal cortex appears to be responsible for retrospective (i.e., sensory-related) memory (Passingham, Rowe, & Sakai, 2004). A well-known task that requires dynamic binding in working memory is the n-back task, in which participants must recognize whether the current item in a stream matches the item presented n places back, where the value of n varies between 1 and 3. Lesions to the PFC have been linked to impaired performance on n-back tasks (Andrews et al., 2013). Christensen and Wright (2010) found that patients with left frontal lesions performed comparably to control participants on 1-back tasks, but they performed significantly more poorly on 2-back tasks.

There is evidence that the dorsolateral regions of the PFC play a role in a verbal working memory test, the letter number sequencing (LNS) subtest of the Wechsler Adult Intelligence Scale (WAIS; Psychological Corporation, 1998). Digits and alphabetic letters are presented in a mixed order, and participants are required to report the digits in ascending order, then the letters in alphabetic order. This requires the encoding of digits and letters in working memory, together with operations that sort them into the correct sequence. In an Event-Related Potential (ERP) study, Hoppenbrouwers et al. (2012) found that with healthy controls, letter-number sequence performance correlated with long-interval intracortical inhibition over the dorsolateral regions of the PFC. In a recent study of hypothesis testing using a modified Wason Selection Task, Cocchi et al. (2013) found that encoding the rule activated a cingulo-opercular network, and processing the cards activated a fronto-parietal network. The latter requires comparison of a conditional rule (of the form *if P, then Q*) with a card potentially confirming or disconfirming the rule. This requires construction of a representation in working memory. This study will be discussed further in chapter 8.

Integrating information

Integration of information is crucial to symbolic processes, and the PFC appears to be specialized for this function. Ramnani and Owen (2004) proposed that the functions of the anterior prefrontal cortex (APFC) can be distinguished, not by cognitive domain, but by the coordination and integration of information processing. This is consistent with the proposal of Christoff and Owen (2006) that the functions of the RLPFC are related more to cognitive complexity than to a cognitive domain. Christoff et al. (2003) also propose that the RLPFC might be specialized for processing of internally generated information. There are still other proposals along the same lines. Huey, Krueger, and Grafman (2006) propose that the human PFC is important for maintaining a stimulus over time and for integrating information. De Pisapia and Braver (2008) examined integration in mental arithmetic using fMRI. Left APFC (BA10/46) showed peak activation in integration relative to control conditions. Burgess, Dumontheil, and Gilbert (2007) propose that the RLPFC (BA10) selects internal versus external sources of activation. The APFC is involved in integrating information represented elsewhere in the brain, such as the parietal cortex (Jung & Haier, 2007), maintaining it in an active state, and switching attention between internal and externally generated information.

There is also evidence for a widespread bilateral fronto-parietal network being recruited during relational integration (Golde, Von Cramon, & Schubotz, 2010). This network included APFC but not premotor cortex (PMC). The PMC was engaged in sequential concatenation of relations, whereas the APFC was engaged in integration.

Premise integration activates certain regions of the PFC, and some studies have isolated this process. Waltz et al. (1999) found a double dissociation in which prefrontal patients were seriously impaired in their ability to integrate relations but unimpaired in episodic memory and semantic knowledge, whereas temporal patients showed the opposite pattern. In an fMRI study of explicit transitive inference (Fangmeier et al., 2006) premise integration activated an additional area in the APFC, the middle frontal (BA 10) and anterior cingulate (BA 32), as compared with premise encoding, which did not. An impairment study by Waechter et al. (2013) found that transitive inference depended on the parietal cortex rather than the prefrontal cortex. However, unlike studies by Fangmeier et al. (2006) and the study by Maybery et al. (1986), premises were presented verbally rather than spatially, which increased the processing required to construct a mental model of the premises. More importantly, premise integration was not differentiated from premise coding, which might have made activation of the PFC less apparent in the data. While there is no reason to doubt that the parietal cortex is involved in transitive inference, this finding does not challenge the conclusion that premise integration activates regions of the PFC.

Implicit transitivity, which does not require premise integration, activates the hippocampus (Preston et al., 2004; Smith & Squire, 2005; Van Elzakker et al., 2003), and BA 46 (Acuna et al., 2002), but it does not appear to activate BA 10, although this might occur if an analytic ordering strategy is used (Libben & Titone, 2008). An fMRI study by Moses et al. (2010) found that the hippocampus and caudate interacted cooperatively, thereby increasing accuracy and awareness, while decreasing reliance on associative learning. Hinton et al. (2010) found that responses based on ordinal position in a dimension activated the inferior frontal cortex, dorsolateral PFC, and parietal cortex. An ERP study of conditional reasoning (modus ponens, modus tollens) by Qiu et al. (2007) showed increased activation in the right anterior cingulate cortex (BA 24) between 700 and 1700 milliseconds when premise integration was expected to occur. The integrative functions of the RPFC have been differentiated further by Bunge, Helskog, and Wendelken (2009) and Wendelken, Chung, and Bunge (2012). These studies further support the role of the RLPFC in integrating different types of input, such as semantic and visuospatial information, thereby supporting higher-level human cognition.

Analogy

Analogy depends on dynamic mappings between representations, and fMRI studies of analogy have indicated activation of the left frontopolar cortex (Bunge et al., 2005), the left frontal pole (BA 9 and BA10; Green et al., 2006), and bilaterally in the PFC (right BA11/47 and left BA45; Luo et al., 2003). A positron emission tomography (PET) study by Wharton et al. (2000) indicated that analogy activated the left prefrontal and inferior parietal cortices.

More recent studies tend to amplify the role of the PFC in analogical reasoning. An fMRI study by Green et al. (2012) showed that frontopolar (left superior frontal gyrus; BA9/10) involvement during the generation of analogical solutions increased as the semantic distance of the analogical mapping increased, even after controlling for task difficulty. An example of an item with greater semantic distance is *blindness: sight:: poverty: ?*, whereas an example item with lesser semantic distance is *blindness: sight:: deafness: ?* Greater semantic distance was interpreted as requiring more creativity.

Several proportional analogies, *A:B::C:D*, were assessed by Krawczyk et al. (2010) in an fMRI study involving three phases: *encoding* (*A:B* presented, encode/induce the relation); *mapping/inference* (*C* term presented, map the *A* term to the *C* term, then infer a *D* term); and *response* (*D* term presented, verify whether *D* completes the analogy). In the encoding phase, there was greater activation in the analogy condition compared to semantic and perceptual control conditions in frontal regions, including the left dorsolateral prefrontal cortex (DLPFC), left inferior frontal gyrus (LIFG), left middle frontal gyrus (LMFG), medial PFC, and posterior medial PFC. The analogy condition required the greatest attention and memory for the *A:B* relation. In the mapping/inference phase, there was greater activation in the analogy condition compared to perceptual control condition in the LIFG. (The semantic condition was intermediate between the other two conditions.) In the response phase, there was greater activation in control conditions than the analogy condition in the left DLPFC, left MFG, and medial PFC (reflective responses were more constrained in the analogy condition and more open-ended in control conditions). An ERP study by Maguire et al. (2012) found differences at the left frontal electrodes during the encoding and mapping/inference phases of analogies relative to semantic and perceptual conditions. The timing of the activity differed according to phase. This research provided neural and behavioral evidence that the analogy problems involve a highly active evaluation of the $A:B$ pair.

Complex relational processing

Selective activation of the PFC has been observed with tasks of high relational complexity. Kroger et al. (2002) parametrically varied the relational complexity of modified Raven's matrix problems and found selective activation of the left APFC. A study of patients with Alzheimer's disease (Waltz et al., 2004) found that dysfunction of the PFC was associated with impaired relational integration. They conclude "that intact PFC is necessary for the on-line integration of relational representations and that this capacity may constitute the essence of executive function" (p. 303). Findings that the most anterior portions of the PFC, especially the fronto-polar cortex, are activated when complex relations are being processed support proposals that the APFC is specialized for integrating representations and processing complex relations.

Developmental cognitive neuroscience evidence

Maturation of the brain involves complex, dynamic processes that begin shortly after conception and continue into late adolescence or adulthood. Measures of synaptic density and elimination (Huttenlocher & Dabholkar, 1997) and of myelination (Paterson et al., 2006) show that prefrontal regions are the last to mature. Dramatic changes in myelination continue in the dorsal, medial, and lateral regions of the frontal cortex during adolescence (Nelson, Thomas, & De Haan, 2006). Glucose metabolism in the frontal and association cortices increases between 8 and 12 months of age (Chugani & Phelps, 1986). Within the frontal lobes, gray matter maturation occurs earliest in the orbitofrontal cortex (BA11), later in the ventrolateral (BA44, BA45, and BA47), and later still in DLPFC (BA9 and BA46), coinciding with its later myelination (Gogtay et al., 2004). A review of functional magnetic resonance imaging with children and adolescents (Casey et al., 2005) has suggested that "brain regions subserving primary functions, such as motor and sensory systems, mature before higher-order association areas that integrate those primary functions (e.g. the prefrontal cortex)." (p. 242). A study of Raven's Matrices performed by 8- to 12-year old children (Crone et al., 2009) showed that children engaged the RLPFC and DLPFC in a similar manner to adults, but the activation was not sustained. This seems to reflect a general tendency for increasingly efficient engagement of more frontal regions with maturation (Bunge & Crone, 2009).

The import of these changes is that higher cognitive functions develop through childhood, and this finding is consistent with behavioral observations that complex cognition develops later. A corollary is that it is unlikely that infants are sufficiently neurologically mature for symbolic processing in the first few months. In these respects, there appears to be consistency between neuroscience evidence and behavioral data, as reviewed in chapters 5 and 6.

Summary of the role of the PFC

The PFC is involved in the fundamental processes of symbolic cognition, the anterior regions being especially important in integrating, and forming mappings between, representations. A region that was little understood until the last decade, the fronto-polar cortex is especially important in higher cognitive functions, especially complex reasoning (Christoff & Gabriele, 2000). We want to avoid overinterpreting neuroscientific evidence given that the field is developing rapidly, and a number of cautionary comments have been made (Mausfeld, 2012; Logothetis, 2008). On the other hand, functional neuroimaging provides an additional source of data that can help to constrain cognitive theories (White & Poldrack, 2013), and the quality of cognitive theories is a factor in interpreting neuroscience findings (Wixted & Mickes, 2013). Our main interest is in studies showing a correspondence between behavioral and neuroscience findings. The neuroscience research available to date seems to provide strong support for the differentiation between basic processes, which we characterize as symbolically structured, and others that we characterize as nonstructured and functionally structured. On the other hand, this evidence might not yet be definitive, and there is scope for further research in which these forms of processing are contrasted systematically. We suggest that our definition of these levels would facilitate such investigations. There is, however, a lot of evidence showing that the processing of relational information consistently involves regions of the PFC (most notably the RLPFC), with links to other regions, such as the fronto-parietal system.

Summary

We have defined relational knowledge as having the properties of structural alignment, symbolization, higher-order representation, accessibility, and generalization. We have shown that, although relations share properties with associations, they also have distinctive properties. Symbolic neural net models have been shown to capture the properties of relational knowledge, providing an existence proof that systems can operate in the proposed way. Ideas from database theory have been explored, to illuminate concepts in relational knowledge. A further property is that relational knowledge is susceptible to complexity in a way that does not apply to nonstructured or functionally structured processes. These complexity effects will be the subject of the next chapter.

4 Cognitive Complexities and Correspondences

Numerous attempts have been made to quantify the complexity of cognitive processes, reflecting the fundamental importance of this parameter. Those that have most relevance to cognitive development have been reviewed by Halford and Andrews (2006, 2011), while those that refer to general cognition have been reviewed by Halford, Cowan, and Andrews (2007) and Cowan (2001). In this chapter, we take account of the contributions that we cited elsewhere, but with a focus on what we see as a coherent and comprehensive account of cognitive complexity principles.

First, we want to mention some issues that have been pervasive in the field. Successful studies on the role of domain knowledge in cognition (Chi, 1978; Chi & Ceci, 1987) sometimes have made it appear that explanations in terms of cognitive complexity and capacity are redundant. A seminal study of short-term memory development by Chi (1978) showed that, whereas recall of digits reflected the usual age trends, recall of chess pieces by 10-year-old chess experts exceeded that of adult chess novices. This research shows that domain knowledge has a powerful effect on short-term recall, but there was no assessment of capacity such as those provided by Cowan (2001) or Andrews and Halford (2002), and so the capacities of these children are unknown. Thus, inferences that there is no age-related increase in memory capacity are unwarranted and have been contradicted by subsequent evidence (Cowan et al., 1999). This is not to deny that there are many powerful techniques for improving memory performance (Jones, 2012; Simon, 1974). However, these studies do not include cognitive complexity effects of the kind that would reveal age differences in working memory development (Andrews & Halford, 2002).

We acknowledge the fundamental importance of knowledge and coding processes in general cognition and in cognitive development. Thus, a theory that proposed that acquisition and organization of knowledge were irrelevant to either of these fields would be patently false, and no such theory has existed to our knowledge. The notion, for instance, that Piaget (1954) eschewed the role of knowledge acquisition is based on confusion. Piaget opposed explanations of cognitive development based on learning theories that were prominent in the early 20th century, such as those by Hull, Spence, Skinner, and Guthrie. He argued for knowledge acquisition based on constructivist processes such as assimilation, accommodation, and equilibration, which now can be seen as more in line with contemporary thinking than were the learning theories that Piaget rejected. Thus, the Discovery of Relations by Analogy (DORA) model of relational knowledge acquisition (Doumas, Hummel, & Sandhofer, 2008) discussed in chapters 3 and 7, is based on unsupervised acquisition of structured knowledge and is arguably consistent with the constructivist processes envisaged by Piaget. However, as we have pointed out elsewhere (Halford & Andrews, 2006, especially pp. 563–600), it is essential that all dimensions that influence cognition be investigated without prior attempts to conflate them into a single variable, regardless of how appealing that variable might be. We consider acquisition processes in chapters 6 and 7, and we will suggest that there are important interactions with complexity. In this chapter, however, we focus on complexity.

An important implication of this position is that research demonstrating an effect of knowledge is not *ipso facto* evidence against complexity. Everyone recognizes the importance of parsimony in science, but this does not mean that we adopt simplistic solutions, which can lead to a proliferation of exceptions (see, e.g., Garcia-Marques & Ferreira, 2011). Parsimony means that we adopt only those dimensions that are necessary to account for the phenomena we study—no more, no less. Failure to give proper recognition to the role of complexity leaves gaps and inconsistencies in our formulations that make coherent theories impossible. Furthermore Halford, Cowan, and Andrews (2007) have shown that complexity and knowledge effects can be separated. Importantly, complexity and knowledge conceptions are not mutually exclusive. Studies that demonstrate an effect of knowledge being a way of providing evidence against capacity can be seen, at best, as a waste of research effort, and at worst, as seriously misleading. One expectation of this formulation is that it might lead to more productive lines of research on these crucial issues.

Another caveat is that complexity effects, and the demonstration of capacity limitations that apply to all of us, are not "pessimistic" in the sense of implying insurmountable obstacles to development or achievement. Much of our work, including some that is considered in this chapter, has been concerned with processes by which we manage to perform complex tasks while operating within the capacity limitations of our cognitions. Furthermore the relational complexity metric that we outline has enabled prediction and subsequent demonstration of previously unrecognized abilities. For example, based on predictions from relational complexity theory, we showed that preschool children understand the effects of weight or distance on the balance scale better than had been known previously (Halford, Andrews, Dalton et al., 2002). We also predict that proportional analogies ($A:B::C:D$), being binary relational, should be possible from age 2 forward. In chapter 6, we will suggest that there should be symbolic processes in 1-year-olds that have not so far been recognized.

Another important consideration is to categorize the cognitive processes that are limited and define the nature of the limitations. Complexity and capacity are crucial to the definition of these categories. Exclusion of complexity and capacity as variables worthy of study precludes achievement of coherence because it makes us unable to categorize some important findings. There have been innovative assessments on which children are more successful than on previous tasks. These include seminal works by Bryant (1972) and Gelman (1972) on conservation of numbers, by Bryant and Trabasso (1971) on transitivity of choice, and by McGarrigle, Grieve, and Hughes (1978) on class inclusion. For example, there is no doubt that the transitivity of choice task in Bryant and Trabasso (1971) is performed better by preschool children than the analytic transitive inference task in chapter 1. In that discussion, we showed that transitivity of choice does not require the symbolic, relational reasoning entailed in analytic transitive inference, and the apparent precocity of preschool children might be attributable to this factor. However, the question that persists is whether apparent improvement, or precocity, is attributable to reduced complexity. We cannot know the answer to this unless complexity is assessed, which is rarely the case.

Thus, while the ongoing resistance to consideration of complexity and capacity as variables in adult cognition, cognitive development, and animal cognition might keep open the opportunity for superficially exciting findings, it also can result in some very misleading conclusions, or at least to conclusions that work against recognition of conceptual coherence. Our concern here is to find an appropriate categorization of the cognitive processes entailed, and at least some versions of transitivity of choice can be performed by much simpler processes than those required for analytic transitive inference. Similar arguments apply to improved performances observed in a number of other contexts, including conservation and class inclusion (Halford & Andrews, 2006).

We need to consider reasons why improved child performance has not been attributed to simpler cognitive processes when this clearly was a possible explanation. There might be resistance to admitting complexity issues because they appear to devalue the cognitive attainments of animals, infants, and young children. This would be inappropriate, and the methodologies that have led to advances in these domains are valuable and often ingenious. It is also the case, however, that categorization by the deep structure of cognitive processes offers coherence and conceptual power that actually increases the significance of these studies. In sum, there have been discoveries of children's cognitions that are more advanced or sophisticated than previously observed, but these in no way preclude the operation of complexity and capacity as cognitive variables. And the use of aphorisms such as "The smarter we become, the better children perform" or "Absence of evidence is not evidence of absence" to support excluding these variables is unjustified and tends to obscure important issues.

Crucially, we are not suggesting that complexity is the only factor that affects performance. There is an unlimited array of variables that affect performance, including declarative knowledge (knowing *what*), procedural knowledge (knowing *how*) and task variables, such as mode of presentation, time allowed, and motivating factors. The study of complexity effects must be conducted with appropriate controls for other variables. In this respect, research on complexity is no different from the study of any other variable in cognitive science. The studies we cite, whether by ourselves or others, have been selected with this consideration in mind.

Boundary conditions

As with all scientific phenomena, it is essential to define boundary conditions for complexity effects. Many claims that complexity effects do not exist have been based on conditions where they would not be expected, while ignoring conditions where complexity does have important effects. A common example of this is studies that demonstrate that children can perform tasks such as proportional analogy (Goswami, 1992) or conservation of quantity (Siegal, Waters, & Dinwiddy, 1988) if they have the requisite knowledge. We have no argument with the finding that the relevant knowledge is essential to these tasks (indeed, it is close to being a tautology). However, the children were all of an age where ternary relational, and *a fortiori* binary relational tasks, can be performed by the majority (Andrews & Halford, 2002; Halford, Wilson, & Phillips, 1998). Capacity limitations can be demonstrated in these tasks if a wider range of ages and a wider range of complexities are sampled; always, of course, with appropriate controls. There are numerous studies indicating age differences in ternary relational tasks using children aged 3–8 years (Andrews & Halford, 2002; Bunch & Andrews, 2012; Andrews et al., 2003; Andrews, Halford, & Boyce, 2012; Andrews et al., 2009; Bunch, Andrews, & Halford, 2007; Halford et al., 2002; Halford, Andrews, & Jensen, 2002; Halford, Bunch, & McCredden, 2007). These studies are controlled with precisely matched tasks in the same domain and same procedure, but at a lower level of complexity. This makes it very difficult to argue that the differences reflect nothing more than knowledge. There are no grounds for arguing against complexity effects when the ages of the children are such that processing capacity effects would not be expected. The formulation of coherent theory requires that we distinguish between conditions where complexity would be observed and conditions where it would not.

Another important development is that improved assessment of working memory, based on latent variables defined by performance on three or more independent measures, has shown that this construct accounts for a high proportion of variance in fluid intelligence. Working memory is an important measure of processing capacity, as we will see in the remainder of this chapter. The implication is that contemporary measures of processing capacity have shown that it is a crucial factor underlying higher cognition, and its role cannot be ignored.

Assessment of relational complexity

Relational complexity theory was proposed by Halford (1993) and Halford, Wilson, and Phillips (1998) as a solution to the problem of defining complexity in cognitive tasks. It was introduced in chapter 1, but we will consider further aspects of the concept here. The essential idea is to define the dimensionality of representations that are activated in performing a cognitive task. Specifically, relational complexity refers to the *arity* of relations; that is, the number of arguments or entities related. Unary relations have a single argument, as in *dog(Fido)*. As in this example, they can be used to express class membership. Binary relations have two arguments, as in *larger(elephant, mouse)*. Ternary relations have three arguments, as in *addition*(2,3,5). Quaternary relations, such as proportion, have four interacting components, as in 2/3 = 6/9, and so on. Each argument corresponds to a *role* or slot that can be filled in a variety of ways. For example, a binary relation has two arguments or two roles, each of which can be filled in a number of ways, such as *larger(horse,dog)*, and *larger(mountain,molehill)*. Thus, each argument corresponds to a variable or dimension and an *n*-ary relation is a set of points in *n*-dimensional space. Halford, Wilson, and Phillips (1998) proposed that the number of related dimensions that must be processed in a single decision is a good measure of cognitive complexity. They outline some key concepts as described next.

Complexity of a cognitive process is the number of variables that must be bound into a representation to perform that process. Complexity of processing also may vary over time within one task, so the critical value is the complexity of the most complex step. Tasks can vary in the number of steps that they require, but this does not necessarily affect processing load because a task with many steps might impose only a low demand for resources at any one time (e.g., counting peas in a box). On the other hand, coordination of steps, as in many hierarchically structured tasks, can impose a processing load, which is taken into account in relational complexity analyses. Higher-order relations entail an additional variable that specifies the level of the step. This is illustrated later in this chapter for the Tower of Hanoi (TOH) task. Some of the basic concepts are defined by Halford, Wilson, and Phillips (1998) as follows: *Processing complexity of a task* is the number of variables that must be bound into a representation to perform the most complex process entailed in the task, using the least demanding strategy available to humans for that task.

Processing demand is the effect exerted by task complexity on a performer, and it reflects the cognitive resources required to perform a task. The core proposal of this chapter is that demand is a function of relational complexity. That is, the more interacting variables that have to be processed in parallel, the higher that demand will be. *Demand* is synonymous with *load* and *effort,* and the three terms tend to be used interchangeably in the psychological literature. It is similar to computational cost in informational technology. Demand can be manipulated experimentally, with other aspects of the task controlled, and a number of examples of this will be considered later.

Resources allocated to a task vary as a function of demand and performance. More resources must be allocated to higher demand tasks to maintain performance. The methodology for dealing with demand and resources is now highly developed, and this is reviewed by Gopher (1994) and Halford (1993, chapter 3). Resources utilized can be measured by physiological arousal indicators (Kahneman, 1973), by neural activity assessed using brain imaging techniques (Carpenter & Just, 1996; Vogel & Machizawa, 2004; Vogel, McCollough, & Machizawa, 2005), by subjective feeling of effort assessed through self-reporting, and by decrement in competing tasks (Navon & Gopher, 1980). Resources invested by an individual in a given task will vary over time as a function of the conditions of performance.

Processing capacity is the limit of resources available. It will vary across individuals and may change over the lifespan (discussed in Halford, Wilson, & Phillips, 1998, §6.3). It is essentially constant within a short time frame, but it can be influenced by factors such as physiological state, diurnal rhythms, and drugs. Empirical evidence (Halford, Wilson, & Phillips 1998, §3.3; Halford, Baker, et al., 2005) indicates that adult humans can process quaternary relations in parallel, although a minority can probably process quinary relations under optimal conditions. The restriction to four entities processed in parallel is consistent with the work of Luck and Vogel (1997) and with evidence reviewed by Cowan (2000). Processing capacity of children increases with age, and present norms suggest they process unary relations at a median age of 1 year, binary relations at a median age of 1½ years, ternary relations at a median age of 5 years, and quaternary relations at a median age of 11 years (Andrews & Halford, 2002; Halford, 1993). The limitation is based on number of independent entities (chunks), regardless of information in each chunk (chunk-size) (Halford, Wilson, & Phillips, 1998, §3.2; Luck and Vogel, 1997).

Method for Analysis of Relational Complexity (MARC)

In this section, we will consider the principles for complexity analysis.

Limiting conditions for relational complexity

Like most scientific phenomena, capacity limitations and processing load effects can be observed only in certain conditions. Thus, short-term memory storage capacity limitations can be observed only where opportunities for recoding, or transferring to long-term memory, are inhibited (Cowan, 2000, §1.2). Similarly, it is necessary to specify the conditions where relational complexity effects can be observed.

Relational complexity does not apply to tasks that are modular or tasks where decisions can be based on perceptual information. Automaticity, which develops due to practice under constant mapping conditions (i.e., where the input–output functions of a task remain constant) also lowers processing loads (Hasher & Zachs, 1979; Logan, 1979; Schneider & Shiffrin, 1977).

Knowledge requirements
It is vital that complexity effects should be assessed in circumstances where adequate procedural and declarative knowledge is available. There are three basic procedures for ensuring this:

1. Use tasks that are appropriate for the sample of participants (e.g., suitable for the relevant species in animal cognition research and for the age group in developmental research). The suitability of the procedures and materials should be beyond reasonable doubt.
2. Ample training must be employed to ensure that the participants are thoroughly familiar with materials, procedure, and task demands. Training should continue to the point where stable performance can be assured, but varied mapping should be used to avoid automaticity. This procedure will not obviate processing load effects. For example, Maybery, Bain, and Halford (1986) found measurable processing load effects in premise integration in transitive inference after hundreds of trials.
3. Control tasks should be used to assess performance with the procedures. In relational complexity research, some test items should require a lower level of relational complexity than the level(s) being studied, and materials and procedures should differ minimally between the levels. This tends to ensure that relevant knowledge is available so that lack of it does not cause failure.

These provisions are implemented in our own studies, as exemplified by Andrews and Halford (2002), Halford et al., (2005) and Maybery, Bain, and Halford (1986).

Role of strategies
The complexity of cognitive tasks can vary considerably depending on the strategies employed. Consequently, the analysis must be based on a cognitive processes model, which needs to be justified independently.

The optimum cognitive strategy for human performers may not correspond to the algorithm that is best theoretically, or to any algorithm that would be used in artificial intelligence. Algorithms that are optimal for von Neumann processors may not be best for biological brains, for two reasons: (a) brains have a non–von Neumann architecture; and (b) brains may "prefer" to use heuristics which, while imperfect, perform better on the space of actual inputs with which brains have to deal. Complexity analyses must be based on strategies used by participants, and this is practicable nowadays because of accumulated information about strategies that underlie a wide range of cognitive performances. One benefit is that it is often possible to devise a task so that a particular strategy or process will be used, thereby enabling prediction, manipulation of complexity effects, or both. It is important, of course, that adequate empirical evidence exists for the strategy that is used.

Processes that reduce complexity

The difficulty of analyzing cognitive complexity and processing capacity is principally due to strategies for making the best use of capacity available. That is, the information required in any step in a task can be greatly reduced so that capacity limitations will not be observed. These strategies are often immensely powerful and have great value in optimizing the power of cognitive processes. However, they can obscure the underlying limitations, which therefore can be studied only in conditions where the strategies can be taken into account. There is nothing mysterious about this: It is just a case of finding the right boundary conditions for observing a scientific phenomenon. Halford, Wilson, and Phillips (1998) proposed two mechanisms whereby the complexity of concepts and their processing loads can be reduced.

Conceptual chunking

Conceptual chunking involves recoding concepts into less complex relations. For example, $speed = distance \,/\, time$ is a ternary relation, but speed can be recoded into a binary relation, $valueOf(speed, 60kph)$, as when speed is indicated by the position of a pointer on a dial. Conceptual chunking reduces processing load, but there is a temporary loss of access to the relations that make up the concept. For example, if speed is represented as a binary relation, changes in speed as a function of time or distance cannot be computed. If we think of speed as a single variable, we cannot answer questions such as, "How does speed change if we cover the same distance in half the time?" The fact that chunked dimensions are inaccessible places a constraint on chunking. The principle is that dimensions cannot be chunked if relations between them must be used to make the current decision. The conditions for chunking are similar to those for automaticity, as both require a constant mapping of stimuli to responses (Logan, 1979; Shiffrin & Schneider, 1977). Automaticity depends on the acquisition of strong associative links and functions at the level of Rank 0 and 1 processes.

Segmentation

The second mechanism for reducing complexity is through the segmentation of tasks into less complex steps, which can be processed serially. Such
serial strategies can be taught, or segmentation can be facilitated by certain
experimental manipulations. However, Halford (1993) and Halford et al.
(1995) argued that the autonomous development of strategies depends on
representing the relational structure of the task, and the self-programming
required to develop serial strategies is also subject to capacity limitations.
This is discussed further in chapter 6.

Limiting conditions for chunking and segmentation

Variables cannot be chunked or segmented if relations between them need
to be processed. This is, therefore, a precondition of both chunking and
segmentation.

Interaction of variables

A useful heuristic is that relational complexity cannot be reduced if the
variables interact. This is analogous to analysis of variance, in which an
interaction cannot be decomposed into the constituent main effects without a remainder. Because each variable influences the effects of the others,
they must be interpreted jointly. Complexity of a cognitive process can be
reduced only if decisions can be made about a subset of variables without
taking the remaining variables into account.

Constraints on decomposition in transitive inference

Interaction of two sources of information is a cause of processing load in
transitive inference. Consider a transitive inference problem such as the
one mentioned in chapter 1: *John is taller than Peter, and Michael is taller
than John; who is tallest?* According to well-validated process models (Halford et al., 1995; Sternberg, 1980, Trabasso, 1977), the inference is made
by integrating the elements into an ordered array. Notice, however, that
no element can be assigned to an ordinal position by either premise alone.
"John is taller than Peter" tells us that John goes in first or second position,
but we do not know which unless we also consider the second premise.
The two premises jointly determine that Michael is in first position. By
similar argument, the other elements can be assigned to a position only
by considering both premises jointly. This places a limit on segmentation
because neither premise can be processed fully without being integrated
with the other. The processing load associated with premise integration

has been validated by Maybery, Bain, and Halford (1986) with university students and by Halford (1984) with children.

MARC

The Method for Analysis of Relational Complexity (MARC; Halford, Cowan, & Andrews, 2007) comprises a set of principles for complexity analysis, based on the fact that variables can be chunked or segmented only if relations between them do not need to be processed (Andrews & Halford, 2002; Birney & Halford, 2002; Halford, Wilson, & Phillips, 1998). Chunking and segmentation mean that the limit is in the number of variables represented, rather than the amount of information represented in each, which is consistent with the findings of Luck & Vogel (1997), Miller (1956), and Simon (1974). The relational complexity metric handles hierarchically structured representations such as TOH tasks (Halford, Wilson & Phillips 1998, §6.1.3), as well as those that are not hierarchically structured, such as simple forms of transitive inference. The relational complexity metric can be applied to tasks involving more than one step, where the complexity of the task is defined by the most complex step (Halford, Wilson, & Phillips, 1998, §3.4; Birney & Halford, 2002; Birney, Halford, & Andrews, 2006).

Certain principles follow from this. One is the principle of *common relations,* which says that where two or more variables are related to all other variables in the representation in the same way, they can be chunked. An example is that if A is compared to B and C (e.g., red is different from blue and green), B and C can be chunked because the relation between them need not be processed and both are related to A in the same way (A is different from both B and C, but this does not specify how B and C differ, if at all). Thus, comparison of A with B, C, ... etc., in this way, is a binary relation. A more complex case of this principle is that where variables are correlated perfectly for the purpose of the decision being made, they can be chunked. Compound statements are chunked where the truth of the compound is at issue, and the truth of components is not considered independently. Components of a compound statement cannot be chunked when they are related in a different way to one or more other propositions.

Hierarchical structuring of variables

Processing load can be reduced by representing complex structures hierarchically and processing one level of the hierarchy at a time. This principle is incorporated into the analogy models of Hummel and Holyoak (1997) and Wilson, Halford et al. (2001). A limiting condition of hierarchical structuring is that variables at different levels of the hierarchy cannot be related. With this procedure, variables that have to be related must be at the same level.

Effective relational complexity determined by decomposition-recomposition

Halford, Wilson, and Phillips (1998, §3.4.3) adapted a technique from relational database theory by which effective complexity can be determined. The idea is that if, for example, a ternary relation can be reduced to two binary relations and then recomposed again without losing information, effective relational complexity is binary, even though three variables are involved. In general, the technique involves decomposing and recombining to determine whether a relation can be reduced to a combination of lower-order relations. If the resulting set of relational instances is identical to the set of instances before decomposition, then the relation is decomposable without loss of information. Otherwise, it is not.

Expertise

Expertise is important for devising strategies that reduce the complexity of relations that have to be processed in parallel, although a lower limit is usually imposed by the structure of the task, so some tasks might be complex even for experts. Expertise incorporates knowledge of the structure of a domain and facilitates recognition of which variables can be chunked or segmented without losing useful information. Thus, when considering heat flow, a person with even modest expertise would recognize that *temp1* and *temp2* can be chunked into a single variable, *tempdiff*, which is related to *heatflow* along a conductor. This reduces complexity of the relations between heat flow and temperature. Similarly, in simple mechanics, *speed* = *distance* × *time*$^{-1}$, but it can be chunked to a single variable, *speed*, written as *v* (velocity), which can be related to acceleration as $a = (v_2 - v_1) / time$. Then acceleration can be chunked and related to further variables, mass (*m*) and acceleration (*a*), thus: $f = ma$, where *f* signifies force, and so on. The reasoning here proceeds by a series of ternary relational expressions at each level of representation, but recognition of how these expressions relate to each other depends on expertise.

An expert and a novice processing the same problem might employ very different cognitive representations, and the former would be less susceptible to processing load effects because of more efficient coding of the problem. It does not follow, however, that experts have no susceptibility to load. Halford et al. (2005) showed capacity limitations in an interpretation of interactions task in which the participants were academics or graduate students in psychology or computer science who had considerable expertise in the domain. This study will be considered in detail later in this chapter.

Processing capacity sets a limit to the number of variables that can be related in a representation that is processed in parallel. Beyond that limit, conceptual chunking or segmentation is required to process the task in a series of steps, none of which exceeds the relational capacity limit. This is the core reason why relational (i.e., analytic, symbolic, Rank 2+) processes entail serial processing that is not required for subsymbolic (Rank 0, 1) processes.

One point to note is that decomposition sometimes might be available to an expert that is not available to a child, or even to an adult acquiring the concept for the first time. Thus, transitive inference can be performed easily using an ordering algorithm, but this approach is not available to the novice acquiring the concept. There is a general problem here, in that it is often difficult to recognize that the cognitive processes involved in a task might be very different for the novice and the expert. Another point is that acquisition of an algorithm often depends on having a mental model of the task, and this mental model requires the kinds of processes that we have described. This is one of the points made by the Transitive Inference Mapping Model (TRIMM) model of acquisition of transitive inference (Halford et al., 1995).

Comparison with contemporary complexity metrics

There are other complexity metrics with which relational complexity theory should be compared, which will be discussed next.

Boolean complexity

Boolean complexity is "an essentially universal measure of the intrinsic mathematical complexity or 'incompressibility' of the propositional concept" (Feldman, 2000, p. 630). It is based on the minimum number of Boolean symbols required to express a concept. For example, $(a \wedge b) \vee (a \wedge \neg b)$ is equivalent to $a \wedge (b \vee \neg b)$, which is equivalent to a. [That is, $(a \cap b) \cup (a \cap \neg b)$ is equivalent to $a \cap (b \cup \neg b)$, which is equivalent to a.] Therefore, it has a Boolean complexity of 1. By contrast, $(a \wedge b) \vee (\neg a \wedge \neg b)$ has no shorter equivalent when expressed in terms of $\wedge$, $\vee$, and $\neg$, and it has a Boolean complexity of 4. Feldman shows that Boolean complexity accounts for performance on a range of conceptual problems.

Relational complexity theory and Boolean complexity are similar insofar as both quantify complexity by the minimum information required to represent a concept, but they differ in significant ways. The derivation of the minimum expression of a concept is defined mathematically in Boolean complexity, but in relational complexity theory, it is defined by psychological processes of chunking and segmentation that take strategies into account. Furthermore, relational complexity theory specifies an empirically determined upper limit to the complexity of a cognitive representations, but it takes account of serial and parallel processes. Thus, any one cognitive representation is limited to approximately four variables, but tasks can be processed in a succession of representations. Relational complexity theory has been applied to a very wide range of cognitive tasks, which attests to its psychological validity.

Cognitive complexity and control
Cognitive complexity and control theory (Zelazo et al., 2003) defines complexity by determining the number of levels of embedding of rules in a hierarchy. A simple rule would be one that links an antecedent condition to a consequent: $a \rightarrow c$. A complex rule would be one in which a setting condition modifies (say, by reversing) the link: e.g., $s_1, a_1 \rightarrow c_1$; $s_1, a_2 \rightarrow c_2$; $s_2, a_1 \rightarrow c_2$; $s_2, a_2 \rightarrow c_1$. Inclusion of the setting condition constitutes a higher-order rule. A well-known example would be the dimensional change card-sort task in which objects that vary in shape and color are sorted by shape under s_1 but by color under s_2. This relatively complex rule is difficult for young children, and it predicts children's performance on complex tasks such as theory of mind (Zelazo et al., 2003). Complexity as defined by cognitive complexity and control theory can be expressed by relational complexity. The complex rule can be expressed by the mappings $\{(s_1, a_1, c_1), (s_1, a_2, c_2), (s_2, a_1, c_2), (s_2, a_2, c_1)\}$ and is a ternary relation. The simple rule is expressed by the mappings $\{(a_1, c_1), (a_2, c_2), ...\}$ and is a binary relation. This is another example of how relational complexity theory encompasses hierarchical structures but also applies to structures that are not specifically hierarchical.

Consistent with relational complexity theory, Halford, Bunch, & McCredden (2007) propose that the complex rule in the dimensional change card sorting task is difficult because the interaction between variables constrains decomposition, requiring a high working memory load. When the task is modified so that it is decomposable into subtasks that can be performed serially, the difficulty is reduced, especially for 3- to 4-year-old children. Thus, whether tasks are hierarchically structured or they have other kinds of structures, such as those in transitive inference or knights and knaves problems, constraint on decomposability is a major factor accounting for cognitive complexity.

Complexity of task models

Duncan et al. (2012) have shown that complex rules for performing a task can result in *goal neglect*, defined as failure to implement some rules in actual performance, even though the rules can be recalled explicitly. They attribute this to the complexity of forming a task model that can be used to control performance. They also show that working memory for complex rules, measured by actual performance rather than recall, correlates with fluid intelligence ($r = 0.57$). The rules can be conceptualized as relational knowledge that is used to direct performance, and the rules used have high relational complexity. Furthermore, they are structured in a way that makes them difficult to decompose into subrules (see Duncan et al., 2012, figure 1). By our count, there are six variables that determine the correct response (whether figures are crossed out, whether figures are identical, the number of birds, properties shared by birds, properties shared by shapes, and which side has the most dots). The rules are interrelated in such a way that they would resist conceptual chunking and segmentation (i.e., there is a hierarchical relation between rules 1 and 2, and rule 4 depends on a conjunction of a number of properties shared by shapes and the side with the most dots). This work has considerable importance for prediction of cognitive performance, and corresponds in important respects with the dimensional change card-sort task (Zelazo et al., 2003) reviewed previously. Specifically, it shows that goal neglect is a variable that is sensitive to complexity, and we propose that it can be analyzed by the relational complexity metric.

Cognitive capacity and working memory

Historical background

In one of the most famous papers in the history of psychology, Miller (1956) assessed processing limitations in short-term memory, absolute judgments, and other domains and proposed the "magical number 7," meaning that our processing capacity is limited to 7 ± 2 independent items. However, Miller also introduced the important concept of chunking, meaning combining elements into a single item, such as when we read "*cat*" as one word rather than as three independent letters. This can greatly increase the information that can be recalled from short-term memory. For example, binary digits can be recoded as octal digits: e.g., 000 = 0, 001 = 1, 010 = 2, ..., 111 = 7. If the coding and decoding are practiced sufficiently to be automatic, then a string of 21 binary digits can be recalled from short-term memory by coding them as 7 octal digits, then decoding them as binary digits. The concept of chunking has been universally accepted in theories of memory ever since Miller's seminal paper.

However, Miller's concept of the "magical number 7" has undergone considerable modification. One of the first challenges was by Broadbent (1975), who found that items tended to be recalled in groups (bursts) of approximately 3 to 4, suggesting that attention was restricted to this number of items. Broadbent therefore proposed that the capacity limit was really 4, and that the "magical number" 7 was the result of two systems, each with capacities of 3–4 items. In a different context, Luck and Vogel (1997) found that the capacity of visual short-term memory was approximately 4 items, though individual differences in capacity might be attributable to the efficiency with which irrelevant items are excluded (Vogel, McCollough, & Machizawa, 2005). Numerous reviews of these studies have emerged since (e.g., Cowan, 2000, 2004; Kane et al., 2004; Oberauer, 2009).

Short-term memory

One of the most wide-ranging reviews of short-term memory capacity was by Cowan (2000), who found considerable converging evidence that short-term memory storage capacity is limited to four chunks. There is an activated portion of long-term memory that has a larger capacity, but the capacity limit occurs because the focus of attention within the activated portion of memory is limited to four chunks. However, Cowan later noted that the limit was observable only in specific circumstances and carefully defined the relevant boundary conditions (Cowan, 2001, §1.2). Perhaps the single most important boundary condition for observation of short-term memory limits is to restrict recoding of items into larger chunks; otherwise, it is impossible to determine how many items are stored. As illustrated previously, decoding 7 octal digits can yield an output of 21 binary digits, but the number of chunks in storage is 7, not 21. It is also necessary to avoid extraneous processing demands, such as the updating of information as required in the *n*-back task, where each item has to be compared to the one that occurred *n* items previously.

Working memory

Research on short-term memory and working memory in the last decade has converged on findings that approximately 60 percent of variance in fluid intelligence is accounted for by working memory capacity. Following an extensive study of working memory as a latent variable, together with an extensive review of the literature, Kane et al. (2004) noted that "we are struck by the limited variation around this estimate." (p. 210). That conclusion still appears valid at this time. Kane et al. employed three measures in each of the domains of verbal and spatial short-term memory and verbal and spatial working memory, and they defined latent variables in each domain, employing a large and cognitively diverse sample of adults. Both verbal and spatial factors were found for short-term memory and working memory, but the verbal and spatial working memory constructs shared 70 percent of their variance, whereas the corresponding short-term memory constructs shared only 40 percent of their variance. Along with other findings, this led to the conclusion that working memory is more domain-general than short-term memory. A total of 13 standardized reasoning tests (5 verbal reasoning, 5 spatial visualization, and 3 of figural, inductive reasoning) were also employed. Path analysis yielded a strong effect of working memory on fluid intelligence (e.g., Kane et al. 2004, figure 5). This paper contributes importantly to the growing consensus that working memory is strongly linked to fluid intelligence, although the constructs remain distinct.

Most tests of working memory have utilized complex span tasks that combine processing and storage. For example, one of the verbal working memory measures employed by Kane et al. (2004) is reading span, in which participants had to read sentences and then remember a word from each sentence. These measures account for a lot of variance in higher cognition, including reasoning, as found by Kane et al. in the study reviewed previously. However, a new conception of working memory by Oberauer (2009) is based, not on storage per se, but on dynamic binding to a coordinate system, which consists of slots linked by relations, but does not necessarily have the specific properties of relations as outlined in chapter 3. Examples of coordinate systems will be given progressively. This theory is eminently applicable to the conception of higher cognition that we are developing.

Oberauer proposed six requirements for working memory, which we paraphrase as follows:

• That it be able to build and maintain new structural representations.
• Selective attention to one or a few elements, and the ability to operate on them.

• A general-purpose mechanism that can be reconfigured flexibly in accordance with a goal. This corresponds to what is broadly understood as an executive function (Andrews et al. 2013) and contrasts with a module that is specialized for a particular function.
• Rapid updating of a structured representation to make it applicable to a current problem (such as solving a chess puzzle).
• Ability to draw on relevant contents of long-term memory.
• Ability to transfer a new structured representation to long-term memory.

This conception of working memory is eminently suitable for application to contemporary theory of human reasoning, as we will show in subsequent pages.

According to Oberauer (2009), working memory comprises three components: activated long-term memory, a direct-access region, and a focus of attention. Activation in long-term memory occurs by perceptual input or association with another representation and includes representation of goals.

The region of direct access "is a mechanism for establishing and holding temporary bindings between contents (e.g., objects, events, words) and contexts (i.e. argument variables in structure templates, or positions in a generic cognitive coordinate system)" (Oberauer, 2009, p. 53). The focus of attention applies to one element and it is used in a cognitive operation (e.g., focusing on one element and ordering it relative to other elements). This seems to imply that the focus of attention can encompass a relation between a number of elements because ordering of elements is included. Oberauer (2009) states that "[t]he ability to maintain strong bindings is, in my view, the main limiting factor in [working memory] capacity" (p. 72). He indicates that the region of direct access has representations of low dimensionality, but he does not suggest a specific value for capacity of working memory. Therefore, this needs to be determined by finding the number of elements that can be bound into a relational representation, to be discussed later in this chapter.

Long-term memory must represent structure because association is not enough. This means that relations, and bindings of elements to appropriate roles in the relational representation, must be specified. Oberauer (2009) illustrates this with "the pastor calmed the businessman." (p. 77). This cannot be represented as associations between these elements because the intended proposition would not be distinguishable from "the businessman calmed the pastor." Notice that this employs the distinction in chapter 2 between association and relational representations because only in the

latter are elements assigned to roles. This calls attention to structural alignment as a defining property of relational knowledge, as specified in chapter
2. However, the contents of long-term memory cannot consist solely of
relations because the bindings must be variable: e.g., *businessman* will not
always be bound to the *agent* role in a specific proposition; rather, it must
be available for binding to an unlimited variety of roles in an unlimited
set of propositions. There is, therefore, no simple translation between
association and relational representations. Oberauer (2009) suggests that
long-term memory is a network of associated chunks, whereas in the direct
access region, structural information is represented explicitly (§3.2). The
chunks in long-term memory contain the bindings between elements and
roles but the bindings become accessible in the direct access region (see
Oberauer, 2009, figure 5). He proposes that the analytic and associative
modes of processing are not "two separate, independent systems of information processing, but ... endpoints of a continuum [that] reflects relative
weight of the analytic subsystem or [working memory] (i.e. the region of
direct access and the bridge, together with the focus of attention and the
response focus) and the associative subsystem (i.e., activated LTM representations and their associations)" (Oberauer, 2009, p. 91).

The conception of working memory by Oberauer and his collaborators
fits well with the processes postulated to underlie relational knowledge and
is eminently applicable to the study of human reasoning. The distinctiveness of the dynamic binding construct is indicated by the findings of
Oberauer et al. (2008) that relational integration shared substantial variance with reasoning that was not accounted for by processing and storage,
or by processing speed. They also argued that relational integration could
not be accounted for by executive functions, of which only one component, updating, predicts fluid intelligence.

However, empirical studies have been largely based on measures that
are a combination of short-term storage and processing (e.g., Kane et al.,
2004). Consequently, there is a comparative paucity of data on dynamic
binding as a predictor of reasoning. Some of the relational complexity tests
that we have investigated arguably entail dynamic binding. For example,
analytic transitive inference (discussed in chapter 1) entails assigning
elements to roles in an ordering schema, and there is good correspondence
between relational reasoning tests of equivalent complexity that (arguably)
entail dynamic binding (Andrews & Halford, 2002). However, working
memory tests are needed that assess dynamic binding independently
of reasoning per se. A test that assessed the recall of words in spatial positions (Oberauer, 2005) provided a clear measure of the dynamic binding

construct. Sets of two to five words were presented, each in a different frame on a screen, followed by a local recognition test, in which participants judged whether probe words appeared in the same frame as previously. The test assessed binding between word and frame and was a good measure of working memory capacity. This binding is dynamic in that it depends on activation of representations and is not based on enduring links. The words are bound to a coordinate system comprising slots that are linked by a left-right spatial relation.

Several other studies of short-term memory recall or recognition provide an important database for determination of capacity. Some of these use quite different methodologies, such as the study of sequential dependencies (reviewed by Cowan, 2000, §3.4.5). A classic study is that of Cleeremans and McClelland (1991), which required sequences of keys to be pressed according to locations on a screen, determined by a finite state grammar that was unknown to participants. There were sequential dependencies between locations of which the participants were unaware. After 20 sessions of training, participants could predict the fourth location given three previous stimuli, but they could not predict a fifth location using the previous four. This limit remained stable after 13 additional training sessions. This type of study provides important converging evidence that the capacity of what can be interpreted as the focus of attention is limited to four entities. While no single study (nor even a single type of study) provides incontrovertible evidence of this limit, the convergence of many different methodologies on broadly consistent findings gives us a lot of confidence in the estimate. One of our arguments in this book is that we should pay more attention to these broad correspondences. While the discrepancies should not be ignored, they should not be allowed to obscure the important larger picture. We should focus on the forest as well as the trees.

The working memory literature provides strong evidence of a limit in short-term storage capacity of four items. However, the theory of relational knowledge requires determination of our capacity for processing relations. Short-term memory capacity can be assessed by the recall or recognition of items, but processing capacity requires determination of the number of variables that can be integrated in a relational representation. Recall that with short-term memory, it was necessary to define the boundary conditions for observation of capacity limits, and this task was carried out by Cowan (2000). To determine processing capacity limitations, we need to know what processes are used to avoid capacity limitations. The two types of processes that reduce the complexity of representations processed are conceptual chunking and segmentation. These load-reduction strategies can be constrained by using a task based on interpretation of interactions (Halford et al., 2005). Interactions cannot be decomposed without loss because interacting variables modify each other's effects. Further measures are needed, however, to constrain other types of recoding that could reduce the complexity of representations actually processed. In addition, care must be taken to ensure that no extraneous sources of difficulty are introduced to the task. In our determination of processing capacity, we used fictitious data relating to everyday phenomena. We also used participants who were academics or graduate students to ensure that expertise in the task was optimal, and participants were also given practice time to ensure that they understood the task demands fully. Performance was contrasted on two-, three-, and four-way interactions, holding other factors constant, including computation of intermediate results.

Participants were given verbal descriptions of an interaction together with a graphical presentation, as shown in figure 4.1.

Bar graphs were used to avoid recoding, and use of arithmetic strategies was discouraged by the instructions. Participants had to make the same decision about each of two data sets (left and right halves of the display in figure 4.1). That is, they made decisions about two two-way interactions. In figure 4.2, they had to make a single decision that integrates both data sets into a single decision about a three-way data set. Thus, both levels require the same amount of information to be processed and the same number of intermediate steps, but they differ in the amount of information required for decision(s).

Amount of information to be processed was controlled by first comparing two two-way interactions (as in figure 4.1) with a three-way interaction (figure 4.2), using eight data points in each case. Binary choices were required in each case. Graphs were first presented with bars of equal length so that participants could familiarize themselves with the variables in the presentation. When they were ready to perform the task, they pressed the two most widely spaced keys, thereby occupying both hands and precluding their use as a means of recoding the task. Then the graphs were presented so as to reveal the data, as shown in figures 4.1 and 4.2. Solution time was measured while the keys were pressed.

Next, this procedure was repeated by comparing two three-way interactions with a four-way interaction, as shown in figures 4.3 and 4.4, respectively. Each participant received two examples of each of the four problem types, with different content (e.g., cakes, cars) in each case. The procedure measured the number of variables that had to be integrated to make a

People prefer **fresh** cakes to **frozen** cakes. The difference depends on the flavor (**chocolate** vs **carrot**), and the type (**iced** vs **plain**).

Left half (black): The difference between **fresh** and **frozen** is □ greater/ □ smaller for **chocolate** cakes than for **carrot** cakes.

Right half (gray): The difference between **fresh** and **frozen** is □ greater/ □ smaller for **chocolate** cakes than for **carrot** cakes.

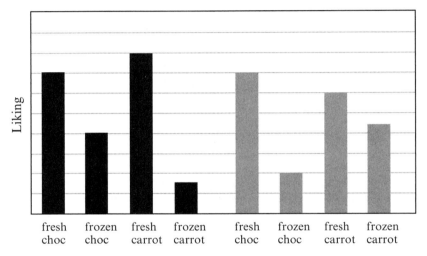

Figure 4.1
Example of a couple of two-way problems. Reproduced from figure 1a by Halford et al., 2005. Copyright © 2005 American Psychological Society. Reproduced by permission.

binary decision. For example, in the four-way problem (figure 4.4), for the participants to answer the question "There is a greater/smaller change in the size of the increase for rich cakes than for low-fat cakes," they must integrate four variables (fresh/frozen, chocolate/carrot, iced/plain, rich/ low-fat).

By contrast, in one of the corresponding three-way problems (figure 4.3), for the participants to answer the question "This increase is greater/ smaller for plain cakes than for iced cakes," they must integrate only three variables (fresh/frozen, chocolate/carrot, iced/plain). A binary decision (greater/smaller) was required in each case.

Accuracy declined with complexity, but was still better than chance in the four- way problems. An extension of the procedure using five-way interactions did not yield better-than-chance performance. Solution time

People prefer **fresh** cakes to **frozen** cakes. The difference depends on the flavor (**chocolate** vs **carrot**), and the type (**iced** vs **plain**).

The difference between **fresh** and **frozen** increases from **chocolate** cake to **carrot** cake.

This increase is ☐ greater/ ☐ smaller for **iced** cakes than for **plain** cakes.

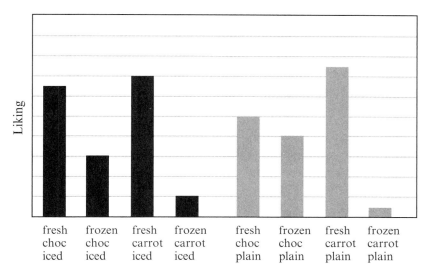

Figure 4.2
Example of a three-way problem. Reproduced from figure 1b by Halford et al., 2005. Copyright © 2005 American Psychological Society. Reproduced by permission.

and confidence data (figure 4.5) show that speed and confidence both declined as complexity increased. Protocol analysis showed that participants experienced information overload with the four-way task. For instance, they would say, "This is what I'm having difficulty holding onto," "Everything fell apart and I had to go back" and "I kept losing information."

The methodology used in the working memory literature (Cowan et al., 2004; Oberauer & Hein, 2012) is very different from the methodology used in our determination of the number of variables that can be integrated in a relational representation, but there is a high degree of consensus about the parameter involved. Both methodologies indicate that working memory capacity is limited to four entities bound in a single representation. We propose that this finding has profound implications for higher cognition.

People prefer **fresh** cakes to **frozen** cakes. The difference depends on the flavor (**chocolate** vs **carrot**), the type (**iced** vs **plain**).

The difference between **fresh** and **frozen** increases from **chocolate** cakes to **carrot** cakes.

Left half (black): This increase is □ greater / □ smaller for **iced** cakes than for **plain** cakes.

Right half (gray): This increase is □ greater / □ smaller for **iced** cakes than for **plain** cakes.

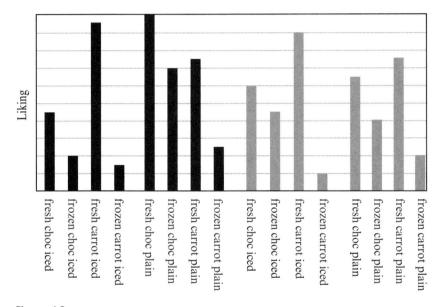

Figure 4.3
Example of two three-way problems. Reproduced from figure 2a by Halford et al., 2005. Copyright © 2005 American Psychological Society. Reproduced by permission.

Applications of the Relational Complexity Metric
In this section, we will show how relational complexity has been determined for a variety of cognitive tasks. This illustrates the principles of MARC and also supports our claim that relational complexity can be regarded as a general cognitive complexity metric. This review includes studies of the development of relational processing capacity, as well as serial and parallel processing and the role of domain expertise.

People prefer **fresh** cakes to **frozen** cakes. The difference depends on the flavor (**chocolate** vs **carrot**), the type (**iced** vs **plain**) and the richness (**rich** vs **low-fat**).

The difference between **fresh** and **frozen** increases from **chocolate** cakes to **carrot** cakes.

This increase is greater for **iced** cakes than for **plain** cakes.

There is a □ greater / □ smaller change in the size of the increase for **rich** cakes than for **low-fat** cakes.

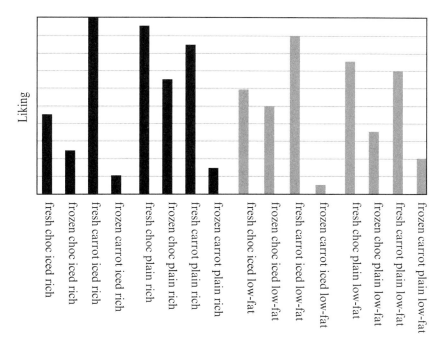

Figure 4.4
Example of a four-way problem. Reproduced from figure 2b by Halford et al., 2005. Copyright © 2005 American Psychological Society. Reproduced by permission.

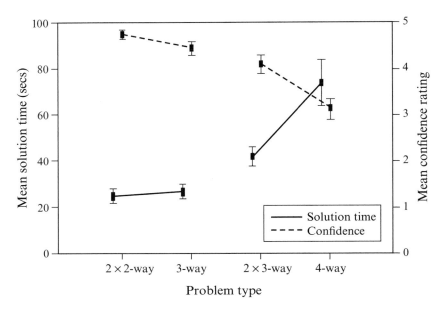

Figure 4.5
Performance on the interpretation of interactions task. Reproduced from figure 3 by Halford et al., 2005. Copyright © 2005 American Psychological Society. Reproduced by permission.

The study of development of relational processing capacity in children by Andrews and Halford (2002) was summarized in chapter 1. The relational complexity of the analytic transitive inference task also has been considered. Here, we consider other applications of the relational complexity metric.

Class inclusion is another task that has been a controversial source of difficulty for young children (Andrews & Halford, 2002). An example is that *apples* and *nonapple-fruit* are included in *fruit*. This is a ternary relation among three classes; *inclusion(fruit, apples, nonapple-fruit)*. There are also three binary relations: *inclusion(fruit, apples)*; *inclusion(fruit, nonapple-fruit)*; and *complement(apples, nonapple-fruit)*. Notice that no single binary relation is sufficient for understanding inclusion. For example, it is not enough to know that *apples* are related to *fruit* because, unless it is recognized that *nonapple-fruit* are also fruit, it is not possible to decide whether *apples* are included in *fruit* or whether *fruit* and *apples* are coextensive. Therefore, the inclusion hierarchy cannot be decomposed into a set of binary relations without losing the essence of the concept.

Conceptual chunking can be illustrated by considering *fruit, apples, bananas, pears,* and *oranges. Bananas, pears,* and *oranges* can be chunked into the single class *nonapple-fruit,* and we still have the inclusion hierarchy *fruit, apples, nonapple-fruit.* So why not chunk *apples, bananas, pears,* and *oranges*? We can, of course, but we will lose the inclusion hierarchy if we do. Then we would have the class of *fruit,* and a class of {*apples, bananas, pears, oranges*}, but we have no complementary subclass. Thus, inclusion hierarchies cannot be reduced to less than a ternary relation, and this imposes a high processing load (Halford & Leitch, 1989).

Theory of mind

A cognitive complexity effect was predicted for theory of mind tasks by Halford (1993, pp. 453–464) before any empirical evidence existed, confirming that it was a genuine prediction, not a postdiction. The influence of the complexity factor now has been confirmed empirically (Davis & Pratt, 1995; Andrews et al., 2003). A complexity analysis of two commonly used theory of mind tasks, appearance-reality and false belief, is shown in figure 4.6. An example of the appearance-reality task would be to show a child a white cardboard cutout of a fish, and then cover it with a blue filter. The child is asked what color the fish appears (blue) and what color it really is (white) (Flavell, Flavell, & Green, 1983). Both answers must be correct for the child to gain credit for understanding the concept. An example of a false belief task would be to allow a child to see an observer watching a chocolate being hidden in a basket, and then, unseen by the observer, a third party moves the chocolate to a box. The child then is asked whether the observer will look for the chocolate in the basket (correct) or in the box (incorrect).

The basis of the relational complexity analysis is that, as shown in figure 4.6, these tasks entail three variables. There is the environmental cue (white color of fish, chocolate in basket), a setting condition (applying a color filter, an unseen transformation of the object's location), and the person's representation. The representation should be a joint function of the environmental cue and the setting condition, and this is a ternary relation, (environmental cue, setting condition, representation). However, it is possible to default to a function of either the environmental cue (as in the connections task) or the setting condition (as in the transformations task), but without taking the other factor into account. These are both binary relations. Appearance-reality and false belief were found to be of equal complexity and to be predicted by other ternary relational tasks, including transitivity, hierarchical classification, cardinality, and class

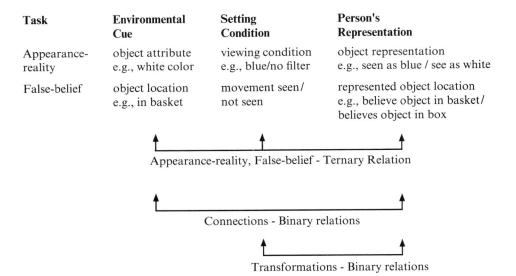

Task	Environmental Cue	Setting Condition	Person's Representation
Appearance-reality	object attribute e.g., white color	viewing condition e.g., blue/no filter	object representation e.g., seen as blue / see as white
False-belief	object location e.g., in basket	movement seen/ not seen	represented object location e.g., believe object in basket/ believes object in box

Appearance-reality, False-belief - Ternary Relation

Connections - Binary relations

Transformations - Binary relations

Figure 4.6
Relational complexity of two theory of mind tasks. Reproduced from Andrews et al. (2003; p. 1748) by permission of John Wiley and Sons.

inclusion, after controlling for performance on the binary relational tasks, which were performed much earlier.

Raven's Matrices

The analysis by Carpenter, Just, & Shell (1990) of Raven's Matrices can be interpreted in terms of the relational complexity metric (Birney, 2002). For example, Carpenter et al. identify a rule that they call "distribution of three values," in which each of three features (e.g., diamond, square, and tri- angle) occurs in a row, a column, or both. The missing value can be deter- mined by complementation, so that if (say) the diamond and square have occurred already, the missing feature must be a triangle. This rule corre- sponds to a ternary relation because every row comprises a set of ordered 3-tuples of the relevant features: *distrib_three_values*{(*diamond, square, tri- angle*), (*square, triangle, diamond*), . . .}. Birney's analyses indicate that Raven's Matrices items mostly comprise superimposed ternary relations, but the difficulty is increased by making the rules hard to recognize. For example, an item analyzed by Carpenter et al. (figure 5) contains rows in which there is a cell with one, a cell with two, and a cell with three horizontal figures, but the horizontal figures differ in shape so that the distribution of number of figures is difficult to detect. Success in Raven's

Matrices also depends on the ability to induce the relevant relation from items that embody it.

The Tower of Hanoi (TOH) Puzzle

The TOH puzzle is a good example of a task that entails planning, which depends on relational knowledge. TOH comprises three pegs and a variable number of discs. The cognitive complexity of the TOH was analyzed by Halford, Wilson, and Phillips (1998; §6.1.3), and a sample of their analysis is reproduced here. The discs are placed initially on peg A with the largest on the bottom, the next largest above it, and so on. The goal is to move all the discs from peg A to peg C without moving more than one disc at a time or placing a larger disc on a smaller one. Complexity in TOH depends on the levels of embedding of the goal hierarchy, a metric that commonly has been used to assess complexity (Just, Carpenter, & Hemphill, 1996). The more difficult moves require more levels of embedding of subgoals in the goal hierarchy (Halford, Wilson, & Phillips, 1998). However, the goal hierarchy metric can be subsumed under the relational complexity metric because moves with more subgoals entail relations with more dimensions of complexity (Halford, Wilson, & Phillips,1998). The first move and every fourth move thereafter are shown because only these require planning (VanLehn, 1991).

Consider a two-disc puzzle. To shift disc 2 from *A* to *C*, it is necessary to shift disc 1 from *A* to *B* first. The main goal is to shift 2 to *C* (2*C*), and the subgoal is to shift 1 to *B* (1*B*). The goal hierarchy, therefore, is 2*C* 1*B*, and it has two levels. Shifting 2 to *C* can be expressed as *shift*(2, *C*), while shifting 1 to *B* can be expressed as *shift*(1, *B*). Here the first argument to "*shift*" is a disc number, and the second is a peg name. The essence of the goal hierarchy is to perform a sequence of moves in order to perform another move. This can be expressed as the higher-order relation *Prior,* the two arguments of which may each be of two types. First, they can be instances of *shift*; as in, *Prior*(*shift*2(_,_), *shift*1(_,_)), meaning that *shift1* is done before *shift2*. Second, they maybe nested *Prior* instances, as in the second argument in *Prior*(*shift*3(_,_), *Prior*(*shift*2(_,_), *shift*1(_,_))). Thus, the task of shifting 1 to *B* before shifting 2 to *C* can be written as the following expression:

Prior(*shift*(2, *C*), *shift*(1, *B*)).

As with other relations, complexity is a function of the number of dimensions or roles to be filled (four in this example), so this task is *prima facie* four-dimensional.

Now consider the more complex three-disc puzzle: In order to shift 3 to *C*, it is first necessary to shift 2 to *B*, and to do that, it is necessary to shift 1 to *C*. There are now three levels of goals, and the corresponding *Prior* expression is also more complex:

Prior(*shift*(3, *C*), *Prior*(*shift*(2, *B*), *shift*(1, *C*)))

There are now six roles, so the task is six-dimensional. By a similar argument, the first move on the four-disc puzzle entails four levels of goals, and can be expressed by the relation

Prior(*shift*(4, *C*), *Prior*(*shift*(3, *B*), *Prior*(*shift*(2, *C*), *shift*(1, *B*))))

This is eight-dimensional. Thus, the number of embedded subgoals corresponds to relational complexity. Conceptual chunking and segmentation can be used to reduce complexity, as with other relational tasks. The first move of the three-disc puzzle can be simplified by chunking discs 1 and 2 as 1/2, and the corresponding pegs as B/C:

Prior(*shift*(3, *C*), *shift*(1/2, *B*/*C*))

Prior(*shift*(1/2, *B*/*C*) can be unchunked, yielding

Prior(*shift*(2, *B*), *shift*(1, *C*))

Thus, conceptual chunking and segmentation enable the task to be divided into two four-dimensional subtasks. This captures the recursive subgoaling strategy that underlies successful performance (VanLehn, 1991), and a conceptual chunk of this kind is called a "pyramid" (Halford, Wilson, & Phillips, 1998, §6.1.3).

Just et al. (1996) have shown that processing resources are related to the number of new goals that have to be generated for a move. Planning only requires the representation of new goals, so the relations that correspond to new goals provide a more realistic estimate of the dimensionality of a move.

Our estimate that humans are limited to processing approximately four dimensions in parallel implies that humans normally process no more than one goal and one subgoal in a single move. That is, they process one relation of the form *Prior*(*shift*(2, *C*), *shift*(1, *B*)), or *Prior*(*shift*(3, *C*), *shift*(1/2, *B*/*C*)). This is consistent with protocol information (VanLehn, 1991; pp. 42–47). A number of predictions based on this analysis have been tested with positive results (Loveday, 1995).

Relational complexity subsumes levels of embedding of a goal hierarchy (Zelazo et al., 2003), as discussed previously. However, the number of levels of embedding can be mapped directly into relational complexity, but there are several differences. Relational complexity also applies to tasks that do not entail subgoals, including tasks where decisions can be made in a single step. Therefore, it has greater generality. Just as important, relational analysis gives insights into the kind of decisions that are made to construct the goal hierarchy. For example, it enables us to determine how much information is likely to be processed in one step when a decision is made that in order to move 3 to C, 1 and 2 must be moved to B. Notice that TOH can be performed without processing steps more complex than a quaternary relation.

There are also reasoning tasks that are difficult for adults because they are structured in a way that constrains decomposition. An example is the knights and knaves task, discussed next.

Knights and knaves task

In the knights and knaves task, a person is either a knight, who always tells the truth, or a knave, who always lies. The aim is to determine which of the two types a person is from a statement that he or she makes. The relational complexity analysis of these tasks by Birney and Halford (2002) can be summarized as follows. Consider this problem: A says, "I am a knave and B is a knave." Some segmentation is possible by hypothesizing that A is a knight. If A were a knight, he would not say that he was a knave, so the hypothesis is contradicted. Therefore, A is a knave. However, this implies that the statement "A is a knave and B is a knave" must be false. Given that we know A is a knave, the only way the statement can be false is if B is a knight. The solution, therefore, is that A is a knave and B is a knight.

This strategy segments the problem into three inferences, but two of them remain complex, so the effective relational complexity of the task is high. The first inference can be expressed as

$knight(A)$ contradicts $says(A, and(knave(A), knave(B)))$, which implies $knave(A)$

There are four sources of variation in this, from left to right, $knight(A)$, A, $knave(A)$, and $knave(B)$. Hence *prima facie* the relational complexity would seem to be 4. However, the processing demand can be reduced using the principles of segmentation and conceptual chunking described in Birney & Halford (2002). Thus $knight(A)$ and the assertor A in the $says(-,-)$ can be chunked together, as can the components of the conjunction. In the Birney & Halford notation, we then have an expression

$\&\text{-}says(knight(A), and(knave(A), knave(B)))$

which because of the chunking has just two sources of variation: $knight(A)$ and $and(knave(A),\ knave(B))$. Further steps with a maximum relational complexity of 2 lead to

$$contradict(knight(A),\ knave(A)) \Rightarrow false(knight(A)) \Rightarrow knave(A))$$

The final inference can be expressed as

$$knave(A) \wedge false(and(knave(A),\ knave(B))) \Rightarrow knight(B)$$

So A is a knave and B is a knight. This is not a full analysis of the knights and knaves task, but it allows us to make several points. The first is that, as with TOH, relational complexity can be applied to tasks that include both serial and parallel processing. The inferences entailed in the reference task described here can be segmented into three distinct steps, and processing is parallel within each step. Relational complexity is assessed for each step in turn. Both relational complexity and the number of steps were found by Birney and Halford (2002) to influence performance, with relational complexity determining the number of correct solutions, and the number of steps being more closely related to solution times. The second point is that, even with the maximum amount of decomposition that is psychologically possible, the task requires some inferences of high structural complexity (i.e., quaternary relations). As the most complex inferences are quaternary relational, the effective complexity of the task is quaternary relational. The third point is that relational complexity analyses take account of expertise because the participant is assumed to understand that the task can be segmented into several steps and therefore can make valid inferences in each step. Relational complexity theory also can explain the difficulty of different forms of the knights and knaves task (Birney & Halford, 2002).

Complexity of sentence comprehension

Sentence comprehension entails assigning words to roles to construct a representation of the events or states that are conveyed by the sentence. For example, in the second sentence in table 4.1, the cow is in the *agent* role and the horse is in the *patient* role. Thus, the meaning of the sentence is a representation of relations such as *followed(cow, horse)*. Comprehension of multiple-role sentences depends on segmenting the sentence into subclauses. For example, in the sixth sentence in table 4.1, "the waiter warned the chef" would be processed first, and then the subordinate clause(s) would be processed. However, object relative sentences (of which sentences 1, 3, 5, and 7 in table 4.1 are examples) resist segmentation because nouns are not in canonical order and precede the verb. As shown in table 4.1, the number of roles in the sentences varies from 2 to 5. In two-role sentences (such as 1 and 2 in table 4.1), "Sally saw" preceded the substantive content of the sentences to control for the number of words to be read, but because this phrase was the same for all sentences, it would contribute minimally to the processing load. Effective relational complexity is determined by the number of roles and decomposability. It would be low (approximately binary relational) for all subject relative sentences, but for object relative sentences, it would increase from (approximately) binary for two-role sentences to quinary for five-role sentences. These hypotheses were assessed by Andrews, Birney, and Halford (2006) with college students by having them read the sentences at their own pace and then answer one comprehension question for each (e.g., "Who touched?").

The relational complexity metric performed similarly to the sophisticated dependency locality theory (Gibson, 2000), but relational complexity is a general metric for a large range of cognitive tasks, whereas dependency locality theory is specialized for sentence comprehension. Measures of relational processing included n-term ordering (which is an extension of transitive inference but entails ordering more elements), and the Latin square task (Birney, Halford, & Andrews, 2006). These measures predicted performance on object-relative sentences after controlling for performance on subject-relative sentences. By contrast, working memory measures, reading span (Daneman & Carpenter, 1980), and forward- and backward-digit span predicted objective-relative performance only before controlling

Table 4.1
Examples of 2-, 3-, 4-, and 5-role object-relative and subject-relative sentences used in Andrews, Birney, and Halford, 2006, Experiments 1, 2, and 3

Form	Roles	Example Sentences
Object	2	Sally saw the horse that the cow followed.
Subject	2	Sally saw the cow that followed the horse.
Object	3	The duck that the monkey touched walked.
Subject	3	The monkey touched the duck that walked.
Object	4	The artist that the waiter warned the chef about talked
Subject	4	The waiter warned the chef about the artist that talked.
Object	5	The clown that the teacher that the actor liked watched laughed.
Subject	5	The actor liked the teacher that watched the clown that laughed.

Note: Reprinted from Andrews, Birney and Halford (2006, table 1).

for subject-relatives. As mentioned with respect to our review of working memory, these processing span measures do not measure working memory as conceived as dynamic binding to a coordinate system.

Categorical (and probabilistic) syllogisms

The relational complexity metric has been applied to categorical syllogism tasks, taking account of strategies and heuristics used by the reasoners (Zielinski, Goodwin, & Halford, 2010). Figures 4.7 and 4.8 show two illustrative problems. Relational complexity is defined by the number of classes of entities that are entailed by premises.

Figure 4.7 illustrates how a subset of these classes is explicitly related for the following syllogism:

Premises: *All X are Y*

All Y are Z

Conclusions: All X are Z. Some Z are X

Representations of the separate premises are shown in lines 1 and 2 of figure 4.7 and of the combined premises in line 3. *All X are Y* is represented by showing entities that are both *X* and *Y* (i.e., *XY*) included in the area that represents *Y*, and ¬*XY* (where ¬ means negation) is also included in *Y*. Areas that are necessary (i.e., they define cases that must exist) according

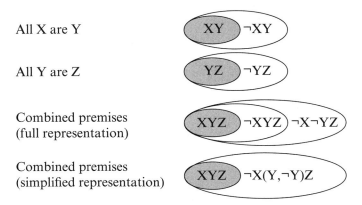

Figure 4.7

Interrelation for a subset of categories corresponding to full and simplified representations of the premises: *All X are Y* and *All Y are Z*. Reproduced from figure 1 by Zielinski, Goodwin, and Halford (2010). © 2009, Psychology Press; reproduced by permission.

to the premises are shaded, and areas that are not shaded are considered possible (i.e., they define cases that may, but do not definitely, exist). The full representation of the combined premises entails three classes of entities: XYZ, $\neg XYZ$, and $\neg X\neg YZ$. The full representation of the combined premises is ternary relational. However, chunking can be applied because the relation between $\neg XYZ$ and $\neg X\neg YZ$ does not need to be processed, and so these two categories can be chunked (fused) into one category. This is shown in line 4 of figure 4.7, which represents a relation between XYZ and $\neg X(Y, \neg Y)Z$. Therefore, effective relational complexity is 2. This application of conceptual chunking is known as the *principle of neglect* (in this case, the status of Y can be neglected).

Now let us consider the following syllogism, shown in figure 4.8:

No X are Y

All Y are Z

Conclusion: Some Z are not X

This problem does not lend itself to simplification. The full representation of combined premises generates the valid conclusion *Some Z are not X*. Four

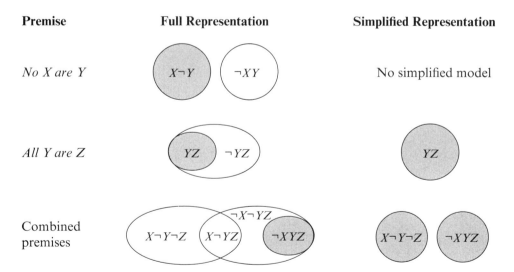

Figure 4.8
Full and simplified representations of the syllogism: *No X are Y* and *All Y are Z*, yielding the conclusion *Some Z are not X*. Reproduced from figure 4 by Zielinski, Goodwin, and Halford (2010). © 2009, Psychology Press, http://www.tandfonline .com/doi/full/10.1080/09541440902830509. Reproduced by permission.

classes of entities are entailed in this representation, so the relational complexity $RC = 4$.

The complexity analysis of categorical syllogisms takes account of both simplified representations that still permit valid conclusions and of heuristics. There are two established heuristics used for these tasks: the figural heuristic (Johnson-Laird & Byrne, 1991; Johnson-Laird & Steedman, 1978) and the atmosphere heuristic (Begg & Denny, 1969; Woodworth & Sells, 1935). The figural heuristic implies that if the figure is $XY - YZ$ (e.g., all X are Y, all Y are Z), then the conclusion should take the form X-Z, while if the figure is $YX - ZY$ (e.g., some Y are X, no Z are Y), the conclusion (after swapping the order of the premises) should take the form Z-X (see Zielinski, Goodwin, & Halford, 2010, table 1). The simplest application of the figural heuristic entails matching the terms of the conclusion to the end terms in the premises, so this strategy is binary relational. The heuristic is likely to be cued by the end terms, so $XY - YZ$ figures cue a conclusion beginning with X, and so on, as suggested by Evans (2006) for other reasoning tasks.

The atmosphere heuristic incorporates attributes of quality (*positive, negative*) and quantity (*universal, particular*). The principle of quality asserts that where one or both premises are negative, the conclusion will be negative; otherwise, it will be positive. This corresponds to the fact *quality(premise1, negative)*. The quality principle links *quality(premise1, negative)* to *quality(conclusion1, negative)*. The principle of quantity asserts that where one or both premises are particular, the conclusion will be particular; otherwise, it will be universal. So we have a rule *quantity(premise1, particular)* $\Longrightarrow$ *quantity(conclusion1, particular)*. Combining these principles gives us *quality(premise1, negative)* $\land$ *quantity(premise1, particular)* $\Longrightarrow$ *quality(conclusion1, negative)* $\land$ *quantity(conclusion1, particular)*. The right-hand side of the rule can be re-expressed as *types(conclusion1, negative, particular)*, which can be regarded as ternary, since *types* is not a source of variation.

The relational complexity metric accounts for approximately the same proportion of problem form variance in categorical syllogisms as the leading domain-specific metric, which is based on the mental models theory of Johnson-Laird (Bucciarelli & Johnson-Laird, 1999)—that is, approximately 80 percent. Relational complexity theory is essentially a mental models theory, but it assesses complexity by the number of distinct categories that are implied by the premises of a syllogism, and it does not assume the construction of more than one mental model. Furthermore, relational complexity theory is a general cognitive complexity metric that is applicable to a wide range of tasks. The relational complexity analysis also integrates heuristic and analytic processes in a single estimate of complexity. Mental models theory will be discussed in greater detail in Chapter 8.

The probability heuristics model of Oaksford and Chater (2007) will be discussed in detail in chapter 8, but we will mention here that it accounts for approximately the same proportion of problem form variance in categorical syllogisms as relational complexity theory. It is based on the principle that premises are probabilistic rather than categorical. The probability heuristics model operates on an implicit ranking of the four premise moods (*All, Some, Some not, None*). According to the *min*-heuristic, which is the main determinant of inferences, individuals tend to draw conclusions that match the mood of the least informative premise. However, Halford (2009) has pointed out that the least informative premise is also the most probable proposition. We will argue in chapter 8 that the theory really amounts to a proposal that there is a constraint between the mood of premises and the mood of conclusions.

Category theory accounts of complexity

In chapter 1, we introduced the idea that cognitive processes can be conceived as functions causing transitions between sets of cognitive states. This was illustrated by accounting for transitive inference and class inclusion in terms of Cartesian products and disjoint unions of sets. In this section, we want to expand this treatment by outlining category theory accounts of cognition proposed by Phillips, Wilson, and Halford (2009) and by Phillips and Wilson (2010, 2011, 2012). For the definition of a category, see box 4.1.

Box 4.1

> **Category**: a (mathematical) category C consists of *objects* and *arrows* (also called *maps* or *morphisms*). Each arrow f in C has a domain and codomain, which are objects in C: we write $f: X \rightarrow Y$ – here, where X is the domain and Y is the codomain. There must be a *composition operator* $\circ$ for arrows: if X, Y, and Z are objects, and $f: X \rightarrow Y$ and $g: Y \rightarrow Z$ are arrows, then there must be an arrow $g \circ f: X \rightarrow Z$, and composition must be *associative*: i.e., if $h: Z \rightarrow W$, then $h \circ (g \circ f) = (h \circ g) \circ f$. Finally, for each object X in C, there must be an identity arrow, written as $1_X: X \rightarrow X$, such that $f \circ 1_X = f = 1_X \circ f$.

To recapitulate part of the discussion in chapter 1, in the transitive inference task in figure 1.4, the premises comprise a green block sitting on top of a red block and a red block sitting on top of a blue block. We can recover the top and bottom blocks of each premise by two functions (projections) that map each pair to its first and second component, respectively: the function *top* maps (*green*, *red*) to *green*, and the function *bottom* maps (*green*, *red*) to *red*. Each set is an object, and each function is a morphism in a category (collection) of sets and functions between sets, which is called **Set.**

In this section, we will elaborate on the introduction to category theory in chapter 1. Mathematical categories study not just objects, but also their maps (see box 4.2). This is what makes category theory a suitable formalism for cognitive processes defined by mappings between representations. So, in this case, the representations are the objects and cognitive processes are, or cause, the transformations or maps. Another feature of category theory models of cognition is that they are not committed to any particular type of representation or process, so there is no *a priori* acceptance of any of the distinctions reviewed previously. We will define the model in general terms here, and mathematical details can be found in Phillips, Wilson, & Halford (2009). Extensions of the theory are contained in Phillips and Wilson (2010, 2011, 2012).

The principal constituents of a category theory model of cognition include objects and arrows (which are also called *maps* or *morphisms*). There also may be transformations between categories, which are termed *functors*. In the context of cognitive science, "an object may be a cognitive state, set of states, or some other entity employing symbolic, or numerical representations, and an arrow may be some cognitive process transforming one state to another" (Phillips, Wilson, & Halford, 2009, p. 2). Often, though not always, arrows are structure-preserving functions.

An example of an arrow/morphism would be the function *log* (logarithm) from the set R^+ of positive real numbers with the usual multiplication operation to the set R of all real numbers with the usual addition operation. We write *log*: $R^+ \rightarrow R$, and we call R^+ the *domain* and R the *codomain* of *log*. An important feature of morphisms is that they are structure-preserving, meaning in this case that the multiplication operation in R^+ corresponds to the addition operation in R in the transformation $log(x \times y) = log\ x + log\ y$. There needs to be a specific category as a setting for all this. In this case, a suitable category would be the category **Grp** of groups: thus, $(R, \times)$ and $(R^+, +)$ are groups; *log*, then, is a morphism between these two groups.

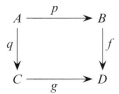

Figure 4.9
This diagram is said to be commutative if $f \circ p = g \circ q$.

The notion of a commutative diagram frequently arises in category theory and in its applications in cognitive science, going back at least to Halford and Wilson (1980), where commutativity was used to express structural consistency between cognitive models. A diagram involving objects and arrows is said to be *commutative* if the compositions of morphisms along any two paths between distinct objects are equal (see figure 4.9). In the familiar case where the objects are sets and the morphisms are functions, commutativity means (in the case of figure 4.9) that for every $a \in A$, $f(p(a)) = q(g(a))$. Figure 2.6 in chapter 2, in fact, is also a commutative diagram, and much of Appendix 2.1 can be expressed in terms of commutativity.

Box 4.2

Categorical products: In some categories, including **Grp** (the category of groups; i.e., sets with a notion of multiplication, an identity, and inverses, subject to some axioms) and **Set** (the category of sets, with sets as objects and functions as arrows), there exist *product objects*. The general definition of these is a little complex, but in **Grp** and **Set**, Cartesian products are product objects. Thus, if G and H are groups (objects in **Grp**), then the set $G \times H = \{(g, h) \mid g \in G, h \in H\}$ is a group too, under the operation $(g_1, h_1) * (g_2, h_2) = (g_1 * g_2, h_1 * h_2)$. The projection morphisms $p_1: G \times H \to G$, such that $p_1(g, h) = g$ and $p_2: G \times H \to H$ such that $p_2(g, h) = h$, are considered part of the product. In summary, we have an object-and-arrow diagram like this:
$G \leftarrow G \times H \to H$.
Products have what is called a *universal property*, which essentially means that they are "optimal" objects Z among diagrams like this one:
$G \leftarrow Z \to H$.
For the full technical definition, see Mac Lane (2000) or Phillips, Wilson, and Halford (2009). Cognitive tasks often involve products in this sense. For example, processing simple sentences like *Mary likes pizza* can be viewed as dealing with points in a (triple) product space of the form *Subject × Relationship × Object*.

Two central notions in basic category theory are products and duality. Products (see box 4.4) in the category **Set** are isomorphic to Cartesian products, which are central to relation theory, if only because relations are by mathematical definition subsets of Cartesian products. Duality (see box 4.3), from our perspective, is a way of pairing off concepts in such a way that properties that hold for one member of the pair have a corresponding property that holds for the other member of the pair.

Box 4.3

Categorical duals: Every category C has a *dual* category C^{op}, which has the same objects, but each morphism $f: X \rightarrow Y$ is replaced by $f^{op}: Y \rightarrow X$, and the composition is replaced by a dual composition: if there is also a $g: Y \rightarrow Z$, then $(g \circ f)^{op} = f^{op} \circ_{op} g^{op}$. The superscript or subscript *op* stands for opposite (direction). Essentially, when you reverse all the arrows in a category theory setup, something interesting happens. Often mathematicians get a theorem "for free" in this way. In the case of products, the dual construct is called a *coproduct*. In the category **Set**, the coproduct turns out to be a *disjoint union*: the disjoint union of sets S and T is $\{(s, 1)|s \in S\} \cup \{(t, 2)|t \in T\}$—i.e., the 1s and 2s serve to ensure that if S and T have members in common, then separate copies of them will end up in the disjoint union.

In the category **Set**, a disjoint union is a categorical *coproduct*. Coproduct is dual to product. Hence, transitive inference and class inclusion are related by the dual notions of product and coproduct. This means that in the more difficult transitive inference and class inclusion concepts achievable by older children (i.e., 6-year-olds), the arity (i.e., number of arguments) of the product or coproduct is binary in the sense that the input to the Cartesian product is comprised of two sets (two arguments). In the easy conditions achievable by both younger (4-year-olds) and older children, the inputs are unary. In transitive inference, this means that only one premise is processed, so the inference might be made by considering only *green* above *red*, while in class inclusion, an inference might be made without computing the disjoint union. In both cases, this means that inferences are made with less information and without integrating the relevant information. Cartesian products and disjoint unions involve integrating information. Thus, category theory provides a theoretical explanation for why older children succeed at both tasks (and other reasoning tasks at the same level of complexity) because older, but not younger, children have the capacity to integrate two sources of information. Phillips, Wilson, and Halford (2009) show that transitive inference and class inclusion tests that are mastered first at a median age of 5 years are connected formally by the dual relationship between product and coproduct (see boxes 4.3 and 4.4). By contrast, the simpler versions of these tasks that are mastered earlier do not involve a product/coproduct, or involve one in a trivial sense. They then proceed to demonstrate a similar point for matrix completion (Halford, 1993), cardinality (Andrews & Halford, 2002), dimensional-change card sorting (Zelazo et al., 2003; Halford, Bunch, & McCredden, 2007), balance-scale (Andrews et al., 2009), and theory of mind (Andrews et al., 2003). Category theory analysis has been extended to account for other fundamental properties of higher cognition, including systematicity (Phillips & Wilson, 2010, 2011, 2012, 2014).

Box 4.4

> **Power transpose of a relation**: There is a natural correspondence between relations r on $A \times B$ and functions $f: A \to \wp B$ (where $\wp B$ is the set of all subsets of B). That is, for each relation, there is a corresponding function. For example, let $A = \{rock, cat, mouse\}$, $B = \{cheese, mouse\}$, and let r be the relation $eats=\{(cat, cheese),(cat, mouse),(mouse, cheese)\}$. Here, r captures the same information as the function $f: A \to \wp B$ which has $f(rock) = \varnothing$, the empty set, $f(cat) = \{cheese, mouse\}$, and $f(mouse) = \{cheese\}$.
>
> In general, for any A and B and relation $r \subseteq A \times B$, define $F(r): A \to \wp B$ by $F(r)(a) = \{b \in B \mid (a, b) \in r\}$. If $f: A \to \wp B$ is a function, define the relation $R(f) \subseteq A \times B$ by $R(f) = \{(a, b) \in A \times B \mid b \in f(a)\}$. It is easy to check that $R(F(r)) = r$ and $F(R(f)) = f$. So we can move back and forth between relations and functions at will. The operator that takes a relation to the associated function is called the *power transpose* operator. Similarly, relations on $A \times B \times C$ are equivalent to functions $A \times B \to \wp C$ and to functions $A \to \wp(B \times C)$, and so on.
>
> Because of this correspondence, functions, relations, and operations can be treated as equivalent for in certain situations.

Categorical products, visual attention, and EEG synchrony

The relationship between categorical product arity and neural activity was examined by Phillips, Takeda, and Singh (2012), using a variation of a visual search task. This study was motivated by the observation that the

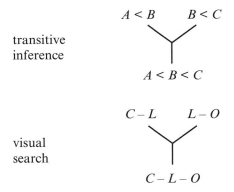

transitive
inference

visual
search

Figure 4.10
Transitive inference involves a join of two (order) relations: $A < B$ and $B < C$. Analogously, visual search involves a join of two feature maps (as relations): color-location (C-L) and location-orientation (L-O).

"standard" model of vision involves Cartesian products of maps of visual features (e.g., color, orientation) that are constrained by object locations (see figure 4.10). Varying the number of feature dimensions that uniquely identify the search target from one (e.g., color) to two (e.g., color and orientation) to three (e.g., color, orientation, and frequency) corresponds to unary, binary, and ternary constrained products, respectively. Analysis of electroencephalogram (EEG) phase synchrony under these three arity conditions revealed a significant increase in frontal-parietal electrode synchrony as a function of product arity.

Visual search as a categorical (Cartesian) product of feature maps constrained by object locations can be seen as analogous to transitive inference as a categorical product of premise relations constrained on common relational attributes (Phillips, Takeda, & Singh, 2012; Supplementary Text S3). The binding of color and orientation is constrained by location, which is analogous to the structure of transitive inference, as shown in figure 1.4 in chapter 1. For example, suppose that a visual field contains rectangular bars as stimuli that vary in color and orientation (e.g., a red-vertical bar and a blue-horizontal bar). Stimuli may appear in one of four possible locations, which are the quadrants of the visual field: i.e., top-left (1), top-right (2), bottom-left (3), and bottom-right (4). In particular, suppose that the visual field contains a red-vertical bar in quadrant 1 and a blue-horizontal bar in quadrant 4. Color and orientation feature maps are binary relations between color and location attributes and orientation and

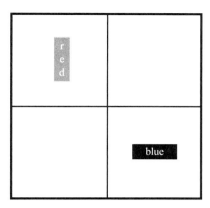

Figure 4.11
Search display containing a red-vertical bar in top-left quadrant (1) and a blue-horizontal bar in the bottom-right quadrant (4).

location attributes, respectively. In the current example, that is the sets of pairs {(*red*, 1), (*blue*, 4)} and {(*vertical*, 1), (*horizontal*, 4)}. The Cartesian product of these two sets constrained at the common locations yields the set of triples {(*red, vertical*, 1), (*blue, horizontal*, 4)}, which correspond to the two bars in the visual field (see figure 4.11).

EEG signals, time-locked to the onset of the search display, were recorded while participants searched for the previously presented target object in the search display, which varied randomly across trials. As expected, participants were significantly slower and less accurate at identifying the target with greater product arity, an effect that is well known for closely related conjunctive and triple conjunctive search conditions in visual attention. Participants also revealed greater frontal-parietal electrode synchrony with arity. This effect also was observed for a subset of conditions equated for behavioral performance (to exclude the possibility that changes were simply due to task difficulty or time spent on the task).

One interpretation of this result is that the increased synchrony results from the need to match more target features held in working memory (frontal cortex) with display object features in the focus of attention (parietal cortex), rather than the binding of visual features to objects per se, in a visual short-term buffer. Visual short-term memory (100 ms to 500 ms) for change detection appears to be impervious to the number of features to an object (up to four), in contrast to the number of objects held in memory (Luck & Vogel, 1997). Mean search times for the visual search task were greater than 700 ms in all three arity conditions. Although more work is needed to identify the role of synchrony in visual search, the important point for our current purpose is that category theory not only provides a formal mathematical basis for relating cognitive structures, it also provides a bridge between cognitive and neural levels of analysis.

Box 4.5

Pullbacks: A *pullback* is a concept somewhat similar to that of a product (see box 4.2). In the category **Set**, the product of two sets A and B is their Cartesian product $A \times B$. Again, in **Set**, the pullback of a collection of objects (sets) A, B, and C, and maps (functions) $f: A \to C$ and $g:B \to C$ is a subset of $A \times B$; namely, $\{(a, b) \in A \times B \mid f(a) = g(b)\}$. We give an example relating to two judo clubs three paragraphs further on. The pullback is often written as $A \times_C B$. Although this notation ignores the crucial roles of f and g in the pullback, it is compact.

Like products, pullbacks have a universal property. Consider objects Z and maps $p: Z \to A$ and $q:Z \to B$, such that $f \circ p = g \circ q$ holds—i.e., the left side of figure 4.12 commutes.

Then the pullback is the "optimal" object Z among setups like the left side of figure 4.12. Technically (Awodey, 2010, p. 91), the pullback is a triple $(A \times_C B, \pi_1, \pi_2)$, as on the right side of figure 4.12, such that for any other triple (Z, p, q), as on the left side of figure 4.12, there is a unique map $u: Z \to A \times_C B$, which makes the whole right side of figure 4.12 commutative. There can be more than one pullback object, but all of them will be isomorphic.

A fairly readily understandable example of a pullback is as follows:

If A and B are the sets of members of two judo clubs, and C is the set of judo belt colors (black belt, brown belt, etc.), and $f: A \to C$ and $g: B \to C$ are functions that map members to their belt colors, then the pullback is the relation of having the same belt color as someone in the other club. That is, (a, b) is in the pullback if a and b have the same belt color.

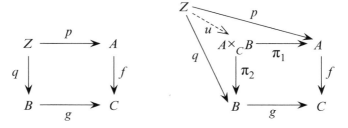

Figure 4.12
Pullback diagrams.

Box 4.5

(continued)

> Natural joins of relations are instances of pullbacks. Pullbacks also arise in the descriptions of seriation and transitivity. For example, if $S \subseteq A \times B$ and $T \subseteq B \times C$ are relations (implemented as tables) in a database (see chapter 3), and $f\colon S \to B$ is the restriction of the projection map $A \times B \to B$ to S, and $g\colon T \to B$ is the restriction of the projection map $B \times C \to B$ to T, then the join of S and T is a pullback of $f\colon S \to B$ and $g\colon T \to B$. In the case where $A = B = C$ and $S = T$, the pullback, which in this case is a "natural join," is the ternary relation $aTbTc$, which arises when modeling transitivity.

Thus, reasons for using category theory concepts in cognitive modeling include at least the following:

• The precision that it provides in establishing structural correspondence via commutative diagrams
• The uniqueness characteristic afforded by constructions like products and pullbacks via universal properties
• The fact that its high level of abstraction allows one to separate the essential structures involved from the implementation details, such as the use of particular grammars, of rule-based systems, and of neural networks of specific types

Conclusion

In this chapter, we have considered a number of longstanding issues in the fields of cognitive complexity and capacity and have argued that attempts to rule out these variables lack justification. This argument is reinforced by developments in the last decade in the field of working memory, which is now shown to account for a high proportion of variance in cognition. We have reviewed contemporary accounts of working memory that are based on assignments to slots in a coordinate system, and we have shown how this offers new insights into processing relational knowledge. We have explained the RC metric in detail, including MARC, which specifies principles that determine when complexity can be reduced by conceptual chunking, segmentation, or both. We have shown that there is an encouraging consensus concerning limits of working memory capacity, which is all the more impressive by being maintained across a wide range of methodologies. We have reviewed other complexity metrics and noted points of similarity and difference to our RC metric. In addition, we have considered several applications of the RC metric that cover a wide range of domains in cognitive development and general cognition, including class inclusion, theory of mind, Raven's Matrices, TOH, knights and knaves, sentence comprehension, and syllogistic reasoning. We suggest that, far from being undesirable concepts, cognitive complexity and capacity can have an integrative effect because they explain the correspondence between tasks in different domains and also explain otherwise mysterious differences in performance between apparently similar tasks. We cannot achieve coherence in cognitive science without taking complexity and capacity into account.

Finally, we have outlined the category theory account of cognitive complexity, which provides a profound analysis of structural correspondences between tasks of equivalent complexity. It links cognitive processes to a body of theory that has wide scientific relevance, and it provides constraints on the predictions generated by this theory.

5 Representational Rank

In chapter 2, we defined three levels of process: nonstructured, functionally structured, and symbolically structured. They are rank-ordered for complexity in the sense that they entail increasingly complex representations and cognitive functions, and the lower-level processes remain accessible while processing the higher levels. The complexity of symbolically structured processes has been defined by the relational complexity metric, as outlined in chapter 4. When relational complexity is combined with the three levels defined earlier in this book, an ordering of cognitive complexity is created, as shown in table 5.1. This yields seven levels of cognitive process, which we define as Representational Ranks 0–6.

The literature that we consider here entails many controversies, and we will not try to resolve all of them in this discussion. Some are purely normative, in the sense that they depend on the assessment of concept mastery as a function of age or species. Others might depend on studies yet to be conducted, and some are based on empirical findings that are themselves subject to controversy. Our purpose here is to define the criteria that enable cognitive processes to be categorized objectively and accurately. Cognitive processes do not emerge simultaneously for all participants; rather, they develop cumulatively, as shown in figure 1.4 in chapter 1. Different researchers adopt different criteria for attainment, which makes the precise comparison of norms difficult in the present state of the field. Therefore, the norms that we suggest are conservative, and the relevant tasks might occur somewhat earlier in development. Our predictions are concerned with correspondences so that, for example, if binary relational processes are observed at 18 months, this adjustment should be applicable to all tasks at this level. Thus, we have presented definitions that include the core properties of cognitive processes at each of the major levels, and that we believe aid in the interpretation of empirical findings. In order to put our proposals in concrete form, now we will

Table 5.1

Tasks assigned to representational ranks with approximate known, or predicted, attainment

Rank	Cognitive Task	Attainment
0	Elemental association	All animals with nervous systems
	Linear transitivity of choice	All animals with nervous systems predicted
1	Conditional discrimination	Birds, mammals, 6-month-old human infants predicted
	Circular transitivity of choice	Birds, mammals, 6-month-old human infants predicted
	Transfer based on computed representations	7-month-old infants, birds, and mammals predicted
	Prototypes	Infants in first year
	Object permanence knowledge	6-month-old infants
	Image schemas	Infants in first year
2	Unary relations	1-year-old infants predicted
	Labeled categories	1-year-old infants predicted
	Match-to-sample	Monkeys, dolphins, 1-year-old infants predicted
	Unary relational analogy	1-year-old infants
	Identity-position binding (stage 5 object permanence)	1-year-old infants
3	Binary relational match-to-sample	Chimpanzees, 2-year-old children predicted
	Accessibility of components of binary relations	Chimpanzees, 2-year-old children predicted
	Tool use	Chimpanzees, 2-year-old children
	Proportional analogy	Chimpanzees, 3- to 4-year-old children, 2-year-old infants predicted
	Inferences about labeled categories	2-year-old children predicted

	Explicit categorization, binary level, with accessibility	2-year-old children predicted
	Weight and distance discrimination on the balance scale	2- to 3-year-old children predicted ahead of data, and confirmed
	Object permanence stage 6	Children late second year
	Mirror self-recognition	Children late second year
	Pretense	Children late second year
	Picture and model interpretation	2- to 3-year-old children
	Representing the representing relation	2- to 3-year-old children
	Awareness of objects (connections task)	Children in second year Chimpanzees
4	Transitive inference	5-year-old children
	Hierarchical classification	5-year-old children
	Conditional discrimination with transfer to isomorphs	5-year-old children (transfer to isomorphs is predicted)
	Theory (Concept) of Mind	4- to 5-year-old children
5	Proportion	Adolescents
	Torque rule on balance scale	Adolescents
	Certain metalogical problems	Adolescents predicted
	Tower of Hanoi (TOH; certain items)	Adolescents predicted
6	Certain categorical syllogisms (e.g., *Some X are Y; some Z are not Y*)	Minority of adults

examine examples of cognitive phenomena that belong to each level of representational rank.

Representational rank was defined in chapter 2 (see box 2.2), but to recapitulate, the term refers to the number of identifiable components bound into a structured representation, such that the components satisfy the constraints imposed by the structure. An example would be a cognitive representation of the binary relations *more-than* and *less-than* defined on a set of positive integers, such as > (3,2), > (5,4) and < (2,5), and < (3,7). There are constraints between the components, including structural alignment so that, for the relation >, the integer in the first position (first role) of each pair must be greater than the integer in the second position (with a corresponding constraint for <). A further constraint is compositionality, so that, for example, given (3,2), the relation must be >. Each instance, such as > (3,2) of a binary relation, has three components, >, 3, and 2, so this representation would be Rank 3. The complexity of a cognitive process depends on representational rank, and higher ranks impose higher processing loads. We will present evidence that there are properties of cognitive performances that are similar within ranks and differ among ranks.

Nonstructured processes are Rank 0 because there is no representation, and therefore, the number of components is zero. Mental states m_i and m_o (as shown in figure 2.2 in chapter 2) represent input and output and do not contribute to rank. The associative link $m_i \rightarrow m_o$ is not a mental state per se, although it might become accessible in some circumstances, as in the Bayesian Analogy with Relational Transformations (BART) model (Lu, Chen, & Holyoak, 2012) discussed in chapter 7.

Functionally structured processes have an internal representation, but they are Rank 1 because the representation functions in a holistic fashion. Even if there is more than one mental state representation, Rank 1 representations are not composed into a structure of the kind required for relational representations as defined in chapter 2.

The rank of symbolically structured processes is one more than the *arity* of the relation because the relation symbol contributes one component to the representation. Unary relations are Rank 2, binary relations are Rank 3, and so on. The representational rank metric ranges from Rank 0 to Rank 6, which covers the full range of cognitive complexities from unstructured, elemental associative processes to the most complex, symbolically structured processes that human information processing capacities make possible.

Predictions of empirical phenomena

Our aims in this section are as follows:

1. To examine tasks of the same representational rank and to match predictions from the theory to empirical data on attainment
2. To contrast phenomena at different levels of cognitive complexity
3. To consider empirical criteria for assigning tasks to levels
4. To assess evidence that tasks of a given rank constitute an equivalence class of equal structural complexity

Predictions are conditional on the boundary conditions discussed in chapter 4, including relevant domain and task knowledge being available to participants.

Nonstructured processes: Rank 0

One paradigm, transitivity of choice, can be switched from Rank 0 to Rank 1 by a seemingly trivial change in the discriminations to be learned, with different properties as a consequence. We will consider Ranks 0 and 1 in turn.

Linear transitivity of choice (Boysen et al., 1993; Chalmers & McGonigle, 1984; McGonigle & Chalmers, 1977; Terrace & McGonigle, 1994; von Fersen et al., 1991) can be performed by elemental association. Participants are trained to choose one member of each pair in a series ($A+B-$, $B+C-$, $C+D-$, $D+E-$, where + indicates a rewarded choice and – indicates a nonrewarded choice); see figure 5.1. Transitivity of choice is assessed with

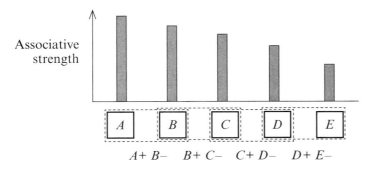

Figure 5.1
Rank ordering of stimuli in a version of the transitivity of choice task according to strength of association with choice response.

untrained nonadjacent pairs, with most interest focusing on *B* and *D*, because *B+* and *B–* occurred equally often in training, as did *D+* and *D–*. Wynne (1995) showed that the Bush-Mosteller (Bush & Mosteller, 1955) and Rescorla-Wagner (Rescorla & Wagner, 1972) models predicted transitive choice (*B* versus *D*) plus serial position effects (De Lillo, Floreano, & Antinucci, 2001) and the symbolic distance effect (better discrimination between elements further apart in the series). Other work corroborates this conclusion (Couvillon & Bitterman, 1992). The production system model of Harris and McGonigle (1994) is consistent with associative models in that it attributes performance to the strength of the tendency, acquired as a function of experience, to respond to each stimulus. This suggests that at least some instances of linear transitivity of choice can be performed by associative learning, and if no more complex process is involved, they would be nonstructured. There are other reasons why these studies cannot be claimed to provide evidence for explicit, symbolically mediated transitive inference. For example, some early studies inadvertently provided cues to the correct order of elements that bypassed the requirement for relational integration (Halford & Kelly, 1984).

There are many variations on this paradigm, with a diversity of processes. One version that arguably comes close to analytic transitive inference was by Lazareva et al. (2004). When crows were taught to associate *A–E* with colored circles that decreased monotonically in size, they selected *B* over *D* even when *D* had greater associative strength. This suggests that crows can respond on the basis of a mental model of the task structure, but it contrasts in important ways with the explicit transitive inference procedure. The ordering was not constructed dynamically in working memory; rather, it was provided by the experimenter because circles of the appropriate size were shown to the crows after they made a choice, and acquisition was incremental rather than dynamic. The representation learned evidently mediates response selection in this restricted context, but there is no evidence for the properties of relational knowledge, such as structural alignment, a relation symbol, representation of roles, accessibility, or mapping based on structural correspondence.

Awareness of the *A–E* sequence influenced human performance in the study by Smith and Squire (2005), but the relatively small amount of training might have precluded implicit transitivity for some participants, requiring them to employ explicit processing. See also Penn, Holyoak, and Povinelli (2008a).

The assignment of this task to Rank 0 is further supported because the transitivity of choice paradigm does not handle variations of the task that can be performed easily by analytic transitive inference. McGonigle & Chalmers (1977) found reduced performance in transitivity of choice on triads, so monkeys were much less efficient at choosing B in the presence of C and D than in the presence of D alone. If the task were performed by integrating relations such as AB, BC ... DE to form an ordered array A,B,C,D,E, as proposed for analytic transitive inference, then it would be predicted that if B is preferable to D, it should be preferable to C and D together because B occurs earlier in the series than both. The relational integration strategy should make it possible to determine the position of an element relative to others in a triad, so we would know that B is better than C or D in the triad BCD. By contrast, both elemental and configural associative models predict a performance that is no better than chance with triads. The failure of monkeys to perform above chance with triads (McGonigle & Chalmers, 1977) suggests that they did not integrate relations and supports the distinction between Rank 0 and higher-rank performances. Performance on triads permits associative and structured processes to be distinguished within the same paradigm, using performance criteria that are appropriate for humans and other animals.

Another performance that is predicted for the relational integration strategy, but would not be predicted by associative learning models, is mapping to isomorphs, based on analogy theory as discussed in chapter 3. The premises *John is taller than Peter* and *Michael is taller than John* define the ordering *Michael taller-than John taller-than Peter* that can easily be mapped to *top-above-middle-above-bottom*, as shown in figure 1.3 in chapter 1. Thus, *top-middle-bottom* can be recognized as an analog of *tallest-middle-shortest*. Notice that the mapping is based on structural correspondence rather than element similarity and requires that relations be represented.

Functionally structured processes: Rank 1

In this section, we consider a number of performances that can be accounted for by the functionally structured model, as defined in chapter 2 (see box 2.5).

Configural association

Elemental association and configural association can be contrasted within the transitivity of choice paradigm.

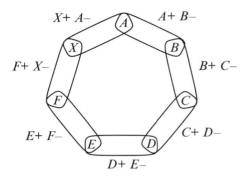

Figure 5.2
Structure of the circular transitivity of choice task.

Circular transitivity of choice

A dramatic difference in performance on the transitivity of choice task can be produced by the seemingly trivial change of adding a pair to a series. If the pair $F+X-$ is added to the series $X+A-$, $A+B-$, $B+C-$, $C+D-$, $D+E-$, $E+F-$, discussed under nonstructured processes, the structure becomes circular rather than linear, as shown in figure 5.2. The task no longer can be learned by elemental association because every element is equally associated with reinforcement and nonreinforcement (in this set of pairs each of A,B,C,D,E,F,X occurs with + and −). However, it can be learned by configural association, and the observed effects are predicted by a configural learning model in which a stimulus (say, B) that acquires associative strength in the presence of C ($B|BC$) is different from a stimulus that acquires associative strength in the presence of A ($B|AB$) (Wynne, 1995). This means that there is a unique configuration for each element in every context where it occurs. Therefore, each pair is learned as a separate discrimination, and nothing is learned that corresponds to the circular structure of the series. Notice that this is like the configurations in conditional discrimination, as shown in figure 2.1D in chapter 2, where each combination of inputs is coded as a unique configuration which avoids associative interference, but means that structure cannot be represented.

The performance of pigeons is lower on the circular transitivity of choice task than on the linear transitivity of choice task, but it is still above chance with discrimination of adjacent pairs. However, performance on the test pair BD is no longer better than chance, and serial position effects disappear (von Fersen et al., 1991). Whereas linear (standard) transitivity of choice is nonstructured, circular transitivity of choice is functionally structured because it is based on configural learning, which conforms to the definition of functionally structured processing. That is, it depends on recoding the stimuli into configurations such as $B|BC$, $B|AB$, etc.

The comparison of linear and circular transitivity of choice illustrates that assignment to a representational rank is based on underlying processes. The former is nonstructured and the latter is functionally structured because of learning processes, even though the tasks are almost indistinguishable in surface form. Performance differences are consistent with representational rank.

Transfer based on functionally structured representations

Several studies of discrimination transfer, independent of content, have findings that are consistent with functionally structured representations. Two are with infants, one with baboons, and one with bees.

Tyrrell, Zingaro, and Minard (1993) trained 7-month-old infants to look at either a pair of identical toys or a pair of nonidentical toys. They showed transfer to new pairs of toys that embodied the relation on which they had been trained.

Marcus et al. (1999) habituated 7-month-old infants to three-word sentences of the form ABA or ABB constructed from an artificial language, then tested them on three-word sentences composed of artificial words not used in habituation. Infants were familiarized with a two-minute speech sample comprising three repetitions of each of 16 utterances (e.g., "ga ti ga," "li ti li"). The test materials comprised 12 sentences with different elements from those used in training. The sentences were either consistent (e.g., "wo fe wo") or inconsistent (e.g., "wo fe fe") with the habituation sequences. Infants looked longer toward the side where the sentences with the novel structure were presented. Thus, they were sensitive to structure even though the content was different. The results were confirmed in two control experiments.

Baboons (specifically *Papio papio*) successfully learned relational match-to-sample discriminations in a task where they could not rely on the identity of the stimuli (Fagot, Wasserman, & Young, 2001). There was a sample stimulus and two choice stimuli, each comprised of a square array of 16 elements. The sample stimulus elements were either all the same or all different. The correct choice stimulus was the one that had the same relation between elements as the sample. If the sample elements were all the same (different), the correct choice elements were all the same (different). All elements of choice stimuli were different from those in the sample, so the correct choice could be made only on the basis of the relations between elements. The baboons achieved 84 percent correct discrimination in training, and when tested with novel stimulus elements in the choice stimuli, they maintained 70 percent correct discrimination. Both performances were much better than chance. Two humans tested on the same procedure learned the task much more quickly, achieving 100 percent correct in test trials. Subsequent experiments suggested that the cue used by baboons was entropy. Reduction in the number of different stimulus elements from 16 to 12 to 8 to 4 to 2 produced a monotonic decrease in the performance of the baboons, from over 80 percent correct to chance level. Their entropy measure is 4 when 16 different items are used and 0 when all the items are the same. Humans were less influenced by entropy and tended to make more categorical judgments. Thus, human performance was distinguishable from that of baboons. Subsequent research has shown successful relational match-to-sample using pairs of stimuli (Fagot & Parron, 2010; Fagot & Thompson, 2011) and with other primate species (Truppa et al., 2011; Vonk, 2003).

Bees have been shown to have similar ability to recognize sameness and difference (Giurfa et al., 2001). They were trained in a delayed matching-to-sample task with the sample placed at the entrance to a Y-maze, and a matching or nonmatching stimulus at the arms of the maze. The bees showed above-chance matching-to-sample on odor, color, and pattern (horizontal versus vertical stripes). They could also transfer between modalities, so that when they were trained on odor, they could transfer to color. Bees can also learn two discriminations such as above-below and left-right simultaneously (Avarguès-Weber et al., 2012).

We have shown that functionally structured processes can mediate transfer based on computed representations of same or different. A functionally structured process was defined in chapter 2 as consisting of functions $f_1: E_i \rightarrow E_h$, $f_2: E_h \rightarrow E_o$ and $f(e_i) = f_2(f_1(e_i)) = e_o$, where E_i, E_h, and E_o are input, hidden, and output elements, respectively. If a process that has this form can perform the artificial grammar task of Marcus et al. (1999), then the task is functionally structured. It is necessary that the representations in E_h represent a regularity that will provide the necessary basis for transfer. There are a number of possibilities here, but it would be sufficient if E_h represented sameness or difference between pairs of elements in the strings, as shown in figure 5.3A. As functionally structured processes can do this, it is clear that transfer observed by Tyrrell et al. (1993) and Marcus et al. (1999) could be based on functionally structured processes. Therefore, representational rank theory helps to resolve the controversy as to whether the infants in the Marcus et al. (1999) study

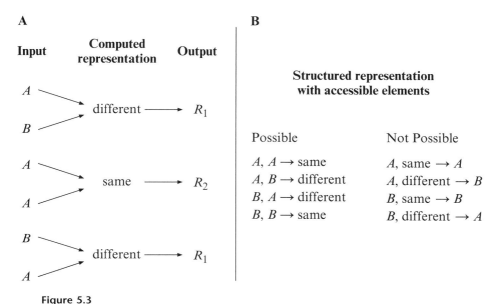

Figure 5.3
A. Representations of *same/different*, computed by functionally structured processes.
B. Some inferences that are possible, and some that are not possible, with function-
ally structured representations.

learned rules (Altmann & Dienes, 1999; Marcus et al., 1999; Seidenberg & Elman, 1999; Shastri, 1999). It is not necessary to postulate rules, or symbolically structured processes, because the task can be performed by functionally structured processes.

The prediction that Rank 1 processes can perform the infant artificial grammar task is borne out by neural net models of this performance. As Eimas (1999) has noted, the *ABA* and *ABB* strings used in Experiments 1 and 2 (Marcus et al., 1999) could be discriminated by focusing on the final pair, as also could pairs *ABB* and *AAB* used in Experiment 3. Strings with patterns *AAB* and *BAB* could be discriminated by the first pair (Marcus, 1999). Other types of strings might be handled by focusing on the first and third elements. Any of these possibilities is consistent with findings that adults sometimes process fragments of strings in artificial grammar experiments (Perruchet, 1994). As shown in figure 5.3, the similarity or difference between the two elements is computed, and then this is associ-ated with an overt response (output). Thus, the function $f_1: E_i \to E_h$ com-putes a representation of same or different based on the input, and the function $f_2: E_h \to E_o$ computes an output based on the same or different representation. It then remains to show that the *same/difference* relation can be computed over novel inputs. A similar interpretation applies to the performance of bees as reported by Avarguès-Weber et al. (2012) because above-below and left-right can be discriminated by computed representations corresponding to E_h based on perceptual input. The bees do not demonstrate relational knowledge conforming to the criteria specified in chapter 2.

Since infants will have heard phonemes similar to those used in the task before, just not in the experimental context, it is reasonable to assume some nonlocal, nonindependent internal representation for both training and testing phonemes, as also noted by McClelland and Plaut (1999). Using a single real-valued dimension to encode all input phonemes, Negishi (1999) presented a simple recurrent net model that accounted for the difference in looking time. Marcus (1999), argued that Negishi's model implements rules, such that "The node in question would represent a variable; its value would represent the instantiation of that variable." (p. 437, note 6). However, variables permit retrieval of a value by the name of the variable that instantiates it. There is no such facility in the simple recurrent net, because input nodes do not have names that lie within the domains of other processes or functions in the net. This implies that a functionally structured process, as implemented in the simple recurrent model, could handle the findings of Marcus et al. (1999), without implementing rules in the sense of referencing variables. The tendency of pigeons to treat stimuli that are associated with a common event as equivalent (Zentall, 2000) appears to be an instance of functionally structured processing, such as that in figure 5.3A, as there is no evidence that any criteria for symbolic processes are met. As the performance of bees observed by Giurfa et al. (2001) also depends on representation of same or different, it also can be modeled by similar Rank 1 processes. The findings of Fagot et al. (2001) with baboons require representation of entropy, of difference between several stimuli. Such a process fits the model of functionally structured processes.

Representational rank theory also suggests a further experiment. A functionally structured process differs from a symbolically structured process in that the functionally structured process does not permit recovery of the elements in the input, so it does not have the property of accessibility as defined in chapter 2. By contrast, figure 5.3B shows a process that performs the same discrimination, but with the elements remaining accessible. That is, given *A,A*, the response is "same," and so on, but given element *A* and the relation "same," we can determine that the other element is *A*, and so on. Evidence of accessibility would be an indicator of symbolically structured processes.

There is a further means of discriminating Rank 1 from Rank 3 processes in the relational match-to-sample task. This is to assess the recoding of the sample (source) to match the relevant dimension in the target. Suppose that the elements in the source differ in two dimensions such as shape and color, while the target elements differ in only one dimension, such as color. Rank 3 processing would permit representation of the relevant dimension; e.g., *different*(*color1*, *color2*). The matching dimension in the source then could be selected, and the response could be based on the relevant dimension. However, if the task is performed by Rank 1 processes, the only representation is a coding of difference between input elements that might reflect either dimension or some composite of both. There is, then, no mechanism for matching relations in source and target. Thus, the ability to recode the source to match the dimension in the target appears to provide a useful means of discriminating Rank 1 from higher-rank representation. To our knowledge, no nonhuman species have been shown to succeed on the recoding task. The most important point for our purposes, however, is that there are at least two ways of checking whether the relational match-to-sample is being performed by Rank 1 or higher-rank processes: accessibility and recoding. There clearly is room for some very interesting research here in both human infants and other animals.

The findings of Tyrrell et al. (1993) and Marcus et al. (1999) that infants can represent a property such as degree of difference between at least two stimuli and use this as a basis for transfer to sets of elements with a similar degree of difference, but dissimilar materials, is an important step toward symbolic processes. The findings of Fagot et al. (2001) and Giurfa et al. (2001) suggest that such presymbolic processes occur in a wide range of nonhuman species. This would probably be adaptive because recognition of change (e.g., that the food supply in a particular location is declining or that critical stimulus patterns have changed) might have survival value. In chapter 6, we will consider the role of these processes in the transition to symbolically structured processes.

The animal cognition literature was reviewed by Penn, Holyoak, and Povinelli (2008a), who concluded that nonhuman animals did not show evidence of conceptual, as distinct from perceptual differences; i.e., they might see a difference but not represent it as a concept that is transferable to equivalent instances. Our position is similar to the extent that, while we readily acknowledge the power and importance of the cognitive processes that have been identified in many nonhuman species, we do not find evidence of symbolic (Rank 2+) cognitive processes, with the possible exception of chimpanzees *(Pan troglodytes)* and bonobos *(Pan paniscus)*. This does not preclude new discoveries, of course.

There is an interesting study by Pepperberg and Carey (2012) of an African Grey parrot *(Psittacus erithacus)* that had been taught words for both ordinal and cardinal numbers 1–6. He was taught ordinal numbers 7 and 8 subsequently and showed generalization to the corresponding cardinal numbers. That is, he discriminated sets of 7 and 8 members better than chance in both comprehension and production. This suggests that he might have performed a mapping from ordinal to cardinal numbers. We expect that the relation between successive numbers would be represented as something equivalent to "more than," so 6 is more than 5, which is more than 4, etc. In training, some recognition of the corresponding relations between ordinal and cardinal numbers 1–6 might have developed. This correspondence could perhaps be extrapolated to numbers 7–8, although the cardinal value of sets of 7 and 8 had not been taught. While it is too early to draw firm conclusions, there is the possibility that the African Grey parrot might be representing binary relations and mapping them between representations. The process by which the correspondence between ordinal and cardinal relations came to be recognized would be an interesting area of study. We consider aspects of this problem in chapter 6.

Prototypes

Prototypes are defined in the literature in two ways. *Prototypes* may be the instance of a category that shares the most features with other category members and the least features with noncategory members (Rosch & Mervis, 1975; Rosch et al., 1976). Alternatively, they may be a collection of central feature tendencies from category members. Thus, the prototype of a bird might be a pigeon, or something like a pigeon, rather than a penguin. Prototypes can be formed by functionally structured processes. So, for example, the prototype for *dog* is a mapping from instances of *dogs* and *nondogs* to a recognition response for *Dog*, mediated by features, such as *tail, furry, four-legs*, etc.

The essential requirement for functionally structured processes is that E_h should represent features that discriminate between instances and noninstances of the category. Correlations between features in E_h will represent statistical links between attributes. However, as with other functionally structured processes, the representation of the features will not be accessible. Thus, knowledge that an entity E is in category C, will not *ipso facto* enable the features of E to be retrieved.

Box 5.1
Functionally structured prototypes

Formally, a functionally structured prototype is a mapping f from an input mental state $m_i \in M_i$ for the instance or non-instance of the prototype to an output state $m_o \in M_o$ representing the prototype, mediated by an internal state $m_h \in M_h$ of prototype features, such that $f_1: M_i \rightarrow M_h$, $f_2: M_h \rightarrow M_o$ and $f(m_i) = f_2(f_1(m_i)) = m_o$. In principle, f_2 could map features of more than one category to M_o; i.e., $f_2': \wp M_h \rightarrow \wp M_o$. (Recall that $\wp S$ is the power set of a set S—i.e., the set of all subsets of S.) For example, if features belonging to the body of a horse and features belonging to the head of a man were mapped to M_o, the interpretation would be *human + horse*, or possibly *centaur*. Thus, functionally structured processes can generate novelty.

Categories that conform to the formal definition of functionally structured prototypes are not compositional and are not structural compositions of other prototypes (see box 5.1). The prototype for *pet fish* may consist of features like *small*, *kept-in-fish-tank*, etc. However, the prototypes of *pet* and *fish* may not consist of these features at all. Whereas the prototype of *pet* may consist of the features *cute* and *furry*, and the prototype for *fish* might be something with *scales*, the prototype for *pet fish* is not something that is *cute* and *furry* with *scales*. This is consistent with the observation that prototypes are not necessarily compositional (Fodor, 1994) so the prototype of *dog* and the prototype of *happy* cannot necessarily be mentally composed to form the prototype of *happy dog*. The prototype of *happy dog* can be acquired by experiencing instances of happy dogs, but there is no assurance that whatever represents *happy* in the prototype of *happy dog* is the same as the representation of *happy* in *happy girl*, etc. The representations of *happy* and *dog* cannot necessarily be recovered from a learned prototype of *happy dog*. Given the parallel between the associative-relational distinction and the implicit-explicit distinction (Phillips et al., 1995), this model is also consistent with acquisition of prototypes through implicit learning, without the intent to learn (Franks & Bransford, 1971; Posner & Boies, 1971). Categories that begin as functionally structured prototypes may become elaborated into higher-rank structures, but in such cases they will acquire the properties of higher-rank processes. This would include linking categories to labels, which we will consider later in this chapter (see section titled "Categories linked to labels").

There is evidence that infants as young as 3 to 4 months can form prototypes and can recognize that a set of objects with similar features, such as geometric shapes (squares, triangles) or animals (dogs, cats), forms a category (Bomba & Siqueland, 1983; Quinn, Eimas, & Rosenkrantz, 1993; Quinn & Johnson, 1997). They are also sensitive to the statistical structure of sets of instances, such as correlation between attributes (Younger, 1985), and can form separate prototypes for related categories at the same time (Quinn et al., 1993; Quinn & Johnson, 1997; Younger, 1993), although categories become more differentiated with age (Younger & Fearing, 1999).

There are neural net models of prototypes that are consistent with the functionally structured definition. A prototype can be formed by superimposing representations of instances (McClelland & Rumelhart, 1985). Each instance of a category is represented as a vector of activation values over a set of neural units, each of which has a modifiable connection to every other unit. Thus, in the *dog* category, each dog is represented by a different vector. The statistical structure of a category is represented by modifying the connection weights between units. Quinn and Johnson (1997) showed that a three-layered net that is consistent with the formal definition of functionally structured processes can model infant categories of animals and furniture, and a similar point is made by Shultz (2012) and by an extensive set of models, which will be discussed in chapter 7.

Object permanence knowledge

Research using the preferential looking paradigm indicates that infants can represent concealed objects (for a review, see Baillargeon, 1995; but see also criticisms of the nativist approach by Allen and Bickhard, 2013). After familiarization, infants aged 3 to 6 months are tested with one event that would have been possible if a concealed object continued to exist and another that would have been impossible. They tend to look longer at the impossible event and are sensitive to specific features of the occluded object, including height (Baillargeon & Graber, 1987) and position (Baillargeon, 1987). The usual interpretation of these data is that infants represent vanished objects, though alternatives based on expectations of physical events (Müeller & Overton, 1998) or perceptual preference (Rivera, Wakeley, & Langer, 1999) have been proposed.

Determination of the rank of early object permanence representations does not require that all aspects of this controversy be resolved. Evidence, at least for the youngest infants, is consistent with a representation being created as a function of input, and then the infant responds based on this representation, without further operation on (or transformation of) the representation. That is, an infant sees an object, creates a representation of it in a particular spatiotemporal frame, then responds on the basis of this representation. The representation is updated by processing of further input, but there are no demonstrated symbolic operations on the representation. This conforms to our definition of a functionally structured process. Consistent with this interpretation, there does not appear to be evidence that the representations have components that are accessible to other cognitive processes and that can be composed into more complex representations while retaining their identity. In this respect, they are more like configurations than like symbolically structured processes. There is also no evidence of representation of relations independent of content, such as would be provided by transfer to isomorphs.

Also, there does not appear to be evidence that infants can make inferences that go beyond the immediate spatiotemporal frame. For example, Halford (1989) suggested that after being shown an event that would have been impossible if the object had still existed, infants with mature object permanence knowledge should infer that the object was not there. Functionally structured object permanence knowledge would not provide a basis for this inference because it requires the transformation of a representation due to a subsequent action that is inconsistent with it. This is a symbolic operation because the infant has not seen that the object is not there (i.e., has not actually seen the vacant space where the object had been). Therefore, the infant must transform the representation of the object to a representation of its absence (i.e., to a vacant space where it had been). The symbolic nature of this operation is indicated because it matches some of the properties of relational knowledge as defined in chapter 2, such as representation of links between different relational instances. Consequently, it is predicted that infants who are operating at the functionally structured level would not make this inference. This test could be a criterion for determining the level to which a particular kind of object permanence knowledge belongs.

This prediction does not appear to have been explicitly tested, but there is suggestive evidence that 6-month old infants may not make this inference. Kotovsky, Mangione, and Baillargeon (cited in Baillargeon, 1995) showed an impossible event that began with a drawbridge lying flat (so no object could have been behind it), then it rotated forward 180°, first up to a vertical position, and then on and down towards the viewer, revealing a clown behind it. In the possible event condition, the drawbridge started from a sloping position that would have made it possible for the clown to be hidden behind it. If the infants represented the display symbolically, they would show more surprise, and longer looking, following the impossible event. No looking preference was observed, suggesting that the infants did not infer that the object could not have been behind the screen in the impossible event condition. There is scope for a wide range of experiments investigating this issue, and they could add a lot of clarification of what is really going on in infant object-permanence studies.

The proposal that young infants' object permanence knowledge is functionally structured is consistent with neural net models. A simple recurrent net model of infants' object permanence knowledge was developed by Munakata et al. (1997). The input comprised successive positions of an object as it moved from left to right, disappeared behind a screen, and then reemerged. The model learned to predict the future position of objects, and to "reach" for the objects, with the latter taking longer to learn. In the model of Mareschal, Plunkett, and Harris (1995), looking was based on the prediction of the position, but reaching depended on coordinating the position with object identity, the extra demands of which explain the later development of reaching. The models agree that the difference between looking and reaching is not purely motor; rather, it is a matter of representational adequacy. These models are functionally structured, in that they have a structure similar to the feedforward and simple recurrent net models discussed previously (see also box 2.5 in chapter 2). That is, there is an internal representation that is computed as a function of input, and the output is a function of that representation. There are no symbolic operations defined on the representation.

Properties of functionally structured processes

Object permanence, prototype formation, and transfer based on computed representations have been demonstrated in infants around 4 to 8 months of age. Representational rank theory hypothesizes that ranks constitute equivalence classes of equal conceptual difficulty, and therefore 4- to 8-month-old infants should be capable of other functionally structured tasks, including conditional discrimination and circular transitivity of choice. Neither of these appears to have been tested, although it would appear quite possible to test them with infants under appropriate conditions. The prediction that conditional discrimination should be possible at 4- to 8-month-olds is radical because all configural learning tasks have proved difficult for children under 4.5 years of age (Gollin, 1966; Gollin & Liss, 1962; Gollin & Schadler, 1972; Rudy, 1991; Rudy, Keith, & Georgen, 1993). There is also evidence that configural learning depends on the maturation of the hippocampus (Rudy et al., 1993; Wickelgren, 1979; but see also Schmajuk & DiCarlo, 1992). However, there are two reasons why previous methodologies might have underestimated infants' and young children's abilities to form conditional discriminations. One is that they were expected to induce the structure without guidance, so their failure may be in recoding of the input, which is known to be difficult in functionally structured tasks, as noted in chapter 2. Substantial improvement can be achieved in configural learning with more guidance (Chalmers & Halford, 2002; Andrews et al., 2012). The second reason is that young children might be trying to understand the task, which means forming a representation of its structure. Representational rank theory predicts that they would be unable to represent the ternary relation that corresponds to conditional discrimination, thus explaining their failure. The issue is capable of resolution because representational rank theory predicts success on conditional discrimination by children who can perform other functionally structured tasks, but transfer to isomorphs with accessibility of components, discussed in chapter 2, should be performed only by children who can perform Rank 4 tasks. We see some value in making this prediction in advance of data. The study by Andrews et al. (2012) with children, discussed in chapter 7, confirmed that transfer to isomorphic conditional discrimination tasks depends on symbolic coding.

Image schemas (Mandler, 2004) are also arguably functionally structured processes but have been shown to be important in the transition to symbolic structure. They are discussed in detail in chapter 6.

Properties of symbolically structured processes

We will consider symbolically structured processes at Ranks 2–4. Ranks 5–6 are considered elsewhere (Halford, Wilson, & Phillips, 1998; Birney & Halford, 2002; Zielinski et al., 2010), and we include illustrative examples of them in table 5.1.

Symbolically structured Rank 2
Rank 2 processes are the simplest symbolically structured processes, as explained in chapter 2. We will consider significant classes of tasks that conform to the definition of this level.

Unary relations
At Rank 2, it is possible to represent unary relations (Halford, Wilson, & Phillips, 1998) or to form representations that link two variables. However, recall from chapter 2 that a symbolically structured Rank 2 process would not create a new symbol representing the combination of the components. This requires a Rank 3 process.

Categories linked to labels
Categories can be related to other cognitive representations, including other categories. A simple case is a binding between a category and a label. This is equivalent to a unary relation $R(a)$, where R is the category label and a represents the set of instances of the category. A category-label binding links a category to other cognitive representations and permits inferences directly from the label. Thus, the proposition that *Ornithorhynchus anatinus* is a mammal can be written as *mammal(Ornithorhynchus anatinus)*. It can be linked to other instances of the same category by the common label, with or without common features: *mammal(rabbit)*, *mammal(cow)*, and *mammal(dolphin)* are all linked to mammal(*Ornithorhynchus anatinus*) by the common label *mammal*, even though few common features may be apparent. Because the components of the representation are accessible, then given *Ornithorhynchus anatinus*, we can retrieve *mammal*, and given *mammal*, we can retrieve *Ornithorhynchus anatinus*, *rabbit*, *cow*, *dolphin*, etc. We can retrieve other instances of the category, and we do not need to know what *Ornithorhynchus anatinus* is (*platypus*). This ability is consistent with single-word use that develops at approximately one year (Clark, 2003).

Match-to-sample
This task is exemplified by the generalized match-to-sample task, in which one of two objects must be selected that matches a sample (e.g., if the sample is a circle, choose the circle rather than the triangle). While any one training problem can be performed by elemental association, transfer must be based on knowledge that is independent of specific stimuli. It requires selection of a choice stimulus that matches the sample, regardless of what the stimuli are. This could be done by encoding the

relation between the sample and each of the choice stimuli: for example, *same*(*circle, circle*) or *same*(*square,square*). This explanation assumes that the relation between sample and choice stimulus is explicitly represented. However, explanations based on contemporary analogy models do not require this assumption (Gentner et al., 1995; Halford, Wilson, & Phillips, 1998; Holyoak & Thagard, 1995; Premack, 1983). The sample and the correct choice can each be represented as the unary relational instances *circle* (*sample-object*) and *circle*(*choice-object*), respectively. A mapping can be formed between these representations using the principles of structural correspondence: that is, *circle*$_{source}$ ↔ *circle*$_{target}$ and *sample-object* ↔ *choice-object*. The mapping is a case of analogical transfer based on a unary relation. This task can be performed by chimpanzees and some monkeys (Oden, Thompson, & Premack, 1988; Tomasello & Call, 1997), as well as dolphins (Herman et al., 1989).

We should note, however, that limited performance on this task could be achieved by functionally structured processes that compute an output that represents the similarity between sample and choice elements, as shown in figure 5.3A. Additional tests would be required to determine whether the representation was Rank 1 or 2. For example, functionally structured processes would decline as featural similarity between sample and choice elements declined, whereas symbolic processes would be more categorical.

Symbolically structured Rank 2 analogy

Generalized match-to-sample can be interpreted as a symbolically structured Rank 2 analogy, as noted previously, but there does not appear to be any specific test of infants' ability to perform this task. However, the study by Chen, Sanchez, and Campbell (1997) does appear to provide evidence of symbolically structured Rank 2 analogy at approximately one year. Two pieces of cloth were presented, with a string lying on each, one string being visibly connected to a desirable toy and the other connected to nothing. Over three problems, infants of 13 months improved in their selection of the cloth and string that was connected to the toy. Infants of 10 months showed less improvement and depended more on cue similarity between problems. The task depends on reaching skills, but there does appear to be a significant cognitive component. Given that infants' representation of each problem is based on a single trial (maximum duration 100 seconds), it is reasonable to expect that there would have been a symbolically structured Rank 2 dynamic binding between the cloth/string combination and the toy to which it was connected. Cloth and string can be processed initially as a chunk because the initial response is either toward or away from both, and then the chunk can be unpacked for serial reaching. This would be similar to a dynamic object-location binding, in that no new representation would be formed, so there would not, for example, be a symbol explicitly representing connection. Lack of detailed process information inevitably makes this analysis more speculative than most in this book, but some predictions can be made. First, performance should decline as a function of delay because dynamic binding is more important in symbolically structured processes. However, decline in featural similarity should have more effect with functionally structured processes. Second, the age of attainment should be as for other symbolically structured Rank 2 tasks. This appears to be supported by the finding that success develops between 10 and 13 months.

Identity-position binding

In the A not-B ($A\bar{B}$) task, infants retrieve a hidden object a number of times from location A, and then see it hidden at B. Between 7 and 12 months, infants tend to search for the object at A. We need to explain, not only the error, but how the error is overcome. However, in the current context, we want to focus on the correspondence between this task and Piagetian object permanence stage 5 (Marcovitch & Zelazo, 1999; Piaget, 1950; Wellman, Cross, & Bartsch, 1986). Representational rank theory predicts that identity-position integration should become possible at the age where other Rank 2 processes emerge (i.e., at about 1 year), which would account for infants *ceasing* to make the $A\bar{B}$ error at that time. Identity-position integration requires that the infant form a representation of an object and dynamically connect it to a representation of its location (i.e., hiding place). This would be an example of a binding between two variables, but without a label for the link, which is one of the possible interpretations of the formal definition of symbolically structured Rank 2 processes discussed previously. The $A\bar{B}$ task could be interpreted as a conflict between this dynamic representation and one formed incrementally by successive retrievals at A (Marcovitch & Zelazo, 1999, 2009). This explanation might complement, rather than exclude, models based on the dynamics of reaching (Smith et al., 1999) or object file representations (Feigenson, Carey, & Hauser, 2002; Xu, Carey, & Welch, 1999). However, it implies that correct performance should be related to emerging higher cognitive processes (Halford et al., 2013). Furthermore, this is consistent with the observed relationship to maturation of the frontal lobes (Diamond, 1991).

Other predictions also follow from this model. First, if children have formed a dynamic binding between an object and a location, then by the principle of accessibility, they should be able to predict the object, given the location, and should be able to predict location, given the object. Therefore, in a task with objects X and Y in locations A or B, where they last saw X at A, they should be surprised by Y at A, or X at B. This combination of performances should not be observed in children who do make the $A\bar{B}$ error. To our knowledge, these predictions have not been tested. Second, performance should decline with delay after seeing X at A because of decay in the dynamic representation. This is consistent with $A\bar{B}$ data (Diamond, 1991). Third, appearance of this ability should be predicted by other Rank 2 performances. The last prediction has not been tested as far as we are aware.

Overcoming the A not-B error recently has been recognized as a portent of the onset of symbolic processes (Halford et al., 2013) and this aspect will be discussed further in chapter 6.

Symbolically structured Rank 3

Relational match-to-sample

We will contrast the performance of apes on the relational-match-to-sample task with the Rank 1 transfer performances discussed previously. Oden, Thompson, and Premack (1990) rewarded infant chimpanzees for choosing a pair of objects that had the same relation as the sample (*BB* if the sample was *AA*; *EF* if the sample was *CD*). The participants could not generalize this discrimination, although in an earlier experiment, the same participants showed generalized discrimination based on handling time. Given a pair *AA* (or *CD*) to handle, they handled *EF* (or *BB*), a new pair with a different relation, longer than *BB* (or *EF*), a new pair with the same relation. This suggests that they were sensitive to the novel relation. The hypothesis that failure is due to the motor components of the match-to-sample task is unlikely because the same participants generalized the single object match-to-sample (Oden et al., 1990). A possible interpretation of the findings is that simpler relations develop before complex relations, and they are integrated with orienting behaviors (looking and exploratory handling) before instrumental behaviors (reaching to pick up). It may be biologically adaptive if competencies that enable infants to obtain information, such as direction of regard and manual exploration, develop before more instrumental competencies. On this hypothesis, instrumental performance of the complex, relational match-to-sample would develop later than the other tasks.

Relational match-to-sample can be interpreted as mapping *same(A,A)* into *same(B,B)*, or mapping *different(C,D)* into *different(E,F)* (Halford, Wilson, & Phillips, 1998; Holyoak & Thagard, 1995; Premack, 1983). It thus entails analogical mapping of binary relations and can appropriately be called the *binary relational match-to-sample task.* This hypothesis is consistent with observations that the relational match-to-sample task is considerably more difficult than same-different discrimination (Fagot et al., 2001). According to representational rank theory, it should require a symbol for the relation because the models of analogical mapping reviewed previously depend on labels for relations, but it should not require language abilities as such. Premack (1983) reported that the only nonhuman primates to succeed were language-trained chimpanzees. However, Thompson, Oden, and Boysen (1997) showed that chimpanzees that had been trained to use plastic tokens to represent the relations *same* and *different* but were not otherwise language-trained, performed the generalized binary relational match-to-sample task. This is consistent with analogy theory and with representational rank theory, which proposes that relational representation should include a symbol for the relation. The performance of apes differs from the Rank 1 generalization performances considered previously, in that they can symbolize relations, show accessibility, and can perform proportional analogies.

Accessibility of components
There is evidence that chimpanzees symbolize relations and can retrieve components of relational representations. Premack (1983) reviews evidence that language-trained chimpanzees will choose a knife in response to being shown an intact and a cut object, or a key in response to an open and a closed lock. Thus, they can use a knife and a key to symbolize the relations *cut* and *open,* respectively. They also show accessibility because, given a closed lock and a key, they can produce an open lock, and so forth. Other evidence reviewed by Tomasello and Call (1997) suggests that binary relations may be processed by primates other than chimpanzees.

Tool use
Tool use entails a binary relation between the tool and its effect, as with the knife discussed in the previous section. Tool use is possible for chimpanzees and 2-year-old human children, as noted by Herrmann et al.

(2010), who also found considerable correspondence between the cognitions of chimpanzees (*Pan troglodytes*) and 2-year-olds.

Proportional analogy

Proportional analogies, of the form $A:B::C:D$ entail mappings of binary relations, as indicated previously. There is evidence that chimpanzees can perform analogies of this form (Oden et al., 1988), although Penn, Holyoak, and Povinelli (2008a) disputed this contention on the grounds that the data are inconclusive. However, we maintain it as a prediction because it is consistent with chimpanzees' ability to perform the binary relational match-to-sample task.

Representational rank theory predicts that 2-year-old human children should be capable of proportional analogy. Although proportional analogies have been demonstrated with 3- to 4-year-olds (Goswami, 1996; Goswami & Brown, 1989), there do not appear to be studies with 2-year-olds, so this too is a novel prediction to be tested. However, 2-year-olds' understanding of exclusivity can be interpreted in terms of binary relational analogies. A child who knows the meaning of the word *cup* and is shown a cup and a painter's palette and then asked, "Which one is the pilson?" tends to indicate the unfamiliar object as the referent of the novel word (Merriman & Stevenson, 1997). They understand that if *pilson* and *cup* each refers to one of the objects (the exclusivity bias) and know which object is the referent of *cup,* it follows that the other object is the referent of *pilson.* This is a form of "fast mapping" (Bloom, 2000; Carey, 1978), and we consider it to be a dynamic process that is characteristic of symbolically structured processes. We could interpret this as indicating that they represent a binary relation of exclusivity that has two roles [i.e., *exclusive*(–,–)], and the words are mapped to these roles, which is another case of analogy. If one object fills one role, the other object fills the other role. Furthermore, the representation is established dynamically following a single presentation.

Structure in categories

Prototypes that are formally equivalent to functionally structured processes do not represent structure and are not compositional, as noted previously. However, categories also can be based on a representation of structure, including naive theories (Gentner & Medina, 1998; Krascum & Andrews, 1998; Medin, 1989). Theories can be expressed as propositions, which can be treated in the same way as relational instances, as discussed in chapter 2. The *weapons* category might be based on propositions such as *kill(sword, people)*, and the *animal* category on propositions such as *have(animals, blood)*. The structural coherence of categories can be expressed as higher-order relations such as "if X has blood, X is an animal" [i.e., *implies(have(X, blood), animate(X))*] and "if X has blood, X can die" [i.e., *implies(have(X, blood), canDie(X))*]. These propositions represent understanding that things that have blood are animate and can die (Gelman & Kalish, 2006). Propositional theories can influence the judging of similarity. For example, gray hair is rated more similar to white hair than to black hair, whereas gray clouds are more similar to black clouds than to white clouds, because of our intuitive theories of aging and weather, respectively (Medin, 1989). We can represent a naive theory of aging by propositions such as *oldPeopleHave(hair, gray)*, *oldPeopleHave(hair, white)*, *youngPeopleHave(hair, black)*, *youngPeopleHave(hair, brown)*, etc. By contrast, a naive theory of weather would include propositions such as *threatening(clouds, gray)*, *threatening(clouds, black)*, *nonthreatening(clouds, white)*, etc. The similarity of gray hair and white hair is due to both being linked to propositions about old people, whereas gray clouds and black clouds are seen as similar because they are linked to propositions about threatening weather. This can be captured by the accessibility property of relational representations. For example:

(clouds, gray) → *threatening, (clouds, black)* → *threatening*

The type of structure represented in the Structured Tensor Analogical Reasoning (STAR) model enables the similarity of these propositions to be recognized in principle, as discussed in chapter 3. The implication is that structures based on categories entail representations of propositions that are distinct from functionally structured prototype representations.

Weight and distance discriminations in the balance scale

Discriminations of weights with distance constant, or distances with weight constant, entail binary relations. For example, recognizing that the side of the balance beam with the greater weight will go down when the distances are equal entails representing the binary relation between two weights, and it is a symbolically structured Rank 3 task. Similarly, recognizing that the side with weights at the greater distance from the fulcrum will go down with constant magnitude of weights entails processing the binary relation between two distances. Consequently, these discriminations should be possible at the age when other symbolically structured Rank 3 concepts are mastered. This prediction was made in advance of evidence (Halford, 1993) and is contrary to previous theory (Case, 1985) and previous empirical observation (Siegler, 1981). It is, therefore, a genuine prediction, not a postdiction, and was confirmed by Halford et al. (2002).

Secondary representations

The distinction between functionally structured representations that are transformations of the input and symbolically structured representations that are guided by structural correspondence bears some correspondence to the distinction between primary and secondary representations (Leslie, 1987), especially as it was reinterpreted by Perner (1991). Primary representation is causally linked to the environment, while secondary representation permits multiple mental models that are detached from the environment (Leslie, 1987; Perner, 1991; Suddendorf & Whiten, 2001).

We will consider the most basic structure of performances that have been linked to secondary representations to determine their representational rank.

Object permanence stage 6
Object permanence stage 6 (Piaget, 1954) is assessed by showing a child an interesting object X that is placed in a container Y, which is immediately hidden at location A. Unbeknownst to the child, X is removed from Y and remains at A. The child then sees Y being moved to location B. The question is whether the child, having failed to find X after searching inside the container Y at B, then will search at A. Searching only inside Y indicates the inability to infer invisible displacements (stage 5). Understanding the location requires representing embedded containment; that is, the *object* is bound to *location$_1$*, which is bound to *location$_2$*. This can be expressed as *location$_2$(location$_1$(object))*, which is a nested unary relation, and in terms of the relational complexity metric, it is equivalent to a binary relation because it has two roles bound into a structure. It is, therefore, Rank 3.

Mirror self-recognition
Mirror self-recognition could be interpreted, hypothetically, as processing relations in the image as analogs of those in reality. The binary relation between a person and a mark (e.g., on the forehead) in the image corresponds to a relation between the real person and a mark on his or her forehead. Mirror self-recognition is achieved by children in the second year, and is also exhibited by chimpanzees (*Pan troglodytes*). See Kärtner et al. (2012) and Suddendorf and Whiten (2001).

Pretense

Tasks that assess pretend-real situations have been analyzed as involving binary relations (Halford, 1993; Suddendorf, Fletcher-Flinn, & Johnston, 1999). Thus, pretending that a banana is a telephone can be represented as *pretend(banana, telephone)*. The relation symbol *pretend* explicitly labels the relationship as *pretense*, distinguishing it from, for example, categorizing the banana as a telephone.

Means-end reasoning

The essence of means-end reasoning is to represent an explicit relation between a means and an end, such as *opens(key, lock)*, *cuts(knife, apple)*, *quenches(water, thirst)*, *breaks(rock, nut)*, etc. Accessibility means that questions such as *cuts(?, apple)*, *breaks(rock, ?)*, can be answered. Accessibility also permits queries such as *?(rock,?)*, which is equivalent to "What can you do with a rock and something else?" If the relational instance *breaks(rock, nut)* is represented, the query *?(rock,?)* would yield a set of outcomes that included *breaks(–, nut)*. Given that action-related prediction is a core function of cognition, as noted in chapter 2, then representation of means-end relations should be a major factor in the development of young children's planning ability.

Picture and model interpretation

The picture-and-model-interpretation task requires a child to find an object hidden in a room by seeing where a model of the object is hidden in a model (or picture) of the room. The basic structure of this task can be interpreted as analogical mapping between relations in a model or picture and relations in the situation represented. Thus, a child can represent *hiddenIn(toy, cupboard)* in the model and map this into *hiddenIn(toy, cupboard)* in the room. This is an analogy based on a binary relation, which is consistent with its attainment by children from approximately 2 years old (DeLoache, 2000).

Awareness, connections, representing the representing relation

When the theory of structured representations was being defined in chapter 2, it was noted that the interpretation mapping was not explicitly represented, implying that representation does not necessarily entail representation of the representing relation. The representing relation, however, can be itself represented in some circumstances; e.g., I can represent (be aware of) the fact that I am representing certain ideas as I write this text. Perner (1991) proposes that this ability develops in the second year. The representing relation is binary because it is a binding between two variables, one representing the represented entity and one representing the representation:

represents(*A*, *B*).

An example would be where the child looks at person *P*, who is seeing object *O*, and represents the fact that *P* perceives (is aware of) *O*:

perceives(*P*, *O*).

These are sometimes called *connections tasks* and are shown in relation to the theory of mind in figure 4.6 in chapter 4. Connections tasks are binary relational (Andrews et al., 2003; Halford, 1993) and are performed by children as young as 2 years old (Flavell, Green, & Flavell, 1990; Lempers, Flavell, & Flavell, 1977; Masangkay et al., 1974). They are structurally simpler than theory of mind tasks, such as perspective taking and false belief, that entail ternary relations.

An interesting example is provided by Senju et al. (2011), who found that 18-month-old infants could infer that a person's awareness of an object depended on whether a blindfold was transparent or opaque. Thus, they recognize that someone who is blindfolded cannot see a particular entity. This means that infants of this age can represent how the mental state of another person is related to input or experience. Importantly, it implies that what develops is not ability to represent mental states per se, but a progression from Rank 3 at 2 years old to Rank 4 at about 4 years old. Thus, it might have been asking the wrong question to focus on representing mental states to the exclusion of cognitive complexity.

In the context of a controversy about infants' theory of mind [see special issue of the *British Journal of Developmental Psychology*, 2012, *30*(1)]. Wellman (2011) has suggested that infants might represent a person's awareness of an object. In terms of relational complexity theory, this would be a binary relational, Rank 3 cognitive process. Representational rank theory predicts that this should be possible at the same age as other Rank 3 processes (Halford et al., 2013).

Correspondence between Rank 3 tasks

All the secondary representation tasks are performed by children of approximately 2 years of age (Perner, 1991) and by the great apes

(Suddendorf & Whiten, 2001). According to our principles, they belong to Rank 3, which supports our hypothesis that concepts of the same rank are mastered at the same point in development or in evolution. However, Rank 3 also includes binary relational match-to-sample, labeled binary relational representations with accessibility of components, proportional analogy, inferences about labeled categories, and weight and distance discrimination on the balance scale, all of which should be mastered at the same approximate age, and these predictions are available for testing. However, existing evidence of performances of Rank 3 tasks is not unimpressive. Relational match-to-sample is performed by chimpanzees, weight or distance discrimination on the balance scale by 2-year-old children, and proportional analogy plus all the secondary representation tasks are performed by both.

Rank 4

Many of the known tasks at this level have been analyzed elsewhere (Andrews & Halford, 1998, 2002; Halford, 1993; Halford, Andrews, & Bowden, 1998; Halford, Andrews, & Jensen, 2002; Halford, Wilson, & Phillips, 1998) and this evidence will be reviewed briefly in the following sections.

Transitive inference

To recapitulate, transitive inference means that if we know *aRb* and *bRc*, where *R* is a transitive relation, then *aRbRc* can be composed and *aRc* necessarily follows (e.g., if $a > b$ and $b > c$, then $a > b > c$ and $a > c$). The task requires that the binary relations *aRb* and *bRc* be integrated into the ternary relation *aRbRc* (Halford, 1993; Andrews & Halford, 1998, 2002). Both premises must be considered to assign elements uniquely to the three positions. Given the premises *John is taller than Peter* and *Michael is taller than John*, the two premises jointly determine that Michael is in first position. The set of three elements can be assigned to unique positions only by considering both premises jointly. This places a limit on segmentation because neither premise can be processed fully without taking the other premise into account. And this occurs because transitive inference entails assigning elements to three roles in a structure in a single decision, so transitive inference is ternary relational (Andrews & Halford, 1998; Halford, 1993) and is therefore Rank 4. The processing load imposed by premise integration has been validated (Maybery, Bain, & Halford, 1986) and shown to involve frontal lobe processes (Fangmeier et al., 2006; Waltz et al., 1999). Transitive inference tasks that entail processing ternary relations are passed by 50 percent of 5-year-olds and 20 percent of 4-year-olds (Andrews & Halford, 1998).

Whereas transitive inference implies an ordinal scale of premise elements, there is no such scale underlying the relationship in transitivity of choice (Markovits & Dumas, 1992). Furthermore, this transitive inference task is performed dynamically in working memory, following a single presentation of premises, whereas transitivity of choice is based on representations created incrementally over many trials and can be performed by associative processes. Transitive inference, though not transitivity of choice, is Rank 4, and (now extensive) normative data indicates that it is attained at a median age of approximately five years. It is, therefore, a marker for the age norms of Rank 4 cognition.

Correspondence between Rank 4 tasks

Rank 4 tasks have been tested with 4- to 8-year-old children in the domains of transitivity, hierarchical classification, cardinality, comprehension of relative clause sentences, hypothesis testing, and class inclusion (Andrews & Halford, 1998, 2002). To assess complexity, Andrews and Halford (2002) devised corresponding Rank 3 tasks for each domain except hypothesis testing and observed a strong effect of relational complexity in each domain. All tasks loaded on a single factor and factor scores were correlated with age ($r = 0.80$), and fluid intelligence ($r = 0.79$). Correspondence across domains for tests at the same rank was observed. Similar results were obtained in a second experiment. Subsequent studies have observed correspondence between hierarchical categories, transitive inference, and class inclusion (Halford, Andrews, & Jensen, 2002); between processing sentences with embedded clauses, hierarchical classification, and transitivity (Andrews, Halford, & Prasad, 1998); between theory of mind, transitivity, hierarchical classification, and cardinality (Halford, Andrews, & Bowden, 1998; Andrews et al., 2003); and between transitivity, class inclusion, dimensional change card sorting, delay of gratification, conditional discrimination, and theory of mind (Bunch & Andrews, 2012). There is, therefore, substantial evidence of correspondence between Rank 4 tasks in a wide range of domains.

Theory of mind tasks (false belief, appearance-reality, and perspective taking) have been analyzed as requiring ternary relations (Halford, Wilson, & Phillips., 1998, §6.2.4.3). The representing relation, *represents*(*A*, *B*), is made conditional on a third variable. For example, a white object viewed through a blue filter is known to be white but is seen as blue, so the person's representation of it as blue or white is conditional on whether it is viewed through the filter or not. Thus, whereas the representing relation is binary relational, concept of mind can be expressed by the ternary relation *represents(person, condition, entity)*.

Theory of mind also has been analyzed by Perner (1991) as requiring metarepresentations, which entail understanding the correspondence between representation and represented entity. There is common ground here because the condition variable effectively modulates this correspondence. That is, the condition variable influences the degree to which the representation corresponds to the represented entity. The addition of the condition variable increases complexity to ternary relational, as shown previously. There is evidence that structural complexity is a factor in children's concept of mind. Performance on it is predicted by the dimensional change card-sort task (Frye, Zelazo, & Palfai, 1995), which is isomorphic to conditional discrimination and is ternary relational (Andrews & Halford, 2002).

Representational rank theory predicts that chimpanzees can perform proportional analogies and binary relational match-to-sample actions, which are Rank 3, and they will also perform Rank 3 theory of mind tasks equivalent to the connections or representations tasks in figure 4.6. This is consistent with the conclusions of Call and Tomasello (2008) that they have a limited theory of mind that represents the link between perception and goal, but they do not succeed on false belief tasks even though they pass the control tasks. We predict that chimpanzees would represent binary relations between percept, action, or situation and goal or intention. There is a need for testing relational complexity of theory of mind in nonhuman primates, equivalent to that performed by Andrews, Halford et al. (2003) with children. So far, we have seen evidence of relations no more complex than binary being processed by nonhuman primates.

Hierarchical classification and category induction
Representational rank theory provides an explanation for the category induction task (Gelman & Markman, 1986, 1987) being performed earlier than the hierarchical classification task (Halford, Andrews, & Jensen, 2002). In category induction, children are given an attribute of an instance of a category (e.g., a rabbit eats alfalfa) and then shown instances of rabbits and other categories of animals that vary in appearance. Even 3-year-olds generalize more to instances of the same category than to different categories. This entails a representation of a category and its complement, and

it is binary relational. When category induction and hierarchical classification are assessed by a common property inference procedure, category induction is readily performed by 3- to 4-year-olds, whereas hierarchical classification is not mastered till a median age of 5 years and is predicted by other ternary relational tasks (Halford, Andrews, & Jensen, 2002). It has often been regarded as an anomaly that young children cannot perform class inclusion but readily perform category induction, both of which appear to require classification ability. The work of Halford, Andrews, and Jensen (2002), however, suggests that they are fundamentally the same paradigm at two levels of relational complexity.

However, we would like to draw attention to an issue here that deserves further investigation. This is that category induction could perhaps be acquired by a mechanism similar to the semantic cognition model of Rogers and McClelland (2004), which will be discussed in chapter 7. If so, it would not necessarily be incompatible with the relational complexity analysis, but it might shed light on an interesting mechanism by which such concepts could be acquired.

Conditional discrimination

When conditional discrimination is performed by configural association, it is functionally structured (Rank 1) and is predicted to be possible at approximately 6 months of age, as noted previously. However, transfer to an isomorphic task, with generation of unknown items, requires symbolically structured representation. The structure is ternary relational (Rank 4) because it comprises ordered triples of the form (*backgroundCue*, *foregroundCue*, *response*) such as (*blue*, *triangle*, *R+*); see figure 2.1 in chapter 2. There is evidence (Gollin & Schadler, 1972; Rudy et al., 1993) that conditional discrimination can be learned at 5 years of age, but transfer to isomorphs with generation of unknown items was not tested until recently. Representational rank theory predicts that this too should be possible at the age at which ternary relations are mastered—that is, 4 to 5 years old.

Andrews, Halford, and Boyce (2012) showed that 4- and 5-year-old children were better able to learn conditional discrimination if they were first taught reversal learning problems. Choice of shape (e.g., triangle or circle) depended on background color (e.g., red or blue) and was selectively rewarded with a happy or sad face. With reversal learning, the background was held constant (gray) and children had to make a choice of only two elements in any one task. This makes the effective relational complexity binary relational, whereas conditional discrimination is effectively ternary

Table 5.2
Awareness questions for conditional discrimination

When the background was red and you chose circle, did you get a happy or a sad face?
When the background was red, and you got a happy face, which shape did you choose, triangle or circle?
When you chose circle and you got a happy face, what color was the background, red or blue?

Adapted from Andrews, Halford, & Boyce (2012, table 1). Copyright © 2012 Elsevier, reproduced by permission.

relational, as we explained previously. The difference between associative and relational learning was indicated by awareness of what had been learned, which is tested by questions as shown in table 5.2.

These questions tested the accessibility of the components bound into relations entailed in the task. Choice of the correct element in conditional discrimination was easier, and occurred at an earlier age, than awareness. There was also more awareness of the simpler, reversal learning task than the more complex conditional discrimination. It appeared that some children who used relational processing on reversal learning reverted to nonrelational processing on conditional discrimination, suggesting that they resorted to nonrelational processing when task complexity increases. Both performance on, and awareness of, reversal learning predicted conditional discrimination, but awareness accounted for unique variance independent of performance. Fluid intelligence predicted interproblem learning in conditional discrimination with children who showed evidence of relational processing, but not with children who relied on associative processing. This study demonstrates that Rank 1 and Rank 3 processes can be discriminated within the same task, revealing different patterns of performance.

Symbolically structured Rank 5

Tasks at the symbolically structured Rank 5 level include proportion, the principle of moments as instantiated in the balance scale, and some categorical syllogism tasks of the kind that were considered in chapter 4. The concept of proportion is defined by relations between four variables, such as $a/b = c/d$, or $2/4 = 3/6$. This makes proportion a difficult concept for children to grasp before age 11, which appears to be the age at which Rank 5 becomes possible, although the normative studies are not as precise about this as about lower ranks. However, proportion can be decomposed into subtasks, so 2/4 and 3/6 can each be chunked and recoded as "half," and then the two halves can be recognized as equal. However, problems still can arise where proportion has to be recognized in other contexts. For example, chunking is more difficult for an example such as 3:7::4:? More frequent errors would be predicted in such cases.

The balance scale comprises a beam on which varying weights can be placed at varying distances from the fulcrum; it has been used extensively in studies of cognitive development. The principle of moments states that the beam balances when the products of weights and distances on the two sides are equal. This is a relation between four variables, comprising weights on each side and distances of weights from the fulcrum. It does not appear to be mastered until adolescence, and is not used even by many adults, who tend to default to less complex ternary relational strategies such as those based on compensation (Halford et al., 2002; Siegler, 1981).

Determination of the relational complexity of categorical syllogisms is considered in detail in chapter 4, based on assessments by Zielinski, Goodwin, and Halford (2010). These authors identified some Rank 5 tasks, such as *All X are Y; some Z are not Y*. Many of the Rank 5 and Rank 6 categorical syllogism tasks have no valid conclusion, but correct answers to this problem can be produced as a default response when participants find the task too difficult. Thus, many of the apparent successes on these tasks are really false positives. Correspondence with Rank 5 tasks in other domains has not been specifically assessed, but if boundary conditions are met, we predict that it will correspond with proportion and the understanding the principle of moments on the balance scale.

Some steps in the Tower of Hanoi (TOH) task entail relating four variables as shown by our analysis in chapter 4. This would mean that they are Rank 5.

Symbolically structured Rank 6

Tasks at the symbolically structured Rank 6 level are relatively rare because of the high working memory loads that they impose, but there is better than chance performance on some tasks at this level. There are Rank 6 categorical syllogism tasks (Zielinski, Goodwin, & Halford, 2010), but they have no valid conclusion and are identified correctly by default "too hard" responses, as noted previously. These are false positives in the sense that they are not based on representation of the relations entailed in a mental model of the premises. Some interpretations of interactions tasks, based on the procedure outlined in chapter 4, are also Rank 6 but are performed by only a minority of participants (Halford et al., 2005). Sentences such as "The boy that the girl that the man saw met slept" require five roles to be filled: *saw(man, girl)*; *met(girl, boy)*; and *slept(boy)*; there are two roles each for "*saw*" and "*met*", and one role for "*slept*." See chapter 4. Such doubly embedded center-embedded sentences are difficult to segment for English speakers, so the words have to be assigned to roles in parallel, which makes the task effectively Rank 6.

Conditions for choosing ranks

A cognitive economy principle would mean that it is normal, although not inevitable, for tasks to be performed by the lowest rank process available. In our analyses of cognitive processes, we attribute the lowest rank process to a performance unless there is independent and objective evidence to the contrary, to avoid unjustified attributions of higher-rank processes. Thus, if a task can be performed by elemental association, procedures that require higher-rank processing are unlikely to be used unless special incentives are offered. One benefit of expertise is that it makes available a repertoire of techniques for reducing processing load. These include conceptual chunking and segmentation, discussed previously.

The procedure used is determined by a strategy selection mechanism, such as that of Siegler and Shrager (1984). The lowest-level strategy available is selected first, and then confidence is assessed. If confidence is above threshold, the strategy is applied. If not, an alternate strategy is sought and the procedure repeated. This often entails moving to a higher-rank procedure. When a strategy is applied, the validity of the output is assessed. If the output is adequate, processing terminates. Otherwise, an alternate strategy is sought. If no strategy can be found, an impasse is reached and strategy development processes are activated. A number of models are consistent with this basic scheme, including Soar (Newell, 1990; Simon & Klahr, 1995) and the Transitive Inference Mapping Model (TRIMM; Halford et al., 1995).

Chapter summary

In this chapter, we have defined three formally distinct levels of cognitive functioning and interpreted them in terms of known psychological processes. We have defined empirical criteria for each level and generated predictions, many of them novel, about performances that are possible at each level. Then we have matched the predictions against a large database over many domains. The theory will be falsified if tasks that are shown to have the formal properties of a given rank conflict with the predictions for that rank. The theory will *not* be disconfirmed if the tasks have only surface similarities to the rank in question. Therefore, tests of the theory need to be based on empirically verified models of cognitive processes, just as we have done in our development of this position. Furthermore, it is important that tasks cannot be assigned to ranks by their labels. For example, there are many tasks that carry the label "analogy" or "transitivity" but which differ in their formal properties. They cannot be assigned to the same rank simply because they have the same label.

We predict that cognitive processes of a given rank will be attainable at similar ages, given the availability of relevant domain and procedural knowledge. However, our predictions should not be confused with those based on some versions of Piagetian stage theory. Working memory is an enabling factor, but there is no implication that all concepts of the same rank will be acquired simultaneously when working memory capacity reaches the requisite level. Concepts are acquired by processes that depend on adaptive interaction with the environment, to be considered in chapter 6.

Nonstructured Rank 0 processes do not entail internal representation other than input and output, and they comprise mainly elemental associative processes. Nevertheless, they can support some impressive performances, such as linear transitivity of choice, that do not entail relationally complex representations. Rank 0 is thought to be universal to all animals with nervous systems.

Functionally structured Rank 1 processes entail a representation that recodes the input and is structured so that an input–output function can be computed. The ability to perform this level of processing is well indicated by the acquisition of conditional discrimination, without transfer to isomorphs. Some classes of neural net models were considered that help to specify the properties of this level of functioning. The formal definition of processes at this level predicts that task structure is not represented, and that this level does not have many of the properties of higher cognitive processes. However, content-independent transfer is possible, although it is restricted by the input–output functions learned. Some recently observed instances of content-independent transfer in infants, baboons, and bees can be explained by processes at this level.

Symbolically structured Rank 2+ processes have representations that are in structural correspondence with input–output functions. Structural alignment is the foundational process that enables this level of cognition. Structural correspondence gives some independence of causal links and allows greater flexibility of representation. At this level, the structure of a task can be represented and the properties of higher cognition become possible. These include rules, propositions, compositionality, accessibility of components, modifiability online, systematicity, higher-order relations, analogy, transfer to isomorphs with generation of unknown items, and processing of variables. Transfer to isomorphs with generation of unknown items is a useful indicator of symbolically structured processes. It makes no demands beyond those made in original learning and can be used with prearticulate and inarticulate participants.

Rank 2+ processes are based on relations, and their complexity can be analyzed by the relational complexity metric of Halford, Wilson, & Phillips (1998) based on the arity (number of arguments) of a relation. This can be integrated with the nonstructured and functionally structured levels to form a scale based on representational rank, defined as the number of components bound into a structured representation, such that the components satisfy the constraints imposed by the structure. Rank is one more than the arity of a relation, so a unary relation is Rank 2, a binary relation is Rank 3, and so on. Nonstructured processes are designated Rank 0, and functionally structured processes are designated Rank 1. The ranks are ordered for structural complexity, and we hypothesize that they constitute equivalence classes with similar psychological properties. We have reviewed empirical evidence that supports this proposal and generated many testable predictions from the theory.

The existence of an intermediate level of cognitive functioning, between elemental association and higher, symbolically structured cognition, facilitates the interpretation of findings that infants and lower animals are capable of content-independent transfer. It means that we can accept evidence for early competencies in infants and young children, while recognizing that much development still has to occur before adult cognitive processes will operate. We can accept both early competence and developmental effects (Wellman, Cross, & Watson, 2001). Similarly, we can accept evidence that content-independent transfer can occur in nonhuman (even in some invertebrate) species without being obliged to attribute human cognitive processes to them, at least until evidence is produced that warrants such attributions. That is, we can conduct very interesting explorations of animal cognition without denying species diversity (Povinelli & Bering, 2002).

The theory has implications for the debate about symbol processing by neural net models by showing that there is a class of processes that yield impressive performances but do not have the properties of higher cognition, such as compositionality, systematicity, and representations based on structural correspondence. Consequently, neural net models of these processes should not be expected to have these properties either. However, some of these models are very important in showing how representations can be formed through interaction with the environment. We would suggest that representational rank theory should help modeling in this area by predicting which sets of properties should cluster together and clarifying evaluation criteria for models.

We have shown that a relatively small set of principles enables a very diverse set of cognitive processes to be interpreted in an orderly way. Drawing both on the published literature and on our own previous work, both going back some decades, we have shown that there are tasks with different surface forms that have equivalent structural complexity, while there are other cases of tasks with similar surface forms that have different structural complexities. This not only generates new predictions, but it obviates intractable issues. Without a method for determining equivalence of cognitive tasks, we cannot resolve debates such as whether transitivity of choice or transitive inference is the correct measure for understanding transitivity. Despite the common label "transitive," these tasks are formally distinct, and it only creates confusion to treat them as measures of the same concept. On the other hand, there are tasks with very different surface forms, such as binary relational match-to-sample and proportional analogy, that are formally similar, and are performed by the same species (chimpanzees).

We conclude that, while representational rank theory is far from solving every problem that it touches, it does point the way to a more orderly interpretation of empirical findings in cognitive psychology and cognitive science.

6 Acquisition of Relational Knowledge and the Origin of Symbols

In chapter 2, we defined categories of cognitive processes corresponding to representational ranks 0–6, and properties of each were discussed with reference to empirical evidence in chapter 5. In this chapter, we consider acquisition processes, with reference to the specific characteristics of each rank.

Rank 0 processes correspond to elemental association, which has been massively researched and well summarized in numerous texts (e.g., Domjan, 2003; Lieberman, 1993). The core process is based on contiguity, and there are highly successful computational models (Rescorla & Wagner, 1972).

Rank 1 corresponds to functionally structured processes and includes configural association and "Type-2" (Clark & Thornton, 1997) processes that entail recoding the input to generate an output. These processes have been researched extensively in paradigms such as conditional discrimination, and we considered them in chapters 2 and 5. We noted there that recoding inputs, such as forming a configuration comprised of background and object cues in the conditional discrimination task in figure 2.1, is a major source of difficulty in acquiring this level of knowledge. Functionally structured processes also have been the subject of theoretical modeling using multilayered neural nets (Shultz, 2012; Thomas & McClelland, 2008). Our focus here will be on acquisition of Rank 2+ symbolically structured processes.

Rank 2+. Acquisition of Rank 2+, symbolically structured cognition has been less researched, and is less well understood, than Ranks 0 and 1. Because lower ranks contribute to higher ranks, we consider the role of Rank 0 and Rank 1 processes in the acquisition of Rank 2+ processes. In chapter 2, we proposed that structural alignment is the core process that differentiates Rank 2+ from lower ranks. Therefore, structural alignment is the foundational process in acquisition of relational knowledge and symbolization, which develop in parallel.

Structural alignment

In chapter 2, we reviewed the processes of structure-consistent mapping between cognitive representations. These mappings apply to both analogical reasoning and the formation of symbolic representations, such as mental models (Holland et al., 1986, chapter 2; Halford & Wilson, 1980; Halford, 1993). These mappings depend on dynamic activations in working memory, reflecting parallel-acting constraints that include element and relational similarity, semantic knowledge, motivational factors such as importance or behavioral significance of certain propositions, and structural correspondence (Gentner, 2010; Holyoak & Thagard, 1989). Structural correspondence criteria are *uniqueness of mapping* and *symbol-argument consistency*, which operate with other factors as soft constraints, and the mapping that best fits the parallel acting constraints is selected. As noted in chapter 1, behavior-relevant prediction is a major role of symbolic representations and depends on appropriate structural alignment, so prediction is a significant driver of structural alignment. In turn, structural alignment leads to recoding inputs and binding them to symbols.

Structure-consistent mapping imposes a processing load that is a function of relational complexity (Halford, Wilson, & Phillips, 1998; Maybery, Bain, & Halford, 1986). Capacity for mapping typically is limited to linking four variables into a single representation (Halford et al., 2005). Relational complexity operates in conjunction with other factors that can contribute to the difficulty of acquiring symbolically structured processes. For example, *larger* and *opposite* are both binary relations, and they would be more difficult than unary relations in the same domain (e.g., *big* compared to *larger*) but might not be equally easy to learn, due to other factors such as accessibility of pairs for comparison. It is easier to recognize examples of *larger* because there are plenty of pairs that differ visibly in size, but *opposite* is harder to represent in a simple visible fashion. Similarly, in the context of the balance scale task, differences in weight have effects that are easy to recognize by the sensation of the downward pull, whereas distance from the fulcrum has effects that are harder to observe (Halford et al., 2002).

One of our conclusions in chapter 2 was that symbolically structured knowledge depends on construction of representations in working memory, which in turn depends on dynamic binding to a coordinate system. Consequently, we propose (Halford et al. 2013) that dynamic binding to a coordinate system should be a portent of the onset of symbolic processes.

Development of dynamic binding to a coordinate system

We now propose that there is evidence for development of dynamic binding to a coordinate system late in the first year of life, but that its significance has been overlooked. Halford et al. (2013) have proposed that a well-known developmental phenomenon, the A not-B ($A\overline{B}$) task should be reinterpreted as evidence of the onset of dynamic binding in infants.

Avoiding the A not-B ($A\overline{B}$) error

The best developmental indicator of dynamic binding to a coordinate system that we are aware of is the *absence* of the $A\overline{B}$ error in infants of approximately 8 months of age. In the $A\overline{B}$ task, infants between 7 and 12 months, having retrieved a hidden object a number of times from location A, and then seeing it hidden at location B, tend to search for it at A. There are a number of reviews (e.g., Marcovitch & Zelazo, 1999; Wellman, Cross, & Bartsch, 1986) and theoretical models (e.g., Diamond, 1988; Marcovitch & Zelazo, 2009; Munakata et al., 1997; Thelen et al., 2001).

The Hierarchical Competing Systems Model

The Hierarchical Competing Systems Model of Marcovitch and Zelazo (2009) offers a unified developmental theory and captures established empirical observations, including effects of age, the number of retrievals from A, and the effect of labeling, delay, and the number and distinctiveness of hiding locations. Also, important for our purposes, it is potentially a theory of development of executive functions throughout the lifespan, which is consistent with our aim of using developmental research to clarify the subsymbolic-to-symbolic transition in general cognition. The model accounts for the $A\overline{B}$ task as a competition between a *habit system* and a *representational system*. The habit system reflects previous retrievals of the object from location A, forming an association that causes the infants to perseverate in reaching toward A despite seeing it hidden at B. The representational system is attributed by Marcovitch and Zelazo (2009) to conscious reflection on the object being at B.

Our conception is based on relational knowledge and working memory as outlined in preceding chapters and summarized in figure 6.1. We accept the habit system, and we interpret the representational system as symbolically structured Rank 2+, which means that it depends on working

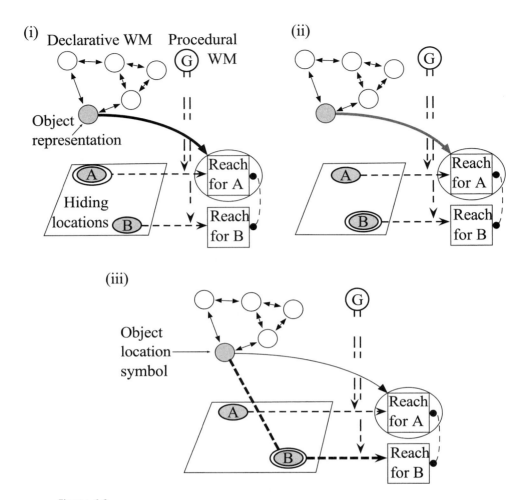

Figure 6.1

Application of the working memory (WM) model of Oberauer (2009) to the $A\bar{B}$ error. All diagrams depict a situation following trials in which the object has been retrieved a number of times from location A. The goal, G, would be to reach for the object where it is believed to be. In (i), the object is now hidden at A (double ellipse): a representation of the object is activated in declarative WM, and there is an association (thick black arc) with reaching for the object at location A, which is correct. In (ii), the object is hidden at B, the association (thick gray arc) reaching to A is still present, and there is no dynamic binding between the object and location B. Therefore, the association dominates performance and the $A\bar{B}$ error occurs. (iii) The $A\bar{B}$ error is not present: there is a dynamic binding (dotted sloping line) between the object and location B. Influenced by the goal G, the motor program to reach for position B is activated, so the correct choice is made to reach for position B. Small circles represent elements of declarative WM and shaded circles represent activation above the baseline. Dotted lines without an arrow represent dynamic bindings, while solid lines with an arrow represent associations and dashed lines with knobs represent inhibitory connections between reaching for A and reaching for B. Reproduced from Halford et al. (2013), figure 3; and adapted from Oberauer (2009), figure 4, with permission.

memory, as outlined in chapter 4. Reflection depends on attention, which is an important factor in working memory (Cowan, 2001). We need to explain not only the error, but how the error is overcome. We propose that infants cease to make the $A\overline{B}$ error when they can form a representation of an object and dynamically connect it to a representation of its location. This means that the habit, formed incrementally by successive retrievals at A, is overcome by mapping the representation of the object into a coordinate system comprised of the set of hiding locations and the spatial relations between them. That is, the error will cease to be made when the infants have a dynamic capability for identity-position integration.

This interprets the $A\overline{B}$ error as a conflict between symbolic and subsymbolic processes. The tendency to continue trying to retrieve an object from A, despite seeing it hidden at B, is a triumph of behavioral mastery over a newly developing (but still relatively weak) dynamic binding to a coordinate system. Thus, *cessation* of the A not-B error represents the triumph of symbolic processes over associative motor learning, which is a subsymbolic process. This explanation implies that correct performance should be related to emerging symbolic processes.

Other evidence of dynamic binding by 1 year of age

Evidence that infants can bind object identity and object position information at 9 months is provided by Káldy and Leslie (2003). Two objects, distinguished by shape and color, were visibly moved behind spatially separated screens. When the screens were lowered, infants looked longer at displays where the objects had been switched, but only if they were identified by shape, not by color. A second experiment showed that the infants appeared to remember both object locations. The locations of the objects were varied from trial to trial, to avoid associating object attributes to locations. Infants of 6.5 months can remember objects by feature (Káldy & Leslie, 2005), but this does not provide evidence of object-location binding. Infants aged 4 months appear not to construct object-location bindings (Mareschal & Johnson, 2003). In a change detection paradigm, Oakes, Ross-Sheehy, and Luck (2006) found that 7.5-month-olds (but not 6.5-month-olds) bound color and location. They concluded that the development of binding occurs between 6 and 8 months after a period of dramatic development of the parietal lobes (which occurs between 3 and 6 months of age).

It is likely that object-location bindings are the first dynamic bindings to a coordinate system that are made by humans. The coordinate system is, in this case, a set of ordered locations in space. Because spatial cognition develops early, spatial location provides an efficient way to begin the cognitively demanding process of binding to a coordinate system. In conclusion, while the evidence is not entirely consistent, it appears that dynamic object-location binding develops late in the first year.

Other predictions follow from this model. First, if children have formed a dynamic binding between an object and a location, then by the principle of accessibility in chapter 2, they should be able to predict the object, given the location, and should be able to predict the location, given the object. Therefore, in a task with objects X and Y in locations A or B, where they last saw X at A, they should be surprised by Y at A, or by X at B. This combination of performances should not be observed in children who make the $A\bar{B}$ error. To our knowledge, these predictions have not been tested. Second, performance on all these tests should decline with delay after seeing X at A because of decay in the dynamic representation. This is consistent with $A\bar{B}$ data (Diamond, 1990). Appearance of this ability should be predicted by other performances that involve dynamic binding to the simplest coordinate systems. These performances should be related to maturation of the BA9, BA10 region in the prefrontal cortex (PFC; Kibbe & Leslie, 2011).

The "X at A, Y at B " procedure differs from hiding an object at one of two ordered locations, then showing a hand removing it from the wrong location, surprising infants. Studies with this procedure (e.g., Baillargeon, DeVos, & Graber, 1989) demonstrate location memory in 8-month-olds, even after 70-second delays. In this procedure, location only needs to be represented because the identity of the object in the specific location is not at issue. In the X at A and Y at B procedure, both object and location must be represented, and if the location of the objects is shown only once, the binding between them must be formed dynamically in working memory. Thus, object-location binding is distinct from location memory.

We can identify the binding of symbols representing objects to symbols representing locations as an example of compositionality only if at least one of the relevant criteria is met. One criterion is accessibility. If we have composed symbols representing X at A and Y at B, we should be able to retrieve components: Thus, given X, we should retrieve A, or given A, we should retrieve X, and the same holds true for Y and B. This is why there should be surprise if the compositions are violated, as with Y at A. Another criterion is that the composition should be independent of associative linkages, so it should be possible to overcome previous learning that X is at B, or Y at A.

Our conclusion is that overcoming the $A\overline{B}$ error reflects dynamic binding to a coordinate system and is an early manifestation of symbolically structured representation. Overcoming the $A\overline{B}$ error should be a predictor of the onset of symbolic processes, and there are hypotheses that could be tested by longitudinal studies, with controls for subsymbolic acquisitions. One prediction concerns language. Infants first produce recognizable words early in the second year (Clark, 2003), and this acquisition should be predicted by ceasing to make the $A\overline{B}$ error, with controls for nonsymbolic processes such as vocalizations without semantic referents, motor development, and nonsymbolic performances. Another early cognitive acquisition that should be predicted by cessation of the $A\overline{B}$ error is theory of mind. In chapter 5, we reviewed a controversy about infants' theory of mind, and we suggested that a symbolic, unary relational conception might be present in infancy. This should be predicted by no longer making the $A\overline{B}$ error.

Further development of dynamic binding

Further developments in object representations have been found to occur later in infancy. In two experiments (Leslie & Chen, 2007), 11-month-olds were shown two pairs of objects in succession. In condition XY/XY, each pair consisted of different objects: i.e., they were shown XY followed by another instance of XY. In condition XX/YY, they were shown two objects that were the same (XX) followed by a different pair of objects that were the same (YY). Three test trials followed immediately on familiarization trials. There was evidence that infants expected a single pair in the XY/XY condition but two pairs in the XX/YY condition. The relation between two objects in a pair appears to be at stake here rather than object-location binding per se, but it is an interesting account of a representational ability that appears to develop in the first year. These findings were interpreted as indicating that at 11 months, infants can use shape to represent pairs of objects. Our interpretation is based on the relations required to represent these displays: XY/XY can be represented by a single pair if the X items are not readily distinguishable, and the situation is similar for the Y items. However, XX/YY cannot be represented by a single XY pair because two instances of X (also two of Y) were presented. As this task is more complex than the object-location binding demonstrated by 8-month-olds, this study appears to indicate some development of object-location binding from 8 to 11 months of age.

There is also evidence that even at 11 months, infants' representations of collections of objects have limited accessibility. Feigenson and Yamaguchi (2009) showed to 11-month-old infants crackers being added sequentially to each of two buckets within their view, and then the infants were allowed to approach the buckets to retrieve the crackers. Preference for the bucket containing more crackers was observed if additions to one bucket were completed before any were added to the next (sequences *ABB* or *AAB*), but not if crackers were added to one bucket, then to the alternate bucket, and then back to the first bucket. That is, they did not recognize that *A* contained more crackers than *B* after the sequence *ABA*. In *ABB* and *AAB*, infants could form a representation of bucket *A*, then of bucket *B*, and compare the two. In *ABA*, they must form a representation of *A*, then of B, and then add to their previous representation of *A*. Failure on *ABA* was not due solely to shifting attention from *A* to *B* because they succeeded with sequence *A(B)AB*, where bucket (*B*) was only touched without adding a cracker before adding a second cracker to bucket *A*. They also succeeded on sequence *ABAA*, where the bucket with the most crackers could be identified without returning to an earlier representation, but not on sequences *AABA*, where return was necessary. Feigenson and Yamaguchi (2009) suggest that "infants can only bind object representations into a set when that set is held in the current focus of attention." (p. 260). Thus, there appears to be a limitation of access to a representation after constructing a second representation, which suggests that accessibility of cognitive representations develops gradually in infancy. Success on *ABB* and *AAB* confirms that infants can store a representation of a single cracker in working memory, update it when a second cracker is added, maintain the representation while attention is shifted to a different location, store a representation of a single cracker in the new location, and compare the two representations. They appear unable, however, to return to a previous representation and update it.

It is clear that infants perform the *AAB* or *ABB* task at 11 months, but we are not aware of any studies that show specifically whether this task is performed by younger infants. The quantification paradigm developed by Wynn (1992) shows that 5-month-olds can represent addition or subtraction of elements to a set (e.g., $1 + 1 = 2$, but not 3) but the *AAB* and *ABB* tasks are more complex in that they require representation of additions to two collections, with subsequent comparisons of the collection so formed. It would be particularly interesting to know whether the *AAB* and *ABB* tasks are mastered at the same age as, or later than, the *A* not-*B* task. It also would be interesting to know whether dynamic object-location bindings become possible when infants cease to make the $A\bar{B}$ error.

Development of object-location binding continues well past infancy (Sluzenski, Newcombe, & Kovacs, 2006). Memory for binding, defined as recognition of combinations (e.g., animal and location) improved between 4 and 6 years of age, independent of memory for components, and was related to episodic memory. Lloyd, Doydum, and Newcombe (2009) found that 4- and 6-year-olds' memory for object-background bindings did not differ in the working memory condition in which each set of four object-background combinations was followed by two test questions. However, the 4-year-olds performed more poorly (higher false alarm rates) than 6-year-olds in the long-term memory condition in which each set of 12 combinations was followed by six test questions. The long-term memory condition incorporated longer delays between study and test, as well as longer study lists (more bindings).

To summarize, binding between attributes of the same object, such as shape and color, appear to be possible at birth. Before about 4 months of age, after seeing an object occluded, infants can recall the objects *or* its location, but they first recall the binding between an object and its location at 7 months. This appears to be the age at which infants first can access object information from location information, and vice versa. At 11 months, they can update representations of objects and compare the updated sets, as in the *AAB* or *ABB* tasks of Feigenson and Yamaguchi, (2009), but they cannot update a previous representation again following processing of an intervening representation (e.g., the *ABA* task of Feigenson & Yamaguchi, 2009). This suggests that previously formed representations are not accessible for further operations after an operation has been performed on another representation. These findings collectively suggest there is development during infancy in the degree to which representations become accessible to other cognitive processes, so the representations of 11-month-olds have greater accessibility than those of 7-month-olds, which in turn are more accessible than those of 4-month-olds. This would be consistent with the development of capacity for dynamic construction of accessible representations in working memory over the period of 4 to 11 months. This process should be significant for the transition to symbolic processes.

There is also a possible link between dynamic object-location bindings and representation of pairs in the relational match-to-sample task, discussed in chapter 5 with respect to the distinction between Ranks 1 and 3. There, we noted that there does not appear to have been a demonstration that animals (e.g., baboons) can recode a sample pair of objects to match a target. For example, to solve a problem like this, where the elements in the source differ in two dimensions (such as shape and color), while the target elements differ in only one dimension (such as color), the animal would need to recode in terms of just color. This appears to require switching between two relational representations, one in the source and one in the target. It would be interesting to compare the procedure of Feigenson and Yamaguchi (2009) with recoding of the match-to-sample task.

Object-location and role-filler bindings

One implication of our analysis is that there is a structural correspondence between object-location bindings and role-filler bindings, discussed in chapter 2. Understanding the sentence "Jane feeds cat" entails dynamically assigning *Jane* to the agent role and *cat* to the patient role, which is structurally similar to the assignment of object X to location A and object Y to location B (see figure 6.2). This structural alignment makes "Jane feeds cat" very different from "cat feeds Jane," although without structural alignment, the difference should not be recognized because the comparison would be based on element similarity, independent of role assignments. It should be possible to construct scenarios (e.g., using puppets) suitable for

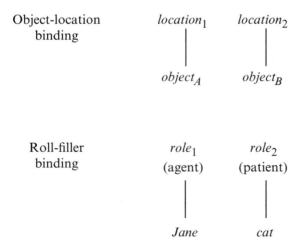

Figure 6.2
Comparison of object-location and role-filler bindings

presentation to infants in order to test their recognition of role-filler bind-ings. That is, if we habituate infants to a binding of puppet A to role 1 and puppet B to role 2, then, assuming that the roles are shown to be recog-nized, they should show increased attention to subsequent presentations in which role assignments are reversed. Furthermore, there should be a correspondence between dynamic role assignment and object-location binding such that the developmental trajectories should be indistinguish-able. Both of these attainments should portend the transition to symbolic processes, including acquisition of word meanings.

Neural correlates of the $A\overline{B}$ task

$A\overline{B}$ performance is associated with maturity of brain systems involving the PFC. Bell and Fox (1992) found that toleration of longer delays in 12-month-olds was associated with more mature patterns of electroencephalogram (EEG) brain activity. Bell (2001) recorded EEG activity while 8-month-olds performed a looking version of the A-not-B task. High-performing infants showed task-related increases in EEG power in four scalp regions (frontal pole, medial frontal, parietal, and occipital), suggesting the involvement of both frontal and nonfrontal brain regions. They also showed increased EEG coherence between medial frontal and parietal sites, suggesting that these regions were working together in the task, and lower coherence between two frontal pairs in the right than the left hemisphere, consistent with more advanced differentiation within the right frontal lobes. Lesion research with nonhuman primates implicates the DLPFC (BA8, BA9, and BA10), but not the hippocampus in $A\overline{B}$ task performance (Diamond, 1990; Diamond, Zola-Morgan, & Squire, 1989).

The $A\overline{B}$ task is subtly different from the delayed response task in that habitual, subsymbolic processes direct retrieval efforts to the wrong posi-tion on B trials following A trials. This increases the demand for symbolic processes on B trials. The delayed response task, without a sequence of A trials preceding the B trial, does not have this conflict, so it does not preclude retrieval using subsymbolic processes. A modification that would make the delayed response task more suitable as a test of mapping to a coordinate system would be to move the apparatus containing the hiding places to a different location to eliminate environmental cues. Location of the hidden food would then require dynamic binding to a location defined by its relation to other potential hiding places within the apparatus. This would be analogous to the procedure of Oberauer (2005), which requires words to be bound dynamically to slots on a com-puter screen.

Relational knowledge in infancy

Very little of the literature has specifically addressed infants' relational knowledge, which makes determination of age-norms for this attainment difficult. However, there is some recent research that can be interpreted in terms of the relational knowledge principles that we have formulated. Experiments by Song and Baillargeon (2007) are representative of a body of research indicating that infants of 9.5 months can represent other people's dispositions to perform certain actions. In habituation, they saw three separate objects moved backward and forward, then in testing, they saw a person choose between a short frame, which did not permit back-and-forth movement, and a long frame, which did. Infants looked longer toward the choice of the short frame, indicating that they had attributed to the person a disposition to move the objects back and forth. Control procedures indicated that the results were not due to preference for any particular action.

Song and Baillargeon (2007) make a subtle but important distinction between a disposition to perform an action and having a goal to reach for an object (to cite one example action). The reaching goal can be learned by observing a person reaching for that object, but the disposition requires seeing the person repeatedly performing one action in preference to another (e.g., reaching for object A in preference to object B, when both are available). Notice that this is analogous to the distinction, made earlier in this chapter, between recall of location (based on seeing an object hidden at a specific place), and object-location binding (based on recognizing that X is at A and Y is at B). The sensitivity to the additional discrimination implies a more elaborate cognitive representation. Interpretation of the Song and Baillargeon (2007) experiment in terms of achieving a goal is unlikely because no goal was apparent in the back-and-forth movement.

Representation of a disposition, as well as its transfer to a novel but isomorphic situation, fulfills the criteria for relational knowledge as embodied in the generativity test. The disposition of a person to perform a specific action, as observed by Song and Baillargeon (2007), implies a relational schema in which the relation symbol *Disposition* is bound to a specific action: *Disposition(Action X)*. This relational schema is induced in the habituation procedure, when infants observe the objects being moved back and forth. Then the schema is mapped into a test situation with the short and long frames. When the infant observes a person choosing the short frame, *Action X* is negated. Because of the binding between *Disposition* and *Action X,* the disposition is inferred to be negated. This would cause surprise in an infant who had attributed that disposition to the person performing the task. This embodies the three abovementioned principles: i.e., induce the schema (moving back and forth), map into a new situation (the test frames), and make inferences about the novel situation (disposition no longer evident). Therefore, we agree with Song and Baillargeon (2007) that a relational representation was probably demonstrated, and our interpretation is that it would have been a unary relation. Thus, this study is consistent with our proposal that dynamic binding of relational schemas is possible at approximately 8 months of age.

If this analysis is confirmed by subsequent research, it would suggest that early evidence of relational knowledge is to be found in infants' theory of mind, as well as in their spatial cognitions. Relational complexity theory, therefore, implies that theory of mind develops from simple, unary relational schemas in infants around 8 months of age to ternary relational schemas in 4- to 5-year-old children, as observed by Andrews et al. (2003) and as predicted by Halford (1993). There also should be binary relational theory of mind, in the form of connections and transformations tasks as discussed in chapter 4 and shown in figure 4.6. There is already some evidence to support this, as correct performance on connections tasks has been reported with 2-year-olds (Senju et al., 2011, chapter 5).

Although relational processing in infancy has not been investigated explicitly in many studies, it could be a productive line of inquiry now. Relational action, dispositions schemas, and spatial knowledge could be templates for other relational knowledge acquisition. Investigation of relational knowledge, in turn, can provide a window into the transition to symbolic cognition, which depends on relational schemas (Halford et al., 2013).

Conclusions about the subsymbolic-to-symbolic transition

Now we can define the transition to symbolic cognition on the basis of processes that are well understood. Acceleration of research into relational knowledge, working memory, neuroscience of the PFC, and its connections to other regions, as well as reassessment of infant cognition and clarification of reasoning processes (including analogy), have opened an entirely new research landscape for investigating the transition to symbolic processes. The subsymbolic-to-symbolic distinction enables tasks to be classified according to cognitive processes entailed, bringing more order and clarity to the domain (Frye & Zelazo, 1998). It permits integration across paradigms without the inconsistencies that have plagued attempts to produce coherent accounts of the field. We also have avoided the circularity inherent in using reasoning or language as a criterion for symbolic processes.

Symbolic processes depend on dynamically forming structured representations in working memory and on forming mappings between representations on the basis of structural correspondence. The essential properties of symbolic processes are outlined, and current evidence indicates that they emerge at about 8 months of age, probably due to maturation of relevant regions of the PFC, interacting with knowledge acquisition in many domains. However, some existing infancy tests can be interpreted as indicators of the ability to map elements to a coordinate system dynamically, and these are predicted to correlate with the onset of symbolic processes. Human infancy offers a unique opportunity to study the processes that underlie the subsymbolic-to-symbolic transition; in this chapter, we have shown how this can be undertaken.

However, perhaps the most important implication of our proposals is that acquisition of symbolic processes depends on relational knowledge. Therefore, relational reasoning and the associated working memory processes need to be included in investigations of the transition to symbolic processes.

Language and early acquisition of relational knowledge

We can learn a lot about the acquisition of structured knowledge from infants' acquisition of relational terms, including verbs, prepositions, adjectives, adverbs, and possessives, that are typically acquired beginning in the second year of life (Clark, 2003). While there is a consensus that innate processes lay a foundation for acquiring language (Golinkoff & Hirsh-Pasek, 2008; Hollich et al., 2000; Mandler, 2004; Tomasello, 1992), there is growing support for the view that domain-general cognitive processes contribute to language acquisition. Relational knowledge is linked closely to word meaning (Dixon & Marchman, 2007), and much of the grammatical structure of language emerges from the meaning of relational terms, especially verbs (Tomasello, 1992). As Golinkoff and Hirsh-Pasek, put it: "Verbs are the gateway to grammar." (p. 397). Comprehension of verbs is a case of relational knowledge as we defined it in chapter 2 and the meaning of verbs includes understanding of conceptual roles, which closely resemble the roles in relational representations. Intransitive verbs have a subject *(Tom laughs)*, transitive verbs have a subject and an object *(Tom sees Bob)*, and some verbs have a subject and a direct and an indirect object *(Tom gives Bob a book)*. Infants and young children are sensitive to the semantic roles of verbs (Naigles, Hoff, & Vear, 2009; Wagner & Lakusta, 2009; Yuan & Fisher, 2009), indicating that the roles are part of their understanding of verbs.

Word learning is a case of learning relations from examples, and there is some appreciation of a larger structure or schema. For example, in learning the meaning of the verb *give,* children might learn that there are three roles, as mentioned previously. This is important to models of structured knowledge acquisition because that means it might begin with links between several entities, and the relational complexity metric would predict that up to four roles might be acquired in parallel. This is an issue to which we will return in the context of computational models (see chapter 7).

The demands entailed in learning relations are indicated by evidence that verbs are more difficult to learn than nouns. The main reasons are that the meaning of nouns can be defined ostensibly (e.g., pointing to a cat and saying "cat"), but the meaning of verbs is more difficult to conceptualize because it is dynamic and transitory, and it might refer to changes of state that are not readily imageable (Golinkoff & Hirsh-Pasek, 2008). The difficulty of learning verbs also varies according to characteristics of the language and linguistic context (Waxman et al., 2013).

A further reason for verbs being more difficult to understand initially is alluded to by Tomasello (1992), although to our knowledge, it has not been fully developed previously. It is that the meaning of verbs is based on more entities than the meaning of nouns. Thus, a full understanding of *giving* entails a relation between three roles: *giver, given object,* and *recipient* (*Tom gives Bob a book*), whereas the meaning of a noun depends primarily on conceptualizing one object. This invokes the relational complexity metric (Halford, Wilson, & Phillips, 1998; Halford, Phillips, & Wilson, 2008), as discussed in chapter 2. Another significant factor is that acquisition of word meaning depends on social processes, including recognition of the intent of the speaker (Tomasello, 1992). With these caveats in mind, we will use word acquisition along with research in other domains to define core processes of acquisition of structured knowledge.

We see the processes that underlie language acquisition as providing at least some indications for the acquisition of relational knowledge generally. A set of general principles for learning structured sequences in language and other domains, including vision, was formulated by Goldstein and his colleagues. The gist of their principles is conveyed by the acronym ACCESS: "Align Candidates, Compare, Evaluate Statistical/Social Significance" (Goldstein et al., 2010, p. 251). Significant structure is identified in small time windows that include *variation sets*, meaning small samples that include partial repetitions and occur in close temporal proximity. Recognition of statistical regularity and alignment of behaviorally significant instances appear to be at the core of structured knowledge acquisition. There are other relevant factors. Thus, Tomasello (2000) pointed out that the linguistic categories entailed in language acquisition are based on usage rather than on abstract linguistic principles. There is also an array of cognitive constraints (Christiansen & Chater, 2008) and benefits from other processes such as shared intentionality (Tomasello, 2008). However, the point that we wish to adopt here is that language acquisition is an instance of largely self-supervised learning from examples occurring in the child's experience. We suggest that this concept is applicable to relational knowledge acquisition in general.

Functionally structured processes in infancy

In chapter 5, we reviewed functionally structured Rank 1 processes, including object concept prototypes and image schemas. In this section, we consider the acquisition of cognitive processes at this level.

Foundational concepts: Image schemas
Mandler (2004) has adopted the term *image schema* for conceptions such as *path, self-motion, containment, up-down, link,* and *agency.* These concepts are relevant to the acquisition of verb meanings that depends on the conceptualization of the relevant activity or change of state. Image schemas are accessible as a whole, making conscious thought and imagination possible but, as we will see, the components are not accessible in the way that components of relational knowledge are accessible. Image schemas are foundational, but not atomic or unitary. Image schemas represent events in a simple, abstract form. They are not visual images; rather, they are *schematic spatial representations.* The image schema *path* entails an object following a trajectory through space, unspecified as to speed, direction, or other figural aspects. An image schema of a container entails a bounded space that has an inside and an outside, but it need not have a particular shape. The image-schema *agency* can be conceptualized in terms of *source-path-goal* (following Lakoff, 1987). Infants can generalize from a known example to a structurally similar example, as when infants substitute opening-closing hands for opening-closing eyes.

The principal process contributing to image schema formation according to Mandler (2004) is *perceptual meaning analysis*, which analyzes perceptual displays into meanings and has been likened to representational redescription (Karmiloff-Smith, 1994). The mechanisms of perceptual meaning analysis are not fully specified, but some processes have been identified. Image schemas utilize the perceptual and motor schemas arising from sensorimotor processes; they develop in parallel with them but are distinct from them.

By this account, image schemas have some elements of structure and constitute the conceptual meanings onto which words will be mapped a little later in development. However, they do not have the explicit structural representations defined in chapter 2. The image-schema *agency* has the components *source-path-goal*, but there is no alignment of components into slots and no explicit symbol for the link, and therefore, no binding between symbol and the entities comprising the structure. A review by Wagner and Lakusta (2009) examining the correspondence between prelinguistic thought and semantics of languages reported that infants can map simple relational schemas into representations of events, as indicated by their detection of subsequent mismatches, but there are limits to generalization, especially in the first year. These findings parallel in some ways our review of the correspondence between thought and relational knowledge. The evidence is consistent with Mandler (2004), in that it shows that infants have early building blocks of relational knowledge. Consequently, image schemas, at least in their most basic form, are functionally structured processes rather than symbolically structured. Later in this chapter, we will consider mechanisms that enable them to be elaborated into relational representations. Our proposal is an alternative to both sides of a controversy, reviewed by Müller and Overton (1998), about whether representations are innate or based on early sensorimotor processes. We propose that early symbolic processes are based on dynamic binding in working memory to a coordinate system. Spatial coordinate systems would be important in this process, as we illustrate through our discussion of the $A\bar{B}$ task, and they might have some innate components, but they would be developed (or least elaborated) through early actions. Dynamic binding in working memory will play a part in this development.

A lot is known about transition processes (see reviews by Fischer & Bidell, 2006; Halford & Andrews, 2006; Siegler, 2006), but until we advanced this formulation, surprisingly little has been known about the subsymbolic-to-symbolic transition. One problem has been that, since we have not had a clear idea of what we are looking for, we might have missed this transition even if it was staring us in the face. We began this chapter by outlining our proposal about the origins of symbolic cognition in infancy, based on dynamic binding to a coordinate system. Now we will expand our consideration of acquisition processes.

Acquisition processes

Self-supervised learning, without prior knowledge that a structure exists, has been identified as a key property of symbolically structured cognition (Doumas et al., 2008; Halford & Busby, 2007). While strategic processes such as hypothesis testing and bootstrapping become important in later acquisition, there must be a mechanism for acquiring structures that are fundamentally new in the sense that there is no prior knowledge to guide acquisition. Associative learning and implicit learning are crucially important here.

Acquisition of links between entities by associative learning arguably provides a starting point for symbolic processes. This means that the acquisition of symbolically structured knowledge is supported by the acquisition of nonstructured and functionally structured knowledge, just as System 2 reasoning is often applied to knowledge acquired by System 1 (Evans, 2003). However, associative knowledge alone is not sufficient for acquisition of relational knowledge, and establishment of structural alignment in working memory is essential. Now we briefly review the processes that we see as responsible for the early stages of acquisition processes.

Mitchell et al. (2009) deny that associative learning consists of automatic formation of associative links, and they argue that all learning, at least in humans, is essentially propositional in character. We accept that propositional representations play a role in human learning, and we agree that there is interaction between automatic and controlled processes in learning. However, a number of lines of evidence cause us to reserve a role for the automatic formation of links in the initial stages of structured knowledge acquisition. These include a role for association in the early stages of language acquisition in infants (Marcus, Fernandes, & Johnson, 2012), associative acquisition of concepts such as animacy (Rakison & Lupyan, 2008), and the sizeable implicit learning literature, as well as classic studies such as that by Cleeremans and McClelland (1991).

Implicit learning

Acquisition of relational knowledge sometimes begins without conscious awareness that there is a structure to be acquired, and it is triggered by relatively automatic recognition of regularities in the environment. Attempts to capture this process have spawned a number of implicit learning paradigms, some of which are reviewed by Pothos (2007).

Self-supervised acquisition of structure is also incorporated in the relational schema induction process of Halford and Busby (2007).

Evidence that implicit learning can contribute to the acquisition of structure has been obtained from a number of paradigms, including control of complex systems (Berry & Dienes, 1993) and hidden covariation detection (Rossnagel, 2001). Despite significant methodological differences, a common factor in many experiments is the absence of any prior information that there is a structure to be acquired. In an attempt to account for unsupervised acquisition of syntax, Reber (1967) showed that artificial grammars can be learned by memorizing strings of elements that conform to the grammar, without explicitly learning the rules and without being told that any structure exists. This implicit learning is developmentally invariant (Reber, 1967), and some form of it would be possible in early infancy. This paradigm yields above-chance transfer that is maintained (although with reduced levels of performance) for dissimilar materials. Reber interpreted the finding as symbolic, but this claim has been controversial; alternative interpretations include similarity-based transfer (Vokey & Brooks, 1992), sensitivity to statistical properties of the material (Pacton et al., 2001), and acquisition of string fragments that can be transferred by analogy (Perruchet, 1994). Thus, if a sequence such as *AABC* is known to be grammatical, the sequence *XXYZ* also is recognized as grammatical.

This paradigm can be accepted as showing that implicit learning results in acquisition of links between elements, and some factors governing this process are known. Acquisition is sensitive to the number of elements needed to predict the next element, consistent with predictability and entropy metrics (van den Bos & Poletiek, 2008), but also with the relational complexity metric (Halford, Wilson, & Phillips, 1998). Acquisition is unrelated to psychometric intelligence (Gebauer & Mackintosh, 2007), but it is not necessarily effortless or unconscious (Shanks, Rowland, & Ranger, 2005). Important for our purposes, there is little evidence that anything more than minimal structural knowledge is acquired. Part of the reason may be, as suggested elsewhere (Halford & Busby, 2007), that the artificial grammars used can be reduced to pairwise links between elements, so there is no requirement to learn a more complex structure.

The issue as to whether the paradigm yields symbolic knowledge (Litman & Reber, 2005) may be somewhat irrelevant because even concrete knowledge, such as specific strings, can be transferred by analogy. Abstraction is not synonymous with the use of symbols, but it can emerge as a result of the structural alignment of sets of specific elements, as we saw in chapter 2. Therefore, it might be more appropriate to reinterpret the Reber paradigm as yielding structural information that forms a building block for relational knowledge.

Implicit learning has been demonstrated for sequences of up to four elements, but consistent with processing capacity limitations discussed in chapter 3, evidence exists showing that it is not possible for sequences of more than four (Cowan, 2001, §3.4.5). [See also the classic study of Cleeremans and McClelland (1991), discussed in chapter 4.] The importance of these findings for the acquisition of structured knowledge is in showing that links between sets of four elements can be learned without awareness, laying the foundation for the acquisition of structures up to the complexity of quaternary relations. This suggests that relational knowledge is acquired by learning links between sets of elements, rather than one role (or one element) at a time. That is, the whole relation is learned in parallel rather than being assembled from pieces learned serially. Recall that this is consistent with observations that verb acquisition entails acquisition of the case roles that comprise the verb meanings. This has implications for computational models of the acquisition of structured knowledge, to be discussed in a subsequent section of this chapter.

Despite the plethora of issues and theories [e.g., the review by Pothos (2007) identifies nine theories], there is one clear implication for the acquisition of structured knowledge: namely, that links between elements can be acquired by self-supervised learning from examples, without prior knowledge that a structure exists and without explicit instruction in the structure. This is a powerful mechanism for starting the acquisition of structured knowledge, but the structures learned in the Reber paradigm are very restricted, and implicit learning needs to be supplemented by other processes, to which we now will turn.

Concept of animacy

Rakison and Lupyan (2008) have proposed that the concept of animacy can be acquired by a domain-general, unsupervised *constrained attentional associative learning* process. Learning that is constrained by attentional biases, some of which are innate, results in representations of statistical regularities, including onset of motion and line of trajectory. Their work provides strong evidence of the role of associative links in the early acquisition of structured knowledge. Rakison and Lupyan (2008) present a feed-forward net model of the representation of animacy (to be considered in chapter 7).

Associative acquisition of order information

The transitivity of choice paradigm (also called *implicit transitive inference*, as discussed in Goel [2007]), discussed in chapters 1 and 2, can be interpreted as showing that associative learning can lead to the acquisition of the order of sets of stimuli. Recall that the paradigm consists of training participants to choose one member of each pair in a series: $A+B-$, $B+C-$, $C+D-$, $D+E-$, where [+] indicates a rewarded choice and [-] indicates a nonrewarded choice (Chalmers & McGonigle, 1984; Terrace & McGonigle, 1994). Transitivity is assessed with untrained nonadjacent pairs, with most interest focusing on B and D, because bias is controlled by $B+$ and $B-$ occurring equally often in training, as do $D+$ and $D-$. Modeling of this paradigm has shown that preference for B over D can be based on relative associative strength, which is maximal for A, and declines monotonically through the series (Wynne, 1995). Performance does not take much effort, and there is no evidence of dynamic binding, but acquisition is inefficient in that it occurs incrementally over many trials (often hundreds of them). In contrast, explicit transitive inference, using dynamic binding in working memory, can occur in a single trial. The critical difference, however, is that there is no mental model of the relations between elements in implicit transitive inference (Markovits & Dumas, 1992), whereas there is such a mental model in explicit transitivity, as we saw in chapter 1. However, such associatively learned orderings might provide a template for the development of symbolically structured transitive inference. This was modeled in the Transitive Inference Mapping Model (TRIMM; Halford et al., 1995).

The importance of the implicit transitive inference paradigm for the acquisition of structured knowledge is that it provides a means by which the order of elements can be learned with little effort or awareness. This could be a useful beginning for the acquisition of structured knowledge, and in some participants, it could be recoded into a more adequate mental model by reflecting on relations between the elements. The further processes required for this are investigated in the relational schema induction paradigm (Halford & Busby, 2007; Halford, Wilson, & Phillips, 1998) and in symbolic connectionist models, considered in chapter 7.

Representational redescription

Karmiloff-Smith (1994) proposed that the implicit-to-explicit transition occurs by representational redescription, which involves three recurrent phases. Phase 1 is essentially subsymbolic, and phase 2 begins the transition to symbolic processes, which is completed in phase 3. This is consistent with other proposals that transitions are made by reflective abstraction (Zelazo et al., 2003). Dixon and Kelly (2007) proposed that children revise theories following error, but they also develop relational representations following correct performance, which they attribute to representational redescription. A common thread here is that there should be processes that can access implicit, nonstructured knowledge and transform it into a structured representation. Thus, if links between successive elements have been learned in a sequence such as *AABC*, this sequence can be activated in long-term memory and a symbolically structured representation can be formed in working memory. This can be applied to the sequence *XXYZ*, as proposed by Perruchet (1994). The representation in working memory would have to take a form like *follows(X, X, Y, Z)*, and this would have to be mapped to a new sequence by the principles of structural correspondence defined in chapter 2.

Relational schema induction

The relational schema induction paradigm (Halford, Bain et al., 1998; Halford & Busby, 2007) is derived from the task used by Halford and Wilson (1980), but adapted for adults. This paradigm depends on learning items in which an operator symbol effects transformations between elements (e.g., *Mary*, symbol $C \rightarrow$ *Kerry*; *Kerry*, symbol $C \rightarrow$ *Jill*; etc.), as shown in figure 6.3. The symbols are geometric figures, so their import is initially unknown. The items are meaningless at first, but they acquire meaning as a relational schema is formed. For example, a circular arrangement of the names can be made so that *C* means to move one step clockwise, *A* means to move one step counterclockwise, and *N* is a null operator, meaning to stay in the same place. Tests for structured knowledge included participants' arrangement of elements by moving them on the computer screen with the mouse, a goodness-of-fit test similar to that used in the Reber paradigm, and a generativity test similar to the one described for conditional discrimination in chapter 2, in which transfer is made to isomorphic tasks and, after initial items to show the correct mapping between old and transfer tasks, unknown items of the transfer task are predicted by analogical inference. The generativity test will be considered further later in this chapter. The task was compared directly to the implicit learning of artificial grammar, and it proved more successful in inducing structural knowledge. In the early stages of acquisition, relational schema induction should

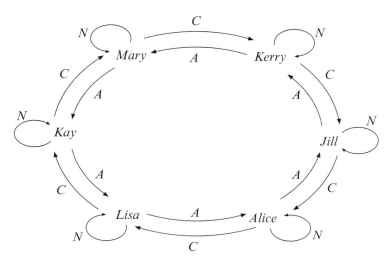

Figure 6.3
Structure emerging from items learned in the relational schema induction task. *C* can be interpreted as a clockwise movement, *A* as counterclockwise, and *N* as a null movement (i.e., remaining in the same state).

depend on temporary binding into a schema, and support for this hypothesis is provided by Reverberi et al. (2005), who showed that rule induction is related to working memory and is localized in the left convexity of the frontal cortex (left lateral frontal cortex).

Structural coherence is manipulated in this paradigm by varying the consistency of the symbols. In the inconsistent condition, symbols have no consistent meaning. An example would be a set of items in which the meaning of *C* corresponds to a clockwise movement when applied to Mary and Kerry, but to a counterclockwise movement when applied to Jill; i.e., Mary, *C* → Kerry; Kerry, *C* → Jill; Jill, *C* → Kerry. The individual items were as valid in the inconsistent condition as in the consistent condition, but the absence of between-item consistency meant that structural alignment and assignment to roles were impossible. This resulted in serious disruption of learning and demonstrates the profound effect of structural alignment in the acquisition of relational knowledge. This paradigm demonstrates that structured knowledge can be acquired by self-supervision, without explicit instruction, provided that structural alignment of instances is possible. It is a more powerful process than the implicit learning of the artificial grammar paradigm of Reber (1967).

Emergence of symbols from relational schema induction

A relational schema will include ordering the state elements and defining operators as movements around the ordered elements. Thus, if the elements are arranged as shown in figure 6.3 (one of the possible valid orderings), then *C* means a clockwise movement, *A* a counterclockwise movement, and so on. Thus, symbols can emerge from formation of a mental model of the task structure. The importance of this is that symbolic processes emerge from, and depend on, structured representations.

The generativity test for relational knowledge

The core process of relational knowledge is the ability to construct mappings between representations on the basis of structure, independent of what can be achieved by element similarity or prior knowledge. The theory that we have outlined here provides a method for distinguishing subsymbolic and symbolic processes that is a direct application of our criteria for symbolic processing, and it is usable in principle with any type of structured material. The generativity test (Halford, Bain et al., 1998; Halford & Busby, 2007) can be used to assess symbolic processes in inarticulate participants, including infants and animals (Halford et al., 2008).

The principles of the generativity test are as follows:

1. Induce a relational schema from repeated exposure to instances of the relation.
2. Map the schema to a novel situation dynamically based on structural correspondence (i.e., analogical mapping).
3. Use the schema to generate inferences about novel situations (including predictions of correct responses to previously unseen stimuli).

This was illustrated in chapter 2 with respect to conditional discrimination: Transfer to the isomorphic task in figure 2.1B enables the prediction of previously unknown elements. The essential requirements for the generativity test are an internal representation of a relation, with evidence of one or more cognitive operations on the representation.

"Learning set" is really relational schema induction

Some kinds of transfer exhibited in the so-called learning set paradigm (Harlow, 1949) qualify as evidence of relational representation. Consider, for example, a two-object discrimination task in which participants are required to choose between two simultaneously presented objects on the basis of a criterion such as shape. In problem 1, choosing a triangle is rewarded, whereas choosing a circle is not (*triangle+; circle–*). When this problem has been learned to the point that the intraproblem learning criterion (e.g., errors reduced below a specified level) is reached, a new problem is introduced, (such as *ellipse+, parallelogram–*). When this is learned to the intraproblem criterion point, the participant progresses to discrimination of a new pair of shapes, and so on through a series of iso-morphic problems. The dependent variable of greatest interest is interprob-lem learning—i.e., the increase in rate of learning across problems. Later problems tend to be learned faster, a phenomenon known as *learning set* or *learning to learn*.

There are numerous accounts of this process (e.g., Medin, 1972; Reese, 1963), but evidence of relational knowledge comes in the form of virtually error-free performance on a new problem. Suppose that, after considerable interproblem training, a new problem is presented consisting of a *cross* and an *hourglass*. Suppose further that the participant chooses the cross and is not rewarded (*cross–*); and then, on the next trial, the hourglass is chosen and is rewarded (*hourglass+*), so it is chosen consistently thereafter. Some nonhuman primates can achieve this level of performance on a new prob-lem (Hayes, Thompson, & Hayes, 1953). If this pattern of behavior occurs consistently on new problems thereafter, it can be interpreted as the evi-dence of a relational representation that is used to predict unknown answers to problems. We would characterize the relational schema as knowledge that only one of two elements will be rewarded: Given $A+$ on the first trial, $B–$ can be predicted, and vice versa. The first trial of a new problem, therefore, constitutes an information trial, in that it indicates which of two stimuli is rewarded.

This behavior can be characterized in terms of the win-stay, lose-shift rule, but that is really only a behavioral description. In terms of relational knowledge theory, the relevant processes involve induction of a relational schema as a result of experience with a succession of isomorphic tasks (Halford & Wilson, 1980; Halford, Bain et al., 1998; Halford & Busby, 2007; Halford, Phillips, & Wilson, 2008). The schema comprises a representation of two elements with an exclusion relation between them: *Exclusive_ reward*($A+$, $B–$). Then the unknown task is mapped into the relational schema. If a stimulus is not rewarded (*cross–*), it is mapped to the unre-warded element of the schema (*cross* $\leftrightarrow$ $B–$). The other element is mapped to the rewarded element (*hourglass* $\leftrightarrow$ $A+$) by the exclusivity criterion (each element is mapped to one, and only one, element in the schema). After the necessary changes have been made, *hourglass* ↔ *A*+ on the information trial results in *cross* ↔ *B*– on the next trial. This is the fundamental process of analogical mapping, which underlies a great deal of higher cognition (Gentner, 2010; Halford, 1993; Holyoak, 2012). It is called the *generativity test* because it assesses the ability to generate information about unknown situations based on previously learned structures. Therefore, the win-stay, lose-shift rule is really evidence for the induction of a relational schema, which connects it to the considerable literature on relational and analogical reasoning.

Corroborative evidence for the relational interpretation is that, after training on many isomorphic problems, participants tend to learn little about specific stimuli in new problems, and associative learning becomes incidental (Bessemer & Stollnitz, 1971). Associative learning is no longer needed because new problems can be performed more efficiently by applying the relational schema induced from previous experience. This is a good example of how previously learned invariant structures can enhance adaptation to new situations.

There are two notable features of the generativity test. The first is that it can be used with inarticulate participants, including other animals (Halford et al., 2008; see also Penn, Holyoak, & Povinelli, 2008a). Use of language constitutes clear evidence of symbolic processes, and this typically occurs toward the end of the first year in human infants. However, an independent criterion is needed if we are to investigate the acquisition of symbolic processes and the role that they play in language development. A second feature of the generativity test is that it imposes no task demands beyond those required to demonstrate associative learning of a single problem. Thus, if, after extended training, a participant (whether animal, infant, child, or adult) applies a relational schema to a new problem, the evidence takes the form of consistent choice of the rewarded stimulus, as indicated by the information trial. At the behavior level, nothing more is required than consistently correct choice of a stimulus, but when it occurs in this way it indicates profound development of cognitive representations.

Comparison and labeling

Numerous studies indicate that comparison of structurally similar situations, provision of common labels, or both promote relational representation. Relational language facilitates relational processing (Loewenstein & Gentner, 2005), but it is not enough by itself, and comparison or mapping between instances appear to be essential. Gentner and Namy (2006) found better transfer to a new category after providing a common label for two instances than if the same label was attached to only one instance. Gick and Holyoak (1983) found that a verbal statement, or a diagram of the convergence principle (e.g., X-rays converging on a tumor or soldiers converging on a military target), did not promote relational encoding unless participants had experienced two embodiments. Thus, mapping between instances of relations appears to be crucial to the acquisition of relational knowledge.

Acquisition involving dynamic binding in working memory

Halford and Busby (2007) described how relational schemas can be acquired as a step toward symbolic processes. They agree with Reber (1967) and with Karmiloff-Smith (1994) that acquisition can begin with the implicit learning of links between elements, enabling unsupervised acquisition of structured knowledge. The importance of structural alignment is shown by the disruptive effect of the inconsistent condition in the relational schema induction paradigm. Structural alignment in turn depends on dynamic binding in working memory and can result in the recoding and acquisition of symbols.

Summary

Structural alignment is important in the transition from constants to variables and from associative to relational knowledge. Structured knowledge acquisition can be achieved by a wide variety of procedures, but all the paradigms that have been successful entail multiple embodiments of a common structure. Labeling and didactic inputs are helpful, but the process is largely self-supervised.

Strategy acquisition and planning

Relational knowledge operations are at the core of planning, which entails the integration of relations to provide a task model, a type of mental model for a sequence of actions. This was demonstrated by Halford, Wilson, and Phillips, (1998, §6.1.3) with the Tower of Hanoi (TOH) task, which is represented in chapter 4. Planning a move entails integrating a prerequisite move with the required move. For example, if Disk 2 has to be moved to peg B, and disk 1 is on top of disk 2 on peg A, then the relevant relations are:

Prior[*shift*(disk 2 to peg B), *shift*(disk 1 to peg C)]

Siegler's microgenetic methods for investigating strategy acquisition (Kuhn, 1995; Siegler, 1995; Siegler & Jenkins, 1989) have shown that more than one strategy is typically available at any one time, strategy strength varies in overlapping waves, and acquisition consists of selective strengthening of strategies. There is also evidence of transfer based on structural correspondence (Chen, Sanchez, & Campbell, 1997).

Structure, analogical mapping, and bootstrapping

Structured knowledge can provide a template for the acquisition of cognitive strategies. This was demonstrated by VanLehn and Brown (1980) for subtraction; and Greeno, Riley, and Gelman (1984) showed how the counting principles proposed by Gelman and Gallistel (1978) guided the acquisition of counting strategies.

Mapping to existing knowledge of even a primitive structure can be a powerful way of developing a symbolic representation. The children's story "Goldilocks and the Three Bears" (*Father bigger-than Mother bigger-than Baby*) can provide an analog for ordered set discrimination (Goswami, 1995). Furthermore, it provided a concept of an ordered set to guide acquisition of strategies in the TRIMM model (Halford et al. 1995). The concept of an ordered set can come from everyday experience, such as the story of the three bears, or nesting cups (*cup 1 fits-in cup 2 fits-in cup 3*, etc.).

Knowledge of ordered sets of at least three elements can be used to assess the outcome of ordering strategies. In the TRIMM model, bootstrapping is used to progress from immature strategies, such as concatenating relations without integration, to more adequate strategies, in which relations are integrated. Thus, given premises $c > d$, $a > b$, a concatenation strategy produces the order c, d, a, b; that is, the elements are ordered within pairs, but the second pair is simply concatenated to the first pair, without integration. However, the order $c > d < a$ does not match the concept of an ordered set as embodied in *Father bigger-than Mother bigger-than Baby* because there is no consistent correspondence between relations in the two structures. However, the order a, b, c, d does match the concept of an ordered set. Subsets $a > b > c$ or $b > c > d$ match *Father bigger-than Mother bigger-than Baby* by the criteria given in chapter 1 and figure 1.3. Once the correct order is recognized by matching to a template of an ordered set, a self-modifying production system generates new productions that integrate premises, yielding the order a, b, c, d, which is consistent with the concept of order, and the productions are strengthened selectively according to the success that they achieved. Thus, representation of structure guides the acquisition of a strategy.

Bootstrapping

Bootstrapping also is used to progress from evolutionarily ancient, innate, core number knowledge to an understanding of the way that numerals represent set sizes of more than four (Carey & Sarnecka, 2006). In the number concept model, Carey and Sarnecka (2006) suggest that the coordinate system comes from language and from learning the number list. These ideas have been taken further in a computational model of bootstrapping in numerical concept learning by Piantadosi, Tenenbaum, and Goodman (2012). Their goal was to account for the transition, at about 3 years and 6 months of age, from learning the individual number words *one, two, three* to understanding the cardinal principle (namely, that counting specifies the number of elements in a set). There are innate processes that enable sets up to about four elements to be quantified, and children learn to count at an early age but do not recognize that the count represents numerosity for sets of more than four elements. For example, they are unable to select the correct number of objects for sets such as *five,* even if they can count to 5 and beyond. Yet after about 3 years, 6 months, children learn the rule that an increase in the count by *one* corresponds to addition of one element to a set, and this principle can be applied recursively to arbitrarily large sets and numerals, thereby achieving a more abstract and far-reaching concept of numerosity. The successor relation *next* between numbers corresponds to the *one more* relation between sets. This constitutes a form of analogical mapping, but these concepts cannot be assumed, and it is the main purpose of this model to show how they can be built up out of primitive functions.

Mapping into a coordinate system is powerful, and it is ubiquitous in the acquisition of symbol systems. It is incorporated into a computational model of relational concept acquisition (Doumas, Hummel, & Sandhofer, 2008), which is discussed in chapter 7. Features are bound to objects yielding one-place predicates such as *big*(*elephant*) and *small*(*mouse*). These are mapped to two-place predicates by analogical processes, bootstrapping the representation to *bigger*(*elephant, mouse*). Mapping between relational representations is an important driver of the transition to symbolic processes and the consequent ability to generate inferences.

Gentner and Kurtz (2006, pp. 163–164) have outlined how analogical mapping is crucial to the acquisition of relational categories. They suggest that experience with relations based on the same dimension (within-dimension triads) leads to re-representation from *little-big-little* or *light-dark-light* to a dimension-independent representation that embodies the concept of symmetry such as *ABA*. This is another case of relational knowledge being acquired by structural alignment.

To summarize this section, mapping into a coordinate system is powerful. It appears to be ubiquitous in the acquisition of symbol systems, and it has been implemented in computational models, which will be considered in chapter 7. In the TRIMM model and in the number concept model, the prior knowledge of elements and relations between them (in one case incidentally acquired, and in the other case partly innate) is used as a coordinate system for developing a new symbolic concept.

Summary and conclusions

The transition to symbolic processes depends on the ability to represent structure, which in turn depends on dynamic assignment to a coordinate system in working memory. There is evidence that this ability develops late in the first year of human life. This evidence comes partly from reinterpretation of the $A\bar{B}$ task, which has been studied extensively over many decades, but its significance in this respect has been overlooked until recently (Halford et al., 2013). However, this proposal is corroborated by other evidence of the development of dynamic binding late in the first year. Our review of the acquisition literature enables us to formulate a number of principles, discussed next.

Acquisition principles

We have defined the essential properties of structured knowledge and reviewed diverse studies relevant to acquisition. What follows is our formulation of the principles that emerge from this work.

Self-supervised acquisition

Structured knowledge can be acquired from examples by self-supervised processes. This has been demonstrated in infant acquisition of verb meanings and of concepts such as animacy, and in the implicit transitive inference and implicit artificial grammar paradigms. Associative learning can yield links between entities and provides an autonomous beginning of structured knowledge acquisition. Structured knowledge also can be acquired through isomorphic tasks that embody the required structure. This last process has been investigated extensively but often has been treated under other conceptual rubrics, such as *learning set*, so its significance as a means of inducing relational schemas has been widely overlooked. However, there have been successful studies of this acquisition process, and there is a lot of potential for further investigation. Multilayered net models have demonstrated mechanisms that can achieve the acquisition of structured knowledge (albeit with limitations) without explicit instruction. Symbolic models have shown how relational representations can be formed by dynamic binding, and this process also has a high degree of autonomy because it is governed by structural correspondence that can be implemented independent of external input.

The *foundation for structured knowledge* can be found in infants in the form of image schemas and spatial schemas. These have structure, but it is not explicit in that the components and links between them are less accessible. It provides a foundation on which explicit structured representations could be built through structural alignment and recoding.

Associative processes can be seen from the paradigms mentioned in this discussion to play an important part in acquiring the foundations for structured knowledge. However, association is not sufficient in itself; it has to be supplemented by other processes.

Structural alignment is the core property from which other properties of relational knowledge emerge. We propose that ultimately, it is driven by prediction of outcomes because consistent alignment tends to optimize prediction. There is scope for deeper understanding of this fundamentally important process.

Formation of structured representations depends on binding a relation symbol and fillers (representations of elements related) into a structure in which the components retain their identity and are accessible to other processes. Symbolic connectionist models, although they differ in some respects, show some degree of consensus about binding mechanisms.

Mappings between structured representations can be formed, based on structural correspondence, which is a major factor governing the acquisition of structured knowledge. It is arguably the process that best distinguishes the acquisition of relational knowledge. This is corroborated by its uniqueness to higher primate (and possibly to human) cognition, and by neuroscience findings that it activates specific regions of the anterior prefrontal cortex (APFC), which are late in evolving and slow to develop. Structural correspondence has been well established in analogy theory and theory of representations; it influences the recognition of similarity and category formation, and it has been shown to be crucial to knowledge acquisition.

Formation of relational slots can occur as a result of aligning relational instances because slots can be defined by sets of entities that occupy one position in a relational representation. This means that positions in a relational representation must be distinguished, but slots need not be represented explicitly in initial acquisition. Once formed, a label needs to be bound to slots so that they can be identified in other cognitive processes.

Representation of variables is among the most important, but rarely recognized, effects of structurally consistent mappings. When instances of a relation are aligned, then the roles effectively function as variables and the acquisition of relational representations makes abstract symbols meaningful. There are neural net mechanisms by which this can occur, but there is potential for much more detailed investigation of these processes.

Verbal symbol formation, recoding, and re-representation are important processes, and symbols can emerge from multilayered nets. However, symbols will not work by themselves, and structural alignment of instances is essential. As Halford and Busby (2007) put it, structure comes before symbols, and structured representations are required to make symbols meaningful. That is, symbols do not create abstraction; rather, they represent abstraction achieved by putting relational representations in correspondence to one another, creating structural commonalities. There is considerable potential to utilize this fact in achieving abstraction in fields such as science and mathematics learning.

Dynamic binding between elements of relations in working memory is essential, both to the formation of relational representations and to mappings between relational representations. It plays a role in at least some structured knowledge acquisition. A model of working memory (Oberauer, 2009) based on dynamic binding to a coordinate system shows considerable promise of accounting for phenomena in this area.

Working memory load is a function of relational complexity, which can limit the structures that can be represented. However, this limit can be overcome in circumstances where the appropriate mapping is indicated by prior knowledge, or where structures can be decomposed, by segmentation, conceptual chunking, or both, into simpler structures that can be processed serially.

Emergence of meaning from initially meaningless, arbitrary materials has been shown to result from structured knowledge acquisition. There is considerable potential to exploit this process in a wide range of contexts.

Self-regulatory processes are crucial to structured knowledge acquisition. They are consistent with constructivist and dynamic systems conceptions of cognitive development (Fischer & Bidell, 2006), In the context of relational knowledge theory, mapping between structures provides a *self-regulatory mechanism* for cognitive growth. Although we have not pursued this issue here, it possibly captures some of what Jean Piaget (1950) and Lev Vygotsky (1962) intended by the assimilatory functions that they saw as foundational in cognitive development. None of this reduces the importance of instruction, but it implies that instruction should be designed to work in cooperation with the powerful autonomous acquisition processes, understanding of which has increased considerably. It also reintroduces logical reasoning which, while once taken as being at the core of thinking, has been displaced by mental models, heuristics, and knowledge access (Halford & Andrews, 2007), but now reappears in the form of structural consistency. Mental models arguably capture important aspects of human reasoning processes, but they are governed by structural correspondence principles, so they are self-regulating to some extent.

Social and cultural inputs are in no way diminished in importance by these principles because they direct attention, indicate goals and intentions, assist with encoding, and provide programs of experiences. However, cultural input needs to be linked to autonomous acquisition processes by using good analogs, as well as by enabling learners to find correspondence between instances of a relation to make relational symbols meaningful. The processes that we have outlined complement the considerable amount of accumulated knowledge of social and cultural factors in structured knowledge acquisition.

Conclusion

We have shown that the integration of contributions from numerous paradigms enables the essential properties of structured knowledge to be defined and shows that much is known about how it is acquired. Empirical studies of processes entailed in the acquisition of language, categorization, and thought can be expanded using this knowledge, while a number of other issues can be seen to warrant less research effort in the future. Rivalry between empirical paradigms such as implicit and explicit transitive inference, and between multilayered and symbolic neural net models, might be replaced by determination of the proper role of each type of process. Of more general importance, there may be no need for rivalry between associative and symbolic relational processes because their roles in structured knowledge acquisition can be seen to be complementary.

7 Neural Nets as Models of Acquisition Processes

In chapter 2, we examined neural net architectures as existence proofs for three levels of cognitive processes. Here, we consider some of the same types of architectures in terms of how effectively they model the acquisition of cognitive processes. In this chapter, we do not attempt to make a comprehensive review of the neural net literature because there are excellent reviews already available (McClelland et al., 2010 Thomas & McClelland, 2008). There is also a collection of papers on computational models of cognitive development edited by Marcovitch and Zelazo (2012). Recall that we see three types of net architectures: two-layered (nonstructured), multilayered (functionally structured), and symbolic connectionist (symbolically structured). These architectures were defined formally in chapter 2, and we considered how they implemented the properties that we attribute to the corresponding cognitive processes. In this chapter, we discuss how these architectures contribute to the acquisition of structured knowledge. Functionally structured and symbolically structured architectures are the most significant as models of structured knowledge acquisition. In addition, we are concerned with the question of whether the distinction between Ranks 1 and 2+ holds up when examined against the architectures and achievements of some of the most important models in the field.

Multilayered (including feedforward) models

In the multilayered nets covered in chapter 2, there is a link between an input, a computed or hidden layer, and an output layer. This corresponds to the multilayered networks that have been used to model multiple cognitive phenomena. Nets with this architecture are associative, in that the input is linked by variable weights to a representation comprising activations in hidden units, which is linked by another set of variable weights to the output.

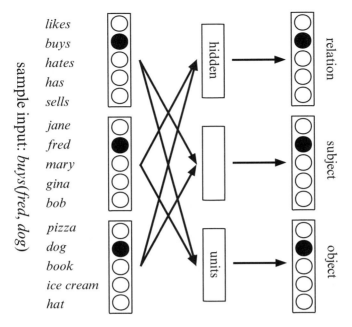

Figure 7.1.
Architecture for a feedforward net designed to achieve the accessibility property. This network tended to overgeneralize.

There are, of course, many variations of this architecture, but we will consider it in its most basic form first. The weights are adjusted incrementally in various ways (e.g., by backpropagation, by deep learning networks, and by autoencoding algorithms) to produce the required output. These processes are effective in adapting to the statistical linkages in the environment, and representations formed in the hidden layer as a result of computing outputs are important early in the acquisition process, but at least in many existing models, they do not result in relational representations that meet our criteria.

Wilson, Marcus, and Halford (2001) tested the extent to which backpropagation could be used to acquire binary relational representations with the accessibility property. Using a network connected as illustrated in figure 7.1, they trained it as an autoencoder.

They found that while the network could be trained on facts like *buys(Mary, book)* in a way that would allow *book* to be retrieved given inputs of *buys* and *Mary*, and also *Mary* to be retrieved given inputs of *buys* and *book*, the network training process tried to generalize from these facts, but did so in invalid ways. For example, when trained on a data set that included *likes(Jane, pizza)*, *likes(Fred, pizza)*, *likes(Fred, dog)*, but not *likes(Jane, dog)*, when *likes(Jane, pizza)* was entered into the trained net, the output signified *likes(Fred+Jane, pizza+dog)*.

There is a multitude of multilayered net models that demonstrate the emergence of cognitive representations as a direct result of learning to compute input–output functions. Rogers and McClelland (2004) modeled a domain-general process for acquisition of semantic knowledge based on the model of Rumelhart (1990), and Hinton (1990) modeled knowledge of family relations. However, a three-layered net of the balance scale by McClelland (1995) clearly demonstrates how structure can emerge from this class of models, and the study captures some crucial developmental findings. The input units represent weights and distances on each side of the balance beam, and the hidden units compare weights and distances. The output units compute the balance state. Metrics for weight and distance emerge due to training to compute the input–output function because the input units representing larger weights, or larger distances, acquire greater connection strengths to the hidden units. This is an elegant demonstration of the emergence of structure from a neural net model that computes input–output functions. The model also matches the observed course of acquisition of the balance scale concept in children.

The computed representation in the hidden units reflects relative weights and distances, but it is a partial representation of the relevant relations. The connection weights compute the effect of weights and distances on the hidden units, but they are not accessible to other cognitive processes. We can inspect the model and determine that $weight_1$ is greater than $weight_2$, which is greater than $weight_3$, etc., but this does not constitute knowledge in any process within the model, other than the process that computes the output. Furthermore, while the model computes the balance state as a function of weight and distance on each side in a way that captures some important developmental phenomena, it does not incorporate accessibility. It could not determine any variable given the other four (e.g., it does not compute weight on the left, given distance on the left, weight and distance on the right, and the balance state), although humans can do this (Halford, 1993), albeit in an approximate and intuitive manner. Also, this model does not enable structure-consistent mapping between relational representations, and therefore it cannot represent principles or rules of the balance beam. Nevertheless, it is a fundamentally important demonstration of how the beginnings of relational representations can emerge from interaction with the environment, through what are essentially associative processes.

The multilayered net developed by Rakison and Lupyan (2008) based on a simple recurrent net architecture (Elman, 1990) modeled the acquisition of correlations between object features and motion characteristics that underpin the concept of animacy. Their success in simulating infancy data supports their claim to have defined a mechanism for learning perceptual regularities, and in our view, they are justified in not claiming that it leads to abstract concepts. This fits well with our assessment of the achievements and limitations of multilayered net models in accounting for the acquisition of structured knowledge. Their model does not cover as wide a range of concepts as the perceptual meaning analysis of Mandler (2004), but it gives a more explicit and detailed account of processes. There seems to be considerable potential to integrate these processes in future research.

A multilayered net model by Leech, Mareschal, and Cooper (2008) demonstrates the role of some elementary processes, including relational priming and relational knowledge, in analogy. We agree that relational processing, including analogy, can emerge from more elementary processes, and this is part of the motivation for neural net models. Symbolic connectionist models also depend on the interaction of simpler processes. However, as Phillips (2008) has pointed out, while the model by Leech, Mareschal, and Cooper (2008) can account for processes that occur early in the acquisition of relations, it must be supplemented by other processes if it is to account for symbolic processes that are manifestly part of child and adult cognition. In their conclusion, the researchers appear to be in broad agreement with this point. This chapter is about these additional processes.

Studies of infant categorization have provided important generalizations about early acquisitions that support the proposals of Rakison and Lupyan (2008). Infants develop prototypes of shapes, animals, or faces (Bomba & Siqueland, 1983; Quinn, Eimas, & Rosenkrantz, 1993; Quinn & Johnson, 1997) as young as 3–4 months of age, and they are sensitive to correlations between features at 9–10 months (Cohen & Cashon, 2006; Mareschal, 2003; Shultz & Cohen, 2004). As discussed in chapter 5, prototypes can be regarded as primitive categories that can be acquired by associative processes such as those in multilayered nets (Cohen & Cashon, 2006; Mareschal, 2003; Shultz & Cohen, 2004), and they are not compositional (Fodor, 1994), but they constitute an excellent early step in the acquisition of conceptual knowledge.

Emergence of structure can be simulated using cascade correlation, an algorithm that adds units to the hidden unit layer of a three-layered net model to take account of extra dimensions in the task (Shultz, 1998, 2012). These models represent serious computational attempts to account for transitions to new levels of structure but, as with other multilayered net models, there is no accessible representation of relations and there are no working memory processes that would permit the formation of mental models (Halford & Andrews, 2006; Halford et al., 2012).

Multilayered nets also have been claimed to provide limited generalization and to be unable to learn rules (Clark & Thornton, 1998) or to exhibit strong systematicity (Phillips, 1998). In their classic criticism of neural nets, Fodor and Pylyshyn (1988) argued cogently that they are not compositional. We agree that this is true of multilayered nets, but we agree with Van Gelder and Niklasson (1994) that many cognitive processes are not compositional, so this should not be a criterion for all models. It is a criterion for relational knowledge, however, and we are not aware of any multilayered nets that fully implement compositionality.

Hidden unit activations in a multilayered neural net can represent relational features such as degree of difference between pairs of elements in the inputs (Altmann & Dienes, 1999; Seidenberg & Elman, 1999) as discussed in chapter 5 (see figure 5.3). For example, they enable discrimination between pairs, by responding *same* to *AA* or *BB*, but *different* to *AB* and *BA*. Activations of hidden units that respond differentially to *same/different* inputs represent a relational feature but do not constitute a symbol for a relation as defined in chapter 2 because there is no binding between the symbol and fillers. One consequence is that a neural net that computes functions *A, A* → *same; A, B* → *different* does not meet the accessibility criterion, so it would not permit responses such as *A, same* → *A*; *A, different* → *B*, etc. Importantly, however, it could be a step toward the acquisition of a relational representation. If units representing relational features become bound to arguments, with structural alignment as in symbolic connectionist models, a relational representation forms.

The multilayered net models that we have considered in this chapter compute representations that generate input–output links. Consequently, they reflect conceptual similarities, including prototypic categories, based on common input–output functions. They are sensitive to statistical regularities, including input–output correlations (Saxe, McClelland, & Gangoli, 2013), which are an important step toward the acquisition of relational knowledge. However, we are not aware of multilayered models that explicitly represent relational instances $R(a_1, ..., a_n)$ in an accessible form, or in a form that implements all the functions of relational knowledge. The representations within the hidden layer or layers are more like configurations than structures because they do not incorporate the properties of relational knowledge (see, for example, the representations in figure 2.1D in chapter 2). They show how symbols can be generated to represent relational features of inputs, but they do not incorporate a symbol that is bound to the slots of a relation; they cannot form structure-consistent mappings between representations; modification is incremental as a function of input–output links, rather than strategic; and representations do not have the accessibility property and cannot be manipulated dynamically in working memory. A major empirical consequence is that they would not account for some cases of transfer between isomorphs that can be predicted by symbolic connectionist models (Phillips & Halford, 1997).

Multilayered models form representations over hundreds or thousands of trials by incremental adjustment of connection weights, so they most closely simulate the formation of representations directly in semantic memory. Some models incorporate fast-learning of new connection weights that expedite the acquisition processes (e.g., Rogers & McClelland, 2004, discussed later in this chapter), but they do not implement dynamic mapping in working memory, which we argue to be essential to the formation of relational knowledge. Nevertheless, these models are important, even to the point of achieving major breakthroughs in many contexts, including plausible mechanisms for laying the foundations of relational knowledge. However, these achievements must be supplemented by symbolic connectionist processes.

Knowledge of family relations (e.g., *father, mother, wife*) is simulated in a neural net model of Hinton (1986, 1990). Given a person in role 1 and a relation as inputs, it produces a person in role 2; for example, (*Penelope, mother-of*) → *James*. As with the Rumelhart (1990) model, it adjusts representations to be appropriate to functions processed. When trained on two isomorphic family trees, one using English names and one Italian, it produced similar representations for corresponding persons in each tree. It also made microinferences based on relations, so that if *person*$_1$ was married to *person*$_2$, and *person*$_1$ was old, it represented *person*$_2$ as old. Thus, two elements have similar representations if they participate in similar relational contexts. The family knowledge net learns concept unit representations that reflect common functional relational contexts. Therefore, it has a conceptual power analogous to that of the semantic cognition model of Rogers and McClelland, based on the similarity of concept representations.

However, the family knowledge model is restricted in its ability to represent and process relations. It does not have the accessibility property because the input always comprises a person in role$_1$ and a relationship, while the output is always a person in role$_2$. It cannot process a query such as "Penelope relationship? James" (i.e., what relationship is Penelope to James?). The model cannot combine or integrate relations. For example, if it knows that *person$_1$* is the father of *person$_2$*, and also the father of *person$_3$*, it cannot infer that *person$_2$* is the brother of *person$_3$*. These points in no way diminish the achievements of this model, but they corroborate the distinction between Rank 1 and Ranks 2+.

A simple recurrent net (Elman, 1990) is like a three-layered net in that it has input units, hidden units, and output units, but it also has context units and recurrent connections that allow the context units to act like a memory to some extent. Activations in the hidden units during a given trial are copied into context units. In the next trial, activations in the hidden units are influenced by activations in both the input units and the context units. The result is that the output of the net is influenced by representations in previous trials, as well as by the current input. Thus, the net takes account of links between events in a sequence.

Simple recurrent net–based models have learned to predict the next word in a sentence, respecting grammatical categories (Elman, 1990), even when they included embedded clauses (Elman, 1993). Cluster analysis of the hidden unit activations showed that words in the same grammatical category, such as nouns or verbs, tended to have similar activations. Semantically similar words, such as those representing animals or foods, also tended to have similar hidden unit representations, although the same word tends to have *slightly* different representations in different contexts. For example, *house* might be represented differently in "cleaning the house" than in "demolishing the house."

It is important to note that the grammatical categories that are recognized by cluster analysis are accessible to the psychologist as an investigator, but they are not accessible to the processes within the net. They are knowledge *in* the system, but not knowledge *to* the system (Clark & Karmiloff-Smith, 1993). The activations in the hidden units are used to compute the input–output function, but they cannot function as grammatical categories for other purposes. Simple recurrent nets typically learn to compute next-item-prediction tasks, e.g., *word* → *next-word,* and the hidden-unit representations that they create while learning the task depend on this prior context. Thus, the representations in Elman's experiments acquired properties that reflect the structure of the environment, which in this case incorporated certain properties of language. But it is important not to project our understanding of grammatical categories onto this model.

The semantic cognition model of Rogers and McClelland

The semantic cognition model of Rogers and McClelland (2004) is shown in figure 7.2 and comprises five layers of interconnected units. A layer of

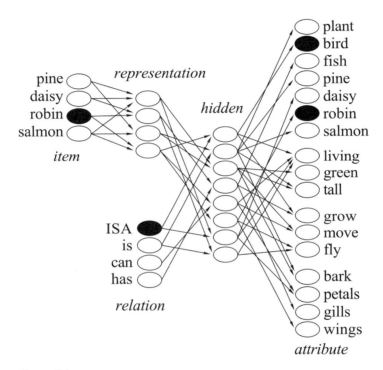

Figure 7.2.
Schematic depiction of the feed-forward net model [Reproduced from figure 3a by Halford, Wilson, and Phillips (2010), which was adapted from Rogers & McClelland (2004), figure 2.2]. The net comprises five layers of units: *item* (input) units represent plants (*pine, oak, rose, daisy*) and animals (*robin, canary, sunfish, salmon*). Each item unit is connected to every unit in a layer of *representation units. Relation units* represent relational inputs or "contexts" (*ISA, is, can, has*). Every representation and relation unit is connected to all units in a layer of *hidden units*, which in turn are connected to all units in a layer of *attribute (output) units* that represent attributes (e.g., *living thing, plant, …, salmon, …, tall, … living, green, … grow, move, … wings, skin*). The activations shown (filled circles) represent *robin ISA bird*.

item units represents plants (*pine, oak, rose, daisy*) and animals (*robin, canary, sunfish, salmon*), while another set of units represents relations (*ISA, is, can,* has). Each item unit is connected to every unit in a layer of *representation units*. Every representation and relation unit is connected to all units in a layer of *hidden units*, which in turn are connected to all units in a layer of *attribute* (output) units that represent such attributes as *living thing, plant, animal, tree, flower, bird, fish, pine, …, salmon, pretty, tall, …, living, …, yellow, grow, move, …, sing, bark, petals, …, roots, skin.* The basic network is depicted in Rogers and McClelland (2004, figure 2.2, p. 57, and an extended network in figure 3.10, p. 115).

The model is derived in part from an earlier model by Rumelhart (1990) and shows how a type of abstraction can emerge from training a feedforward network to predict attributes of objects, given a relational context. For example, given the pair of inputs *canary* and *can*, outputs are produced such as *move* (canary can move), *fly* (canary can fly), etc. The network is trained using a backpropagation algorithm to activate attribute units in the output layer in response to an item and relation pair in the input.

Activations in representation and hidden units are distributed (i.e., represent elements by multiple units) and are initially neutral (activations set to zero), but as a result of training, they gradually come to represent the similarities and differences of kinds of objects but do not represent explicit semantic properties of objects. This is a subtle feature of the model, which enables the simulation of some fundamentally important phenomena. One of these is the ability to interpret and use new information, such as *a sparrow is a bird* (assuming that the net has not been trained on *sparrow*). This is achieved by *backpropagation-to-representation*, utilizing knowledge that is stored in the network in the form of connection weights between units. The process can be summarized as follows (précis of Rogers & McClelland, p. 64):

A neutral representation is created on representation units (all activations set to zero), appropriate input and relation units (e.g., *sparrow* and *ISA*) are activated, and activation is fed forward to the output units. The output is compared to the correct activation of the appropriate output unit, and an error signal is generated to adjust activations in the representation layer. This process is iterated, making a small adjustment each time, until the error signal becomes zero-order. The process can be applied to several propositions about an object, and the resulting activations of the representation units come to resemble the pattern for objects with similar attributes (e.g., birds such as canary and robin). The new information is stored by fast-learning of new connection weights between the item and representation units and between the latter and the hidden units [in a process that reflects the operation of the hippocampus according to the model of McClelland, McNaughton & O'Reilly (1995)]. The network then becomes able to infer new propositions based on similarity of new items to previously learned items: That is, after being told *"a sparrow is a bird,"* it infers *"sparrow can fly," "sparrow has wings,"* etc. This is an important inference that occurs relatively automatically because of a newly created representation of *sparrow* that is similar to representations of other birds and is similarly connected to the hidden and output layers.

This achievement occurs because their model captures the effect of "coherent covariation of properties" (Rogers & McClelland, 2004, pp. 91 *ff.*) across different items. In essence, this occurs because similar items, such as *robin* and *canary,* lead to similar sets of attributes being activated in the output layer (both are living, animal, bird, have skin, etc.), which produces similar error signals to the representation layer. The representations in that layer become adjusted (by backpropagation-to-representation) so that they reflect the covariation of properties. This effect is modulated by the level of the hierarchy so that, for example, *robin* and *canary* are most similar and *robin* and *salmon* are less similar than *robin* and *canary,* but as both are animate, they are more similar than (say) *oak* and *canary,* which are both living but not both animate.

One important property of the model is that representations become adjusted so that they represent "semantic similarity relationships" (p. 62) that have not been perceived. Similarities reflected in the representations layer reflect attributes that have become associated with items (e.g., canaries can fly, have wings, etc.), and this information becomes linked to new input, such as sparrows. The model also simulates progressive differentiation from holistic categories to higher-order categories (*animate* versus *inanimate*) to basic (*fish* versus *bird*) to subordinate (*canary* versus *robin*)—a phenomenon that has been observed frequently in children's acquisition of categories.

One implication of the model is that the structure of representations comes to reflect implicit knowledge of similarities at different levels of the hierarchy. Importantly, this yields the ability to recognize features of conceptual hierarchies without explicit knowledge, so the model (and, by implication, children whose cognitive development is simulated) can make judgments based on similarities that they have not perceived, but which are implied by what they know. Thus, the similarities of their representations of different birds (e.g., canaries and robins) allow them to generalize about the properties of birds, but without necessarily knowing explicitly that canaries and robins are both birds. This gives the model the ability to account for category induction as observed in young children, and as discussed in chapter 5 (also see the review by Gelman & Kalish [2006] and the analysis by Halford & Andrews [2006]). The basic logic is that children are shown a picture of an entity from a familiar category (e.g., *dog*), are told an unfamiliar but plausible fact about the entity (has a spleen), and then are found to generalize more on the basis of category membership than perceptual similarity (generalize more to a dissimilar dog than to a similar animal from another category). A plausible hypothesis is that the generalization is based on similarity of representations of members of the same category, independent of perceptual similarity of input, and that the model offers an existence proof of a process that could yield representations with the appropriate similarity properties. It is also consistent with the idea that categories can develop through observation of events in which entities take part (Mandler, 2000; Halford, Wilson, & Phillips, 2010). Thus, we might categorize *bicycles* and *ships* together because both are used to move people. The semantic cognition model provides a plausible account of these important phenomena, and in some ways, it complements our relational complexity account of children's category inductions, outlined in chapter 5.

On the other hand, as Halford, Wilson, and Phillips (2010) have pointed out, the semantic cognition model does not include an explicit representation of structure, such as inclusion relations, as discussed in chapters 1 and 5. Therefore, given a proposition such as "In city X, there are both boys and girls," it would not be able to infer that there are more children than boys. There is also no mapping based on structural correspondence, and no active construction of relational representations in working memory. Thus, the model features some very impressive achievements, but it does not invalidate the distinction between functionally structured (Rank 1) and symbolically structured (Rank 2+) cognition.

Semantic similarity effects in analogy

A recurrent neural net model by Kollias and McClelland (2013) entails training a network to represent relations of the form *aRb* and *cRd,* and then to find the best-fitting analogy of two choices; that is, given *aRb,* it finds the best analog of cRd_1 or cRd_2 (e.g., *pig:boar::dog:wolf* or *cat*). The better solution is *wolf,* because the relation (*wilder version of*) is closer to the relation between *pig* and *boar*. Relational components *ab*, *aR*, and *Rb* are each presented one-third of the time, and the net was trained to produce the remaining component (i.e., to produce *R* when given *ab*, *b* when given *aR*, and *a* when given *Rb*). Representations of relations were formed in hidden units during training. The net was tested on analogies without further training, and it succeeded in finding the solution with the *cd* relation that was most similar to the *ab* relation. This model simulates some important effects of relational semantic similarity, it advances our knowledge of how relational representations can be trained, and it includes a version of the accessibility property that is absent from many of the models that we have considered. There is also a form of structural alignment where *aRb* is aligned with *cRd*, but the alignment is built into the architecture and is not formed in working memory by structural correspondence.

Symbolic connectionist models

There are neural net models, usually known as *symbolic connectionist models*, that implement the criterial properties of structured knowledge defined in chapter 2 (Doumas, Hummel, & Sandhofer, 2008). The essence of these models is a mapping between two relational representations, based on structural correspondence and with a composition operation defined on the relations (as in premise integration, discussed in chapters 2 and 4, with respect to transitive inference, categorical syllogisms, and other types of reasoning). This mapping is dynamic and attentional, imposes a processing load in working memory, and corresponds to conscious experience. These models implement dynamic bindings between relation symbols and fillers: i.e., the components retain their identity in the binding and are accessible to other cognitive processes. New operations come into play at this level, including recoding of structures, joining (combining and integrating), accessing components by their roles (projecting) or fillers (selecting), chunking representations, and forming higher-order relations (Phillips, Halford, & Wilson, 1995). Whereas functionally structured processes are *online*, meaning that they are connected to input–output functions, symbolically structured processes are *offline*, meaning that they do not include an inherent link to output. They must be supplemented by planning functions, motor programming functions, or both, but absence of the constraint to compute input–output functions directly increases the flexibility of representations and enables higher levels of abstraction.

The Discovery of Relations by Analogy (DORA) model

The Discovery of Relations by Analogy (DORA) model (Doumas et al., 2008) is an outgrowth of the Learning and Inference with Schemas and Analogies (LISA) connectionist model of analogies and schema induction (Hummel & Holyoak, 1997, 2003). Relations are represented in DORA by four layers of units and the connections between them, as shown in figure 7.3. At the top are *P (Proposition)* units (e.g., *loves(John,Sally)*), which are linked to *PO (predicate-object)* units (*John, lover; Sally, beloved*) via *RB (role-binding)* units (*John + Lover, Sally + beloved*). The PO units are connected to semantic units that represent features of objects (e.g., *male, adult, ..., has-emotion*). RB units bind objects to roles in the proposition, so *John* is bound to the *lover* role in the proposition *loves(John, Sally)*, and so on. The P→PO→RB links effectively bind the predicate (relation symbol) to the arguments, as required for relational representations as described in chapter 2. In DORA and LISA, as in earlier models like SHRUTI (Shastri & Ajjanagadde, 1993), the role (in this case *lover*) is represented explicitly, but this is not true in models such as the Structured Tensor Analogical Reasoning (STAR) model, to be considered later in this chapter.

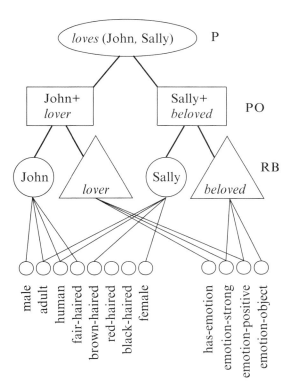

Figure 7.3
Outline of the architecture of the DORA model (adapted from figure 2b in Doumas, Hummel and Sandhofer [2008]). Copyright © American Psychological Association, by permission.

The structural alignment property of symbolically structured processes is implemented by role-filler bindings. The bindings are dynamic and are coded by firing synchronously, as in LISA, or SHRUTI, or in close temporal proximity, as in DORA (see also the discussion in chapter 3). For example, to represent *loves(John, Sally)*, the units representing the *lover* role fire in close temporal proximity with units representing *John*, while units representing *loved* fire in close temporal proximity with *Sally*. Units representing the *lover* role fire out of synch with units representing the *loved* role, as do their fillers, so *John* fires out of synch with *Sally*. This is illustrated in figure 3.1 in chapter 3. Retrieval from long-term memory occurs due to activation that originates with the P unit and passes through RB and PO units to semantic units, which excite units in long-term memory. Mapping occurs by concurrent activation of units in two analogs, aided by mapping hypotheses linking corresponding units (mapping P to P, RB to RB, etc.). These processes take account of semantic similarity effects. Structural alignment and mapping are important in the acquisition of relational/symbolic processing. DORA implements these acquisition processes using role-filler bindings and synchronous firing.

Structured Tensor Analogical Reasoning (STAR) model

The STAR model (Halford, Wilson & Phillips, 1998; Wilson, Halford et al., 2001) was outlined in chapter 3, but it is considered further here for comparison with DORA and other models. STAR is one of a number of conjunctive coding models (e.g., Plate, 1995), and was based on a memory model (Humphreys, Bain, & Pike, 1989) and an analogy model by Smolensky (1990). In STAR, relational representations are formed by binding the relation symbol and arguments into an array, as shown in figure 3.2. For example, the relation *likes(John, Sally)* is represented by activations on three sets of input units, representing *likes, John,* and *Sally.* A mathematical treatment is given in box 3.3 in chapter 3. The activations of the binding units are formed dynamically in working memory as the direct result of activations in the input units. Thus, the relational representation can be formed in a single trial, and it lasts as long as the activations persist. The relation *likes(Ken, Tina)* is represented by an array formed by different sets of input units, giving a different pattern of activation in the binding units, as shown in figure 3.2B.

The relation symbol and roles are represented by positions in the representation, so the symbol *loves* and roles *lover* and *loved* correspond to different ranks of the array. This gives a natural correspondence to relational representations in predicate calculus expressions such as *loves(John, Sally)* and often also in natural language constructions (*John loves Sally*), where *lover* and *loved* occupy specific positions in the sentence.

The representations of relational instances can be superimposed, so the representation of *likes(Ken, Tina)* in figure 3.2B can be superimposed on *likes(John, Sally)* to form a composite representation, as shown in figure 3.2C. Notice that this is distinguishable from the superimposed representations of *loves(John, Tina)* and *loves(Ken, Sally)* in figure 3.2D. The components (symbol and arguments) retain their identities in the composite representation, and the role assignments are maintained. (This is achieved in the LISA and DORA models by having distinct P nodes for the different relational instances—thus, the P nodes serve in LISA/DORA to bind the relation symbol and the arguments/fillers, as well as the role symbols.)[1]

Superposition enables the recognition of commonalities because common features have more influence on the output. It also can provide a representation of relational slots because a slot corresponds to all the elements in a specific position in the representation. Given a structural alignment mechanism, relational representations can be formed initially without explicit representation of slots. The representation of *loves* could originate as a relational feature in a multilayered net, but it is the binding of the feature to the arguments (*John* and *Sally*) that enables it to function as a relational symbol.

Both LISA/DORA and STAR models implement many properties of relational knowledge. We consider that Doumas, Hummel, and Sandhofer (2008) are justified in their claim that "DORA serves as an existence proof that relational representations can be learned from examples, thereby addressing one of the fundamental problems facing symbolic models of cognition" (p. 30). We also see a consensus that LISA and DORA model analogy and relational schema induction and provide a plausible (if limited) mechanism for cognitive development, and there is some supporting neurological evidence for synchronous activation as a binding mechanism.

STAR also implements many properties of relational knowledge (Halford, Wilson, & Phillips, 1998; Wilson, Halford et al., 2001). It has accessibility because any component can be retrieved from the relational representation, it can determine the truth value of a proposition, and it implements systematicity, strategic modifiability, analogical reasoning, structural correspondence, and representation of variables. It can account for processing load increases as a function of cognitive complexity and for capacity limitations, and it implements higher-order relations. The Relational Concept (Relcon) model (Gray et al., 2006) shows how relational categories that exhibit prototypicality and context sensitivity can be formed with the STAR architecture. In addition, similarity judgments that respect structural alignments can be simulated.[2]

Complexity and capacity

One of the most important implications of these models is that LISA/DORA and STAR account for processing load and, indirectly, for capacity limitations (Halford, Wilson, & Phillips, 1998; Hummel & Holyoak, 2003). This is illustrated in figure 3.1 in chapter 3. In LISA/DORA, representational rank corresponds to the number of distinct phases, so the Rank 3 representation, *loves,* requires three phases (as shown in figure 3.1A) and the Rank 4 counterpart, *gives,* requires four phases (figure 3.1B). In STAR, representational rank is identical to the rank of the tensor representation (figure 3.1C). Capacity limitations are predicted because there is a limit to the number of distinct phases that can be represented (Hummel & Holyoak, 2003; Doumas, Hummel, & Sandhofer, 2008). In STAR, there is a limit to the number of ranks that can be bound into a representation. The reason is that if each vector comprises n elements, the number of binding units required (as in figure 3.2) is n^r where r is rank. This leads to an exponential increase in processing load as a function of representational rank.

Structured knowledge can be acquired by cumulative storage of instances of relations. This can be illustrated using the balance scale model. The balance state depends on moments on the two sides, where moments are products of weights and distances on that side. For simplicity, we will consider the left side only (as the same argument applies to the right side). The weights, distances, and moments on each side of the balance can be represented by vectors; e.g., on the left side, we have $v_{weightL}$, $v_{distanceL}$, and $v_{momentL}$. Each instance of this relation can be represented by the outer products of three vectors, which can be superimposed to represent cumulative knowledge.

Symbolic connectionist models effectively implement mapping between relational representations, which we propose to be a driver of the transition to symbolic processes, and the consequent ability to generate inferences. This means that structural alignment would be the principal means by which foundational structures, such as the image-schema agency discussed in chapter 5, can be formed into explicit relational concepts. If the components *source, path,* and *goal* are aligned in successive instances of agency, then a binding to a symbol can be formed, and the components become individually accessible through their occupancy in the slots of the resulting structure. Perhaps the most important implication of these symbolic connectionist models is that both demonstrate the role of dynamic working memory processes in the acquisition and processing of relational knowledge.

Although multilayered and symbolic connectionist models are both composed of elementary processes, it is clear that they operate in very different ways. The symbolic connectionist models, LISA/DORA and STAR, show how the properties of relational knowledge can be implemented. Multilayered neural net models complement symbolic models by showing how representations can emerge from processing input–output functions, but they do not result in the representation of relations that meet our criteria in chapter 2 for symbolically structured cognition. The acquisitions modeled by two layered nets can lay foundations for relational knowledge by forming links between elements. All these architectures provide an existence proof for processes entailed in the acquisition and operation of relational processes, but at this time, none tells the whole story.

Bayesian Analogy with Relational Transformations (BART) model

The Bayesian Analogy with Relational Transformations (BART) model (Lu, Chen, & Holyoak, 2012) is a computational model that acquires relational representations from experience with perceptually available nonrelational features. Learning is efficient, requiring only a small number of instances, and can proceed from exclusively positive instances (i.e., negative instances can be utilized but are not essential to acquisition). It shows more adequate generalization to novel instances than is typical of neural net models; it can perform a variety of functions; including analogy; and it can account for and simulates important phenomena such as the symbolic distance effect (i.e., better discrimination among representations that are more different). Its most significant advance is that it begins with featural, nonrelational inputs, whereas symbolic connectionist models such as DORA and STAR require handcrafted input representations. It effectively integrates some properties of Bayesian and symbolic models of cognition. Specifically: "Given feature vectors corresponding to pairs of objects, the model uses statistical learning to update weights associated with feature dimensions for various comparative relations (e.g., larger, fiercer), and then uses its learned weights to decide whether novel pairs instantiate a specified relation." (Lu, Chen, & Holyoak, 2012, p. 622). On the other hand, it appears that the objects are assigned to slots (larger, smaller, etc.).

The problem of how to assign elements to slots remains to be solved for computational models of relational knowledge. BART begins with features and proceeds to forming relations between pairs (binary relations) by bootstrapping from single-place predicates. One restriction of BART is that it might be difficult to apply to predicates such as *opposite* or *between*, which are not readily reducible to sets of features. However, BART represents a promising new direction in models of relational knowledge acquisition.

Halford, Wilson, and Phillips (2010) suggest that the multilayered net and symbolic connectionist models simulate "[c]omplementary but distinct processes" (p. 503). The multilayered net models show powerful learning mechanisms that appear to lay the foundation for relational knowledge, but there are properties such as structural alignment and structure-consistent mapping that are not captured by these models, at least in their present form. They also do not incorporate a role for working memory in forming structured representations. Given that working memory accounts for a high proportion of variance in fluid intelligence, as discussed in chapter 5, this suggests that there is still a significant gap between multilayered models and higher cognition. Therefore, we continue to claim that there are properties of symbolically structured cognition that are unique.

Neural net models of acquisition

Neural net models have captured a wide range of phenomena in structured knowledge acquisition. Some very significant acquisition mechanisms have been demonstrated, from laying the foundation for relational knowledge as in multilayered nets to capturing the properties of high-level relational knowledge, as in symbolic connectionist models. An important feature of these models is that they show, in their diverse ways, how new structured representations can emerge from more elementary processes. There is the potential for an answer to the fundamentally important problem of how new structured knowledge can be acquired. As with the proposals of Allen and Bickhard (2013a,b), structured knowledge acquisition research frees theorists from excessive dependence on innate foundations. The literature that we review here suggests the answer lies in deeper and more wide-ranging acquisition mechanisms that enable the emergence of higher cognition from more elemental processes. Investigation of all the different types of models, whether multilayered or symbolic, has value in pursuing this important goal.

The differences between multilayered models and symbolic models demonstrate the reality of process differences being observed empirically. No single model has yet accounted for the entire process, and we have outlined some crucial issues that remain, but the achievements so far give one plenty of encouragement to accept structured knowledge acquisition as a major phenomenon in cognition and cognitive development.

Notes

1. The vector representing an element remains constant across bindings, as Holyoak and Hummel (2000) acknowledge (see, for example, their figure 9.1). We consider that their further claim that tensor representations are not constant because they occur in different vector spaces (p. 244) is untenable because it would mean that symbols in general lose their identity when they occur in different spaces or in different media. Thus, *CAT* in print would not be the same symbol as when it appears on a computer screen, nor would it retain its identity when it is transmitted to different brain regions.

2. It is useful to clarify the relationship between the *symbol-argument-argument* representation of relations used in STAR and the *role-filler* representation used in LISA/DORA. LISA/DORA build into the representation of relational instances the names of roles like *lover* and *beloved*, while STAR retrieves this information, when needed, from semantic memory in the form of schemas like *schema(loves, [lover, beloved])*. The two systems become formally equivalent for representing relational instances once this is recognized (cf. Doumas and Hummel, 2004). LISA/DORA also have semantic or microfeatural units (shown at the bottom of figure 7.3.).

The equivalence is via a reified version of the LISA/DORA representation: Using the setup in figure 7.3 as an example, the *P* unit is expressed (reified) using a name such as *loves1*, and then the three predicates *instance(loves, loves1)*, *roleFiller(loves1, lover, John)*, and *roleFiller(loves1, beloved, Sally)* capture the content of figure 7.3. The "*John+lover*" *PO* node together with its subordinate *RB* nodes "*John*" and "*lover*" corresponds to *roleFiller(loves1, lover, John)*. Once the *schema(loves, [lover, beloved])* is accessed, the STAR representation *loves(John, Sally)* can be converted into the format just described. Conversely, the three predicates can be used to reconstruct the schema and the *symbol-argument-argument* version. These conversions can be done entirely automatically, by an algorithm with no special knowledge of the meanings being encoded.

8 Human Reasoning and Relational Knowledge

In this chapter, we examine some state-of-the art models of inference to assess how our conception of relational knowledge fits with some advanced forms of cognition. Conceptions of human reasoning underwent major transformations in the 20th century. While George Boole (1951) regarded his treatise on logic as defining the laws of thought, an enormous body of subsequent research raised doubts as to whether logic could be regarded as the norm of human reasoning. Many alternatives were proposed, including psycho-logic (Braine, 1978: Piaget, 1950, 1957), logical rules of inference (Rips, 2001), information-processing models (Anderson 1983; Newell & Simon, 1972), heuristics (Gigerenzer & Goldstein, 1996; Kahneman & Tversky, 1973; Kahneman, Slovic, & Tversky, 1982; Tversky & Kahneman, 1973), mental models (Johnson-Laird, 1983), modular processes (Cosmides & Tooby, 1992), and Bayesian rationality (Oaksford & Chater, 2007). Human susceptibility to fallacies, as revealed in many studies on reasoning (e.g., Kahneman & Tversky, 1973), tended to cast doubt on our inherent rationality—a rather somber conclusion when you reflect on the necessity of rationality in dealing with the world. Fortunately, a conception of adaptive rationality (Anderson, 1990) replaced the normative conception that appeared to suggest an overwhelming susceptibility to fallacy. The essential idea is that heuristics are more rational than they seem when the nature of the environment is taken into account.

The fragmentation implied by these diverse theories is rather daunting to anyone who wants to see even minimal coherence, but the picture becomes much more optimistic if we cease to focus exclusively on differences and instead look for common ground. We do this in many contexts throughout this book, but at this point, it is appropriate to outline the essence of our proposal in more detail. In this chapter, we consider a number of important cognitive processes to illustrate how some issues can become more tractable if analyzed in terms of our relational knowledge formulation.

We have proposed that relational knowledge captures many core properties of higher cognition, but this apparently conflicts with some other theories, such as those based on heuristics. The essence of heuristic accounts is that they require little cognitive effort and frequently yield valid solutions. Thus, heuristics are ecologically rational (Arkes, 2012). One of the most notable heuristic accounts is Bayesian rationality theory (Oaksford & Chater, 2007), which offers quantified predictions of performance in conditional reasoning, categorical syllogisms and Wason Selection Tasks, all of which have been major areas of interest to theorists of reasoning. We considered categorical syllogisms in chapter 4, where we showed that relational complexity theory accounts for as much problem form variance as the probability heuristics model (Oaksford & Chater, 2007), both being at the realistic maximum. However, relational complexity applies to a sufficiently wide range of cognitive processes to be regarded as a general complexity metric. In this chapter, we consider categorical syllogisms further and analyze the Wason Selection Task, including the previously neglected role that cognitive complexity plays in it. We consider essential points of comparison between Bayesian rationality and relational knowledge theory and propose that relational knowledge offers a more integrated account of both domains.

Bayesian rationality

Oaksford and Chater (2001) proposed that propositions as used in reasoning should be interpreted as conditional probabilities: "Thus the statement that *birds fly* claims that the conditional probability of something flying, given that it is a bird, is high." (p. 350, italics in original). They go on to derive conditional probabilities for conditionals (if *p*, then *q*) and show that it can account for some important findings, such as modus ponens being easier than modus tollens. We fully accept the claim that most propositions, as understood by humans engaged in natural reasoning (i.e., reasoning not based on formal logic or mathematics), is essentially probabilistic. However, as we pointed out in chapter 2, relational knowledge captures probabilities in the extension of relational representations, so this claim does not inherently conflict with the relational knowledge account of higher cognition. Furthermore, mental models, which are arguably relational representations as discussed in chapter 2, can represent probabilities (Johnson-Laird et al., 1999; Johnson-Laird, & Byrne, 2002). This is done by having more than one mental model of a proposition with relative probabilities specified for each model. Thus, the conditional probability conception of reasoning does not inherently conflict with either mental models or relational knowledge. Furthermore, relational knowledge increases the predictive power of reasoning because it enables predictions that go beyond previous experience. Even the simple example of transitive inference (as shown in figure 1.3 in chapter 1) produces an inference that is independent of semantic knowledge.

However, a reasonably detailed comparison of relational knowledge and heuristic accounts is important to our argument, and we approach this by reviewing one of the most advanced heuristic models. Our analysis of categorical syllogisms in chapter 4 provides a foundation that facilitates the comparison of heuristic reasoning models with relational knowledge models. To recapitulate, a categorical syllogism consists of two premises, such as *All X are Y, No Y are Z*, together with a conclusion, which in this instance might be *No X are Z*. (In this case, there is another possible valid conclusion: *No Z are X*.) There are four premise quantifiers (*All*, *Some*, *Some not*, and *None*), which define the "mood" of the premise. Four moods, applied to each of two premises and four figures (*XY-YZ*; *YX-ZY*; *XY-ZY*; *YX-YZ*), yield 64 possible syllogisms, of which 27 have valid conclusions.

The probability heuristics model

The probability heuristics model (Oaksford & Chater, 2007, chapter 7; 2009a) accounts for performances on different forms of categorical syllogisms on the basis of heuristics that are considered to optimize information gain in reasoning. The model is based on heuristics for generating probable conclusions from premises according to the form of the premises. The quantifiers *few* and *most* have been added to the quantifiers standardly used in categorical syllogisms. Quantifiers of premises are rank-ordered according to their theoretical informativeness, which is based on a rarity assumption. That is, "most natural language predicates are mutually exclusive" (Oaksford & Chater, 2007, p. 221). The essential idea here is that statements of the form "Some *X* are not *Y*" are almost universally true in the natural world. Thus, "Some elephants are not planets" and "Some mountains do not fly" are inevitably true. Because informativeness is inversely proportional to the likelihood that a proposition is true (Shannon & Weaver, 1949), the premises of the mood *Some-not* have low informativeness. By contrast, premises "All *X* are *Y*" are much less likely to be true and are therefore more informative. According to the analysis in Oaksford and Chater (2007, 2009a), the order of premise moods, from most to least informative, is *All, Most, Few, Some, None, Some not.*

The probability heuristics model entails a number of heuristics that are based on premise informativeness. According to the *min*-heuristic, the quantifier of the conclusions should be the same as the quantifier in the least informative premise (Oaksford & Chater 2007, p. 217). This can be illustrated with the following syllogism, adapted from Oaksford and Chater (2009a, p. 82):

All X are Y (max-premise)

Some Z are not Y (min-premise)

By the *min*-heuristic, the conclusion will be of the form *Some not.*

There is an *attachment heuristic* that provides a way of generating a conclusion: "If just one possible noun phrase (e.g., *some* Z) matches the subject noun phrase of just one premise, then the conclusion has that noun phrase." (Oaksford & Chater, 2009a, p. 82, italics in original; *P, Q,* and *R* have been changed to *X, Y,* and *Z* to be consistent with our notation).

This generates the following conclusion:

Some Z are not X

There are also two test heuristics. The first is the *max*-heuristic, which holds that confidence in the conclusion is proportional to the informativeness of the most informative premise. In our example, confidence would be based on the premise *All X are Y.* The second is the *Some not* heuristic, which recommends avoiding or not accepting *Some not* conclusions because of their lack of informativeness. This has been a somewhat simplified account of the probability heuristic model, and accounts by Oaksford and Chater (2007, 2009a) show more capabilities of the model.

This theory has been the subject of considerable controversy, as exemplified by the many comments on Oaksford and Chater's (2009a) target article; and the authors' response to those comments (Oaksford & Chater 2009b). There are also important reviews of the field by Khemlani and Johnson-Laird (2012). We will not review that controversy, but certain points are relevant to our argument.

The foundation for the probability heuristics model is partly that there is considerable constraint between mood of the premises and the mood of the conclusion, for those syllogisms that have valid conclusions. This constraint can be seen by inspecting table 6 of Khemlani and Johnson-Laird (2012). The constraint is captured in part by the figural and atmosphere heuristics, both of which were discussed in chapter 4, and the probability heuristics model provides a more comprehensive way of generating conclusions from this set of constraints. Heuristics take less cognitive effort than the generation of mental models, such as those shown for categorical syllogisms in figures 4.7 and 4.8 in chapter 4. The cognitive complexity of mental models of categorical syllogisms can be quantified by the relational complexity metric, which also can be applied to the figural and atmosphere heuristics, as discussed in chapter 4. In general, heuristic solutions have a lower cognitive complexity than mental models, but the latter can generate valid solutions (at least potentially) to all syllogisms, and fallacies that arise from heuristics can be avoided. Given that heuristics and mental models can both generate conclusions to categorical syllogisms, and both are tractable to complexity analysis, there is no inherent conflict between heuristic theory and relational knowledge theory.

There are two propositions that are unique to the probability heuristics model, however. The first is that heuristics employ a quantification of informativeness defined in the probability heuristics model. That is, it is not merely that a particular quantifier is employed, but that it is employed because of some recognition of its informativeness. There is no doubt that cognitive processes obtain information to maximize adaptation to the world, as we noted in chapter 1. Inferences help make our world more predictable. However, the informativeness defined in the probability heuristics model is not uniquely indicated by the empirical findings. As we noted previously, similar levels of predictions are obtained by mental models, and relational complexity theories that do not employ the informativeness ranking of the probability heuristics model. And there does not appear to be any independent evidence that the inferences made are due to cognitive representation of the relative informativeness of the premises.

The problem here is that according to information theory (Shannon & Weaver, 1949), informativeness is the inverse of probability, so it is reasonable to ask whether the heuristics that are attributed to informativeness might be based on perceived probability. Therefore, we could reinterpret the *min*-heuristic as choosing the most probable conclusion based on the mood of the premise. That is, perhaps people have heuristics such as *Some-not is more likely than All*, or *Some-not is more likely than None*. Such heuristics perhaps could be likened to pragmatic reasoning schemas (Cheng & Holyoak, 1985) that are induced from life experience. That is, people might have learned from experience that it is more likely that some people are honest than that all people are honest; it is more likely that some birds fly than that all birds fly. Correspondingly, it is more likely that some people do not own cars than that no people own cars, and so on.

The second unique proposition is that confidence in the conclusion is proportional to the informativeness of the most informative (i.e., *max*) premise. This is an anomaly because, as Halford (2009) pointed out, the *max* premise is also the least probable, so one wonders why confidence should be based on it, rather than on a more probable premise. In their rejoinder, Oaksford and Chater (2009b) argue that "surely the more information you are given, the stronger conclusions you can draw?" (p. 114). This misses the point, however, because it does not explain why the least probable conclusions inspire the most confidence. More important, Oaksford and Chater make no comment on Halford's main point, which is that high confidence is confounded with low complexity:

"An alternative hypothesis is that high confidence is associated with *lowest* complexity, because the least probable forms according to the Probability Heuristics Model are also the least complex according to complexity metrics. The simplest syllogisms according to the Relational Complexity metric, those based on binary or ternary relations, have at least one A (All) premise, or at least one I (Some) premise. A (All) premises are the most informative (least probable) and I (Some) premises the second most informative in the Probability Heuristics Model. Thus, *the most informative, and least probable, syllogisms are of low complexity*, which is a more plausible basis for confidence than low probability." (Halford, 2009, p. 91; italics in the first sentence in original, those in the last sentence added here).

These criticisms of the probability heuristics model do not deny the validity of heuristic theories; rather, they show that heuristics need to be supplemented by representations of relations that capture the meaning of premises, as in mental models and the relational complexity metric.

As we have seen in chapter 4, complexity metrics, based on mental models and relational complexity, can account for problem form variance approximately, as does the probability heuristics model. There are a number of issues related to the assumptions underlying each theory, and the effect of estimated parameters, which we cannot consider here. We accept that people reason with heuristics and that inferences are greatly simplified as a result. Therefore, any model of reasoning must take heuristics into account, but the probability heuristics model is not the only model that can do this. In a meta-analysis of syllogistic theories, Khemlani and Johnson-Laird (2012) found that all theories had merit, but that overall, theories based on models performed better than heuristic theories, though no theory performed perfectly. Khemlani and Johnson-Laird (2013) presented a new model, *mReasoner*, which includes heuristics for construction of mental models (in a way that is reminiscent of the theory of Evans 2006, 2008, but takes the process much further). *mReasoner* performed best of the seven types of theories subjected to the meta-analysis. Therefore, the other unique feature of probability heuristics model, that reasoning is accounted for exclusively by heuristics without active construction of mental models in working memory, does not appear viable at this time.

One problem with this issue is that mental models, relational complexity, and the probability heuristics model overlap to a considerable extent, and it is not possible to manipulate the relevant factors independently. This might be helped by the enlarged corpus of problems defined by Roberts (2005). However, the formulation of processes that have wide application also helps to avoid getting sidetracked by idiosyncratic phenomena that are of little general relevance. Our approach is that, while we identify differences, we try to focus on the often neglected common ground among different approaches. In the case of reasoning, there is a vast mass of evidence that heuristics are employed and provide a serviceable way of making everyday inferences, with low demands on working memory. However, construction of mental models that provide cognitive representations of relations implied by the task is also necessary, and the theory of mental models generates important predictions. Oaksford and Chater (2009a) claim that logic has little application to everyday reasoning. Heuristic reasoning utilizes links that are learned in the course of adapting to the world, and it is very serviceable. However, the thing that makes relational reasoning necessary is that we sometimes have to go beyond experience to deduce things that are implied by propositions that we encounter. We accept that such reasoning is not done according to the rules of standard logic, and analyses such as that by Khemlani and Johnson-Laird (2012) indicate that mental models provide the best account so far of such reasoning.

As mentioned in chapter 1, it is common ground that cognitive processes are motivated by the quest for informativeness and ability to predict the environment. Thus, this proposition does not uniquely favor models such as the probability heuristics model. Reasoning processes that go beyond stored knowledge by constructing representations of possibilities consistent with premises, as with mental models, actually increase the predictive scope and power of cognition. Thus, mental models theory potentially optimizes information gain to a greater extent than models such as the probability heuristics model.

Mental models theory takes account of heuristics and is based on knowledge. The fleshing out of mental models is influenced by the ease with which information can be retrieved from semantic memory (Markovits, 2000; Markovits & Barrouillet, 2002). In conditional reasoning, a premise such as *All tables have legs* might be represented by the following mental model, as a first approximation:

Table legs

Given the minor premise *X has legs,* this mental model would support the inference *X is a table.* This occurs because any conclusion can be drawn that is consistent with the mental model. In this case, the mental model comprises simply the pair *Table legs*, which is consistent with tables being the only things that have legs. This inference is an instance of affirmation of the consequent, which is a fallacy. However, the mental model can be fleshed out by providing additional antecedents as discussed next.

Table legs

Non-table legs

Affirmation of the consequent no longer is generated because the second component of the mental model comprises non-table entities that have legs (e.g., dogs). This fleshing out is more likely with well-known examples such as tables because it is easy to retrieve instances of non-tables with legs, so fallacies such as affirmation of the consequent are less common with premises that relate well-known domains. Construction of mental models is dynamic and depends on structural correspondence, as discussed in chapter 2. Thus, mental models theory depends in some ways on analogy theory, which addresses the question of how structural correspondence is established, as considered in chapter 3. However, as the abovementioned example illustrates, mental models reflect semantic knowledge as well as structural consistency.

Our conclusion from this discussion is not necessarily to support one specific theory, because theories in this area are undergoing constant development, but to show that there is a reasoning function that includes relational representations, is constructed in working memory, is consistent with the premises, and is capable in principle of going beyond past experience. Currently, mental models theory appears to be the best way of fulfilling this reasoning function. We have reviewed state-of-the-art models of reasoning in order to show that our formulation of categories of cognition is consistent with contemporary thinking on the issue. We now present a reinterpretation of a classical reasoning problem, the Wason Selection Task, and consider whether it offers a resolution of some long-standing issues.

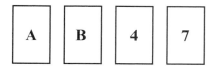

Figure 8.1
The Wason Selection Task

Wason Selection Task

In one commonly used version of the Wason Selection Task, four cards are presented as shown in figure 8.1. Participants are (1) told that each card has a letter on one side, and a number on the other, and (2) given a rule, such as *If there is an A on one side, there is a 7 on the other side* (*P* implies *Q*, which we will write as *P* → *Q*); after which (3) they are asked: *Which cards would you have to turn over to see if the rule is being violated?* The correct answer is cards A and 4 (*P and not-Q*).

The Wason Selection Task (Evans & Ball, 2010) has been widely interpreted as demonstrating the limits of human reasoning because, although apparently simple, it is performed poorly by all but a small minority of participants. There are two main types of error. The first is to choose 7 (*Q*), but turning over the 7 and finding that there is no *A* on the other side does not disconfirm the rule. The canonical interpretation of the rule is that it is unidirectional, corresponding to the conditional, *A* → 7, so it is not implied that 7 on one side will be accompanied by *A* on the other side. This choice, therefore, could be motivated by a bidirectional (biconditional) interpretation of the rule, *A* ↔ 7. Alternatively, it might reflect a simplistic choice of cards that match terms in the rule (i.e., a matching strategy). The second main type of error is failing to choose card 4 (i.e., the *not-Q* card), which would disconfirm the rule if an *A* is on the reverse side.

The low level of performance on this test has given rise to numerous theories about human reasoning, one of the most influential being that of Cosmides and Tooby (1992), who claim that successful performance depends on social contract processes, such as an innate "cheater detection" module. The essence of this proposal is that if the rule is in the form of a social contract, such as "to gain *benefit B, condition C* must be fulfilled," then people will turn over the *not-C* card because failure to fulfill this condition would be cheating, and humans have a cheater detection module that is part of their innate adaptive ability. Stenning and Van

Lambalgen (2008) argue that this view is mistaken. We will consider whether the account of cognition that we have developed should cause us to agree in principle with that judgment. We do not disagree with innate modules having an influence on reasoning, but the question is how much of reasoning can be explained plausibly in this way. It is also important to consider whether concentration on modules has obscured the role of domain general processes such as relational knowledge. We will analyze the relational processes entailed in the Wason Selection Task, including the hitherto neglected factor of relational complexity, to determine whether an explanation for otherwise mysterious difficulties becomes apparent.

A further issue is that, while fewer than 10 percent of participants typically respond correctly on abstract versions of the task, performance can be much improved when they are presented with familiar, concrete versions. One of the best-known versions is the drinking rule task (If you drink alcohol, you must be at least 18 years old), in which 73 percent correctly chose cards *beer* and *16 years,* and not cards *coke* and *22 years* (Griggs & Cox, 1982). Later in this chapter, we will suggest that this finding is interpretable in terms of the complexity factor.

Performance on abstract versions of the test has been explained in terms of confirmation bias (avoiding negative instances), matching bias (repeating the elements in rule), and acquired pragmatic reasoning schemas. However, after four decades of research, no consensus has emerged, and a possible reason for this is that many processes are blended in the task, impeding analysis of the relevant factors. We propose some innovations to identify and isolate relevant processes and offer further explanations for task difficulty. First, however, we analyze what we believe are some of the important factors that underlie performance on the task.

The two most common errors need to be examined more closely. Choice of Q might reflect matching the elements in the rule, but it is also consistent with the biconditional interpretation, $P \leftrightarrow Q$, which implies that if there is a Q on one side, there will be a P on the other. This response is scored as an error because the canonical interpretation of the rule is the conditional $P \rightarrow Q$. However, the biconditional interpretation is consistent with an adaptive (Anderson, 1990) conception of rationality as distinct from a normative one. For example, the rule might be interpreted as a *prediction* that P will be accompanied by Q, and the biconditional corresponds to a higher correlation (and therefore a better prediction) than the conditional (Halford, 1993). Therefore, the biconditional interpretation is arguably rational, and if so, it is appropriate to score the selection of Q not as an error. Another common error (sometimes attributed to confirmation bias) is the failure to select *not-Q*, even though it has the potential to falsify (and thus to test) the rule. Regardless of whether choice of Q is interpreted as a matching or a biconditional response, these two choices (selecting Q and failure to select *not-Q*) should be scored separately, as they reflect different processes. More important, selecting *not-Q* requires an inference of significant complexity, and this factor has been largely overlooked.

Relational complexity of the Wason Selection Task

In the Wason Selection Task, derivation of the conjunction that violates the rule is as follows:

P implies Q is equivalent to *not-P or Q* (by truth tables) and the negation of *not-P or Q* is equivalent to *P and not-Q* (by de Morgan's theorem).

Therefore, *P and not*-Q negates *P implies Q*. A more psychologically realistic process is to construct a mental model of the rule in working memory, as described next.

To recognize that *not-Q* can falsify the rule requires the combination *P and not-Q* to be related to the rule *P implies Q*. The minimal mental model of the rule is the pair (*P, Q*), and that of the disconfirming conjunction is (*P, not-Q*). The relation between these two is one of incompatibility [i.e., *incompatible*((*P, Q*), (*P, not-Q*))]. There are four roles (two in the rule and two in the falsifying combination), and this process is at the limit of human processing capacity (Halford et al., 2005) as discussed in chapter 4. Consequently, participants might fail to choose *not-Q* because of the complex inference entailed.

In familiar contexts, such as the drinking rule task of Griggs and Cox (1982), this process is bypassed because the violating conjunction (such as *a person drinking beer who is less than 18 years*) is already known, and there is less need to derive it by analytic reasoning or by constructing the relevant mental model. Therefore, the processing load associated with this process does not occur. Thus, better performance of familiar versions of tasks can be obtained because cognitive complexities are bypassed, reducing the working memory load, although this important point often goes unrecognized.

The processing load might influence construction of the task model that guides performance, as discussed in chapter 4. Once a task model is formed, it can be reduced to a criterion equivalent to *P and not-Q*, which entails a binary relation. This means that processing load effects might be low when deciding whether to turn over cards. However, construction of the task model depends on recognition that *P and not-Q* is incompatible with $P \rightarrow Q$, which entails a representation equivalent to *incompatible((P, Q), (P, not-Q))* mentioned earlier. The complexity of this decision means that tutoring in the rules of the Wason Selection Task, as conducted by Cocchi et al., (2014) and Osman (2007), would be difficult, particularly with respect to inducing the understanding that *not-Q* cards should be turned over. Processing load effects when turning over cards might be variable depending on whether construction of the task model is still going on, or a simpler criterion (choose the cards that correspond to *P* and *not-Q*) already has been fully determined.

Modifications to the Wason Selection Task paradigm

In our research on this question, we have sought to analyze the component processes in the task by using the following innovations (note that not all innovations were used in every experiment):

• Presenting the cards successively in some conditions of the experiments, in contrast to the usual procedure of presenting them simultaneously (see figure 8.2). Successive presentation would facilitate a strategy of considering one card at a time, thereby enabling the implications of elements that could be on the opposite sides of the cards to be recognized. If participants are attempting a rational test of the rule in this way, performance should improve with successive presentation.

• The rule was specified separately for each card, so it was different for every problem. This was enabled by successive presentation because with simultaneous presentation, the same rule necessarily applied to all four cards. Independent rule specification for each item could be important because the task essentially entails computing the correspondence between the rule and the elements on the card in order to determine whether in principle, the card could falsify the rule. If the same rule applies to several cards, computing this correspondence becomes less demanding.

• The letter-number instantiations were varied (e.g., *"if* A *then* 7*"* versus *"if* 3 *then* Z*"*). This modification ensured that cards had to be processed by mapping between card elements and rule elements, and it was not possible to simplify the task by matching elements.

• Failure to select the *not-Q* card (i.e., 4) should be scored separately from selection of the *Q* (i.e., 7) card. The latter is arguably not an error according to an ecological interpretation of the rule, as discussed previously. Either way, these selections represent different processes, and failure to select the *not*-Q card is more diagnostic of a logical error in reasoning. It is also predictive of high processing loads.

• Training was given to ensure that the demands of the task were fully understood, including the conditional ($P \rightarrow Q$) interpretation of the rule, as distinct from the biconditional interpretation ($P \leftrightarrow Q$). The aim was primarily to reduce variance in strategies.

• The presentation of one or two possible elements on the reverse side of the card was indicated in a shaded area beneath each card, as shown in figure 8.2. The idea is that, if participants are reasoning logically about what might be on the opposite side of the card, this should facilitate correct selections.

• Participants were asked to rate the difficulty of their decision concerning each card on a five-point scale (this also necessitated successive presentation).

• Electroencepholgram (EEG) and functional magnetic resonance imaging (fMRI) measures were taken to assess processing demands and brain regions activated.

An example of the methodology as used by Cocchi et al. (2014) can be summarized as follows:

Each trial commenced with a central fixation cross (800 ms) followed by a short blank interval (500 ms), before a logical rule establishing a relation between two alphanumeric variables (e.g., "If A, then 7") was presented for 3,000 ms. Rules always consisted of a single letter and a single digit (1 to 9), with letters and digits presented with equal frequency as the first and second elements of the rule across runs. A total of 180 different rules were presented throughout the experiment. Following a randomly varied time period of 3,000–5,000 ms, a single digit or letter (where a digit or a letter appeared an equal number of times) was displayed for 3,000 ms. Participants were instructed to consider this character as one side of a card and to indicate, as quickly and as accurately as possible, if the card was potentially able to *disconfirm* the rule, assuming that the other side of the card could contain any possible letter (if the face side contained a number) or digit (if the face side contained a letter). Critically, participants were instructed that the rule was not bidirectional. Thus, for example, the rule "If A, then 7" does not imply "If 7, then A."

Our findings are reported in detail elsewhere (Cocchi et al., 2014), but to summarize, we found that successive presentation had methodological benefits but did not promote large increases in performance relative to

Each card has a letter on one side, and a number on the other. Below the card is written the letter or number that appears on the other side. The rule is **if there is an X on one side, there is a 3 on the other side**.

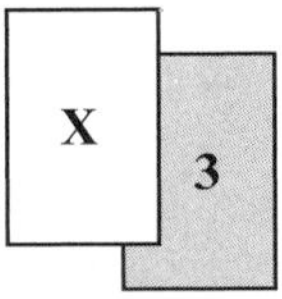

Would you have to turn the card over to see if the rule is being violated? Yes/No

Please rate the difficulty of this decision from 1 (very easy) to 5 (very difficult)

| 1 | 2 | 3 | 4 | 5 |

Each card has a letter on one side, and a number on the other. Below the card is written the letter or number that may appear on the other side. The rule is **if there is a Z on one side, there is a 9 on the other side**.

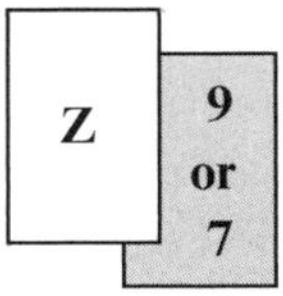

Would you have to turn the card over to see if the rule is being violated? Yes/No

Please rate the difficulty of this decision from 1 (very easy) to 5 (very difficult)

| 1 | 2 | 3 | 4 | 5 |

Figure 8.2
Examples of a test item in a modified version of the Wason Selection Task. In the first case, one element only is indicated for the reverse side; in the second case, two possible elements are indicated for the reverse side. The difficulty scale is shown beneath each item.

simultaneous presentation, and that provision of two possible elements on the reverse side also had very little benefit. These findings suggest that participants do not attempt to reason about possible elements on the reverse side of the card; rather, they attend only to the visible elements. Thus, they frequently made selections that simply matched the visible elements (e.g., with the four cards presented in figure 8.1, they selected A and 7, consistent with the matching hypothesis of Evans 2008). Matching is an accurate behavioral description, but we propose that matching might be a default response due to the complexity of the task, or to lack of clear understanding as to what was required. In one experiment where adequate training was used, we observed very high success rates, the lowest being 87 percent on the *not*-Q card (Cocchi et al., 2014). In another study, provision of one possible element on the reverse side raised correct performance to around 80 percent because it is easy to recognize the correct selection with that procedure. This suggests that failure to consider the possible element on the reverse side reflects the cognitive complexity of the relevant inferences. When it is easy to interpret the element on the reverse side, as in the one-element condition, it is processed successfully. Thus, correct performance is easily obtained where task demands were well understood and where processing load is low.

Separate presentation of the rule and the card enabled the determination of brain activations associated with encoding the rule as distinct from processing the cards, which, by our analysis, entails relating rule and card elements, as discussed previously. The findings of Cocchi et al. (2014) indicated different brain activation patterns for these two components of the task. Encoding the rule activated a cingulo-opercular network, and a fronto-parietal network was activated when processing the cards. As mentioned earlier in this chapter during the relational complexity analysis of the Wason Selection Task, encoding the rule requires a simpler representation, comprising two elements in its mental model, whereas matching a card to the rule is more complex, with a mental model comprising up to four elements. While our findings are not definitive on all the issues raised, they support the hypothesis that rule processing and card processing entail different processes. This opens up some new lines of investigation.

Our contention, therefore, is that the mysteriously low levels of performance that have been observed so often with the Wason Selection Task are explicable with reinterpretation of the task (especially scoring of the selection of the Q card as correct, or at least treating it separately from the error of failing to select the *not*-Q card), with adequate communication of the task demands, and with due consideration of the complexity effects. These proposals arguably made interpretations based on modular processes or the probability heuristics model unnecessary, except perhaps on specific versions of the task that tend to induce these processes. Thus, we agree with Stenning and Van Lambalgen (2008) to the extent that the case for specific processes, such as specialized deontic reasoning processes or cheater detection modules, disappears when the Wason Selection Task is analyzed in greater depth and when the inherent complexity of reasoning in the task is recognized.

Pragmatic reasoning schemas

Pragmatic reasoning schemas (Cheng & Holyoak, 1985) also have been proposed as a basis for performing the Wason Selection Task. Pragmatic reasoning schemas include such things as permission, and they can be induced from ordinary life experience. Our environment abounds in instances of permission: paying for a hamburger gives permission to eat it, a driver's license gives permission to drive a car, and so on. Enhancement of Wason Selection Task performance by presentation in the form of a permission (Cheng & Holyoak, 1985) has yielded two main classes of hypotheses. One is that improvement is due to the specialized domain of deontic reasoning, which includes reasoning about permissions and obligations. However, Almor and Sloman (1996) have argued persuasively that there are no compelling reasons to regard deontic reasoning as special. The other hypothesis is that the permission concept might be an analog. Halford (1993) has pointed out that there is a close structural correspondence between permission and the conditional, in that they can be expressed by isomorphic truth tables. This would mean that at least part of the benefit of the permission version of the Wason Selection Task is that it induces a conditional (i.e., one-way) interpretation of the task. The permission schema also might reduce the cognitive load incurred by generating a task model because the disconfirming instance, *P and not-Q*, is analogous to the *action-without-permission* element in the schema. Analogy is a reasoning process that has great generality, and it might have implications for the Wason Selection Task that have not yet been fully recognized. It is not our function here to resolve all these specific issues about the Wason Selection Task, but it is important to point out that the possibility of an account based on principles of considerable generality might have been overlooked.

Executive functions

In chapter 3, we reviewed numerous neuroscience studies of the role of the prefrontal cortex (PFC) in processing relations, including a classic study by Luria (1980). We argued that patients with lesions to the frontal regions of the cortex appeared to have difficulty processing complex relations. In this section, we briefly consider a proposal that relational knowledge might account for some aspects of executive functions, thereby possibly bringing more cohesion to this diverse field (Andrews et al., 2013; Halford et al., 2010). Based on magnetic resonance imaging (MRI) records, the study compared stroke patients with lesions to frontal regions of the PFC with patients with nonfrontal lesions and matched controls. The participants were tested on a battery of standard executive function tests and a battery of relational processing measures at three levels of cognitive complexity. Composite measures of both executive function and relational processing were sensitive to the effects of frontal damage, and there was special sensitivity at the intermediate ternary-relational level of complexity. The relational processing measures accounted for over half the variance in executive function (Halford et al., 2010). The ternary- and quaternary-relational measures accounted for unique variance even when variance associated with the control measures and stroke status was controlled. While research on this question is not yet definitive, the results indicated that relational processing theory might offer a unifying conceptualization of some aspects of executive functions, with benefits including a common set of cognitive processes and methods for inducing the acquisition of executive functions. The results also add to the growing body of evidence that attests to the power of the relational complexity metric.

Latin square task

The Latin square task, a psychometric test based on the relational complexity metric, was developed recently by Birney, Halford, and Andrews, (2006). Although this test is still at an early stage of development (Perret, Bailleux, & Dauvier, 2011), it does suggest the possibility of psychometric tests being developed that are explicitly based on relational complexity. However, assessment of relational complexity theory requires independently validated accounts of the cognitive processes actually performed in the task. While Perret, Bailleux, and Dauvier's (2011) methodology has some admirable features, their secant and nonsecant problems require different inferences. Thus, the greater difficulty of the nonsecant problems (see their figure 4) is due to the different inferences required rather than differences in relational complexity. Furthermore, the lack of difference between the notionally ternary, quaternary, and quinary problems is because they can all be chunked to the same level of complexity. The authors do recognize these issues, and there is potential to refine the test using Method for Analysis of Relational Complexity (MARC) principles.

Representational rank and cognitive development

Piaget (1950) proposed that cognitive development occurs through a succession of stages: sensorimotor, preoperational (with substages preconceptual and intuitive), concrete operational, and formal operational (Flavell, 1963; Halford, 1982; Hunt, 1961). There have been many reinterpretations of Piaget's stages, some of which are included in our review of information processing models of cognitive development (Halford & Andrews, 2011). There was also a period of intense controversy in this area that lasted from approximately 1970 to 2000. Our current formulation is not specifically intended to address this controversy, although we have reviewed it extensively (see, for example, Halford, 1982, 1989, 1993; Halford & Andrews, 2006). Our conclusion was that the Piagetian research demonstrated phenomena that needed to be explained. Critical examples would be the difficulty that young children have with transitive inference, class inclusion, and conservation of quantity. These findings have survived decades of research, and while they undoubtedly reflect acquisition and organization of knowledge, they cannot be wholly explained without invoking cognitive complexity as a factor. Our purpose here is to link Piagetian research to our conceptualization of levels of cognitive processes, captured in the concept of representational rank. This link builds on the formulation of Halford and Andrews (2011) and is summarized in figure 8.3. The essential idea is that cognitive development depends to a considerable extent on progression through relational representations of increasing complexity. This conception captures the phenomena that Piaget explained by stages of cognitive development, while subsuming a much wider range of cognitive processes.

Piaget's sensorimotor stage has been replaced in our formulation with a discussion of processes that have been identified in subsequent research. These include the subsymbolic to symbolic transition (Halford et al., 2013), image schemas (Mandler, 2004) and a number of neural net models of object concept representation, prototype foundation, and other processes, discussed in previous chapters. We will not attempt a detailed

Piagetian Stage	Rank	Cognitive Processes	Typical Tasks	PDP Implementation
Preconceptual	2	Binary relations	match-to-sample, identity position, category label distinct from category	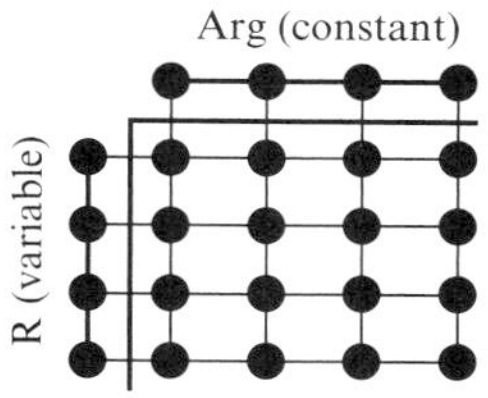 Arg (constant) / R (variable)
Intuitive	3	Binary relations, Univariate functions	relational match-to-sample, A-not-B, complementary categories	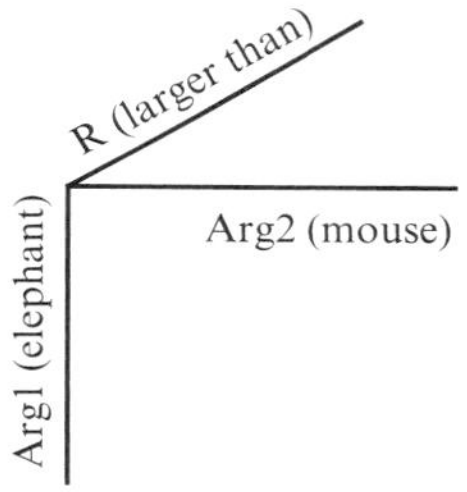 R (larger than) / Arg1 (elephant) / Arg2 (mouse)
Concrete Operational	4	Ternary relations, Binary operations, Bivariate functions	transitive inference, hierarchical categories, concept of mind	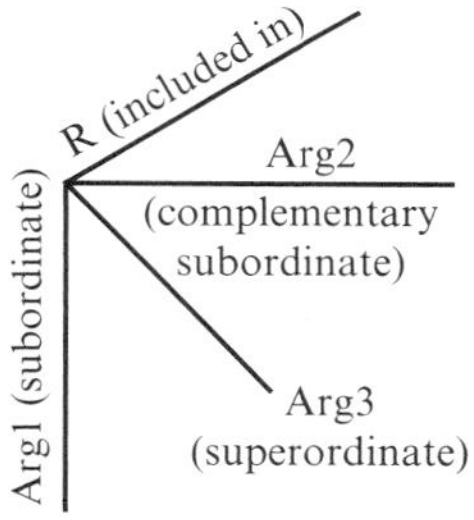 R (included in) / Arg1 (subordinate) / Arg2 (complementary subordinate) / Arg3 (superordinate)
Formal Operational	5	Quaternary relations, Composition of binary operations	proportion, balance scale	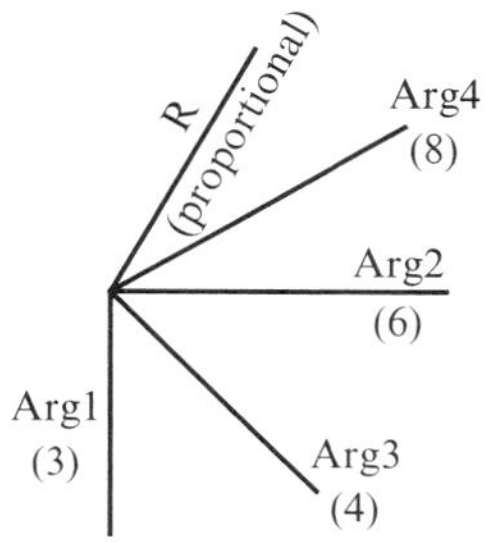 R (proportional) / Arg1 (3) / Arg4 (8) / Arg2 (6) / Arg3 (4)

Figure 8.3

Correspondence between Piagetian levels of reasoning and representational rank. Reproduces figure 1 in Halford & Andrews (2011). Copyright © 2011 Blackwell Publishing Ltd. Reproduced by permission of John Wiley & Sons.

reconciliation with Piaget's theory here, but we note that this formulation is broadly consistent with his notion of sensorimotor processes, at least in the first few months of life.

However, the contemporary account of infant cognition is much more elaborate, in many ways, than envisaged in Piaget's now historically significant writings.

We do not identify a single level of process with Piaget's preoperational stage; rather, we specify a correspondence between the preconceptual substage and unary relational processes, and between the intuitive substage and binary relational processes. Also, we do not specify ages of attainment, as we consider this a normative question that should be addressed in empirical work. For example, Andrews and Halford (2002) specified the percentage of children passing ternary relational tasks as a function of age (see figure 1.4 in chapter 1). The ages are not inherently predicted by relational knowledge theory, but correspondence between tasks of the same rank, whether in the same or different domains, is predicted, provided that the boundary conditions are observed (e.g., domain knowledge is demonstrated by the methods specified in chapter 4). One reason why correspondence was not observed with Piagetian tasks is that too many processes were required within one task. When careful and extensive efforts are made to isolate the concepts that the task is intended to assess, research has demonstrated correspondence across tasks (Andrews & Halford, 2002; Andrews et al. 2003; Halford et al. 2002, Halford, Andrews, & Jensen, 2002; Bunch & Andrews, 2012). This isolation of core processes was the result of very extensive study, our own as well as that of many other researchers', which identified the component processes. Our contention is that relational complexity is one factor that underlies the increases in reasoning sophistication as children developed.

Our treatment of Piagetian phenomena was based on the isolation of underlying processes and is consistent with our treatment of other cognitive tasks. Thus, we handled deductive inference by isolating the core process of premise integration (Halford, 1984; Maybery, Bain, & Halford, 1986). Furthermore, our isolation of what we believe are the core relational processes in the Wason Selection Task, discussed earlier in this chapter, is the result of a similar process of identifying the components of the task that had been reported in some four decades of research in the literature.

To conclude this section, we propose that Piaget's findings concerning the development of concepts and reasoning in children can be reinterpreted in terms of progression through representational ranks, enabled by increasing working memory capacity.

Conclusion

Principles

We have considered how relational knowledge theory, including the relational complexity metric, accounts for some key areas of higher cognition, including deductive inference, Bayesian rationality, the probability heuristics model, mental models, the Wason Selection Task, pragmatic reasoning schemas, the Latin square task, executive functions, and Piagetian cognitive development.

Relational knowledge theory is not inherently in conflict with alternative accounts of reasoning, such as those based on heuristics. Relational representations and heuristics are not incompatible, but they can be blended in reasoning. This is essentially consistent with the formulation by Evans (2003, 2006, 2008), discussed in chapter 1, and the point is developed in greater detail in the *mReasoner* model (Khemlani & Johnson-Laird, 2013). Relational representations enable knowledge to be used to predict the environment and guide adaptation. We have reviewed one of the most prominent heuristic theories, the probability heuristics model, and argued that it does not inherently conflict with relational knowledge theory; indeed, the two are complementary in certain respects. We also have argued that there are some limitations of the probability heuristics model that could be overcome using relational knowledge theory, especially with respect to the neglected factor of cognitive complexity.

While we do not discount the role of modular processes in reasoning, such as those that are concerned with social contracts, including cheater detection, we have shown that there is a role for domain-general processes such as mental models and accessible representations of relations. Processes by which representations that capture essential relations in a problem can be constructed in memory are indispensable to higher cognition. While it is not our function in this book to discriminate between alternative models, it appears at the present time that mental models theory provides the best account of this aspect of reasoning.

We have demonstrated the benefit of reinterpreting established paradigms and findings, including the Wason Selection Task and some of the Piagetian literature, to show that there are general principles that have not always been recognized.

Questions for further investigation

More research is needed to show how mental models of relational representation can be constructed, starting from associative links (redescription). Interest in this problem has been diminished by competing proposals based on heuristics, but nothing in that literature really denies the importance of the construction of representations in working memory.

9 Applications of Relational Knowledge Theory

The 21st century is arguably the age of complexity, in that life has never been as complex as it currently is and the portents indicate increasing complexity, at least for the foreseeable future. Both work demands and the growth of technology have contributed to rapid increases in the complexity of human performance. It is beyond the scope of this book to review the human factors literature on this topic (see, for example, Vicente, 2003), but in this chapter, we indicate how relational complexity theory can be applied to problems in human performance. Some of our proposals here are based on experience with human factors contexts, and systematic data have not always been collected.

The importance of complexity in modern life

It is well recognized that a lot of the complexity that influences our lives comes from our use of technology, and the human factors literature is replete with examples of human error caused by the human—technology interface. An example of enormous task complexity would be the situation with Qantas flight QF32 in an A380 aircraft after it left Changi Airport in Singapore on November 3, 2010. Captain Richard de Crespigny (2012; http://qf32.aero) described the situation as follows:

The aircraft was so injured, and so many of the 250,000 sensors were complaining, that I had reached the limit of my ability to absorb them all. The ECAM *[Electronic Centralised Aircraft Monitoring]* threw up so many failures, degradations, and check-lists—especially in the fuel system—that I could not evaluate all the interactions and consequences of the cascading failures. I just wasn't confident how much of the aircraft we had left. So I wanted to be ready for the worst possible contingency——a no-engine landing. (p. 173; words in brackets added from p. 156)

And later:

We went back to the basics and it became easy: "All right, let's keep this simple. We can't transfer fuel, we can't jettison it. The trim tank fuel is stuck in the tail and the transfer tanks are useless. The only useable fuel is the fuel in the three feed tanks sitting on top of each engine. I don't care which fuel pumps have failed because we are below our fuel gravity ceiling, so fuel will drip into each engine. So forget the pumps, forget the other eight tanks, forget the total fuel quantity gauge, and instead let's concentrate only on the fuel in the feed tanks above each engine. We're burning 3 tonnes of fuel per engine per hour, and I see 8 tonnes of fuel in feed tank 1 and 11 tonnes of fuel in feed tanks 3 and 4. So we have two and a half hours of fuel in feed tank 1, although it's leaking fuel very fast, and we have three and a half hours of fuel in Engines 3 and 4.

"I say we forget analysing the fuel system any more. We concentrate only on feed tanks 1, 3, and 4. We have up to two and a half hours of flight time before we lose Engine 1. We'll monitor the feed tank fuel and our endurance every five minutes. I'm happy. Do any of you have any thoughts?"

"No," came the reply from everyone. (p. 198)

This statement succeeded in simplifying the representation of the situation to make it cognitively manageable. This process continued:

My overriding philosophy was still to focus on what was working. The fuel was okay—we had as many as two and a half hours on Engine 1. Hydraulics were okay—we had two pumps powering one system, plus reserves. Flight controls were okay—we had control in all axes, for the moment. (p. 203)

Thus, the captain used his basic understanding of an aircraft, developed during his career that is beautifully described in the earlier chapters of the book, to identify the factors that really mattered: fuel to keep the airplane flying, hydraulics to actuate essential functions, and control. The captain's reasoning comprises links between a small number of variables that collectively represent the essential aspects of the situation, and which can be accessed effectively to draw inferences about a wide range of issues. It illustrates the power and flexibility of human cognition proceeding from basic understanding of a situation to effective problem solving. This capacity helped save the lives of the 469 persons on board flight QF32.

Treatment of complexity

Human operators and decision makers often experience overload in the amount of information that needs to be attended to at one time. Typically, the person has all the requisite knowledge and skills for the task, but difficulties arise due to the amount of information that must be integrated in a single decision. The problem can be particularly acute in command

and control tasks where large amounts of information are concentrated in one location to be processed by a single operator. Often the person is only dimly aware that information overload is the cause of the difficulty because the problem is not generally well understood. It is, however, very common, both in work and everyday life, and an analysis that led to effective remediation would have a considerable benefit.

The first thing to notice is that a problem is not always recognized as being caused by complexity, and it might be attributed instead to other factors such as motivation or fatigue. It is often the case that neither workers nor managers are trained to estimate processing loads, so even where estimates are attempted, they might have little validity. However, the common factor is information overload, so we need to specify what this means.

Information overload can be recognized by the following signs:

1. A subjective feeling of effort that does not seem to have any apparent explanation. The operators might be highly competent, and they may be even be able to explain clearly what should be done in a given situation. The problem, however, is that too much information needs to be processed in each decision.
2. The appearance of unexplained errors by otherwise competent operators in otherwise satisfactory work environments.
3. Unexplained but apparently intractable difficulties in training or in achieving mastery of a task.

Experts in a task develop highly effective strategies for processing large amounts of information without overloading their capacity. Relational complexity theory accounts for these strategies by coding and decomposition procedures that limit the amount of information that has to be processed in any one step of the task, as described for conceptual chunking and segmentation in chapter 4. However, difficulties can arise in unusual circumstances for which strategies are not fully efficient. Such strategies are often developed by trial and error, without real insights into the causes of the problem. Not only is this process likely to be slow, but also it may have more serious disadvantages, particularly in safety-critical industries or those where error is costly.

This type of problem is particularly acute with tasks that have to be performed under time pressure, or where unusual combinations of circumstances are likely to arise. Modern high-technology industries produce many situations of this kind because of the number of variables that have to be taken into account in decision making. The fact that processes normally function smoothly, with a minimum of operator intervention, means there may be little opportunity for the gradual acquisition of efficient strategies to reduce the information processing load. Insight into the causes of information overload is vital in such circumstances.

The lack of an effective means of analyzing processing loads often has meant that even highly sophisticated systems have not been designed with adequate recognition of this factor. All too often, it can be recognized only after the event, when correction can be costly, and failure to correct may even be disastrous. Great gains in efficiency could be achieved by recognizing such problems in advance or by performing remediation before an existing work situation causes trouble. Such analyses require specialized expertise, which can be provided using the products of research into this problem.

As we have defined the term *complexity,* it refers to factors that affect performance due to the number of variables or components that have to be related or integrated to perform a task. In this section, we consider some of the ways that complexity can affect performance.

As discussed in chapter 4, *cognitive complexity* refers to aspects of work that increase the *processing load* (or *mental load*) on the human operator, or which impede performance due to the number of task elements or amount of information that must be processed. Processing load is best measured by the number of variables that have to be processed at each step in the task. Processing load corresponds to the subjective feeling of effort, but also to various objective indicators of arousal or brain activation. High mental loads contribute to increased error rates, longer decision times, increased fatigue, mental stress, and difficulty in learning.

Capacity limitations and the ability to deal with cognitive complexity

Humans are limited in the number of variables or factors that they can take into account in decision making at any time. As shown in chapter 4, the limit is approximately four variables related in any one cognitive representation, although this can be influenced by individual differences. However, in this context, we want to consider how this limited capacity is utilized to perform complex tasks. Tasks with more than four variables can be processed by *segmenting* them into components that do not overload the capacity to process information in parallel. An example would be the way that humans segment a complex manual multiplication task into subtasks that deal with one column at a time. However, relations between variables in different segments become inaccessible while a particular segment is being processed. Hence, carrying digits from one column to another imposes an additional processing load and is a cause of error in children's arithmetic.

Processing loads can also be reduced by *conceptual chunking,* which is equivalent to compressing variables. For example, *velocity = distance/time,* but can be recoded to a binding between a variable and a constant (e.g., speed = 50 miles per hour). Conceptual chunking reduces processing load, but chunked relations become inaccessible (e.g., if we think of velocity as a single variable, we cannot determine what happens to velocity if we travel the same distance in half the time). The application of segmentation and conceptual chunking depends on expertise in the task domain.

Experts tend to recognize how a task can be subdivided (segmentation), or reconceptualized (conceptual chunking) in a way that captures the important relations, whereas novices are unable to do this and consequently may experience unmanageable task loads. They might roam around a problem indefinitely without seeing a way to handle it. Expertise requires that the task structure remains constant, or that a provision be made to adapt to changes, probably guided by understanding of the underlying structure. People with high levels of expertise can use their conceptual knowledge to devise new strategies for segmentation and conceptual chunking.

Processing load in a job typically varies over time, so a single quantitative indicator applicable to all jobs might not be sufficient. In figure 9.1,

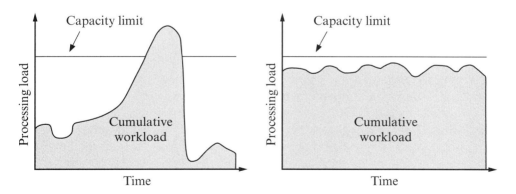

Figure 9.1

Two different processing load distributions. Total work done in the two scenarios is represented by the areas under the two curves. In the left hand graph, with lower total work, the peak processing load exceeds the capacity limit, so that errors are likely. In the right graph, even though total work is higher, peak processing load does not exceed the capacity limit.

the left panel shows a load that is generally low, but with a peak that exceeds capacity. The right panel shows a job with a more constant load but with a higher mean. The impacts of these work environments will be quite different. The one in the left panel may cause short-term overload, while that in the right panel is more likely to produce fatigue or stress. In the first case, load is best measured by the complexity of the most complex step, whereas in the second case, it is best measured by the complexity of all the steps (i.e., by the area under the curve).

We need to consider how complexity can arise in a task. The relevant factors include number of elements, knowledge requirements, matching knowledge to the task, planning, and memory load.

Number of elements

The number of steps (or subtasks) required for a task, or the number of elements or components in a situation, can affect complexity. For example, work can be complex because of the number of customers who have to be serviced, the number of tasks that have to be performed for each customer, the number of separate pieces of information that have to be accessed, and other aspects. We can refer to these generically as *number of elements*. Number of elements probably will be related to work time. It will not necessarily be related to processing load because at any one time, a task can have a lot of elements but a low processing load. For example, a telephone book contains many elements (names and phone numbers), and reading it would take a long time, but it is not complex because only one subscriber can be processed at a time (segmentation). However, if time is the only measure available, number of elements might be difficult to distinguish from processing load because both can increase work time. If this distinction is important, it is necessary to employ one or more measures that assess processing load independent of number of elements. Physiological arousal indicators that have been used for this purpose include pupil dilation (Kahneman, 1973), probe reaction time (Maybery, Bain, & Halford, 1986) and Event Related Potential (ERP) measures (Vogel et al., 2005; Vogel & Machizawa, 2004). However, these are often hard to use in practical situations, and ratings of mental effort frequently suffice. In our investigation of the Wason Selection Task, summarized in chapter 8, we found that difficulty ratings were effective measures of processing load.

The number of task elements required to process industrial work has been investigated using statistical information from the records of an organization. In one of our industry consultations, staff were surveyed regarding the frequency with which each topic (task) was seen to be complex. They were asked to rate frequency from 0 (never complex) to 4 (always complex). This count was added to the estimates of degree of complexity from 1.0 (complex) to 3.0 (extremely complex) to provide an indicative complexity measure. These statistical data are very useful, although they are subject to a number of limitations and need to be supplemented with information based on direct observation of the work activities of staff.

Number of elements can contribute to errors. One reason is simply that the number of opportunities for error increases with the addition of task elements due to the way probabilities accumulate. Second, large numbers of elements tend to encourage the development of short cuts to enable the task to be completed with what is seen as appropriate accuracy and effort in an appropriate time.

The distinction between processing load and number of elements depends in an important way on whether the task can be decomposed so that a small number of elements can be processed at one time. Those tasks that impose the highest loads are often those that are structured in a way that resists decomposition into simpler subtasks. In chapter 4, we showed how decomposability influenced effective relational complexity. Thus, transitive inference was shown to impose a processing load with both children and adults because the premises had to be interpreted jointly to construct a mental model that would generate a conclusion. Similar effects were demonstrated with categorical syllogisms and many other cognitive tasks. Decomposability has a similar effect on complexity in human factors contexts. In our human factors consultations, we found cases where rules that had to be implemented were modified by other rules in a way that corresponded to interactions between variables in reasoning tasks.

On the other hand, tasks that can be proceduralized so that they can be performed by a sequence of well-learned steps tend to impose low processing loads, even if many elements are involved. Thus, assembling an order from a list of required items imposes a low load because it can be decomposed easily into a myriad of subtasks that can be performed one at a time.

Working memory

Reasoning and other symbolically structured processes depend on the construction of relational representations in working memory, as discussed in chapter 4. In human factors, working memory plays a major role in planning and modifying procedures. Human factors management, therefore, depends on designing tasks so the working memory load never exceeds available capacity, which means that it must not be necessary to relate more than four variables.

An issue that is very relevant to human factors is whether working memory can be increased by training. The literature on this topic is reviewed by Shipstead, Redick, and Engle (2012), and they concluded that improvements are possible but might be limited to task-specific contexts. Alternatively, working memory capacity might be increased but the effect will not extend to fluid intelligence (Harrison et al., 2013). That is, there might not be a general improvement in working memory that will facilitate performances with a high degree of novelty. We cannot resolve this issue here, but we can make one suggestion: that the crucial function of working memory in symbolically structured cognition is dynamic binding to a coordinate system. We saw the importance of this in chapter 4, but it is also important in the acquisition of higher cognitive processes, as discussed in chapter 6. Thus, even the origin of symbolic processes depends on dynamic binding to a coordinate system. The possibility that a general increase in working memory capacity could be achieved by training dynamic binding to a coordinate system does not appear to have been investigated specifically. If a general increase in the efficiency of dynamic binding could be achieved, this might offer a new approach to achieving domain-general increases in working memory capacity, possibly with an improvement in fluid intelligence.

Responses to excessive complexity

Most cases of excessive complexity and consequent information overload do not result in a total breakdown of performance. Indeed, they might pass unnoticed, which is part of the reason for the lack of due attention to the complexity problem. However, the illusory success in dealing with information overload can lead to progressive deterioration in the quality of performance, and this can be seriously detrimental. Therefore, it is important to be aware of the effects of excessive complexity.

A common response is *defaulting to simpler representations* of the task. In classical reasoning tasks such as transitivity or class inclusion (discussed in chapter 5), children often respond on the basis of a single premise. Consider, for example, the problem discussed in chapter 1: *John is taller than Peter, and Michael is taller than John; who is tallest?* A person who cannot integrate the premises, such as a child under the age of 4 years, might make an inference based on only one premise and respond that John is the tallest. In our discussion of the Transitive Inference Mapping Model (TRIMM) in chapter 6, we showed how a concatenation strategy, in which premises are considered one at a time without integration, can lead to errors.

In industrial contexts, workers dealing with excessively complex rules are found to adopt simpler approximations to the rules. In our consulting work, we have found cases where workers reduced excessively complex tasks to a form that we designated as *Simple, Serviceable, Suboptimal*. This action results in performance that is right some (perhaps even most) of the time, so the errors may go undetected until problems arise subsequently, leading to wasteful rework. In the context of mathematics education, children adopt *malrules,* or rules that are approximations to correct rules (English & Halford, 1995). Thus, the distributive law of multiplication over addition might be overgeneralized to the distribution of addition over multiplication: $2(3 + 4) = (2 \times 3) + (2 \times 4)$, but $2 + (3 \times 4) \neq (2 + 3) \times (2 + 4)$; yet children have been known to treat these rules as equivalent.

Goal neglect, discussed in chapter 4, is a common response to information overload, as is the related effect of forgetting intentions (Einstein et al., 2003). Another response to information overload is fragmentation of knowledge. This means that tasks such as firefighting might be broken down into simpler subtasks in which factors are treated in isolation. Thus, the effect of wind on a fire might be considered in one representation, and the slope of the terrain might be considered in another representation. However, the interaction between these factors might not be recognized, so there can be a failure to recognize that slope and wind velocity can each magnify the effect of the other; a strong wind has more effect when a fire is burning uphill than when it is burning downhill.

Knowledge requirements

Tasks can be complex because of the knowledge required. This might entail long periods of training, but retrieval of knowledge from memory or from external sources such as handbooks or reference works can impose high processing loads at the time that the knowledge is used. This is particularly true where information about several factors must be retrieved.

Changes in procedures that require relearning can contribute to processing load even more than original learning because of interference from previously learned but superseded knowledge. That is, *proactive interference* is likely to be a factor.

Knowledge is of two main kinds: declarative and procedural. Declarative knowledge ("knowing that") is more factual, whereas procedural knowledge ("knowing how") is more closely related to skills. Declarative knowledge can support the acquisition of procedural knowledge; for example, understanding a task such as flying a plane or sailing a yacht is a help in acquiring the necessary skills to do the task. However, declarative knowledge is not synonymous with procedural knowledge, as a person can have a lot of declarative knowledge about a task and not know how to perform it (e.g., an aviation buff who has read a lot about flying planes but when placed in a cockpit cannot do anything safely until further instruction is provided).

Reciprocally, procedural knowledge does not necessarily imply declarative knowledge, as witnessed by findings that acknowledged experts in a field often cannot explain the basis of their skills. The relevance to training in organizations is that declarative knowledge often means knowing about something without mastery, and without acquiring the procedural knowledge that is required for adequate job performance.

The declarative-procedural distinction is important in training (particularly in retraining) because it means that merely telling staff about new procedures will not necessarily enable them to perform the relevant tasks. They might need practice in implementing the procedures before they will exhibit the requisite procedural knowledge.

Accessibility of knowledge is an important factor in complexity because, if the required knowledge is not readily accessible, it might be necessary to conduct searches of memory or reference works, and the search processes can themselves impose a processing load.

Matching knowledge to the task

Knowledge has to be matched to features of the task for appropriate decisions to be made. This involves first understanding the verbal statement of relevant rules or concepts and then constructing a mental model or task model, as discussed in chapter 4. It is likely to entail switching back and forth from knowledge representation to task representation to find appropriate matches. Where problems are presented in a way that is not clearly related to the relevant knowledge, this factor can be an important contributor to task difficulty.

Planning

Planning entails constructing a mental model of the task using relevant knowledge. It requires a representation of the current state of the task, the goals that have to be achieved, and the means of progressing from the current state to the goal state, often through intermediate steps that entail subgoals. Planning requires that the relations between task elements match the relations stored in memory so that, for example, a step will be selected that will effect the desired transition between the current state and the next goal, based on knowledge of the situation. If the right matches are not predefined, this can entail searching a problem space, and the size of the space can have a big impact on task complexity. Selecting appropriate actions often involves taking account of complex relationships, especially where multiple constraints must be satisfied. This is likely to be the case where complex rules have to be observed and where other demands of the situation have to be satisfied. The relations involved in planning can be a major factor influencing processing load. Thus, planning can itself impose a high cognitive load.

Memory load

The requirement to remember elements of a task while making decisions can impose a high load if the work environment does not provide suitable support in the form of memory aids or an efficiently organized sequence of steps. Memory for actions to be taken in the future, known as *prospective memory,* can increase the operator's processing load. Having to remember elements of incomplete work or having to recall the state of the task before interruptions or distractions occurred can increase task complexity significantly.

Assessment of complexity

We have applied the knowledge accumulated in cognitive science to the analysis of complexity in staff operations, which has necessitated some changes in the way that task analyses are usually carried out. Standard ways of representing work processes (e.g., as binary decision trees) are valuable for designing and organizing work, but they are not necessarily a psychologically realistic way to analyze the complexity of decisions. In binary decision trees, variables are processed one at a time, whereas in real-life decisions, two or more variables often interact. Processing is

often assumed to be hierarchical, but this also might not be psychologically realistic. Sometimes variables that were processed in earlier steps
can be processed in combination with different variables in subsequent
steps.

We have analyzed the tasks that staff must perform in certain industrial contexts, trying to determine as accurately as practicable the cognitive processes employed in carrying out a task. This approach is expensive
in terms of the amount of data and the complexity of the analyses
required. We believe that this approach is worthwhile, however, because
it enables the appreciation of factors that would not be observable in
transaction records. Tasks with the same number of transactions can differ significantly in the complexity of the processes needed to carry them
out. This factor can be assessed to some extent by appropriately structured ratings by staff. However, these ratings are subject to potential
biases and are limited to processing loads of which staff have at least
some awareness. As some important sources of complexity are possibly
not consciously recognized, this limitation could distort the assessment.
There is value, therefore, in supplementing these ratings by objective
observation.

The complexity of significant but covert activities can be detected by
competent observers through direct observation. An example would be the
complexity of planning, organizing, or sequencing the steps required to
perform a task. Unless this is externalized by notes on a scratchpad, by
"thinking aloud," by protocol analysis, or by some similar attempt to
externalize the process, planning goes on "in the head" and is not observable. Furthermore, staff are probably not even aware of the processing load
that they experience in planning. Estimates of processing load do not correspond to recognized work activities, which might reduce the face validity
of ratings. The complexity of planning activity is actually likely to preclude
the recognition of how complex it is because the high processing load
might inhibit reflection on the task. Our observation and analysis methods
are designed to detect cases of complexity that would escape other types
of assessment.

Much of the challenge of complexity analysis is in detecting when
decomposition cannot be used. The guiding principle is that variables cannot be chunked or segmented for a given step if relations between them
must be processed, as defined in chapter 4. Another case is where a novel
combination of variables occurs, such as when a previously learned procedure has to be modified by a new variable or by a new value on an old
variable.

Scientific thinking and relational knowledge

We will not review the extensive literature on cognition in science, technology, and mathematics, although we have contributed to this field in earlier publications (Andrews et al., 2009; English & Halford, 1995; Halford, 1993; Halford & Andrews, 2006; Halford et al., 2002, 2005). For this discussion, we will just indicate how the relational knowledge that we defined in chapter 2 relates to these fields.

Time, distance, and mass are basic physical dimensions, while concepts such as volume, speed, and density are composed of these dimensions. These concepts are essential to an understanding of matter, which in turn lies at the core of much knowledge in the physical sciences. These concepts are inherently relational. Volume is the product of length, breadth, and height, and is *prima facie* quaternary relational, although it can be reduced to lesser dimensions by conceptual chunking; (e.g., we can chunk length and breadth into area, so volume then becomes the product of area and height). The restrictions on chunking defined in chapter 2 apply, of course, so that questions that entail processing the relation between length and breadth cannot be answered without unchunking area into its constituent dimensions. Speed = distance/time and density = mass/volume are two further examples of a similar sort.

It is often difficult for children to master symbolic concepts (Smith, 2007), and these difficulties can persist well into high school. While we do not pretend to provide a quick or easy answer to this problem, we draw attention to the implication of relational knowledge theory that symbols depend on structure, without which symbols are essentially meaningless. Acquisition of structure depends critically on structural alignment, so it is likely that this process lies at the core of acquiring symbolic concepts. Modifying teaching materials and approaches on the basis of relational complexity theory might be fruitful.

It is important that we distinguish between recognition of an already known concept and acquisition of a genuinely new concept that is "incommensurable" with preexisting cognitions (Fischer & Bidell, 2006; Carey, 2009; Halford & Andrews, 2006). Our observation is that familiarity with a concept might mean that complexity is underestimated. Complexity might be much greater for someone who is unfamiliar with the task. Failure to recognize this fact can have major impacts in both educational and industrial settings. The acquisition of concepts that are incommensurable with those existing previously is a major source of difficulty for children. An example would be the concepts of density and proportion discussed previously, where new relations between variables have to be represented. Such acquisitions are a major source of difficulty to children at a number of points in their schooling (Smith, 2007), and relational knowledge theory suggests that they can be facilitated by better induction of relational representations. Acquisition is based on experience with relational instances and is partly autonomous and self-supervised, as discussed in chapter 6. It can be triggered by relatively automatic recognition of regularities in the environment, without explicitly structural information; and it can be validated by structural correspondence with a coordinate system, which can be established autonomously, by processing information in the task without explicit instruction. These factors make acquisition difficult to observe and manipulate experimentally, and successful teaching methodology must take them into account. Structural alignment of a set of instances to a coordinate system should be of value in this context, as illustrated in table 9.1, because it indicates how density relates to other variables.

An integrated structure incorporating the properties of relational knowledge must be formed. Language undoubtedly plays a role in the acquisition of complex concepts, but concept acquisition also depends on learning the relations among the relevant dimensions (e.g., among V, D, and M), so verbal labels alone are not sufficient. Symbols depend on operating systems that are inherently relational. Integration is a defining property of relational knowledge and occurs by dynamic mapping to a coordinate system. It is also a distinguishing neuroscience feature, in that it activates the frontopolar cortex (lateral BA 10), as discussed in chapter 3.

Verbal explanations of density should be more effective once the relations such as those in table 9.1 are known. Once the effect of density is recognized in the set of aligned instances, participants will be able to benefit from instructions such as "these objects are made of different kinds of stuff—some kinds of stuff are heavier than others, so this one (iron) is heavier than this one (aluminium), which is heavier than this one (wood),

Table 9.1

Coordinate system for understanding density, defined as mass divided by volume ($D = MV^{-1}$)

Schema	V	D	M
Instance 1 (Iron)	10 cm³	Unknown	79 gm
Instance 2 (Aluminium)	20 cm³	Unknown	52 gm
Instance 3 (Wood)	15 cm³	Unknown	13 gm

etc." However, verbal explanations of density will not be meaningful without experience of aligned instances. The general principle is that the acquisition of many complex concepts depends on acquiring a representation of the appropriate structure which, as in this case, means assignment to a coordinate system. Carey (2009) proposes Quinian bootstrapping as the transition mechanism, which is essentially consistent with assignment to a coordinate system, but relational knowledge theory offers many detailed principles that can enhance the effectiveness of procedures for inducing the acquisition of new concepts, as discussed in chapter 6.

Our criteria for integrated relational representations are *accessibility* and *generativity,* as discussed in chapter 3. In the context of density, accessibility means inferring any one of V, D, or M given the other two. For example, in table 9.1, if $V \approx 10$ cm^3 and $M \approx 79$ gm, then $D \approx 7.9$. The generativity test requires transferring to isomorphic structures and accessing the relational representation to predict values of new items.

An experiment (Mingon, 2012) in which 5- to 7-year-old children were trained to assign blocks to a matrix (as shown in figure 9.2) supports the effect of structural alignment. Children trained at structural alignment showed more improvement as a result of verbal instruction than children who did not understand structural alignment. Performance on accessibility and generativity tests predicted relational processing in the post-test. This is obviously only a limited study, but it illustrates how we apply relational knowledge to the acquisition of a basic scientific concept.

Concept of the Earth

The concept of the Earth is inherently relational, and the work of Vosniadou and Brewer provides some beautiful examples of representations that are constructed to meet conflicting constraints, such as depiction of a spherical Earth with a platform inside on which people can stand (see Vosniadou & Brewer, 1992, figure 1). A person's everyday understanding, in the absence of scientific instruction, is represented in more psychologically realistic fashion by mental models than by equations, although the mental models ultimately provide a stepping-off point to the more precise understanding based on mathematics. Here, we just want to make a few points about the nature of the required mental models.

One issue is a conflict between the cultural conception of the Earth as a sphere and our everyday experience that, allowing for topographic ups and downs, it appears more flat than round. The cultural input provides verbal information that the Earth is round or spherical (children are told

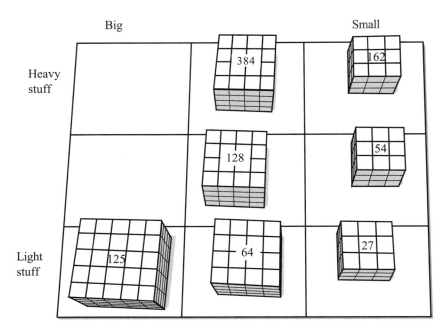

Figure 9.2
Structural alignment training. Blocks are assigned to a matrix according to volume (indicated by squares) and mass (indicated by digits). Volumes and masses are clearly discriminable, and participants have extensive experience with both before making assignments.

the Earth is round), globe maps provide useful visual information about the form of the Earth, and photographs from space tend to reinforce the evidence that it is spherical. The conflicting conceptions can be reconciled to some extent by understanding that the enormous size of the Earth makes it appear flat to an observer on the ground, and Hayes et al. (2003) found that children were helped to form a spherical world model if they received information about both size and gravity. However, understanding this conception still entails some difficulties. We define understanding as having a mental model that represents the relevant relations.

First, the spherical nature of the Earth means that some of its inhabitants must somehow stand on what is depicted in most maps as the lower side of the Earth (i.e., "down under"). This conflicts with the everyday understanding of gravity as something that pulls things down (when you drop a stone, it goes down). A coherent mental model of the Earth needs to include representation that "pulling down" actually corresponds to attraction toward the center of the Earth. Thus, a person standing in Norway experiences gravity in the same way as a person standing in Australia in that the "downward pull" is really attraction toward the center of the Earth. There is a correspondence between two relations here that we can express this way: *corresponds*(*object, pulled_down; object, pulled_toward_Earth_center*). Some conceptual chunking can possibly occur here (e.g., *object* is an element of both component relations), and this is an issue to be investigated. However, the important point for our present purposes is that a correspondence between two relations must be represented to provide a realistic conception of gravity on the Earth. Thus, relational knowledge is at the core of an intuitive understanding of the Earth.

Another issue with a spherical concept of the Earth is that objects disappear over the horizon. There are limited opportunities to observe this, although it can be experienced by standing on a beach or a headland and watching a boat sail away. Understanding can be promoted further by imagining oneself rising vertically in a helicopter above the observation point, and realizing that the vanishing object should become visible again (subject to how far it has moved).

Other aspects of the concept of the Earth include the day-night cycle produced by the rotation of the Earth. This can be neatly demonstrated by shining a directed light source on a model globe in a darkened room, but representation of the relations involved is by no means simple. Then there is the seasonal variation caused by "tilting" the Earth through approximately 45 degrees as it completes its annual orbit of the Sun. A mental model of orbital motion also needs to include the effect of gravitational attraction in causing the Earth to adopt a curved path around the Sun. Understanding phases of the moon depends on a mental model of the moon's orbit around the Earth, and this model is applicable to artificial satellites.

This has been a necessarily brief and simple account of the concept of the Earth, but our purpose has been to draw attention to some of the relational representations that are inherent in such a concept. There have been a number of valuable investigations, of which we have mentioned only a small sample (see also Halford & Andrews, 2006). Future research into this domain could shed a lot of new light on acquisition of relational knowledge.

Cognitive complexity of mathematics education

Relational knowledge theory, including the relational complexity metric, has been applied extensively to mathematics education. Relations pervade even elementary mathematics: e.g., "3" is defined to be the equivalence class of sets with 3 elements, so by an equivalence relation. A variable, however, is defined by reference to other terms in the expression ("$X + 3 = 5$" defines X by its relation to another addend and a sum). Mathematical operations are defined by more complex relations, so addition is defined by union of disjoint sets, and so on (see boxes 2.1 and 2.6 in chapter 2).

These considerations have a lot of implications for the acquisition of mathematical concepts. Concrete aids such as arithmetic blocks are essentially analogs and function in accordance with analogy theory. Their effectiveness depends on how readily learners can map the structure of the analog to the structure of the concept, and the performance of many teaching aids can be accounted for on this basis (English & Halford, 1995; Halford, 1993). Thus, the transition from arithmetic to algebra is not a matter of substituting letters for numbers but of representing the relevant structures. This point is consistent with the subsymbolic-to-symbolic transition that we considered in chapter 6. Complexity has a strong but often unrecognized effect. Thus, proportion, known to be difficult for young children, is defined by relations between four variables ($p/q = r/s$) and is inherently quaternary relational in that it necessarily relates four variables. However, it can be chunked and segmented so that acquisition can begin with binary relations such as a half (1/2), which can be understood by young children. It can form a building block to more complex concepts but should not be mistaken as a substitute for those concepts. These matters have been examined in great detail in existing literature (see English & Halford, 1995), and our purpose here has been simply to draw attention to the links between relational knowledge theory and acquisition of mathematical concepts.

Complexity in air traffic control

Air traffic control is well known to be a task that entails considerable cognitive complexity, which has great importance because of its safety-critical nature. One point that has always been clear is that the number of aircraft in a given control area (i.e., the number of aircraft using a specific air traffic control frequency) is not a valid measure of complexity. There might be 20 aircraft traveling through an area, but if they are separated by altitude or horizontal distance, there might be no problem. On the other hand, a small number of aircraft can cause excessively high processing demands on a controller. In this section, we will briefly summarize a project (Boag et al., 2006) that applied the Method for Analysis of Relational Complexity (MARC), which we outlined in chapter 4, to this problem.

One component of the project entailed critical interviews with a group of controllers who were invited to outline one important or memorable event in their careers. One such episode is shown in figure 9.3. We want to emphasize that it was not a safety-critical incident, but it does illustrate how MARC applies to the task.

Dealing with complexity

In chapter 4, we considered conceptual chunking and segmentation as ways of reducing the complexity of cognitive tasks. In applied contexts, there are a number of strategies for dealing with complexity, all of which depend in some way on expertise and are consistent with the processes discussed in chapter 4, in that they reduce the complexity of relational representations employed in any step of the task.

Proceduralization

Complexity can be handled by various forms of proceduralization. For example, a complex process can be handled by performing and checking off one step at a time. This is a form of segmentation, as discussed in chapter 4. Proceduralization might not work, however, where the task is so varied that standardized procedures are impractical, where the criteria are modified by a number of supplementary rules that require additional information to be taken into account, or where rules are changed so frequently that procedures cannot be established.

Development of strategies

Instruction in a task often includes learning strategies for efficient performance. Such strategies entail recoding, in the form of conceptual chunking, or segmenting procedures into smaller steps that require less information to be processed. Once a task is well understood, the operator can devise strategies for performing it efficiently, without cognitive overload. However, when a task is changed, the strategies must be modified, or even relinquished and replaced. Replacement of strategies can impose

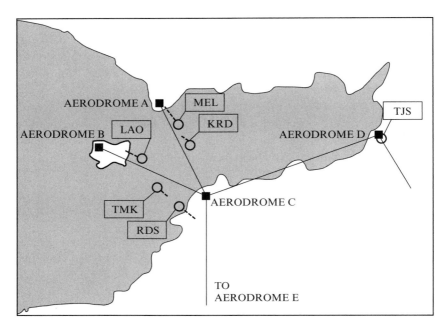

Figure 9.3
A situation that was reported to impose a high, but not safety-critical, processing load on a controller. Locations and aircraft identifications have been disguised. Aircraft are shown by small circles with "history dots" trailing behind. Letters in rectangles represent aircraft call signs (e.g., TMK, "tango mike kilo"). MEL and KRD were climbing out of Aerodrome A, while LAO was climbing out of Aerodrome B. TMK and RDS were descending into Aerodrome B. These five aircraft needed to use the same airspace for climbing or descending. At the point where the controller had to decide what instructions to issue, TJS requested departure (takeoff) clearance from Aerodrome D. Unable to make all the decisions required, the controller told TJS to stand by. The incident illustrates that it is the relations between the aircraft that determines the controller's cognitive load (Boag et al., 2006).

considerable cognitive workload on the person charged with performing the task.

Automaticity

Automaticity can develop as a way of coping with complexity. With extensive practice, tasks become automatic, so they impose minimum load on the performer. The cost of this is that the performance becomes less modifiable, as it is no longer under strategic control (i.e., it becomes a "habit").

The result is sometimes the continuation of procedures after they become inappropriate (e.g., persistence of habitual searching for something in a place where it is no longer kept).

Automaticity develops under conditions of *constant mapping;* that is, where the relations between elements of the task remain constant. When mappings vary, automaticity no longer produces relatively effortless correct performance, and considerable effort may be required to establish a new set of procedures. In effect, it reduces the processing to unstructured (Rank 0) or functionally structured (Rank 1), as defined in chapters 2 and 5.

Lookup table procedures

Well-learned knowledge can be stored in memory structures that sometimes are called *lookup tables,* where they can be accessed with little error or effort. An example would be that educated adults can access the sum of two single-digit numbers quickly, effortlessly, and without error. Again, however, this requires a work environment in which there is constant mapping. Lookup table retrievals work for arithmetic because addition and multiplication facts remain constant.

Complexity: A summary

The limitations on human ability to process information are now understood and have been quantified with reasonable precision. There are well-established processes by which people can handle complexity, in addition to well-known processes for coping with change. However, complexity and change tend to magnify each other's effects, so change is harder to cope with in conditions of high complexity, and vice versa.

Those tasks that have the highest effective complexity are the ones in which procedures or strategies are constrained by some feature of the task or the work environment. Achieving efficient procedures tends to require considerable effort, and a large amount of an organization's resources may need to be devoted to it. Superficial learning that leads to knowing about a topic, but not mastery, will lead to mounting dissatisfaction in a complex environment.

The complexity of most tasks is not a fixed quantity; rather, it depends in a major way on conditions of performance. A task that can be performed according to a well-learned procedure that remains constant over time can impose a low processing load, and it also can have short decision times and a low error rate, despite being inherently complex. By contrast, a task that is different every time that it is performed and where the operator has to plan a procedure with each performance, accessing all the relevant information from a relatively disorganized set of reference material, can impose very high loads, with consequent slow decisions and high error rates. There are exceptional tasks that do not lend themselves to efficient proceduralization, and these may impose loads that are difficult to reduce. However, it is a fair generalization that there is a lot of scope to reduce the complexity of tasks for the performer by good job design, thorough training, and efficient maintenance of expertise.

The large number of factors that influence processing load means that the relative complexity of tasks varies considerably depending on the circumstances. A task that would be easy for an expert who had a well-rehearsed procedure for performing it might be very difficult for a person who had to devise a completely new plan for tackling it. A task that might be easy to perform with good support for decision making, for keeping track of the current state of the work, and for remembering steps that need to be taken in the future could be very difficult without any of these aids. Tasks can be rank-ordered for complexity only if other factors are held constant, which is rarely the case in a real work environment. Therefore, while rank ordering for complexity is possible in principle, we believe at the present time that careful consideration of the relevant factors is more beneficial. If the conditions of performance are specified, precise quantification could be achieved with further investigation. With this caveat in mind, the way that factors combine clearly makes some tasks very complex. The most important point, however, is that the principles governing complexity, as well as other aspects of performance where it is based on higher cognition, now are sufficiently well understood that there is no reason why human factors problems should be intractable.

10   Conclusion

In this book, we have shown that it is possible to distinguish categories of cognitive processes in a way that corresponds to identifiable cognitive architectures and is supported by converging evidence from numerous paradigms. In addition, we have demonstrated that the categories distinguish cognitions by features that can be regarded as foundational, in that they relate to numerous and important properties of cognitive performance. In the process, we suggest that we have brought into focus issues that have tended to be neglected by many otherwise admirable research paradigms. In this chapter, we present the essence of our contribution and summarize the implications.

The core distinction is between subsymbolic and symbolic processes. This distinction goes back to the early history of the discipline, but it has been neglected due to a number of factors. There has been a perception that it is difficult to define, there has been a belief that it would be preferable to conceptualize all cognition in terms of a single set of processes, and there has been some anxiety that the distinction diminishes the significance of specific findings in domains such as infancy and animal cognition. We believe that all these reservations are unjustified. We have provided formal definitions and empirical criteria for the categories of cognition. We acknowledge the numerous processes that are shared by all the categories, but there are also specific properties that determine category membership. The significance of many infancy and animal cognition findings has increased rather than decreased due to our formulations.

The key to distinguishing between subsymbolic and symbolic cognition is to define the structure on which symbolic processes depend. Structure has played a major part throughout the history of theorizing in cognitive psychology, but it has had many different meanings and has been hard to relate clearly and rigorously to empirical operations. We propose that relational knowledge provides the core of symbolic processes because it provides a successful approach to defining the structural properties of higher cognition, but it also can be linked to subsymbolic processes such as association.

Structural alignment

The essential difference between subsymbolic and symbolic processes is that the latter depend on structural alignment. This idea also has a history in the field, but we have identified it as the core of symbolic processes. Relational knowledge provides the operating system that gives meaning to symbolic processes. Structural alignment is essential to relational knowledge, which entails binding to roles or slots. Relational knowledge has the further merit that it shares many properties with association, which has played a fundamental role in cognition throughout history. Relational knowledge is differentiated from association by structural alignment, which depends on dynamic binding to a coordinate system in working memory. This links the theory of symbolic processes to research showing that working memory shares a high proportion of variance with fluid intelligence. There are numerous fundamental properties of higher cognition that flow from this formulation, and these were outlined in chapter 2.

Structural alignment also has enabled a new approach to the longstanding and difficult problem of the subsymbolic-to-symbolic transition. In the process, it adds new significance to the extensively investigated phenomenon of the A not-B ($A\bar{B}$) error, discussed in chapter 6. When infants, having repeatedly retrieved a hidden object from location A, are shown it being hidden at location B, they still tend to retrieve it from A. This is interpreted as a conflict between associative knowledge that it can be retrieved from A and dynamic binding of the object to B. Ceasing to make the $A\bar{B}$ error, therefore, indicates dynamic binding in working memory, a capacity that is at the core of symbolic processes. This development, which occurs late in the first year of life, portends the acquisition of many symbolic processes, including dynamic binding to slots in relational representations and representation of the meaning of a child's first words.

The dynamic binding to spatial coordinates that occurs in the $A\bar{B}$ task should apply to role-filler binding, as in understanding the proposition "Jane feeds cat," where *Jane* and *cat* are assigned to the *agent* and *patient* roles, respectively. This proposal was made in chapter 6. This novel approach to the subsymbolic-to-symbolic transition was enabled because we have made representation of structure (relational knowledge) the foundation of symbolic processes, which gives new significance to evidence that dynamic representation of structure occurs late in the first year. This is one of numerous examples of longstanding phenomena receiving increased significance through coherent foundations of cognition.

Structural alignment also has the merit that it can be indicated by simple and tractable empirical procedures. Consider the three propositions discussed in chapter 2:

Jane feeds cat (1)

Bob feeds dog (2)

Cat feeds Jane (3)

With structural alignment, (1) is more similar to (2) than to (3), but without structural alignment; that is, if the judgment is based solely on element similarity without regard to roles, then (1) and (3) would be more similar. This could be developed into a test for infants and other animals: If (1) were enacted by puppets in a habituation sequence, then infants who align elements to roles should be more surprised by the switch from (1) to (3) than from (1) to (2). Participants who do not make structural alignments would see more similarity between (1) and (3) and would show more surprise at the switch from (1) to (2). It would be necessary to control for ecological factors, as there might be inherent surprise at a cat feeding a woman, but this factor could be controlled by ingenuity that is readily available to researchers in the field. This paradigm potentially provides a new approach to assessing symbolic processes in inarticulate participants, and it avoids the confounds inherent in using tests that require language competence. Our formulation implies that the acquisition of relational knowledge, including dynamic binding to coordinate systems, plays a role in language acquisition, which means that we cannot always assume that language provides the foundation for acquisition of higher cognition. There are strong links between acquisition of language and relational knowledge, and we cannot assume that the causal influences always go in the same direction. We believe that the excessive ease with which cognitive processes can be attributed to language can lead to simplistic explanations that tend to hinder the quest for important underlying factors. Reinterpreting the role of relations in the symbolic transition, we believe, points the way to deeper understanding of the core of cognition.

Structural alignment also plays a role in the acquisition of relational knowledge throughout the lifespan, and it is particularly relevant to the acquisition of symbolic concepts. If symbols are meaningless without structure, and the acquisition of structured knowledge depends on structural alignment, then solutions to the well-known problems with acquisition of symbolic concepts should depend on structural alignment. There is still considerable unused potential for this factor to be exploited in pedagogy, especially in the all-important domains of science, technology, and mathematics learning.

The structural properties of symbolic processes now have been well defined and include accessibility and systematicity. The conceptual basis for these properties has been derived from a more abstract domain, mathematical category theory, which provides criteria for the structural properties of cognition and obviates the arbitrariness that might once have induced some skepticism toward structurally based models.

Complexity

Complexity is arguably the biggest issue in the 21st century, yet it tends to be neglected and often even seems to be avoided in research. However, there are problems that cannot be solved without it. For example, it is hard to assess the benefits of pedagogical innovations if we cannot rule out the possibility that something simpler is being learned, but without assessment of complexity, this issue cannot be addressed in a systematic way. One reason for skepticism about complexity and cognitive capacity has been the difficulty of distinguishing contexts where it operates from those where it does not. Thus, there are tasks that appear to be complex, such as the sophisticated inductive inferences performed by young children (as discussed in chapter 5), but where capacity limitations are not observed. On the other hand, there are apparently simple tasks, like the Wason Selection Task (discussed in chapter 8) and the knights and knaves task, and comprehension of compound, object-relative sentences (such as "The boy that the girl that the man saw met slept."), both discussed in chapter 4, where complexity effects are strong. Some of these observations have tended to engender skepticism about the reality of capacity limitations, but when the nature of cognitive capacity is adequately defined, it can be seen as a powerful explanation for many phenomena. When we appreciate the widespread effects of complexity in modern life, the as yet unexplored potential of this construct is prodigious.

The relational complexity metric provides a way of quantifying the complexity of cognitive processes, as discussed extensively in chapter 4. The essence of the metric is the number of independent entities bound into a relational representation, with the amount of information in each entity having comparatively little effect. This explains why chunking is effective—namely, because information in one entity can be increased without affecting relational complexity. There are, however, limitations to this process because relations between variables in that single chunk cannot be processed. The theory also means that complexity effects belong mainly to relational representations and have much less effect on subsymbolic processes such as elemental association (Rank 0) and processes that depend on computed internal representations that directly produce output (Rank 1). As these nonrelational processes are often used in processes such as heuristic reasoning, complexity effects there will be minimal.

One benefit of the relational complexity metric is that it has enabled specification of boundary conditions for complexity and capacity effects. Heuristics can occur in cognitive processes that are symbolic and were formed by relational processing in working memory. For example, categorical syllogisms sometimes can be performed by using heuristics that link the mood of a premise (*All, Some, None, Some not*) with the mood of a conclusion, as discussed in chapters 4 and 8. Here, knowledge of links between entities is being used to simplify reasoning and avoid the processing loads associated with relational knowledge. There are powerful strategies for reducing complexity of cognitive processes that have to be performed in any step of a task, but that power has given rise to the misperception that complexity effects are eliminated, which subsequent research has disconfirmed. Another benefit of the relational complexity metric is that it specifies the conditions under which decomposition of cognitive tasks can be performed and shows where the limitations operate. In essence, decomposition cannot be employed where variables interact, and this has been elaborated into several principles defined in chapter 4. The serial processing that is characteristic of higher cognition is attributable to high processing loads that cause decomposition into simpler subtasks that are performed serially. Subsymbolic processes do not impose such high processing loads and more often are performed by parallel acting constraints.

Working memory

Considerable improvement in assessment of working memory has been seen in the last decade. One advance was measurement by latent variables, based on three or more distinctly different tests, as a result of which working memory was found to account for considerably more variance in fluid intelligence than previously. A second advance was the theory of working memory as dynamic binding to a coordinate system. This conception is eminently applicable to higher cognition, in that it provides a mechanism for structural alignment, which is essential to relational representations, which in turn form the foundation of symbolic cognition. According to relational knowledge theory, the acquisition of symbolic representations depends on the construction of a relational representation in working memory. This means that working memory plays a major role in symbolic processes, consistent with the high correlation between working memory and fluid intelligence. As noted previously, there are basic processes that operate at all levels, and associative links can be acquired between symbols once those symbols have been formed and given meaning by being embedded in relational representations. Thus, we have an association between clouds and rain even though we no doubt have a relational (and indeed sophisticated) concept of clouds and their formation. Whether we operate at the associative or relational level depends on factors such as task demands and motivational state. As we saw in chapter 8, deductive reasoning depends in part on the construction in working memory of representations (currently best characterized as mental models) that correspond to information in premises. However, some deductions are generated by heuristics that utilize associations between properties such as moods of premises and moods of conclusions.

Subsymbolic cognition

Subsymbolic cognition is less unified than cognition at the symbolic level, and we have separated modular processes as a distinct category on the grounds that they do not entail internal and accessible representations of structures. This would not preclude analysis in terms of relational knowledge if accessible relational representations were found to be employed in modular processes, but we are not aware of any such cases at this time. We have identified two levels of subsymbolic processes: nonstructured (Rank 0) and functionally structured (Rank 1). Nonstructured processes entail a link between two entities and correspond to elemental association, which we believe plays an important role in knowledge acquisition because it is an efficient and relatively effortless way of learning links in the environment. Importantly, it can occur automatically, without any prior knowledge that a structure is to be learned and without specific instruction about the structure. We proposed in chapter 6 that nonstructured processes play an initial role in the acquisition of structured knowledge, and it corresponds to implicit learning, which has been widely investigated in this context. Nonstructured processes are, therefore, a powerful mechanism for knowledge acquisition, but they have limitations such that, as we saw in chapter 2, there are some links that they cannot learn due to factors such as associative interference.

Functionally structured (Rank 1) processes entail a link between an input and a computed internal representation, and a further link between the internal representation and an output, as defined in chapter 2. The internal representation can be a recoding of the input and is important in computing an appropriate output. The functionally structured level is a powerful means of computing input–output functions that match environmental contingencies, and consequently architectures of this type have been utilized to simulate an enormous range of phenomena. They differ from our symbolically structured level discussed previously in that they do not produce an internal and accessible representation of relations, at least in the forms that we have examined. One reason for this is that, as we have defined them, they do not incorporate structural alignment, which is crucial to the symbolically structured level. Another reason for the importance of Rank 1 and 2 cognitions is that they can support some processes, including transfer based on properties such as same-different, or left-right, that are sophisticated but subsymbolic. This is where the fundamental difference between subsymbolic and symbolic has to be made.

Symbolically structured processes can be conceptualized as inherently relational and depend on structural alignment in working memory. Relational representations are validated by structural correspondence so that, for example, mental models used in deductive reasoning are in structural alignment to premises. There is a sizeable list of properties of higher cognition that follow from this formulation, as defined in chapter 2. Another important property, noted in chapter 6, is that the acquisition of relational knowledge is partly self-supervised because structural correspondence can be established by internal working memory processes that do not necessarily require external input. As pointed out in chapter 1, we do not need to be told that a mental model of the order of three elements in a transitive inference task is in correspondence to relations in the premises. Thus, structured knowledge sometimes can be acquired from examples, without specific instruction in the nature of the structure. This is an important feature of structured knowledge acquisition because it is partly autonomous, as when children learn grammatical rules without instruction from adults. However, as explained in chapter 6, there is still a role for good pedagogy to guide experience with examples of structure, to facilitate structural alignment, and to articulate the structure learned, but the

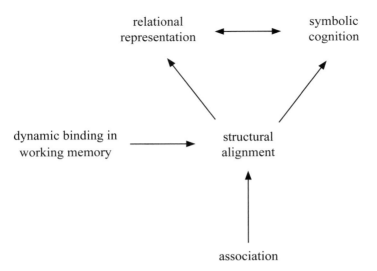

Figure 10.1
Links between processes entailed in symbolically structured, Rank 2+ cognition. Structural alignment, based on dynamic binding in working memory, is crucial to the transition from association to relational representation, which develops in parallel with symbolic cognition.

pedagogy depends on the autonomous underlying acquisition processes. A graphic summary of the links between association, structural alignment, dynamic binding in working memory, relational representations, and symbolic cognition is provided in figure 10.1.

The nonstructured, functionally structured, and symbolically structured levels correspond to two-layered, three-layered, and symbolic connectionist classes of neural net models, as discussed in chapters 2 and 3. A comprehensive review and evaluation of these models is well beyond the scope of this book, but we take the neural net and symbolic connectionist models as providing validation for the existence of the categories of cognition that we have defined. That is, they demonstrate that cognitive processes can operate according to the principles that we have attributed to these categories of processes, and they assist with deriving the properties of each category. This does not preclude further development of these models, but they belong to the categories we have defined only if they conform to the properties that we specify. Thus, if a multilayered feedforward net is produced that models structural alignment dynamically, as distinct from incrementally over multiple trials, then that neural net will simulate symbolically structured processes. We are not aware of any multilayered feed-forward neural net that does this, though.

Categorization by deep structure

In chapter 1, we set the goal of defining a system for categorizing cognitions by their deep structure, thereby bringing increased coherence to the field. The question is to what extent we have achieved that goal. Now we would like to propose that it has been achieved in the following senses:

• Cognitive processes are assigned to categories according to core or foundational properties based on the level of structure that is represented. This in turn affects the ability to form mappings (i.e., establish correspondences) between cognitive representations. There is a mathematical basis for this property, as outlined in chapters 1 and 4. This ability depends on dynamic structural alignment in working memory, and many properties of cognition follow from this, as specified in chapter 2.

• Cognitive processes can be assigned to equivalent categories despite belonging to different domains or being investigated by different paradigms. Thus, categories transcend paradigms and domains.

• The categories are discriminable by empirical criteria that are applicable across a wide range of domains.

• There are empirical tests, including some tests for higher cognitive processes, that are applicable to inarticulate participants. Thus, cognitive capabilities can be assessed uncontaminated by dependence on language. Language does influence conceptualization and reasoning, but relational knowledge underlies both, and they need to be manipulated independently to determine whether the influence really reflects language or relational representations.

One important implication of our formulation is that we can no longer categorize cognitions by the behaviors that are produced. In essence, the problem with this longstanding behaviorist conception is that there is no constant mapping between cognitions and behaviors. The same output can be produced by many different cognitive processes, and the same process can produce many different outputs, depending on the history of the performer and other factors. Consider the processes that can yield a transitive inference, as discussed in chapters 1 and 2. If the participants have been trained to discriminate between pairs of objects over hundreds of trials, as in the transitivity of choice paradigm, the inference might be based on elemental association. On the other hand, if the inference is produced by a single presentation of verbally stated premises, it might reflect dynamic binding in working memory. Converging evidence from other tests would be required, of course, but distinct processes are identifiable.

To be clear, recognition that the observation of behavior is a fundamentally important source of data for psychology was one of the great insights of the 20th century. But we cannot categorize phenomena solely by behaviors, and we need theories connecting observations to the underlying phenomena. This need has long been recognized in other sciences and now must be taken more seriously in psychology. The theories have to be validated, of course, and considerable effort might be required, but we believe that there is an abundance of modeling expertise to fulfill this need. If we do not make the effort required, we will forfeit the opportunity for a coherent and unified discipline.

Benefits

The tendency to treat all cognitions as belonging to the same category, implying a common deep structure applicable to all, produces inconsistencies and exceptions and discourages some important lines of investigation. For example, investigation of thinking has tended to be discouraged by putative demonstrations that it is evident in infants or other animals, whereas many of these achievements, although undoubtedly of great importance, are properly categorized as subsymbolic cognitions. Failure to distinguish subsymbolic and symbolic processes has tended to discourage investigation of the latter. Our categories of cognition open up many potential lines of investigation in this and many other areas. Another example would be that complexity has tended to be neglected, despite its manifest importance as a 21st century issue, because determining that some cognitions are of lower complexity might be seen as diminishing the importance of the research. We strongly urge that this is a misconception, and the significance of these lines of research is actually embellished by a coherent conception of cognition. The subsymbolic-symbolic distinction has been neglected (or even avoided) due to lack of adequate definition or a belief that it can be handled by the distinction between prelinguistic and language-based categorizations. It also has been eschewed because of anxieties that it will diminish the significance of some findings in domains such as infancy and animal cognition. We believe these anxieties are unjustified.

Parsimony is increased by the categorization of cognitions according to common sets of properties. With our system of categorization, we have identified many links and correspondences that had not been recognized. In the process, we have identified a small set of principles that account for a very wide range of cognitive processes.

There are also technical questions that could be investigated in a way that would increase our understanding of some important processes. One of these is the formation of structured representations in working memory. Enough is known to establish this as an important process, but it has not received the depth of investigation that it deserves. The conception of working memory as dynamic binding to a coordinate system plays a very important role in contemporary cognitive theory, but there is considerable scope for further investigation. For example, whereas there are complex span tasks for assessing simultaneous processing and storage conceptions of working memory, there does not appear to be a measure of dynamic binding to a coordinate system in the context of symbolically structured processes. Another possibility is to investigate whether working memory capacity can be improved, as discussed in chapter 9.

One of the most important implications of the formulation is that we need to determine whether any cognitive architectures can implement the properties of higher cognition without dynamic structural alignment. A lot of research effort has been justifiably expended to establish whether higher cognition can emerge from interaction between elementary processes. Many of the resulting computational models have been based on the architecture of feedforward or other types of multilayered nets, as discussed in chapters 2, 3, and 7. We suggest that none of these models has the property of dynamic structural alignment, and we also have not found any that support the essential properties of higher cognition. This does not show that nets with this type of architecture are inherently incapable of dynamic structural alignment or of higher cognition, and we need to remain open to the possibility that dynamic structural alignment might be implemented by entirely new architectures, which might also implement higher cognition. But the question remains whether any architecture can implement higher cognition without dynamic structural alignment.

In addition, there are issues that can be seen as unproductive and undeserving of investigation. For example, we do not need to decide whether cognition is heuristic or analytic because roles can be found for both types of processes. We also can dispense with associative versus structured conceptions because both manifestly play a role. One important thing about this book is that it indicates how and when these factors are manifest. Because we have defined the properties of different categories of cognition, we do not say *if* cognition is heuristic or analytic, but we say *when* it is heuristic and *when* it is analytic and provide empirical criteria for both. Similarly, we can say when acquisition is based on association or when it is based on structure, and we can specify the consequences of each option.

Our most important conclusion is that we can shift the emphasis away from "isms" and toward foundational properties of cognition. We see our formulation as pointing the way to many productive developments within the enormous and exciting field of cognition, which also has implications for other areas, including psychology, cognitive science, neuroscience, information technology, artificial intelligence, anthropology, education, and human factors.

Glossary of Terms and Abbreviations

A not-B ($A\bar{B}$) error   A task in which an infant sees an object hidden one or more times at location A, retrieves it each time, and then sees it hidden at B; subsequently, the infant tends to try to retrieve the object at A.

Accessibility   A property of symbolically structured processes whereby each component of a relational representation can be retrieved from any of the other components of that representation.

ACME   An early model that successfully implemented mapping by parallel constraint satisfaction; the acronym means "Analogical Constraint Mapping Engine."

ACT-R   A model of memory developed by John Anderson that specified a networked memory comprised of working memory, declarative memory and procedural memory; the acronym means "Adaptive Control of Thought—Rational."

Analog   The target (or source) of an analogical mapping. *See also* Analogy.

Analogy   A mapping between two representations (one called a *source* or *base*, the other called a *target*) based on correspondence between relations in the representations.

Animacy   A concept that captures the correlations among features and motion characteristics that underpin the living-nonliving distinction.

APFC   A part of the prefrontal cortex (PFC) area of the brain; the acronym means "anterior prefrontal cortex." *See also* PFC.

Attention   Cognitive resources, mental effort, or concentration devoted to a cognitive process.

BA   A system for mapping the cortex of the brain based on the architecture of its cellular structure; the acronym means "Brodmann area," named for German anatomist Korbinian Brodmann. His original system demarcated 52 areas.

Backpropagation   A method of training a neural network to learn a target function by minimizing error (the difference between a target and network response) as a function of connection weights by employing the *chain rule* for calculating the derivative (i.e. the slope) of the error surface; errors and weight changes are effectively propagated backward from the output units along afferent connections until the input units are reached.

BART   A computational model that acquires relational representations from experience with perceptually available nonrelational features; the acronym means "Bayesian Analogy with Relational Transformations."

Bayesian   Based on Bayes's theorem, a mathematical prescription for estimating the probability of a hypothesis given the evidence taking into account the prior probability of the hypothesis and (conditional) probability of obtaining evidence.

Binary operation   A binary function sending pairs of elements to elements that are all taken from the same set. Addition and multiplication are examples. Unary and ternary operations are defined similarly.

Bindings   *See* Dynamic binding, Role-filler binding, and Object-location binding.

Cartesian product   The Cartesian product of two sets, *A* and *B*, comprises all ordered pairs of combinations of the elements from *A* and the elements from *B*. Cartesian products are examples of categorical products. *See also* Universal mapping property.

Category, categorical   The word *category* and the associated adjective *categorical* are used in three distinct senses in this book.

• In mathematical category theory, a collection of objects and morphisms (relations or transformations between objects), and a composition operation for morphisms into other morphisms, that satisfies certain axioms. In this context, a "categorical approach" would be an approach based on category theory.
• Categorical syllogisms are inference schemas composed of two premises and a conclusion. The premises and conclusion are all *categorical propositions*, that is, propositions such as "*All men are mortal*" that relate two categories such as *men* and *mortal*. Categorical propositions may be of one of four types, known as moods: "*All X are Y*"; "*Some X are Y*"; "*Some X are not Y*"; and "*No X are Y*."
• The term category is defined in various ways in psychology. For example, a grouping of items sharing one or more similarities; a class of stimuli that can be treated in an equivalent manner; the set of entities or examples "picked out" by a mental concept.

Category theory   Category theory is the study of properties of categories (*see* first definition for Category).

Chunking   The process whereby individual units of information are combined into larger units. *Conceptual* chunking is reducing a relational representation to fewer dimensions, thereby reducing processing load.

Class inclusion   If a superordinate class (A) contains two nonempty subclasses (B, B'), then A must be more numerous than either B or B'.

Complex span tasks   Tasks (e.g., operation span, reading span) that require the simultaneous storage and manipulation of information in working memory.

Compositionality   A representation of a complex entity is constructed from the representations of its constituents, such that they retain their identity in the composition.

Conditional discrimination   Involves learning that a particular response will be rewarded and another response will not be rewarded in one context, and that the contingencies will be reversed when the context changes. More generally, C1: A+ B−; C2: A− B+, where C1 and C2 represent two different contexts, A and B represent two different responses, and + and − indicate whether the responses lead to positive or negative outcomes. The task structure corresponds to the structure of *exclusive-or (XOR)*.

Configuration   Two or more elements combined in a way that they are no longer distinguishable or accessible.

Conservation   A term introduced by Jean Piaget for a child's (or an adult's) under-standing that quantitative aspects of a stimulus display are not affected by arbitrary transformations of the display itself.

Coordinate system   A system comprising of one or more dimensions of ordered values that are reference points (coordinates) for aligning or grounding the roles of a relation together with a capacity to bind roles to those positions.

DLPFC   A part of the prefrontal cortex (PFC) area of the brain; the acronym means "dorsolateral prefrontal cortex." *See also* PFC.

DORA   The acronym means "Discovery of Relations by Analogy."

Dynamic binding   A link between two representations that is readily modifiable.

EEG   The recording of electrical activity along the scalp, used as a measure of brain activity; the acronym means "electroencephalography."

ERP   The measured brain response that is the direct reaction to a specific sensory, cognitive, or motor event; the acronym means "event-related potential."

Feedforward network   An acyclic network consisting of a collection of input units, a collection of output units, and sometimes one or more collections of intermediary units, called *hidden units*. The fact that it is acyclic entails that there are no feedback loops in the network.

Figure   Refers to the order of mention of the categories in a premise. *See also* Syllogism.

fMRI   A neuroimaging procedure using magnetic resonance imaging (MRI) to measure brain activity by monitoring blood flow during the performance of a cognitive task; the acronym means "functional magnetic resonance imaging."

Function   A mapping such that each element from the source (*domain*) set is mapped to just one element in the destination (*codomain*) set. A mapping is a special case of a relation, in which each domain element is related to exactly one codomain element. *See also* Relation.

Functionally structured   The link between the mental states representing input and output is mediated by an internal representation that recodes the input and functions in an holistic fashion; therefore, Rank = 1. *See also* Representational rank.

Generalization   The process of inferring a response from a novel input based on previous responses to other inputs.

Heuristic   A rule of thumb or shortcut method used in thinking, reasoning and/or decision making. A rule or procedure that helps solve a problem but does not guarantee success.

Higher-order relation   A relation where one or more of the related elements is a relational instance. For example, *knows(Jane, likes(Mary, John))* is a higher-order relation, since the second element, *likes(Mary, John)*, is itself an instance of the relation *likes*. *See also* Relation.

IFG   A ridge of the frontal lobe of the brain; the acronym means "inferior frontal gyrus."

Inner (dot) product   The dot product of two vectors in n-dimensional Euclidean space, $\mathbf{a} = (a_1, \ldots, a_n)$ and $\mathbf{b} = (b_1, \ldots, b_n)$ is the sum of the products of their n coordinates, $\mathbf{a} \bullet \mathbf{b} = \Sigma_i a_i b_i$.

Inverse relation   The inverse $R°$ of a binary relation R between sets A and B is the relation between B and A defined by $bR°a$ if and only if aRb. For example, the relation "<" (less than) is the inverse of the relation ">" (greater than), and *"parent_of(Parent, Child)"* is the inverse of *"child_of(Child, Parent)."* Also called *converse relation*. *See also* Relation.

Isomorphism   An isomorphism is a morphism $f: A \to B$ that has an inverse morphism $g: B \to A$, whose compositions in both directions are identity maps: $g \circ f = 1_A$ and $f \circ g = 1_B$. *See also* Morphism.

Latent variable   Confirmatory factor analysis yields latent variables reflecting a variance common to multiple tasks selected to assess the same construct (e.g., updating in working memory). Latent variables are more stable measures than those based on a single task.

LIFG   Left inferior frontal gyrus. *See also* IFG.

LISA   A computational model of analogical inference and schema induction; the acronym means "Learning and Inference with Schemas and Analogies."

Long-term memory   Memory for information that has been processed and integrated with one's general knowledge. The long-term memory store is presumed to be without limit in terms of its capacity and the duration for which information can be retained. *See also* Short-term memory.

MARC   A set of principles for estimating the relational complexity of cognitive tasks; the acronym means "Method for Analysis of Relational Complexity."

Match-to-sample   A task where one selects an item from a list of alternative items that is the same as the cue.

Medial PFC   A part of the prefrontal cortex (PFC) of the brain.

Modifiability   The capacity to substitute one operation for another operation, consequently changing the response for a given input. This capacity is akin to treating functions as input data, or having the capacity to compute higher-order functions (i.e., functions that take or return other functions).

Modus ponens   Reasoning of the following form: if P, and P implies Q, then Q.

Modus tollens   Reasoning of the following form: if not Q, and P implies Q, then not P.

Mood of premise   Refers to the quantifier (one of *All, Some, None,* and *Some not*) used in a premise. *See also* Syllogism.

Morphism   A morphism $f: A \rightarrow B$ is a (structure-preserving) mapping from an object A to an object B in a category. Morphisms must be able to be composed, so that given morphisms $f: A \rightarrow B$ and $g: B \rightarrow C$, a composite morphism $g \circ f: A \rightarrow C$ must exist. Thus fundamentally a morphism is just a directed link from one object to another in a category, with this composition property. The specific nature of morphisms depends on the category. In the category **Set**, a morphism is simply a function, and composition is given by $(g \circ f)(a) = g(f(a))$. Morphisms are also known as *arrows* or *maps*. *See also* Category *and* Structure-preserving mapping.

Natural join   Natural join is an operation that takes two relations with a common attribute (or attributes) and returns a relation whose instances are obtained by combining pairs of instances from the two relations that have the same value for the common attribute(s). For example, the natural join of a (*Mother, Child*) relation and a (*Father, Child*) relation, produces a relation whose instances are triples (*Mother, Father, Child*) consisting of both parents and the *Child*. *See also* Pullback.

Nonstructured   A link between a mental state representing input and a mental state representing output. There are no intervening mental states; therefore, Rank = 0. *See also* Representational rank.

Object-location binding   A link between the representation of an object and the representation of the object's location in a particular space.

Object permanence   Recognition that a hidden object still exists.

Outer product   The outer product of two vectors, $\mathbf{a} = (a_1, ...,a_m)$, and $\mathbf{b} = (b_1, ..., b_n)$, is an $m \times n$ matrix $\mathbf{M}$, where element M_{ij} is the product of the ith coordinate of A and the jth coordinate of B; that is, $M_{ij} = a_i b_j$. The outer product generalizes to products of matrices, and is then called the Kronecker product, and to products involving more than two vectors.

PET   A functional imaging technique that analyzes the amount of metabolic activity taking place in various parts of the brain during performance of cognitive tasks; the acronym means "positron emission tomography."

PFC   The anterior part of the frontal lobes of the brain; the acronym means "prefrontal cortex."

Planning   Working out how some action or procedure will be carried out in order to achieve a goal. For example, in Tower of Hanoi (TOH) problems, respondents must devise a series of moves to reach the goal state. This involves representing the relations between the current state, subgoals, and the goal.

PMC   A region in the posterior portion of the frontal lobe of the brain that helps to plan movements; the acronym means "premotor cortex."

PPC   A region of the brain involved in planning movement; the acronym means "posterior parietal cortex."

Primary and secondary representations   Primary representation is causally linked to the environment, while secondary representation permits multiple mental models that are detached from the environment. *See also* Representation.

Project, projection   Projection is an operation that takes a relation and a list of attribute names, that returns a relation consisting of instances restricted to those attributes. For example, a projection of a (*Mother, Father, Child*) relation, onto the *Mother* and *Child* attributes, returns the pairs of *Mother*s and their *Child*ren that appeared in the original relation, effectively forgetting the *Father*s.

Proportional analogy   An analogy of the form "*A* is to *B* as *C* is to *D*" often written as *A:B::C:D*. For example dog:kennel::rabbit:hutch. *See also* Analogy.

Prototype   This term may refer to the representation of either an idealized or most typical instance of a category; these may be different. An idealized category member is a possibly non-existent construct that shares the most attributes with other members of the same category and the least attributes with members of different categories. The most typical instance is an actual member of the category that is as close as possible to the ideal.

Psycho-logic A form of logic that specifically matches human reasoning even though it is different from standard logic.

Pullback Pullback is a concept from mathematical category theory, which generalizes categorical product. A pullback of sets takes two sets A and B and functions f: $A \to C$ and g: $B \to C$ for some third set C, and produces the set of ordered pairs (a, b) from the Cartesian product of A and B that satisfy $f(a) = g(b)$. It can be shown that natural joins are pullbacks, along with other relations of interest in cognition. *See also* Cartesian product, Natural join.

Rank *See* Representational rank, Symbolically structured representation.

Rationality—adaptive A reason or action that is rational in the sense that it permits effective adaptation to the environment; for example, a memory that reflects what needs to be remembered.

Rationality—normative A mode of reasoning that conforms to the established criteria for logical validity. *See also* modus ponens, modus tollens.

Raven's Progressive Matrices Test A test of fluid intelligence or performance IQ that consists of designs (*matrices*), each with a missing part. Respondents select the omitted part from a set of alternatives. The matrices vary from simple designs to abstract logical relations.

Relation Mathematically, a relation R between sets A and B is a subset of the Cartesian product $A \times B$. If $(a, b) \in R$, we write aRb or $R(a, b)$. For example, if (*Mary, John*) $\in$ *likes*, we write *Mary likes John*, or *likes(Mary, John)*. In cognition, each relation may be augmented by a schema that specifies the roles played by the members of the sets A and B: in the *likes* example, the schema would be *likes(Liker, Liked)*.

Relational match-to-sample A task where one selects a pair of items with the same relationship as the cue pair from a list of alternative pairs. *See also* match-to-sample.

Relational complexity A metric for defining the complexity of a cognitive process based on the number of entities that vary across relational instances, that are linked in a single cognitive representation.

Relational instance A member or instance of a relation. For example, in the relation *smaller* = {(1, 2), (2, 3), (3, 4), (1, 3), (2, 4), (1, 4)}, (2, 3) is a relational instance [and it might also be written *smaller*(2, 3), or 2 *smaller* 3]. *See also* Relation.

Representation Cognitive representations are internal states that contain information that can be used by the animal, whether human or nonhuman, to interact with the environment in an adaptive manner.

Representational rank The number of components bound into a structured representation plus one. *See also* Symbolically structured representation.

RLPFC A part of the prefrontal cortex (PFC) area of the brain; the acronym means "rostrolateral prefrontal cortex." *See also* PFC.

Role-filler binding A link between a representation of the role that an element (known as a *filler*) plays in a relation, and that filler.

Schema of a relation *See* Relation.

Segmentation A strategy used to reduce complexity by decomposing complex relations into less complex components that can be dealt with in succession.

Select, selection Selection is an operation that takes a relation and a proposition, that returns a relation consisting of instances of the original relation that satisfies the proposition. For example, a selection of the (*Mother, Father, Child*) relation using the proposition *Father = John* returns the triples of the form (*Mother, John, Child*).

Short-term memory (STM) Memory that contains recently presented information that has received minimal processing or interpretation. STM capacity is limited to 4 ± 1 chunks and its duration is brief. *See also* Working Memory.

STAR A model in which the relation-symbol and roles (*arguments*) are each represented by the vectors, and the binding is represented by the outer product of these vectors; the acronym means "Structured Tensor Analogical Reasoning."

Structural alignment The assignment of elements to slots or roles in a structure; the process of finding a structural correspondence between two representations.

Structural correspondence A mapping from a source (*base*) representation to a target representation so that the components and their relationships in the source representation are preserved as components and their relationships in the target representation. *Preserved* means that each component a in the source is mapped to the component a' in the target, and the relation R in the source is mapped to the relation R in the target such that the relationship aRb holds if and only if the relationship $a'R'b'$ holds. *See also* Representation.

Structure A set of elements with relations defined over them.

Syllogism A deductive reasoning problem that consists of two premises and a conclusion. In categorical syllogisms the premises and conclusion relate categories. For example, *All X are Y; Some Y are Z; therefore Some X are Z. See also* the second sense of Category, categorical, which describes categorical syllogisms. In linear syllogisms, the premises and conclusions consist of instances of an asymmetric, transitive relation, and yield linear orderings; e.g. aRb and bRc yields the inference $aRbRc$. *See also* Transitive inference.

Symbol A representation that stands in for either another representation or some external entity, the meaning of which depends on a processing system or some other type of structure.

Symbolically structured representation   Having an explicit, accessible, and internal representation of relations. Each relation has a symbol, which is bound to the arguments (*fillers*). Rank is one more than the number of arguments, being 2, 3, 4, and 5 for unary, binary, ternary, and quaternary relations, respectively. *See also* Representational rank.

Symbol system   A system comprising of a collection of symbols and operations for manipulating symbols.

Symbolic distance effect   The greater the distance between two concepts on a relevant dimension, the faster the decision can be made; e.g., for the questions "Which is smaller: 1 or 2?" versus "Which is smaller: 1 or 4?" the answer is reached faster on the latter question.

Systematicity   A property of cognition where having some cognitive capacity (*ability*) implies having some other (structurally related) cognitive capacity.

Theory of mind   An individual's recognition that others have mental lives, beliefs, plans, and desires that can influence their actions. False belief and appearance-reality tasks are frequently used to evaluate children's theory of mind. Theory of mind also involves the ability to infer what is in another person's (or, perhaps, animal's) mind, based on information such as what the person has seen.

Tower of Hanoi (TOH)   TOH comprises three pegs, referred to as A, B, and, C, and a variable number of disks of graded size, each with a hole in the center. The disks are placed initially on peg A with the largest on the bottom, the next largest above it, and so on. The goal is to move all the disks from peg A to peg C without moving more than one disk at a time or placing a larger disk on a smaller one.

Transitive inference   A form of deductive reasoning in which the relation is transitive, such that given the premises *aRb* and *bRc*, the conclusion *aRc* necessarily follows. For example, given that *Tom is taller than Pete* and *Pete is taller than Joe*, the conclusion *Tom is taller than Joe* necessarily follows.

Transitivity   A property of a binary relation *R*, where *R* is transitive if whenever *aRb* and *bRc* both hold, *aRc* also holds.

Transitivity of choice   Participants are trained to choose one member of each pair in a series (e.g., *A* + *B*–, *B* + *C*–, *C* + *D*–, and *D* + *E*–, where + indicates a rewarded choice and – indicates a nonrewarded choice). Then they are tested on untrained nonadjacent pairs, with most interest focusing on *B* and *D*. The choice of B is interpreted as evidence of transitivity of choice.

Tuple   An *n*-tuple is an ordered list of *n* items.

Universal mapping property   A property of certain constructions in a mathematical category (for example a categorical product) that specifies the existence and uniqueness up-to-isomorphism properties of a structure. Uniqueness up-to-isomorphism means that there can be more than one structure with the property, but all such will be isomorphic. A universal mapping property is sometimes called just a *universal property*. A construction that has a universal mapping property may be called a *universal construction*. *See also* Cartesian product.

Wason selection task   A task that involves reasoning based on the conditional rule, If *P*, then *Q*. Four cards displaying stimuli that correspond to *P*, not *P*, *Q*, not *Q*, are presented. The respondents' task is to decide which cards to turn over to test the rule.

Working memory   A limited capacity system used to hold and operate on information relevant to the current cognitive task or problem. *See also* Short-term memory.

Working memory span   An index of working memory capacity usually derived from performance on simple or complex span tasks. *See also* Working memory.

References

Acuna, B. D., Eliassen, J. C., Donoghue, J. P., & Sanes, J. N. (2002). Frontal and parietal lobe activation during transitive inference in humans. *Cerebral Cortex*, 12(12), 1312–1321.

Aizawa, K. (2003). Cognitive architecture: The structure of cognitive representations. In S. Stich & T. Warfield (Eds.), *The Blackwell guide to philosophy of mind* (pp. 172–189). Malden, MA: Blackwell.

Allen, J. W. P., & Bickhard, M. H. (2013a). The pendulum still swings. *Cognitive Development, 28*(2), 164–174. doi: http://dx.doi.org/10.1016/j.cogdev.2013.01.009.

Allen, J. W. P., & Bickhard, M. H. (2013b). Stepping off the pendulum: Why only an action-based approach can transcend the nativist—empiricist debate. *Cognitive Development, 28*(2), 96–133. doi: http://dx.doi.org/10.1016/j.cogdev.2013.01.002.

Almor, A., & Sloman, S. A. (1996). Is deontic reasoning special? *Psychological Review*, 103(2), 374–380.

Altmann, G. T. M., & Dienes, Z. (1999). Rule learning by seven-month-old infants and neural networks. *Science*, 284, 875.

Anderson, J. R. (1983). *The architecture of cognition*. Cambridge, MA: Harvard University Press.

Anderson, J. R. (1990). *The adaptive character of thought*. Hillsdale, NJ: Erlbaum.

Anderson, J. R. (1991). Is human cognition adaptive? *Behavioral and Brain Sciences*, 14, 471–517.

Anderson, J. R. (1993). *Rules of the mind*. Hillsdale, NJ: Erlbaum.

Anderson, J. R. (2005). Human symbol manipulation within an integrated cognitive architecture. *Cognitive Science*, 29(3), 313–341.

Anderson, J. R., Bothell, D., Byrne, M. D., Douglass, S., Lebiere, C., & Qin, Y. (2004). An integrated theory of the mind. *Psychological Review*, 111(4), 1036–1060.

Anderson, M. (1992). *Intelligence and development: A cognitive theory*. Oxford, UK: Blackwell.

Anderson, N. H. (1980). Information integration theory in developmental psychology. In F. Wilkening, J. Becker, & T. Trabasso (Eds.), *Information integration in children* (pp. 1–45). Hillsdale, NJ: Erlbaum.

Andrews, G., Birney, D., & Halford, G. S. (2006). Relational processing and working memory capacity in comprehension of relative clause sentences. *Memory & Cognition*, 34(6), 1325–1340.

Andrews, G., & Halford, G. S. (1998). Children's ability to make transitive inferences: The importance of premise integration and structural complexity. *Cognitive Development*, 13(4), 479–513.

Andrews, G., & Halford, G. S. (2002). A cognitive complexity metric applied to cognitive development. *Cognitive Psychology*, 45(2), 153–219.

Andrews, G., & Halford, G. S. (2011). Recent advances in relational complexity theory & its application to cognitive development. In P. Barrouillet & V. Gailard (Eds), Cognitive development and working memory: A dialogue between neo-Piagetian and cognitive approaches (pp. 47–68). Hove, East Sussex: Psychology Press.

Andrews, G., Halford, G. S., & Boyce, J. (2012). Conditional discrimination in young children: The roles of associative and relational processing. *Journal of Experimental Child Psychology*, 112, 84–101.

Andrews, G., Halford, G. S., Bunch, K. M., Bowden, D., & Jones, T. (2003). Theory of mind and relational complexity. *Child Development*, 74, 1476–1499.

Andrews, G., Halford, G. S., Murphy, K., & Knox, K. (2009). Integration of weight and distance information in young children: The role of relational complexity. *Cognitive Development*, 24(1), 49–60.

Andrews, G., Halford, G. S., & Prasad, A. (1998). *Processing load and children's comprehension of relative clause sentences*. Paper presented at the 15th Biennial Conference of the International Society for the Study of Behavioral Development, Berne, Switzerland, July 1–4, ERIC document Accession number ED 420 091.

Andrews, G., Halford, G. S., Shum, D., Maujean, A., Chappell, M., & Birney, D. (2013). Relational processing following stroke. *Brain and Cognition*, 81, 44–51.

Andrich, D., Lyne, A., Sheridan, B., & Luo, G. (1998). *Rasch Unidimensional Measurement Models* (v. 2.7q). Perth: RUMM Laboratory.

Arbib, M. A., & Manes, E. G. (1975). *Arrows, structures and functors: The categorical imperative*. New York: Academic Press.

Arkes, H. R. (2012). Heuristics can be ecologically rational. *Trends in Cognitive Sciences*, 16(5), 260–261.

Atran, S. (1993). *Cognitive foundations of natural history: Towards an anthropology of science.* New York: Cambridge University Press.

Avarguès-Weber, A., Dyer, A. G., Combe, M., & Giurfa, M. (2012). Simultaneous mastering of two abstract concepts by the miniature brain of bees. *Proceedings of the National Academy of Sciences of the United States of America*, 109, 7481–7486.

Awodey, S. (2010). *Category Theory* (2nd ed.). Oxford, UK: Oxford University Press.

Baillargeon, R. (1987). Young infants' reasoning about the physical and spatial properties of a hidden object. *Cognitive Development*, 2(3), 179–200.

Baillargeon, R. (1995). A model of physical reasoning in infancy. In C. Rovee-Collier & L. P. Lipsitt (Eds.), *Advances in infancy research* (Vol. 9, pp. 305–371). Norwood, NJ: Ablex.

Baillargeon, R., DeVos, J., & Graber, M. (1989). Location memory in 8-month-old infants in a non-search AB task: Further evidence. *Cognitive Development*, 4(4), 345–367.

Baillargeon, R., & Graber, M. (1987). Where's the rabbit? 5.5-month-old infants' representation of a hidden object. *Cognitive Development*, 2(4), 375–392.

Bell, M. A. (2001). Brain electrical activity associated with cognitive processing during a looking version of the A-Not-B task. *Infancy*, 2, 311–330.

Bell, M. A., & Fox, N. A. (1992). The relations between frontal brain electrical activity and cognitive development during infancy. *Child Development*, 63, 1142–1163.

Berry, D. C., & Dienes, Z. (1993). *Implicit learning: Theoretical and empirical issues.* Hillsdale, NJ: Lawrence Erlbaum Associates.

Bessemer, D. W., & Stollnitz, F. (1971). Retention of discriminations and an analysis of learning set. In A. M. Schrier & F. Stollnitz (Eds.), *Behavior of nonhuman primates* (Vol. 4, pp. 1–58). New York: Academic Press.

Binet, A., & Simon, T. (1980; orig. 1905). *The development of intelligence in children.* Nashville, TN: Williams Printing Co.

Birney, D. P. (2002). *The Measurement of Task Complexity and Cognitive Ability: Relational Complexity in Adult Reasoning.* Ph.D. dissertation, University of Queensland, St Lucia, Brisbane, Australia.

Birney, D. P., & Halford, G. S. (2002). Cognitive complexity of suppositional reasoning: An application of the relational complexity metric to the knight-knave task. *Thinking & Reasoning*, 8(2), 109–134.

Birney, D. P., Halford, G. S., & Andrews, G. (2006). Measuring the influence of complexity on relational reasoning: The development of the Latin square task. *Educational and Psychological Measurement*, 66(1), 146–171.

Blanchette, I., & Dunbar, K. (2000). How analogies are generated: The roles of structural and superficial similarity. *Memory & Cognition*, 28(1), 108–124.

Bloom, P. (2000). *How children learn the meaning of words*. Cambridge, MA: MIT Press.

Boag, C., Neal, A., Loft, S., & Halford, G. S. (2006). An analysis of relational complexity in an air traffic control conflict detection task. *Ergonomics*, 49(14), 1508–1526.

Bomba, P. C., & Siqueland, E. R. (1983). The nature and structure of infant form categories. *Journal of Experimental Child Psychology*, 35(2), 294–328.

Bonner, C., & Newell, B. R. (2010). In conflict with ourselves? An investigation of heuristic and analytic processes in decision making. *Memory & Cognition*, 38(2), 186–196.

Boole, G. (1854/1951). *An investigation of the laws of thought, on which are founded the mathematical theories of logic and probabilities*. New York: Dover Publications.

Boysen, S. T., & Himes, G. T. (1999). Current issues and emerging theories in animal cognition. *Annual Review of Psychology*, 50, 683–705.

Boysen, S. T., Berntson, G. G., Shreyer, T. A., & Quigley, K. S. (1993). Processing of ordinality and transitivity by chimpanzees (*Pan troglodytes*). *Journal of Comparative Psychology*, 107(2), 1–8.

Braine, M. D. S. (1978). On the relation between the natural logic of reasoning and standard logic. *Psychological Review*, 85, 1–21.

Brainerd, C. J., & Gordon, L. L. (1994). Development of verbatim and gist memory for numbers. *Developmental Psychology*, 30(2), 163–177.

Brainerd, C. J., & Kingma, J. (1984). Do children have to remember to reason? A fuzzy-trace theory of cognitive development. *Developmental Review*, 4, 311–377.

Broadbent, D. E. (1975). *The magic number 7 after fifteen years*. London: Wiley.

Bryant, P. E. (1972). The understanding of invariance by very young children. *Canadian Journal of Psychology*, 26, 78–96.

Bryant, P. E., & Trabasso, T. (1971). Transitive inferences and memory in young children. *Nature*, 232, 456–458.

Bucciarelli, M., & Johnson-Laird, P. N. (1999). Strategies in syllogistic reasoning. *Cognitive Science*, 23, 247–303.

Bunch, K. M., & Andrews, G. (2012). Development of relational processing in hot and cool tasks. *Developmental Neuropsychology*, 37(2), 134–152.

Bunch, K., Andrews, G., & Halford, G. S. (2007). Complexity effects on the children's gambling task. *Cognitive Development*, 22, 376–383.

Bunge, S. A., & Crone, E. A. (2009). Neural correlates of the development of cognitive control. In J. M. Rumsey & M. Ernst (Eds.), *Neuroimaging in developmental clinical neuroscience* (pp. 22–37). New York: Cambridge University Press.

Bunge, S. A., Helskog, E. H., & Wendelken, C. (2009). Left, but not right, rostrolateral prefrontal cortex meets a stringent test of the relational integration hypothesis. *NeuroImage*, 46(1), 338–342.

Bunge, S. A., Wendelken, C., Badre, D., & Wagner, A. D. (2005). Analogical reasoning and prefrontal cortex: evidence for separable retrieval and integration mechanisms. *Cerebral Cortex*, 15(3), 239–249.

Burgess, P. W., Dumontheil, I., & Gilbert, S. J. (2007). The gateway hypothesis of rostral prefrontal cortex (area 10) function. *Trends in Cognitive Sciences*, 11(7), 290–298.

Bush, R. R., & Mosteller, F. (1955). *Stochastic models for learning*. New York: Wiley.

Call, J., & Tomasello, M. (2008). Does the chimpanzee have a theory of mind? 30 years later. *Trends in Cognitive Sciences*, 12(5), 187–192.

Carey, S. (1978). The child as word learner. In M. Halle, J. Bresnan, & G. A. Miller (Eds.), *Linguistic theory and psychological reality* (pp. 264–293). Cambridge, MA: MIT Press.

Carey, S. (2009). *The origin of concepts*. New York: Oxford University Press.

Carey, S., & Sarnecka, B. W. (2006). The development of human conceptual representation: A case study. In Y. Munakata & M. H. Johnson (Eds.), *Processes of change in brain and cognitive development* (pp. 473–496). Oxford: Oxford University Press.

Carpenter, P. A., & Just, M. A. (1996). Functional and neuroscience approaches to working memory. *International Journal of Psychology*, 31(3/4), 325.

Carpenter, P. A., Just, M. A., & Shell, P. (1990). What one intelligence test measures: A theoretical account of the processing in the Raven Progressive Matrices Test. *Psychological Review*, 97, 404–431.

Case, R. (1985). *Intellectual development: Birth to adulthood*. New York: Academic Press.

Casey, B. J., Galvan, A., & Hare, T. A. (2005). Changes in cerebral functional organization during cognitive development. *Current Opinion in Neurobiology*, 15(2), 239–244. doi: http://dx.doi.org/10.1016/j.conb.2005.03.012.

Chalmers, K. A., & Halford, G. S. (2002). Young children's understanding of oddity: Reducing complexity by simple oddity and "most different" strategies. *Cognitive Development*, 106, 1–23.

Chalmers, M., & McGonigle, B. (1984). Are children any more logical than monkeys on the five-term series problem? *Journal of Experimental Child Psychology*, 37(2), 355–377.

Chen, Z., Sanchez, R. P., & Campbell, T. (1997). From beyond to within their grasp: The rudiments of analogical problem solving in 10- and 13-month-olds. *Developmental Psychology*, 33(5), 790–801.

Cheng, P. W., & Holyoak, K. J. (1985). Pragmatic reasoning schemas. *Cognitive Psychology*, 17, 391–416.

Chi, M. T. H. (1978). Knowledge structures and memory development. In R. S. Siegler (Ed.), *Children's thinking: What develops?* (pp. 73–96). Hillsdale, NJ: Erlbaum.

Chi, M. T. H., & Ceci, S. J. (1987). Content knowledge: Its role, representation, and restructuring in memory development. *Advances in Child Development and Behavior*, 20, 91–142.

Chomsky, N. (1980). Rules and representations. *Behavioral and Brain Sciences*, 3(1), 1–61.

Christensen, S., & Wright, H. H. (2010). Verbal and non-verbal working memory in aphasia: What three *n*-back tasks reveal. *Aphasiology*, 24(6–8), 752–762.

Christiansen, M. H., & Chater, N. (2008). Language as shaped by the brain. *Behavioral and Brain Sciences*, 31(05), 489–509.

Christoff, K., & Gabrieli, J. D. E. (2000). The frontopolar cortex and human cognition: Evidence for a rostrocaudal hierarchical organization within the human prefrontal cortex. *Psychobiology*, 28, 168–186.

Christoff, K., & Owen, A. M. (2006). Improving reverse neuroimaging inference: Cognitive domain versus cognitive complexity. *Trends in Cognitive Sciences*, 10(8), 352.

Christoff, K., Ream, J. M., Geddes, L. P., & Gabrieli, J. D. (2003). Evaluating self-generated information: anterior prefrontal contributions to human cognition. *Behavioral Neuroscience*, 117(6), 1161–1167.

Christoff, K., Prabhakaran, V., Dorfman, J., Zhao, Z., Kroger, J., Holyoak, K. J., & Gabrieli, J. D. (2001). Rostrolateral prefrontal cortex involvement in relational integration during reasoning. *NeuroImage*, 14, 1136–1149.

Chugani, H. T., & Phelps, M. E. (1986). Maturational changes in cerebral function in infants determined by 18FDG positron emission tomography. *Science*, 231(4740), 840.

Clark, A. (1992). The presence of a symbol. *Connection Science*, 4(3–4), 193–205.

Clark, A. (2013). Whatever next? Predictive brains, situated agents, and the future of cognitive science. *Behavioral and Brain Sciences*, 36, 181–253.

Clark, A., & Karmiloff-Smith, A. (1993). The cognizer's innards: A psychological and philosophical perspective on the development of thought. *Mind & Language*, 8(4), 487–519.

Clark, A., & Thornton, C. (1997). Trading spaces: Computation, representation, and the limits of uninformed learning. *Behavioral and Brain Sciences*, 20(1), 57–90.

Clark, A., & Thornton, C. (1998). Reading the generalizer's mind. *Behavioral and Brain Sciences*, 21(2), 308–310.

Clark, E. V. (2003). *First language acquisition*. New York: Cambridge University Press.

Cleeremans, A., & McClelland, J. L. (1991). Learning the structure of event sequences. *Journal of Experimental Psychology: General*, 120(3), 235–253.

Cocchi, L., Halford, G. S., Zalesky, A., Harding, I. H., Ramm, B. J., Cutmore, T., Shum, D. H., & Mattingley, J. B. (2014). Complexity in relational processing predicts changes in functional brain network dynamics. *Cerebral Cortex.*, 24(9), 2283–2296. doi:10.1093/cercor/bht075.

Codd, E. F. (1990). *The relational model for database management: Version 2*. Boston: Addison-Wesley.

Cohen, L. B., & Cashon, C. H. (2006). Infant cognition. In D. Kuhn & R. S. Siegler (Eds.), Handbook of child psychology (Vol. 2). *Cognition, perception, and language* (6th ed., pp. 214–251). Hoboken, NJ: John Wiley & Sons.

Coombs, C. H., Dawes, R. M., & Tversky, A. (1970). *Mathematical psychology: An elementary introduction*. Englewood Cliffs, NJ: Prentice-Hall.

Cosmides, L., & Tooby, J. (1992). Cognitive adaptations for social exchange. In J. H. Barkow, L. Cosmides, & J. Tooby (Eds.), *The adapted mind: Evolutionary psychology and the generation of culture* (pp. 163–228). New York: Oxford University Press.

Couvillon, P. A., & Bitterman, M. E. (1992). A conventional conditioning analysis of "transitive inference" in pigeons. *Journal of Experimental Psychology: Animal Behavior Processes*, 18(3), 308–310.

Cowan, N. (2000). Processing limits of selective attention and working memory: Potential implications for interpreting. *Interpreting*, 5(2), 117–146.

Cowan, N. (2001). The magical number 4 in short-term memory: A reconsideration of mental storage capacity. *Behavioral and Brain Sciences*, 24(1), 87–185.

Cowan, N., Chen, Z., & Rouder, J. N. (2004). Constant capacity in an immediate serial-recall task: A logical sequel to Miller (1956). *Psychological Science*, 15(9), 634–640.

Cowan, N., Nugent, L. D., Elliott, E. M., Pomomareo, E., & Scott Saults, J. (1999). The role of attention in the development of short-term memory: Age differences in the verbal span of apprehension. *Child Development*, 70, 1082–1097.

Crone, E. A., Wendelken, C., Van Leijenhorst, L., Honomichl, R. D., Christoff, K., & Bunge, S. A. (2009). Neurocognitive development of relational reasoning. *Developmental Science*, 12(1), 55–66.

Daneman, N., & Carpenter, P. (1980). Individual differences in working memory and reading. *Journal of Verbal Learning and Verbal Behavior*, 19, 405–438.

Davis, H. L., & Pratt, C. (1995). The development of children's theory of mind: The working memory explanation. *Australian Journal of Psychology*, 47(1), 25–31.

de Crespigny, R. C. (2012). *QF32*. Sydney: Pan Macmillan. http://qf32.aero.

De Lillo, C., Floreano, D., & Antinucci, F. (2001). Transitive choices by a simple, fully connected, backpropagation neural network: Implications for the comparative study of transitive inference. *Animal Cognition*, 4(1), 61–68.

DeLoache, J. S. (2000). Dual representation and young children's use of scale models. *Child Development*, 71, 329–338.

De Neys, W. (2006). Dual processing in reasoning: Two systems but one reasoner. *Psychological Science*, 17(5), 428–433.

De Pisapia, N., & Braver, T. S. (2008). Preparation for integration: The role of anterior prefrontal cortex in working memory. *Neuroreport*, 19(1), 15.

Diamond, A. (1988). Abilities and neural mechanisms underlying A not-B performance. *Child Development*, 59, 523–527.

Diamond, A. (1990). The development of neural bases of memory function as indexed by the AB and delayed response tasks in human infants and rhesus monkeys. In A. Diamond (Ed.), *The development and neural bases of higher cognitive functions* (pp. 267–317). New York: New York Academy of Sciences (Vol. 608).

Diamond, A. (1991). Neuropsychological insights into the meaning of object concept development. In S. Carey & R. Gelman (Eds.), *The epigenesis of mind: Essays on biology and cognition* (pp. 67–110). Hillsdale, NJ: Erlbaum.

Diamond, A., Zola-Morgan, S., & Squire, L. R. (1989). Successful performance by monkeys with lesions of the hippocampal formation on AB and object retrieval, two tasks that mark developmental changes in human infants. *Behavioral Neuroscience*, 103(3), 526–537.

Dixon, J. A., & Kelley, E. (2007). Theory revision and redescription: Complementary processes in knowledge acquisition. *Current Directions in Psychological Science*, 16(2), 111–115.

Dixon, J. A., & Marchman, V. A. (2007). Grammar and the lexicon: Developmental ordering in language acquisition. *Child Development*, 78, 190–212.

Domjan, M. P. (2009). *Principles of learning and behavior*. Belmont, CA: Cengage Learning/Wadsworth.

Doumas, L. A., & Hummel, J. E. (2004). A fundamental limitation of symbol-argument-argument notation as a model of human relational representations. In K. Forbus, D. Gentner & T. Regier (Eds), *Proceedings of the 26th Annual Conference of the Cognitive Science Society* (pp. 327–332). Mahwah, NJ: Erlbaum.

Doumas, L. A., Hummel, J. E., & Sandhofer, C. M. (2008). A theory of the discovery and predication of relational concepts. *Psychological Review*, 115(1), 1–43.

Dunbar, K. (2001). The analogical paradox: Why analogy is so easy in naturalistic settings, yet so difficult in the psychological laboratory. In D. Gentner, K. J. Holyoak, & B. K. Kokinov (Eds.), *The analogical mind: Perspectives from cognitive science* (pp. 313–334). Cambridge, MA: MIT Press.

Dunbar, K., & Klahr, D. (1989). Developmental differences in scientific discovery processes. In D. Klahr & K. Kotovsky (Eds.), *Complex information processing: The impact of Herbert A. Simon* (pp. 109–143). Hillsdale, NJ: Lawrence Erlbaum.

Duncan, J., Schramm, M., Thompson, R., & Dumontheil, I. (2012). Task rules, working memory, and fluid intelligence. *Psychonomic Bulletin & Review*, 19(5), 864–870.

Dupré, J. (2006). Scientific classification. *Theory, Culture, & Society*, 23(2–3), 30–32.

Edelman, S. (2012). Six challenges to theoretical and philosophical psychology. *Frontiers in Psychology*, 3, 219. doi:10.3389/fpsyg.2012.00219.

Eilenberg, S., & Mac Lane, S. (1945). General theory of natural equivalences. *Transactions of the American Mathematical Society*, 58(2). 231–294.

Eimas, P. D. (1999). Do infants learn grammar with algebra or statistics? *Science*, 284, 435–436.

Einstein, G. O., McDaniel, M. A., Williford, C. L., Pagan, J. L., & Dismukes, R. (2003). Forgetting of intentions in demanding situations is rapid. *Journal of Experimental Psychology: Applied*, 9(3), 147–162.

Elman, J. L. (1990). Finding structure in time. *Cognitive Science*, 14(2), 179–211.

Elman, J. L. (1993). Learning and development in neural networks: The importance of starting small. *Cognition*, 48(1), 71–99.

English, L. D., & Halford, G. S. (1995). *Mathematics education: Models and processes*. Hillsdale, NJ: Erlbaum.

Evans, J. S. B. (1984). Heuristic and analytical processess in reasoning. *British Journal of Psychology*, 75, 451–468.

Evans, J. S. B., & Ball, L. J. (2010). Do people reason on the Wason selection task? A new look at the data of Ball et al. (2003). *Quarterly Journal of Experimental Psychology*, 63(3), 434–441.

Evans, J. S. B., & Stanovich, K. E. (2013a). Dual-process theories of higher cognition: Advancing the debate. *Perspectives on Psychological Science*, 8(3), 223–241.

Evans, J. S. B., & Stanovich, K. E. (2013b). Theory and metatheory in the study of dual processing: Reply to comments. *Perspectives on Psychological Science*, 8(3), 263–271.

Evans, J. S. B. T. (2003). In two minds: Dual-process accounts of reasoning. *Trends in Cognitive Sciences*, 7(10), 454–459.

Evans, J. S. B. T. (2006). The heuristic-analytic theory of reasoning: Extension and evaluation. *Psychonomic Bulletin & Review*, 13(3), 378–395.

Evans, J. S. B. T. (2008). Dual-processing accounts of reasoning, judgment, and social cognition. *Annual Review of Psychology*, 59, 255–278.

Fagot, J., & Parron, C. (2010). Relational matching in baboons (*Papio papio*) with reduced grouping requirements. *Journal of Experimental Psychology: Animal Behavior Processes*, 36(2), 184–193.

Fagot, J., & Thompson, R. K. R. (2011). Generalized relational matching by guinea baboons (*Papio papio*) in two-by-two-item analogy problems. *Psychological Science*, 22(10), 1304–1309.

Fagot, J., Wasserman, E. A., & Young, M. E. (2001). Discriminating the relation between relations: The role of entropy in abstract conceptualization by baboons (*Papio papio*) and humans (*Homo sapiens*). *Journal of Experimental Psychology: Animal Behavior Processes*, 27(4), 316–328.

Falkenhainer, B., Forbus, K. D., & Gentner, D. (1989). The structure-mapping engine: Algorithm and examples. *Artificial Intelligence*, 41(1), 1–63.

Fangmeier, T., Knauff, M., Ruff, C. C., & Sloutsky, V. (2006). fMRI evidence for a three-stage model of deductive reasoning. *Journal of Cognitive Neuroscience*, 18(3), 320–334.

Feigenson, L., & Yamaguchi, M. (2009). Limits on infants' ability to dynamically update object representations. *Infancy*, 14(2), 244–262. doi:10.1080/15250000802707096.

Feigenson, L., Carey, S., & Hauser, M. (2002). The representations underlying infants' choice of more: Object files versus analog magnitudes. *Psychological Science*, 13(2), 150–156.

Feldman, J. (2000). Minimization of Boolean complexity in human concept learning. *Nature*, 407(6804), 630–632.

Fischer, K. W., & Bidell, T. R. (2006). Dynamic development of action and thought. In R. M. Lerner & W. Damon (Eds.), *Handbook of child psychology: Theoretical models of human development* (6th ed., Vol. 1, pp. 313–399). Hoboken, NJ: John Wiley.

Fitch, W., Hauser, M. D., & Chomsky, N. (2005). The evolution of the language faculty: Clarifications and implications. *Cognition*, 97(2), 179–210.

Flavell, J. H. (1963). *The developmental psychology of Jean Piaget*. Princeton, NJ: Van Nostrand.

Flavell, J. H., Flavell, E. R., & Green, F. L. (1983). Development of the appearance-reality distinction. *Cognitive Psychology*, 15, 95–120.

Flavell, J. H., Green, F. L., & Flavell, E. R. (1990). Developmental changes in young children's knowledge about the mind. *Cognitive Development*, 5(1), 1–27.

Fodor, J. A. (1975). *The language of thought*. New York: Thomas Y. Crowell Company.

Fodor, J. A. (1983). *Modularity of mind: An essay on faculty psychology*. Cambridge, MA: MIT Press.

Fodor, J. A. (1994). Concepts: A potboiler. *Cognition*, 50, 95–113.

Fodor, J. A. (2000). Why we are so good at catching cheaters. *Cognition*, 75, 29–32.

Fodor, J. A., & Pylyshyn, Z. W. (1988). Connectionism and cognitive architecture: A critical analysis. *Cognition*, 28(1–2), 3–71.

Frank, M. J., Cohen, M. X., & Sanfey, A. G. (2009). Multiple systems in decision making: A neurocomputational perspective. *Current Directions in Psychological Science*, 18(2), 73–77.

Franks, J. J., & Bransford, J. D. (1971). Abstraction of visual patterns. *Journal of Experimental Psychology*, 90(1), 65–74.

Frye, D., & Zelazo, P. D. (1998). Complexity: From formal analysis to final action. *Behavioral and Brain Sciences*, 21(6), 836–837.

Frye, D., Zelazo, P. D., & Palfai, T. (1995). Theory of mind and rule-based reasoning. *Cognitive Development*, 10, 483–527.

Gallistel, C. R. (1990). Representations in animal cognition: An introduction. *Cognition*, 37, 1–22.

Garcia-Marques, L., & Ferreira, M. B. (2011). Friends and foes of theory construction in psychological science. Vague dichotomies, unified theories of cognition, and the new experimentalism. *Perspectives on Psychological Science*, 6(2), 192–201.

Gebauer, G. F., & Mackintosh, N. J. (2007). Psychometric intelligence dissociates implicit and explicit learning. *Journal of Experimental Psychology: Learning, Memory, and Cognition*, 33(1), 34.

Gelman, R. (1972). Logical capacity of very young children: Number invariance rules. *Child Development*, 43, 75–90.

Gelman, R., & Gallistel, C. R. (1978). *The child's understanding of number*. Cambridge, MA: Harvard University Press.

Gelman, S., & Kalish. (2006). Conceptual development. In D. Kuhn & R. Siegler (Eds.), *Handbook of child psychology: Cognitive, language and perceptual development* (6th ed., Vol. 2, pp. 687–731). Hoboken, NJ: John Wiley.

Gelman, S. A., & Markman, E. M. (1986). Categories and induction in young children. *Cognition*, 23(3), 183–209.

Gelman, S. A., & Markman, E. M. (1987). Young children's inductions from natural kinds: The role of categories and appearances. *Child Development*, 58, 1532–1541.

Gentner, D. (1983). Structure-mapping: A theoretical framework for analogy. *Cognitive Science*, 7(2), 155–170.

Gentner, D. (2010). Bootstrapping the mind: Analogical processes and symbol systems. *Cognitive Science*, 34(5), 752–775.

Gentner, D., & Gentner, D. R. (1983). Flowing waters or teeming crowds: Mental models of electricity. In D. Gentner & A. L. Stevens (Eds.), *Mental models* (pp. 99–129). Hillsdale, NJ: Erlbaum.

Gentner, D., & Kurtz, K. J. (2006). Relations, objects, and the composition of analogies. *Cognitive Science*, 30(4), 609–642.

Gentner, D., & Medina, J. (1998). Similarity and the development of rules. *Cognition*, 65(2–3), 263–297.

Gentner, D., & Namy, L. L. (2006). Analogical processes in language learning. *Current Directions in Psychological Science*, 15(6), 297–301.

Gentner, D., Rattermann, M. J., Markman, A., & Kotovsky, L. (1995). Two forces in the development of relational similarity. In T. Simon & G. S. Halford (Eds.), *Developing cognitive competence: New approaches to process modelling* (pp. 263–313). Hillsdale, NJ: Erlbaum.

Gentner, D. et al. (1997). Analogical reasoning and conceptual change: A case study of Johannes Kepler. *Journal of the Learning Sciences*, 6(1), 3–40.

Gibson, E. (2000). The dependency locality theory: A distance-based theory of linguistic complexity. In Y. Miyashita, A. Marantz, & W. O'Neil (Eds.), *Image, language, brain* (pp. 95–126). Cambridge, MA: MIT Press.

Gick, M. L., & Holyoak, K. J. (1980). Analogical problem solving. *Cognitive Psychology*, 12, 306–355.

Gick, M. L., & Holyoak, K. J. (1983). Schema induction and analogical transfer. *Cognitive Psychology*, 15(1), 1–38.

Gigerenzer, G., & Goldstein, D. G. (1996). Reasoning the fast and frugal way: Models of bounded rationality. *Psychological Review*, 103(4), 650.

Giurfa, M., Zhang, S., Jenett, A., Menzel, R., & Srinivasan, M. V. (2001). The concepts of "sameness" and "difference" in an insect. *Nature*, 410, 930–933.

Gluck, M. A., & Thompson, R. F. (1987). Modeling the neural substrates of associative learning and memory: A computational approach. *Psychological Review*, 94(2), 176–191.

Goel, V. (2007). Anatomy of deductive reasoning. *Trends in Cognitive Sciences*, 11(10), 435–441.

Goel, V., & Dolan, R. J. (2003). Explaining modulation of reasoning by belief. *Cognition*, 87(1), 11–22.

Gogtay, N. et al. (2004). Dynamic mapping of human cortical development during childhood through early adulthood. *Proceedings of the National Academy of Sciences of the United States of America*, 101(21), 8174–8179.

Golde, M., Von Cramon, D. Y., & Schubotz, R. I. (2010). Differential role of anterior prefrontal and premotor cortex in the processing of relational information. *NeuroImage*, 49(3), 2890–2900.

Goldstein, M. H. et al. (2010). General cognitive principles for learning structure in time and space. *Trends in Cognitive Sciences*, 14(6), 249–258.

Golinkoff, R. M., & Hirsh-Pasek, K. (2008). How toddlers begin to learn verbs. *Trends in Cognitive Sciences*, 12(10), 397–403.

Gollin, E. S. (1966). Solution of conditional discrimination problems by young children. *Journal of Comparative and Physiological Psychology*, 62(3), 454–456.

Gollin, E. S., & Liss, P. (1962). Conditional discrimination in children. *Journal of Comparative and Physiological Psychology*, 55(5), 850–855.

Gollin, E. S., & Schadler, M. (1972). Relational learning and transfer by young children. *Journal of Experimental Child Psychology*, 14(2), 219–232.

Goodwin, G. P., & Johnson-Laird, P. N. (2005). Reasoning about relations. *Psychological Review*, 112, 468–493.

Gopher, D. (1994). Analysis and measurement of mental load. In G. d'Ydewalle, P. Eelen, & P. Bertelson (Eds.), *The state of the art* (pp. 265–291). Hillsdale, NJ: Erlbaum.

Goswami, U. (1992). *Analogical reasoning in children*. Hove, UK: Erlbaum.

Goswami, U. (1995). Transitive relational mappings in three- and four-year-olds: The analogy of Goldilocks and the three bears. *Child Development*, 66, 877–892.

Goswami, U. (1996). Analogical reasoning and cognitive development. In H. Reese (Ed.), *Advances in child development and behaviour* (pp. 91–138). San Diego: Academic Press.

Goswami, U., & Brown, A. L. (1989). Melting chocolate and melting snowmen: Analogical reasoning and causal relations. *Cognition*, 35, 69–95.

Gray, B., Wilson, W. H., Halford, G. S., & McCredden, J. (2006). Relcon: A tensor model of relational categorization. In R. Sun (Ed.), *CogSci/ICCS 2006 Proceedings* (28th Annual Conference of the Cognitive Science Society, in cooperation with the 5th International Conference of Cognitive Science, Vancouver, BC, Canada). (pp. 99–100). Mahwah, NJ: Erlbaum.

Green, A. E., Fugelsang, J. A., Kraemer, D. J., Shamosh, N. A., & Dunbar, K. N. (2006). Frontopolar cortex mediates abstract integration in analogy. *Brain Research*, 1096(1), 125–137.

Green, A. E., Kraemer, D. J. M., Fugelsang, J. A., Gray, J. R., & Dunbar, K. N. (2012). Neural correlates of creativity in analogical reasoning. *Journal of Experimental Psychology: Learning, Memory, and Cognition*, 38(2), 264–272. doi:10.1037/a0025764.

Greeno, J. G., Riley, M. S., & Gelman, R. (1984). Conceptual competence and children's counting. *Cognitive Psychology*, 16, 94–143.

Griggs, R. A., & Cox, J. R. (1982). The elusive thematic-materials effect in Wason's selection task. *British Journal of Psychology*, 73(3), 407–420.

Halford, G. S. (1982). *The development of thought*. Hillsdale, NJ: Erlbaum.

Halford, G. S. (1984). Can young children integrate premises in transitivity and serial order tasks? *Cognitive Psychology*, 16(1), 65–93.

Halford, G. S. (1989). Reflections on 25 years of Piagetian cognitive developmental psychology, 1963–1988. *Human Development*, 32, 325–387.

Halford, G. S. (1992). Analogical reasoning and conceptual complexity in cognitive development. *Human Development*, 35, 193–217.

Halford, G. S. (1993). *Children's understanding: The development of mental models*. Hillsdale, NJ: Erlbaum.

Halford, G. S. (1997). Recoding can lead to inaccessible structures but avoids capacity limitations. *Behavioral and Brain Sciences*, 20(01), 75.

Halford, G. S. (2009). Complexity provides a better explanation than probability for confidence in syllogistic inferences. *Behavioral and Brain Sciences*, 32(01), 91.

Halford, G. S., & Andrews, G. (2006). Reasoning and problem solving. In D. Kuhn & R. Siegler (Eds.), *Handbook of child psychology* (Vol. 2). *Cognitive, language and perceptual development* (6th ed., pp. 557–608). Hoboken, NJ: John Wiley.

Halford, G. S., & Andrews, G. (2007). Domain general processes in higher cognition. In Roberts, M. J. (Ed.) *Integrating the mind: Domain general versus domain specific processes in higher cognition* (pp. 302–331). Hove, UK: Psychology Press.

Halford, G. S., & Andrews, G. (2011). Information processing models of cognitive development. In U. Goswami (Ed.), *The Wiley-Blackwell handbook of childhood cognitive development* (pp. 697–722). Oxford, UK: Wiley Blackwell.

Halford, G. S., Andrews, G., & Bowden, D. (1998). *Complexity as a factor in children's theory of mind.* Paper presented at the poster session of the 15th Biennial Conference of the International Society for the Study of Behavioral Development, Berne, Switzerland, July 1–4, ERIC document accession number ED 421 673.

Halford, G. S., Andrews, G., & Jensen, I. (2002). Integration of category induction and hierarchical classification: One paradigm at two levels of complexity. *Journal of Cognition and Development*, 3(3), 143–177.

Halford, G. S., Andrews, G., Dalton, C., Boag, C., & Zielinski, T. (2002). Young children's performance on the balance scale: The influence of relational complexity. *Journal of Experimental Child Psychology*, 81, 417–445.

Halford, G. S., Andrews, G., Phillips, S., & Wilson, W. H. (2013). The role of working memory in the subsymbolic-symbolic transition. *Current Directions in Psychological Science*, 22(3), 210–216.

Halford, G. S., Andrews, G., Shum, D., Chappell, M., Birney, D., & Maujean, A. (2010). *Does relational processing account for executive functions? A stroke study.* Paper presented at the 37th Australasian Experimental Psychology Conference, University of Melbourne.

Halford, G. S., Andrews, G., Wilson, W. H., & Phillips, S. (2012). Computational models of relational processes in cognitive development. *Cognitive Development*, 27(4), 481.

Halford, G. S., Bain, J. D., Maybery, M., & Andrews, G. (1998). Induction of relational schemas: Common processes in reasoning and complex learning. *Cognitive Psychology*, 35(3), 201–245.

Halford, G. S., Baker, R., McCredden, J. E., & Bain, J. D. (2005). How many variables can humans process? *Psychological Science*, 16(1), 70–76.

Halford, G. S., Bunch, K., & McCredden, J. (2007). Problem decomposability as a factor in complexity of the dimensional change card sort task. *Cognitive Development*, 22(3), 384–391.

Halford, G. S., & Busby, J. (2007). Acquisition of structured knowledge without instruction: The relational schema induction paradigm. *Journal of Experimental Psychology: Learning, Memory, and Cognition*, 33(3), 586–603.

Halford, G. S., Cowan, N., & Andrews, G. (2007). Separating cognitive capacity from knowledge: A new hypothesis. *Trends in Cognitive Sciences*, 11(6), 236–242.

Halford, G. S., & Kelly, M. E. (1984). On the basis of early transitivity judgements. *Journal of Experimental Child Psychology*, 38, 42–63.

Halford, G. S., & Leitch, E. (1989). Processing load constraints: A structure-mapping approach. In M. A. Luszcz & T. Nettelbeck (Eds.), *Psychological development: Perspectives across the life-span* (pp. 151–159). Amsterdam: North-Holland.

Halford, G. S., Maybery, M. T., & Bain, J. D. (1988). Set-size effects in primary memory: An age-related capacity limitation? *Memory & Cognition*, 16(5), 480–487.

Halford, G. S., Phillips, S., & Wilson, W. H. (2008). The missing link: Dynamic, modifiable representations in working memory. *Behavioral and Brain Sciences*, 31(02), 137–138.

Halford, G. S., Phillips, S., Wilson, W. H., McCredden, J., Andrews, G., Birney, D., et al. (2007). Relational processing is fundamental to the central executive and it is limited to four variables. In N. Osaka, R. Logie, & M. D'Esposito (Eds.), *The cognitive neuroscience of working memory* (pp. 261–280). Oxford, UK: Oxford University Press.

Halford, G. S., Smith, S. B., Dickson, J. C., Maybery, M. T., Kelly, M. E., Bain, J. D., et al. (1995). Modelling the development of reasoning strategies: The roles of analogy, knowledge, and capacity. In T. Simon & G. S. Halford (Eds.), *Developing cognitive competence: New approaches to cognitive modelling* (pp. 77–156). Hillsdale, NJ: Erlbaum.

Halford, G. S., & Wilson, W. H. (1980). A category theory approach to cognitive development. *Cognitive Psychology*, 12(3), 356–411.

Halford, G. S., Wilson, W. H., Guo, J., Gayler, R. W., Wiles, J., & Stewart, J. E. M. (1994). Connectionist implications for processing capacity limitations in analogies. In K. J. Holyoak & J. Barnden (Eds.), *Advances in connectionist and neural computation theory: Vol 2. Analogical connections* (pp. 363–415). Norwood, NJ: Ablex.

Halford, G. S., Wilson, W. H., & Phillips, S. (1998). Processing capacity defined by relational complexity: Implications for comparative, developmental, and cognitive psychology. *Behavioral and Brain Sciences*, 21(6), 803–831.

Halford, G. S., Wilson, W. H., & Phillips, S. (2010). Relational knowledge: the foundation of higher cognition. *Trends in Cognitive Sciences*, 14(11), 497–505.

Harlow, H. F. (1949). The formation of learning sets. *Psychological Review*, 42, 51–65.

Harnad, S. (1990). The symbol grounding problem. *Physica D. Nonlinear Phenomena*, 42, 335–346.

Harris, M. R., & McGonigle, B. O. (1994). A model of transitive choice. *Quarterly Journal of Experimental Psychology*, 47B(3), 319–348.

Harrison, T. L., Shipstead, Z., Hicks, K. L., Hambrick, D. Z., Redick, T. S., & Engle, R. W. (2013). Working memory training may increase working memory capacity but not fluid intelligence. *Psychological Science*, 24, 2409–2419.

Hasher, L., & Zacks, R. T. (1979). Automatic and effortful processes in memory. *Journal of Experimental Psychology: General*, 108, 356–388.

Hayes, B. K., Goodhew, A., Heit, E., & Gillan, J. (2003). The role of diverse instruction in conceptual change. *Journal of Experimental Child Psychology*, 86(4), 253–276.

Hayes, K. J., Thompson, R., & Hayes, C. (1953). Discrimination learning sets in chimpanzees. *Journal of Comparative and Physiological Psychology*, 46, 99–104.

Herman, L. M., Hovancik, J. R., Gory, J. R., & Bradshaw, G. L. (1989). Generalization of visual matching by a bottlenosed dolphin (*Tursiops truncatus*): Evidence for invariance of cognitive performance with visual and auditory materials. *Journal of Experimental Psychology: Animal Behavior Processes*, 15(2), 124–136.

Herrmann, E., Hernández-Lloreda, M. V., Call, J., Hare, B., & Tomasello, M. (2010). The structure of individual differences in the cognitive abilities of children and chimpanzees. *Psychological Science*, 21(1), 102–110.

Heyes, C. M. (1998). Theory of mind in nonhuman primates. *Behavioral and Brain Sciences*, 21(1), 101–134.

Hinton, E. C., Dymond, S., von Hecker, U., & Evans, C. J. (2010). Neural correlates of relational reasoning and the symbolic distance effect: Involvement of parietal cortex. *Neuroscience,* 168(1), 138–148. doi: http://dx.doi.org/10.1016/j.neuroscience.2010.03.052.

Hinton, G. E. (1986). Learning distributed representations of concepts. *Proceedings of the Eighth Conference of the Cognitive Science Society* (pp. 1–12). Hillsdale, NJ: Erlbaum. Reprinted in Morris, R. G. M. (Ed), Parallel distributed processing: Implications for psychology and neurobiology, Oxford, UK: Clarendon Press (1989). http://www.cs.toronto.edu/~hinton/absps/families.pdf; accessed November 15, 2013.

Hinton, G. E. (1990). Mapping part-whole hierarchies into connectionist networks. *Artificial Intelligence*, 46, 47–75.

Hofstadter, D. R. (2001). Analogy as the core of cognition. In D. Gentner, K. J. Holyoak, & B. N. Kokinov (Eds.), *The analogical mind: Perspectives from cognitive science* (pp. 499–538). Cambridge, MA: MIT Press.

Holland, J. H., Holyoak, K. J., Nisbett, R. E., & Thagard, P. R. (1986). *Induction: Processes of inference, learning, and discovery.* Cambridge, MA: MIT Press.

Hollich, G. J. et al. (2000). Breaking the language barrier: An emergentist coalition model for the origins of word learning. *Monographs of the Society for Research in Child Development,* 65, Serial No. 123.

Holyoak, K. J. (2012). Analogy and relational reasoning. In K. J. Holyoak & R. G. Morrison (Eds.), *Oxford handbook of thinking and reasoning* (pp. 234–259). New York, NY: Oxford University Press.

Holyoak, K. J., & Hummel, J. E. (2000). The proper treatment of symbols in a connectionist architecture. In E. Dietrich & A. Markman (Eds.), *Cognitive dynamics: Conceptual change in humans and machines* (pp. 157–185). Mahwah, NJ: Erlbaum.

Holyoak, K. J., & Hummel, J. E. (2001). Toward an understanding of analogy within a biological symbol system. In D. Gentner, K. J. Holyoak, & B. N. Kokinov (Eds.), *The analogical mind: Perspectives from cognitive science* (pp. 161–195). Cambridge, MA: MIT Press.

Holyoak, K. J., & Thagard, P. (1989). Analogical mapping by constraint satisfaction. *Cognitive Science,* 13(3), 295–355.

Holyoak, K. J., & Thagard, P. (1995). *Mental leaps.* Cambridge, MA: MIT Press.

Hoppenbrouwers, S. S. et al. (2012). Inhibitory deficits in the dorsolateral prefrontal cortex in psychopathic offenders. *Cortex,* 49(5), 1377–1385.

Huey, E. D., Krueger, F., & Grafman, J. (2006). Representations in the human prefrontal cortex. *Current Directions in Psychological Science,* 15(4), 167–171.

Hull, C. L. (1943). *Principles of behavior.* New York: Appleton Century Crafts.

Hummel, J. E., & Holyoak, K. J. (1997). Distributed representations of structure: A theory of analogical access and mapping. *Psychological Review,* 104, 427–466.

Hummel, J. E., & Holyoak, K. J. (2003). A symbolic-connectionist theory of relational inference and generalization. *Psychological Review,* 110(2), 220–264.

Humphrey, G. (1951). *Thinking: An introduction to its experimental psychology.* London: Methuen.

Humphrey, G. (1963). *Thinking: An introduction to its experimental psychology.* New York: John Wiley.

Humphreys, M. S., Bain, J. D., & Pike, R. (1989). Different ways to cue a coherent memory system: A theory for episodic, semantic, and procedural tasks. *Psychological Review,* 96(2), 208–233.

Humphreys, M. S., Wiles, J., & Dennis, S. (1994). Toward a theory of human memory: Data structures and access processes. *Behavioral and Brain Sciences*, 17, 655–667.

Hunt, E. B. (1962). *Concept learning: An information processing problem*. New York: Wiley.

Hunt, J. M. (1961). *Intelligence and experience*. New York: Ronald Press.

Huttenlocher, P. R., & Dabholkar, A. S. (1997). Regional differences in synaptogenesis in human cerebral cortex. *Journal of Comparative Neurology*, 387(2), 167–178.

James, W. (1890). *Principles of psychology*. New York: Holt, Rinehart, & Winston.

Johnson-Laird, P. N. (1983). *Mental models*. Cambridge, UK: Cambridge University Press.

Johnson-Laird, P. N. (2010). Mental models and human reasoning. *Proceedings of the National Academy of Sciences of the United States of America*, 107(43), 18243–18250.

Johnson-Laird, P. N., & Byrne, R. M. J. (1991). *Deduction*. Hillsdale, NJ: Erlbaum.

Johnson-Laird, P. N., & Byrne, R. M. J. (2002). Conditionals: A theory of meaning, pragmatics, and inference. *Psychological Review*, 109(4), 646–678.

Johnson-Laird, P. N., & Steedman, M. (1978). The psychology of syllogisms. *Cognitive Psychology*, 10, 64–99.

Johnson-Laird, P. N., Legrenzi, P., Girotto, V., Legrenzi, M. S., & Caverni, J.-P. (1999). Naive probability: A mental model theory of extensional reasoning. *Psychological Review*, 106(1), 62–88.

Jones, G. (2012). Why chunking should be considered as an explanation for developmental change before short-term memory capacity and processing speed. *Frontiers in Psychology*, 3, 167. doi:10.3389/fpsyg.2012.00167.

Jung, R. E., & Haier, R. J. (2007). The parieto-frontal integration theory (P-FIT) of intelligence: Converging neuroimaging evidence. *Behavioral and Brain Sciences*, 30(2), 135–154.

Just, M. A., & Carpenter, P. A. (1992). A capacity theory of comprehension: Individual differences in working memory. *Psychological Review*, 99(1), 122–149.

Just, M. A., Carpenter, P. A., & Hemphill, D. D. (1996). Constraints on processing capacity: Architectural or implementational? In D. Steier & T. Mitchell (Eds.), *Mind matters: A tribute to Allen Newell* (pp. 141–178). Mahwah, NJ: Erlbaum.

Kahneman, D. (1973). *Attention and effort*. Englewood Cliffs, NJ: Prentice-Hall.

Kahneman, D., & Tversky, A. (1973). On the psychology of prediction. *Psychological Review*, 80(4), 237–251.

Kahneman, D., Slovic, P., & Tversky, A. (Eds.). (1982). *Judgment under uncertainity: Heuristics and biases.* New York: Cambridge University Press.

Káldy, Z., & Leslie, A. M. (2003). Identification of objects in 9-month-old infants: Integrating "what" and "where" information. *Developmental Science, 6*(3), 360–373.

Káldy, Z., & Leslie, A. M. (2005). A memory span of one? Object identification in 6.5-month-old infants. *Cognition, 97*(2), 153–177.

Kane, M. J., Hambrick, D. Z., Tuholski, S. W., Wilhelm, O., Payne, T. W., & Engle, R. W. (2004). The generality of working memory capacity: A latent-variable approach to verbal and visuospatial memory span and reasoning. *Journal of Experimental Psychology: General, 133*(2), 189.

Karmiloff-Smith, A. (1990). Constraints on representational change: Evidence from children's drawing. *Cognition, 34*(1), 57–83.

Karmiloff-Smith, A. (1994). Precis of beyond modularity: A developmental perspective on cognitive science. *Behavioral and Brain Sciences, 17*, 693–745.

Kärtner, J., Keller, H., Chaudhary, N., & Yovsi, R. D. (2012). The development of mirror self-recognition in different sociocultural contexts. *Monographs of the Society for Research in Child Development, 77*(4), 1–87.

Keane, M. T., Ledgeway, T., & Duff, S. (1994). Constraints on analogical mapping: A comparison of three models. *Cognitive Science, 18*, 387–438.

Kendler, H. H., & Kendler, T. S. (1962). Vertical and horizontal processes in problem solving. *Psychological Review, 69*, 1–16.

Khemlani, S., & Johnson-Laird, P. (2012). Theories of the syllogism: A meta-analysis. *Psychological Bulletin, 138*(3), 427–457.

Khemlani, S., & Johnson-Laird, P. (2013). The processes of inference. *Argument and Computation, 4*, 1–20. doi:10.1080/19462166.2012.674060.

Kibbe, M. M., & Leslie, A. M. (2011). What do infants remember when they forget? Location and identity in 6-month-olds' memory for objects. *Psychological Science, 22*(12), 1500–1505.

Kinderman, P., Dunbar, R., & Bentall, R. P. (1998). Theory-of-mind deficits and causal attributions. *British Journal of Psychology, 89*, 191–204.

Knowlton, B. J., & Holyoak, K. J. (2009). Prefrontal substrate of human relational reasoning. In M. Gazzaniga (Ed.), *The cognitive neurosciences IV* (pp. 1005–1017). Cambridge, MA: MIT Press.

Kollias, P., & McClelland, J. L. (2013). Context, cortex, and associations: A connectionist developmental approach to verbal analogies. *Frontiers in Psychology, 4*, 857.

Kotovsky, L., Mangione, C., & Baillargeon, R. (1995; unpublished manuscript). Infants' responses to impenetrability violations.

Krascum, R. M., & Andrews, S. (1998). The effects of theories on children's acquisition of family-resemblance categories. *Child Development*, 69, 333–346.

Krawczyk, D. C., McClelland, M. M., Donovan, C. M., Tillman, G. D., & Maguire, M. J. (2010). An fMRI investigation of cognitive stages in reasoning by analogy. *Brain Research*, 1342, 63–73.

Kroger, J., Sabb, F. W., Fales, C., Bookheimer, S. Y., Cohen, M. S., & Holyoak, K. (2002). Recruitment of anterior dorsolateral prefrontal cortex in human reasoning: A parametric study of relational complexity. *Cerebral Cortex*, 12, 477–485.

Kuhn, D. (1995). Microgenetic study of change: What has it told us? *Psychological Science*, 6, 133–139.

Lakoff, G. (1987). *Women, fire, and dangerous things: What categories reveal about the mind*. Chicago: University of Chicago Press.

Lashley, K. S. (1938). Conditional reactions in the rat. *Journal of Psychology*, 6, 311–324.

Lazareva, O. F., Smirnova, A. A., Bagozkaja, M. S., Zorina, Z. A., Rayevsky, V. V., & Wasserman, E. A. (2004). Transitive responding in hooded crows requires linearly ordered stimuli. *Journal of the Experimental Analysis of Behavior*, 82(1), 1–19.

Leech, R., Mareschal, D., & Cooper, R. P. (2008). Analogy as relational priming: A developmental and computational perspective on the origins of a complex cognitive skill. *Behavioral and Brain Sciences*, 31(4), 357–377.

Lempers, J. D., Flavell, E. R., & Flavell, J. H. (1977). The development in very young children of tacit knowledge concerning visual perception. *Genetic Psychology Monographs*, 95(1), 3–53.

Leslie, A., & Keeble, S. (1987). Do six-month-old infants perceive causality? *Cognition*, 25, 265–288.

Leslie, A. M. (1987). Pretense and representation: The origins of "theory of mind." *Psychological Review*, 94(4), 412–426.

Leslie, A. M., & Chen, M. L. (2007). Individuation of pairs of objects in infancy. *Developmental Science*, 10(4), 423–430.

Libben, M., & Titone, D. (2008). The role of awareness and working memory in human transitive inference. *Behavioural Processes*, 77(1), 43–54.

Lieberman, D. A. (1993). *Learning: Behavior and cognition* (2d ed.). Pacific Grove, CA: Brooks/Cole.

Litman, L., & Reber, A. S. (2005). Implicit cognition and thought. In K. Holyoak & R. G. Morrison (Eds.), *Cambridge handbook of thinking and reasoning* (pp. 431–455). New York: Cambridge University Press.

Lloyd, M. E., Doydum, A. O., & Newcombe, N. S. (2009). Memory binding in early childhood: Evidence for a retrieval deficit. *Child Development*, 80, 1321–1328.

Locke, J. [1690] (1924). In A. S. Pringle-Pattison (Ed.), *An essay concerning human understanding*. Oxford: Clarendon Press.

Loewenstein, J., & Gentner, D. (2005). Relational language and the development of relational mapping. *Cognitive Psychology*, 50(4), 315–353.

Logan, G. D. (1979). On the use of a concurrent memory load to measure attention and automaticity. *Journal of Experimental Psychology: Human Perception and Performance*, 5, 189–207.

Logan, G. D. (2003). Executive control of thought and action in search of the wild homunculus. *Current Directions in Psychological Science*, 12(2), 45–48.

Logothetis, N. K. (2008). What we can do and what we cannot do with fMRI. *Nature*, 453(7197), 869–878.

Loveday, W. (1995). *The effect of complexity on planning in the Tower of Hanoi problem*. Honours thesis, University of Queensland, Brisbane, Australia.

Low, J., & Perner, J. (Eds.). (2012). Implicit and explicit theory of mind. [Special issue]. *British Journal of Developmental Psychology*, 30(1).

Lu, H., Chen, D., & Holyoak, K. J. (2012). Bayesian analogy with relational transformations. *Psychological Review*, 119(3), 617–648.

Luck, S. J., & Vogel, E. K. (1997). The capacity of visual working memory for features and conjunctions. *Nature*, 390(6657), 279–281.

Luder, W. F. (1943). Electron configuration as the basis of the periodic table. *Journal of Chemical Education*, 20(1), 21–26.

Luo, Q. et al. (2003). The neural substrate of analogical reasoning: An fMRI study. *Cognitive Brain Research*, 17(3), 527–534.

Luria, A. R. (1980). *Higher cortical functions in man* (2nd ed.). (Haigh, B., Trans.). New York: Basic Books.

Mac Lane, S. (1971). *Categories for the working mathematician*. New York: Springer-Verlag.

Mac Lane, S. (2000). *Categories for the working mathematician* (2nd ed.). New York: Springer.

Maguire, M. J., McClelland, M. M., Donovan, C. M., Tillman, G. D., & Krawczyk, D. C. (2012). Tracking cognitive phases in analogical reasoning with event-related potentials. *Journal of Experimental Psychology: Learning, Memory, and Cognition*, 38(2), 273.

Mandler, J. M. (2000). Perceptual and conceptual processes in infancy. *Journal of Cognition and Development*, 1, 3–36.

Mandler, J. M. (2004). *The foundations of mind: Origins of conceptual thought*. New York: Oxford University Press.

Mandler, J. M., & Mandler, G. (1964). *Thinking: From association to gestalt*. New York: John Wiley & Sons.

Marcovitch, S., & Zelazo, P. D. (1999). The A-not-B error: Results from a logistic meta-analysis. *Child Development*, 70, 1297–1313.

Marcovitch, S., & Zelazo, P. D. (2009). The need for reflection in theories of executive function: Reply to commentaries. *Developmental Science*, 12(1), 24–25.

Marcovitch, S., & Zelazo, P. D. (2012). Introduction to special issue: "The potential contribution of computational modeling to the study of cognitive development: When, and for what topics?" *Cognitive Development*, 27(4), 323–325. doi: http://dx.doi.org/10.1016/j.cogdev.2012.07.001.

Marcus, G. F. (1999). Response to Altmann and Dienes: Rule learning by seven-month-old infants and neural networks. *Science*, 284, 875.

Marcus, G. F., Fernandes, K. J., & Johnson, S. P. (2012). The role of association in early word-learning. *Frontiers in Psychology*, 3, 283. doi:10.3389/fpsyg.2012.00283.

Marcus, G. F., Vijayan, S., Bandi Rao, S., & Vishton, P. M. (1999). Rule learning by 7-month-old infants. *Science*, 283(5398), 77–80.

Mareschal, D. (2003). Connectionist models of learning and development in infancy. In P. T. Quinlan (Ed.), *Connectionist models of development: Developmental processes in real and artificial neural networks. Studies in developmental psychology* (pp. 43–82). New York: Psychology Press.

Mareschal, D., & Johnson, M. H. (2003). The "what" and "where" of object representations in infancy. *Cognition*, 88(3), 259–276.

Mareschal, D., Plunkett, K., & Harris, P. (1995). Developing object permanence: A connectionist model. In J. D. Moore & J. F. Lehman (Eds.), *Proceedings of the 17th Annual Conference of the Cognitive Science Society* (pp. 170–175). Hillsdale, NJ: Erlbaum.

Markovits, H. (2000). A mental model analysis of young children's conditional reasoning with meaningful premises. *Thinking & Reasoning*, 6(4), 335–348.

Markovits, H., & Barrouillet, P. (2002). The development of conditional reasoning: A mental model account. *Developmental Review*, 22, 5–36.

Markovits, H., & Dumas, C. (1992). Can pigeons really make transitive inferences? *Journal of Experimental Psychology: Animal Behavior Processes*, 18(3), 311–312.

Marsh, T., & Boag, S. (2013). Evolutionary and differential psychology: conceptual conflicts and the path to integration. *Frontiers in Psychology*, 4, 655. doi:10.3389/fpsyg.2013.00655.

Masangkay, Z. S., McCluskey, K. A., McIntyre, C. W., Sims-Knight, J., Vaughn, B. E., & Flavell, J. H. (1974). The early development of inferences about the visual percepts of others. *Child Development*, 45, 357–366.

Mausfeld, R. (2012). On some unwarranted tacit assumptions in cognitive neuroscience. *Frontiers in Psychology*, 3, 67.

Maybery, M. T., Bain, J. D., & Halford, G. S. (1986). Information processing demands of transitive inference. *Journal of Experimental Psychology: Learning, Memory, and Cognition*, 12(4), 600–613.

Mayr, E., & Bock, W. J. (2008). Classifications and other ordering systems. *Journal of Zoological Systematics and Evolutionary Research*, 40(4), 169–194.

McClelland, J., McNaughton, B., & O'Reilly, R. (1995). Why there are complementary learning systems in the hippocampus and neocortex: Insights from the successes and failures of connectionist models of learning and memory. *Psychological Review*, 102(3), 419–457.

McClelland, J. L. (1995). A connectionist perspective on knowledge and development. In T. Simon & G. S. Halford (Eds.), *Developing cognitive competence: New approaches to cognitive modelling* (pp. 157–204). Hillsdale, NJ: Erlbaum.

McClelland, J. L. et al. (2010). Letting structure emerge: Connectionist and dynamical systems approaches to cognition. *Trends in Cognitive Sciences*, 14(8), 348–356.

McClelland, J. L., & Plaut, D. C. (1999). Does generalization in infant learning implicate abstract algebra-like rules? *Trends in Cognitive Sciences*, 3(5), 166–168.

McClelland, J. L., & Rumelhart, D. E. (1985). Distributed memory and the representation of general and specific information. *Journal of Experimental Psychology: General*, 114(2), 159–188.

McClelland, J. L., Rumelhart, D. E., & Hinton, G. E. (1986). The appeal of parallel distributed processing. In D. E. Rumelhart & J. D. McClelland (Eds.), Parallel distributed processing: Vol 1. Foundations (pp. 3–44). Cambridge, MA: MIT Press.

McGarrigle, J., Grieve, R., & Hughes, M. (1978). Interpreting inclusion: A contribution to the study of the child's cognitive and linguistic development. *Journal of Experimental Child Psychology*, 26(3), 528–550.

McGonigle, B. O., & Chalmers, M. (1977). Are monkeys logical? *Nature*, 267, 355–377.

McLaughlin, B. P. (2009). Systematicity redux. *Synthese*, 170(2), 251–274.

Medin, D. L. (1972). Role of reinforcement in discrimination learning set in monkeys. *Psychological Bulletin*, 77, 305–318.

Medin, D. L. (1989). Concepts and conceptual structure. *American Psychologist*, 44(12), 1469–1481.

Meiser, T. (2011). Much pain, little gain? Paradigm-specific models and methods in experimental psychology. *Perspectives on Psychological Science*, 6(2), 183–191.

Merriman, W. E., & Stevenson, C. M. (1997). Restricting a familiar name in response to learning a new one: Evidence of a mutual exclusivity bias in two-year-olds. *Child Development*, 68), 211–228.

Miller, G. A. (1956). The magical number seven, plus or minus two: Some limits on our capacity for processing information. *Psychological Review*, 63(2), 81–97.

Miller, G. A., Galanter, E., & Pribram, K. H. (1960). *Plans and the structure of behavior*. New York: Holt, Rinehart and Winston.

Mingon, M. (2012). *Complex concept acquisition: Density, relational knowledge, and the education of children*. Honours thesis, Griffith University, Mt. Gravatt, Australia.

Mitchell, C. J., De Houwer, J., & Lovibond, P. F. (2009). The propositional nature of human associative learning. *Behavioral and Brain Sciences*, 32(02), 183–198.

Mitchell, M., & Hofstadter, D. R. (1990). The emergence of understanding in a computer model of concepts and analogy-making. *Physica D. Nonlinear Phenomena*, 42(1–3), 322–334.

Monsell, S. (2003). Task switching. *Trends in Cognitive Sciences*, 7(3), 134–140.

Moore, K. (2012). Brains don't predict; They trial actions. *Frontiers in Psychology*, 3, 417. doi: 10.3389/fpsyq.2012.00417.

Morewedge, C. K., & Kahneman, D. (2010). Associative processes in intuitive judgment. *Trends in Cognitive Sciences*, 14(10), 435–440.

Moses, S. N., Brown, T. M., Ryan, J. D., & McIntosh, A. R. (2010). Neural system interactions underlying human transitive inference. *Hippocampus*, 20(8), 894–901. doi:10.1002/hipo.20735.

Müller, U., & Overton, W. F. (1998). How to grow a baby: A reevaluation of image-schema and Piagetian action approaches to representation. *Human Development*, 41(2), 71–111.

Munakata, Y., McClelland, J. L., Johnson, M. H., & Siegler, R. S. (1997). Rethinking infant knowledge: Toward an adaptive process account of successes and failures in object permanence tasks. *Psychological Review*, 104(4), 686–713.

Naigles, L. R., Hoff, E., & Vear, D. (2009). *Flexibility in early verb use: Evidence from a multiple-n diary study*. Monographs of the Society for Research in Child Development, 74. (Serial No. 293). Wiley-Blackwell.

Navon, D., & Gopher, D. (1980). *Task difficulty, resources, and dual task performance*. Hillsdale, NJ: Erlbaum.

Negishi, M. (1999). Do infants learn grammar with algebra or statistics? Letter: A comment on G. F. Marcus et al. (1999), "Rule learning by seven month-old infant." *Science*, 284(5413), 433.

Nelson, C. A., Thomas, K. M., & de Haan, M. (2006). Neural bases of cognitive development. In D. Kuhn & R. Siegler (Eds.), *Handbook of child psychology (Vol. 2). Cognitive, language and perceptual development* (6th ed., pp. 3–57). Hoboken, NJ: John Wiley.

Newell, A. (1980). Physical symbol systems. *Cognitive Science*, 4, 135–183.

Newell, A. (1990). *Unified theories of cognition*. Cambridge, MA: Harvard University Press.

Newell, A., & Simon, H. A. (1972). *Human problem solving*. New York: Prentice-Hall.

Norman, D. A. (1986). Reflections on cognition and parallel distributed processing. In J. L. McClelland & D. E. Rumelhart (Eds.), *Parallel distributed processing: Vol. 2. Psychological and biological models* (pp. 531–546). Cambridge, MA: MIT Press.

Novick, L. R. (1988). Analogical transfer, problem similarity, and expertise. *Journal of Experimental Psychology: Learning, Memory, and Cognition*, 14(3), 510–520.

O'Reilly, R. C., & Munakata, Y. (2000). *Computational explorations in cognitive neuroscience: Understanding the mind by simulating the brain*. Cambridge, MA: MIT Press. A Bradford Book.

Oakes, L. M., Ross-Sheehy, S., & Luck, S. J. (2006). Rapid development of feature binding in visual short-term memory. *Psychological Science*, 17(9), 781–787.

Oaksford, M., & Chater, N. (2001). The probabilistic approach to human reasoning. *Trends in Cognitive Sciences*, 5(8), 349–357.

Oaksford, M., & Chater, N. (2007). *Bayesian rationality: The probabilistic approach to human reasoning*. New York: Oxford University Press.

Oaksford, M., & Chater, N. (2009a). Précis of Bayesian rationality: The probabilistic approach to human reasoning. *Behavioral and Brain Sciences*, 32(1), 69–84.

Oaksford, M., & Chater, N. (2009b). The uncertain reasoner: Bayes, logic and rationality. *Behavioral and Brain Sciences*, 32(1), 105–120.

Oberauer, K. (2005). Binding and inhibition in working memory: Individual and age differences in short-term recognition. *Journal of Experimental Psychology: General*, 134(3), 368.

Oberauer, K. (2009). Design for a working memory. In B. H. Ross (Ed.), *Psychology of Learning and Motivation: Advances in Research and Theory* (Vol. 51, pp. 45–100). San Diego, CA: Elsevier Academic Press.

Oberauer, K., & Hein, L. (2012). Attention to information in working memory. *Current Directions in Psychological Science*, 21(3), 164–169.

Oberauer, K., Süss, H.-M., Wilhelm, O., & Wittmann, W. (2008). Which working memory functions predict intelligence? *Intelligence*, 36(6), 641–652.

Oden, D. l., Thompson, R. K. R., & Premack, D. (1988). Spontaneous transfer of matching by infant chimpanzees (*Pan troglyodytes*). *Journal of Experimental Psychology: Animal Behavior Processes*, 14(2), 140–145.

Oden, D. L., Thompson, R. K. R., & Premack, D. (1990). Infant chimpanzees (*Pan troglodytes*) spontaneously perceive both concrete and abstract same/different relations. *Child Development*, 61, 621–631.

Osman, M. (2007). Can tutoring improve performance on a reasoning task under deadline conditions? *Memory & Cognition*, 35(2), 342–351.

Pacton, S., Perruchet, P., Fayol, M., & Cleeremans, A. (2001). Implicit learning out of the lab: The case of orthographic regularities. *Journal of Experimental Psychology: General*, 130(3), 401–426.

Paivio, A. (1971). *Imagery and verbal processes*. New York: Holt, Rinehart, & Winston.

Passingham, R. E., Rowe, J. B., & Sakai, K. (2004). Prefrontal cortex and attention to action. In G. Humphreys & J. Riddoch (Eds.) *Attention in Action: Advances from Cognitive Neuroscience* (pp. 263-286). Hove, East Essex: Psychology Press.

Paterson, S. J., Heim, S., Thomas-Friedman, J., Choudhury, N., & Benasich, A. A. (2006). Development of structure and function in the infant brain: Implications for cognition, language and social behaviour. *Neuroscience & Biobehavioral Reviews*, 30(8), 1087–1105. doi: http://dx.doi.org/10.1016/j.neubiorev.2006.05.001.

Pearce, J. M. (1994). Similarity and discrimination: A selective review and a connectionist model. *Psychological Review*, 101(4), 587–607.

Pears, R., & Bryant, P. (1990). Transitive inferences by young children about spatial position. *British Journal of Psychology*, 81(4), 497–510.

Penn, D. C., Holyoak, K. J., & Povinelli, D. J. (2008a). Darwin's mistake: Explaining the discontinuity between human and nonhuman minds. *Behavioral and Brain Sciences*, 31(2), 109–130.

Penn, D. C., Holyoak, K. J., & Povinelli, D. J. (2008b). Darwin's triumph: Explaining the uniqueness of the human mind without a deus ex machina. *Behavioral and Brain Sciences*, 31(2), 153–178.

Penn, D. C., Holyoak, K. J., & Povinelli, D. J. (2012). So, are we the massively lucky species? *Behavioral and Brain Sciences*, 35(4), 236–237.

Pepperberg, I. M., & Carey, S. (2012). Grey parrot number acquisition: The inference of cardinal value from ordinal position on the numeral list. *Cognition, 125*(2), 219–232. doi: http://dx.doi.org/10.1016/j.cognition.2012.07.003.

Perner, J. (1991). *Understanding the representational mind*. Cambridge, MA: MIT Press.

Perret, P., Bailleux, C., & Dauvier, B. (2011). The influence of relational complexity and strategy selection on children's reasoning in the Latin square task. *Cognitive Development*, 26(2), 127–141.

Perruchet, P. (1994). Learning from complex rule-governed environments: On the proper functions of nonconscious and conscious processes. In C. Umilta & M. Moscovitch (Eds.), *Attention and performance XV: Conscious and nonconscious information processing* (pp. 811–835). Cambridge, MA: MIT Press.

Phillips, S. (1998). Are feedforward and recurrent networks systematic? Analysis and implications for a connectionist cognitive architecture. *Connection Science*, 10(2), 137–160.

Phillips, S. (1999). Systematic minds, unsystematic models: Learning transfer in humans and networks. *Minds and Machines*, 9(3), 383–398.

Phillips, S. (2000). Constituent similarity and systematicity: The limits of first-order connectionism. *Connection Science*, 12(1), 45–63.

Phillips, S. (2008). Abstract analogies not primed by relations learned as object transformations. *Behavioral and Brain Sciences*, 31(4), 393–394. doi:10.1017/S0140525X08004639.

Phillips, S. (2014). Analogy, cognitive architecture and universal construction: A tale of two systematicities. *PLoS ONE*, 9(2), e89152.

Phillips, S., & Halford, G. S. (1997). Systematicity: Psychological evidence with connectionist implications. In M. G. Shafto & P. Langley (Eds.), *Proceedings of the 19th Annual Conference of the Cognitive Science Society* (pp. 614–619). Mahwah, NJ: Erlbaum.

Phillips, S., & Wilson, W. H. (2010). Categorial compositionality: A category theory explanation for the systematicity of human cognition. *PLoS Computational Biology*, 6(7), e1000858.

Phillips, S., & Wilson, W. H. (2011). Categorial compositionality II: Universal constructions and a general theory of (quasi-) systematicity in human cognition. *PLoS Computational Biology*, 7(8), e1002102.

Phillips, S., & Wilson, W. H. (2012). Categorial compositionality III: F-(co)algebras and the systematicity of recursive capacities in human cognition. *PLoS ONE*, 7(4), e35028.

Phillips, S., & Wilson, W. H. (2014). A category theory explanation for systematicity: Universal constructions. In P. Calvo & J. Symons (Eds.), The Architecture of Cognition: Rethinking Fodor and Pylyshyn's *Systematicity Challenge*. (pp. 227-249) Cambridge, MA: MIT Press.

Phillips, S., Halford, G. S., & Wilson, W. H. (1995). The processing of associations versus the processing of relations and symbols: A systematic comparison. In J. D. Moore & J. F. Lehman (Eds.), *Proceedings of the 17th Annual Conference of the Cognitive Science Society* (pp. 688–691). Pittsburgh: Lawrence Erlbaum.

Phillips, S., Takeda, Y., & Singh, A. (2012). Visual feature integration indicated by phase-locked frontal-parietal EEG signals. *PLoS ONE*, 7(3), e32502.

Phillips, S., Wilson, W. H., & Halford, G. S. (2009). What do transitive inference and class inclusion have in common? Categorical (co)products and cognitive development. *PLoS Computational Biology*, 5(12), e1000599.

Piaget, J. (1950; orig. 1947). *The psychology of intelligence* (Piercy, M., & Berlyne, D. E., Trans.). London: Routledge & Kegan Paul.

Piaget, J. (1954; orig. 1950). *The construction of reality in the child* (Cook, M., Trans.). New York: Basic Books.

Piaget, J. (1957). *Logic and psychology*. New York: Basic Books.

Piantadosi, S. T., Tenenbaum, J. B., & Goodman, N. D. (2012). Bootstrapping in a language of thought: A formal model of numerical concept learning. *Cognition*, 123(2), 199–217.

Plate, T. A. (1995). Holographic reduced representations. *IEEE Transactions on Neural Networks*, 6(3), 623–641.

Polk, T. A., & Newell, A. (1995). Deduction as verbal reasoning. *Psychological Review*, 102(3), 533–566.

Polya, G. (1954). *Mathematics and plausible reasoning. I. Induction and analogy in mathematics*. Princeton, NJ: Princeton University Press.

Posner, M. I., & Boies, S. J. (1971). Components of attention. *Psychological Review*, 78, 391–408.

Postle, B. R. (2006). Working memory as an emergent property of the mind and brain. *Neuroscience*, 139(1), 23–38.

Pothos, E. M. (2007). Theories of artificial grammar learning. *Psychological Bulletin*, 133(2), 227.

Povinelli, D. J., & Bering, J. M. (2002). The mentality of apes revisited. *Current Directions in Psychological Science*, 11(4), 115–118.

Prabhakaran, V., Narayanan, K., Zhao, Z., & Gabrieli, J. (2000). Integration of diverse information in working memory within the frontal lobe. *Nature Neuroscience*, 3(1), 85–90.

Premack, D. (1983). The codes of man and beasts. *Behavioral and Brain Sciences*, 6(1), 125–167.

Preston, A. R., Shrager, Y., Dudukovic, N. M., & Gabrieli, J. D. E. (2004). Hippocampal contribution to the novel use of relational information in declarative memory. *Hippocampus*, 14(2), 148–152. doi:10.1002/hipo.20009.

Preuss, T. M. (2000). What's human about the human brain? In M. S. Gazzaniga (Ed.), *The new cognitive neurosciences* (pp. 1219–1234). Cambridge, MA: MIT Press.

Psychological Corporation. (1998). *Wechsler Adult Intelligence Scale—3rd Edition Australian Adaptation*. Marrickville, Australia: Harcourt Brace & Company (Australia) Pty Ltd.

Pylyshyn, Z. W. (1999). Is vision continuous with cognition? The case for cognitive penetrability of visual perception. *Behavioral and Brain Sciences*, 22(3), 341–423.

Qiu, J. et al. (2007). The neural basis of conditional reasoning: An event-related potential study. *Neuropsychologia*, 45(7), 1533–1539.

Quinn, P. C., & Johnson, M. H. (1997). The emergence of perceptual category representations in young infants: A connectionist analysis. *Journal of Experimental Child Psychology*, 66, 236–263.

Quinn, P. C., Eimas, P. D., & Rosenkrantz, S. L. (1993). Evidence for representations of perceptually similar natural categories by 3-month-old and 4-month-old infants. *Perception*, 22, 463–475.

Raichle, M. E. (2010). Two views of brain function. *Trends in Cognitive Sciences*, 14(4), 180–190.

Rakison, D. H., & Lupyan, G. (2008). Developing object concepts in infancy: An associative learning perspective: I. Introduction. *Monographs of the Society for Research in Child Development*, 73(1), 1–29.

Ramnani, N., & Owen, A. M. (2004). Anterior prefrontal cortex: Insights into function from anatomy and neuroimaging. *Nature Reviews Neuroscience*, 5(3), 184–194.

Reber, A. S. (1967). Implicit learning of artificial grammars. *Journal of Verbal Learning and Verbal Behavior*, 6(6), 855–863.

Reed, S. K. (1987). A structure-mapping model for word problems. *Journal of Experimental Psychology: Learning, Memory, and Cognition*, 13, 124–139.

Reed, S. K., Ackinclose, C. C., & Voss, A. A. (1990). Selecting analogous problems: Similarity versus inclusiveness. *Memory & Cognition*, 18(1), 83–98.

Reese, H. W. (1963). *Discrimination learning set in children*. New York: Academic Press.

Rescorla, R. A., & Wagner, A. R. (1972). A theory of Pavlovian conditioning: Variations in the effectiveness of reinforcement and nonreinforcement. In A. H. Black & W. F. Prokasy (Eds.), *Classical conditioning II: Current theory and research* (pp. 64–99). New York: Appleton-Century-Crofts.

Reverberi, C., Lavaroni, A., Gigli, G. L., Skrap, M., & Shallice, T. (2005). Specific impairments of rule induction in different frontal lobe subgroups. *Neuropsychologia*, 43(3), 460–472.

Riley, C. A., & Trabasso, T. (1974). Comparatives, logical structures, and encoding in a transitive inference task. *Journal of Experimental Child Psychology*, 17(2), 187–203.

Rips, L. J. (2001). Two kinds of reasoning. *Psychological Science*, 12(2), 129–134.

Rivera, S. M., Wakeley, A., & Langer, J. (1999). The drawbridge phenomenon: Representational reasoning or peceptual preference? *Developmental Psychology*, 35(2), 427–435.

Roberts, M. J. (2005). Expanding the universe of categorical syllogisms: A challenge for reasoning researchers. *Behavior Research Methods*, 37(4), 560–580.

Robin, N., & Holyoak, K. J. (1995). Relational complexity and the functions of prefrontal cortex. In M. S. Gazzaniga (Ed.), *The cognitive neurosciences* (pp. 987–997). Cambridge, MA: MIT Press.

Rogers, T. T., & McClelland, J. L. (2004). *Semantic cognition: A parallel distributed processing approach*. Cambridge, MA: MIT Press.

Rosch, E., & Mervis, C. B. (1975). Family resemblences: Studies in the internal structure of categories. *Cognitive Psychology*, 7, 573–605.

Rosch, E., Mervis, C. B., Gray, W. D., Johnson, M. D., & Boyes-Braem, P. (1976). Basic objects in natural categories. *Cognitive Psychology*, 8(3), 382–439.

Rossnagel, C. S. (2001). Revealing hidden covariation detection: Evidence for implicit abstraction at study. *Journal of Experimental Psychology: Learning, Memory, and Cognition*, 27(5), 1276–1288.

Rudy, J. W. (1991). Elemental and configural associations, the hippocampus, and development. *Developmental Psychobiology*, 24(4), 221–236.

Rudy, J. W., Keith, J. R., & Georgen, K. (1993). The effect of age on children's learning of problems that require a configural association solution. *Developmental Psychobiology*, 26(3), 171–184.

Rumelhart, D. E. (1990). Brain style computation: Learning and generalisation. In S. F. Zornetzer, J. L. Davis, & C. Lau (Eds.), *An introduction to neural and electronic networks* (pp. 405–420). Cambridge, MA: MIT Press.

Rumelhart, D. E., Hinton, G. E., & Williams, R. J. (1986). Learning internal representations by error propagation. In D. E. Rumelhart & J. L. McClelland (Eds.), *Parallel Distributed Processing: Explorations in the Microstructure of Cognition* (Vol. 1: Foundations, pp. 318–362). Cambridge, MA: MIT Press.

Saxe, A. M., McClelland, J. L., & Ganguli, S. (2013). Learning hierarchical category structure in deep neural networks. In M. Knauff, M. Pauen, N. Sebanz, & I. Wachsmuth (Eds), *Proceedings of the 35th Annual Conference of the Cognitive Science Society* (pp. 1271–1276). Austin, TX: Cognitive Science Society.

Schmajuk, N. A., & DiCarlo, J. J. (1992). Stimulus configuration, classical conditioning, and hippocampal function. *Psychological Review*, 99(2), 268–305.

Schneider, W., & Shiffrin, R. M. (1977). Controlled and automatic human information processing: I. Detection, search, and attention. *Psychological Review*, 84, 1–66.

Seidenberg, M. S., & Elman, J. L. (1999). Do infants learn grammar with algebra or statistics? *Science*, 284, 433.

Senju, A., Southgate, V., Snape, C., Leonard, M., & Csibra, G. (2011). Do 18-month-olds really attribute mental states to others? A critical test. *Psychological Science*, 22(7), 878–880.

Shanks, D. R., Rowland, L. A., & Ranger, M. S. (2005). Attentional load and implicit sequence learning. *Psychological Research*, 69(5), 369–382.

Shannon, C. E., & Weaver, W. (1949). *The mathematical theory of communication*. Urbana, IL: University of Illinois Press.

Shastri, L. (1999). Infants learning algebraic rules. *Science*, 285, 1673.

Shastri, L., & Ajjanagadde, V. (1993). From simple associations to systematic reasoning: A connectionist representation of rules, variables, and dynamic bindings using temporal synchrony. *Behavioral and Brain Sciences*, 16(3), 417–494.

Shiffrin, R. M., & Schneider, W. (1977). Controlled and automatic human information processing: II. Perceptual learning, automatic attending, and a general theory. *Psychological Review*, 84, 127–190.

Shipstead, Z., Redick, T. S., & Engle, R. W. (2012). Is working memory training effective? *Psychological Bulletin*, 138(4), 628.

Shultz, T. R. (1998). A computational analysis of conservation. *Developmental Science*, 1, 103–126.

Shultz, T. R. (2012). A constructive neural-network approach to modeling psychological development. *Cognitive Development*, 27(4), 383-400.

Shultz, T. R., & Cohen, L. B. (2004). Modeling age differences in infant category learning. *Infancy*, 5(2), 153–171.

Siegal, M., Waters, L. J., & Dinwiddy, L. S. (1988). Misleading children: Causal attributions for inconsistency under repeated questioning. *Journal of Experimental Child Psychology*, 45, 438–456.

Siegler, R. S. (1981). Developmental sequences within and between concepts. *Monographs of the Society for Research in Child Development*, 46, 1–84.

Siegler, R. S. (1995). How does change occur? A microgenetic study of number conservation. *Cognitive Psychology*, 28, 225–273.

Siegler, R. S. (2006). Microgenetic analyses of learning. In D. Kuhn & R. Siegler (Eds.), *Handbook of child psychology (Vol. 2). Cognitive, language, and perceptual development* (6th ed., pp. 464–510). Hoboken, NJ: John Wiley & Sons

Siegler, R. S., & Jenkins, E. A. (1989). *How children discover new strategies*. Hillsdale, NJ: Erlbaum.

Siegler, R. S., & Shrager, J. (1984). Strategy choices in addition and subtraction: How do children know what to do? In C. Sophian (Ed.), *Origins of cognitive skills* (pp. 229–293). Hillsdale, NJ: Erlbaum.

Simon, H. A. (1974). How big is a chunk? *Science*, 183, 482–488.

Simon, T., & Klahr, D. (1995). A computational theory of children's learning about number conservation. In T. Simon & G. S. Halford (Eds.), *Developing cognitive competence: New approaches to process modeling* (pp. 315–353). Hillsdale, NJ: Erlbaum.

Simon, T., Newell, A., & Klahr, D. (1991). *A computational account of children's learning about number conservation*. San Mateo, CA: Morgan Kaufmann.

Simon, T. J., Hespos, S. J., & Rochat, P. (1995). Do infants understand simple arithmetic? A replication of Wynn (1992). *Cognitive Development*, 10(2), 253–269.

Sloman, S. A. (1996). The empirical case for two systems of reasoning. *Psychological Bulletin*, 119, 3–22.

Sloman, S. A. (2002). Two systems of reasoning. In T. Gilovich, D. Griffin, & D. Kahneman (Eds.), *Heuristics and biases: The psychology of intuitive judgment* (pp. 379–396). New York: Cambridge University Press.

Sluzenski, J., Newcombe, N. S., & Kovacs, S. L. (2006). Binding, relational memory, and recall of naturalistic events: A developmental perspective. *Journal of Experimental Psychology: Learning, Memory, and Cognition*, 32(1), 89.

Smith, C., & Squire, L. R. (2005). Declarative memory, awareness, and transitive inference. The *Journal of Neuroscience*, 25(44), 10138–10146.

Smith, C. L. (2007). Bootstrapping processes in the development of students' common-sense matter theories: Using analogical mappings, thought experiments, and learning to measure to promote conceptual restructuring. *Cognition and Instruction*, 25(4), 337–398.

Smith, E. E., Langston, C., & Nisbett, R. E. (1992). The case for rules in reasoning. *Cognitive Science*, 16, 1–40.

Smith, L. B., Thelen, E., Titzer, R., & McLin, D. (1999). Knowing in the context of acting: The task dynamics of the A-not-B error. *Psychological Review*, 106(2), 235–260.

Smith, R., Keramatian, K., & Christoff, K. (2007). Localizing the rostrolateral prefrontal cortex at the individual level. *NeuroImage*, 36(4), 1387–1396.

Smolensky, P. (1990). Tensor product variable binding and the representation of symbolic structures in connectionist systems. *Artificial Intelligence*, 46(1–2), 159–216.

Song, H., & Baillargeon, R. (2007). Can 9.5-month-old infants attribute to an agent a disposition to perform a particular action on objects? *Acta Psychologica*, 124(1), 79–105.

Spearman, C. E. (1923). *The nature of intelligence and the principles of cognition*. London: MacMillan.

Srinivasan, M. V. (2011). Honeybees as a model for the study of visually guided flight, navigation, and biologically inspired robotics. *Physiological Reviews*, 91(2), 413–460.

Stanovich, K. E., & West, R. F. (2000). Individual differences in reasoning: Implications for the rationality debate? *Behavioral and Brain Sciences*, 23(5), 645–665.

Stenning, K., & van Lambalgen, M. (2008). *Human reasoning and cognitive science*. Cambridge, MA: MIT Press.

Sternberg, R. J. (1980). Representation and process in linear syllogistic reasoning. *Journal of Experimental Psychology: General*, 109, 119–159.

Stuss, D. T., & Alexander, M. P. (2005). Does damage to the frontal lobes produce impairment in memory? *Current Directions in Psychological Science*, 14(2), 84–88.

Suddendorf, T., Fletcher-Flinn, C., & Johnston, L. (1999). Pantomine and theory of mind. *Journal of Genetic Psychology*, 160(1), 31–45.

Suddendorf, T., & Whiten, A. (2001). Mental evolution and development: Evidence for secondary representation in children, great apes, and other animals. *Psychological Bulletin*, 127(5), 629–650.

Sun, R., & Zhang, X. (2004). Top-down versus bottom-up learning in cognitive skill acquisition. *Cognitive Systems Research*, 5(1), 63–89.

Suppes, P., & Zinnes, J. L. (1963). Basic measurement theory. In R. D. Luce, R. R. Bush, & E. Galanter (Eds.), *Handbook of mathematical psychology* (pp. 1–76). New York: Wiley.

Sutton, R. S., & Barto, A. G. (1981). Toward a modern theory of adaptive networks: Expectation and prediction. *Psychological Review*, 88(2), 135–170.

Terrace, H. S., & McGonigle, B. (1994). Memory and representation of serial order by children, monkeys, and pigeons. *Current Directions in Psychological Science*, 3(6), 180–185.

Thelen, E., Schöner, G., Scheier, C., & Smith, L. B. (2001). So what's a modeler to do? *Behavioral and Brain Sciences*, 24(01), 70–80.

Thomas, M. S. C., & McClelland, J. L. (2008). Connectionist models of cognition. In R. Sun (Ed.), *The Cambridge handbook of computational psychology* (pp. 23–58). London: Cambridge University Press.

Thompson, R. K. R., Oden, D. L., & Boysen, S. T. (1997). Language-naive chimpanzees (*Pan troglodytes*) judge relations between relations in a conceptual matching-to-sample task. *Journal of Experimental Psychology: Animal Behavior Processes*, 23(1), 31–43.

Tomasello, M. (1992). *First verbs: A case study of early grammatical development*. New York: Cambridge University Press.

Tomasello, M. (2000). Culture and cognitive development. *Current Directions in Psychological Science*, 9(2), 37–40.

Tomasello, M. (2008). *Origins of human communication*. Cambridge, MA: MIT Press.

Tomasello, M., & Call, J. (1997). *Primate cognition*. New York: Oxford University Press.

Trabasso, T. (1977). The role of memory as a system in making transitive inferences. In R. V. Kail & J. W. Hagen (Eds.), *Perspectives on the development of memory and cognition* (pp. 333–366). Hillsdale, NJ: Erlbaum.

Truppa, V., Mortari, E. P., Garofoli, D., Privitera, S., & Visalberghi, E. (2011). Same/ different concept learning by capuchin monkeys in matching-to-sample tasks. *PLoS ONE*, 6(8), e23809.

Tversky, A., & Kahneman, D. (1973). Availability: A heuristic for judging frequency and probability. *Cognitive Psychology*, 5, 207–232.

Tweney, R. D. (1998). Toward a cognitive psychology of science: Recent research and its implications. *Current Directions in Psychological Science*, 7(5), 150–154.

Tyrrell, D. J., Zingaro, M. C., & Minard, K. L. (1993). Learning and transfer of identity-difference relationships by infants. *Infant Behavior and Development*, 16(1), 43–52.

van den Bos, E., & Poletiek, F. H. (2008). Effects of grammar complexity on artificial grammar learning. *Memory & Cognition*, 36(6), 1122–1131.

Van Elzakker, M., O'Reilly, R. C., & Rudy, J. W. (2003). Transitivity, flexibility, conjunctive representations, and the hippocampus. I. An empirical analysis. *Hippocampus*, 13(3), 334–340. doi:10.1002/hipo.10083.

Van Gelder, T., & Niklasson, L. (1994). Classicalism and cognitive architecture. In A. Ram & K. Eiselt (Eds.), *Proceedings of the Sixteenth Annual Conference of the Cognitive Science Society* (pp. 905–909). Atlanta: Erlbaum.

VanLehn, K., & Brown, J. S. (1980). Planning nets: A representation for formalizing analogies and semantic models of procedural skills. In R. E. Snow, P. A. Federico & W. E. Montague (Eds.), *Aptitude learning and instruction. Vol. 2. Cognitive process analyses of learning and problem solving* (pp. 95–137). Hillsdale, NJ: Erlbaum.

VanLehn, K. (1991). Rule acquisition events in the discovery of problem-solving strategies. *Cognitive Science*, 15(1), 1–47.

Vicente, K. (2003). *The human factor: Revolutionizing the way people live with technology*. New York: Routledge.

Vogel, E. K., & Machizawa, M. G. (2004). Neural activity predicts individual differences in visual working memory capacity. *Nature*, 428(6984), 748–751.

Vogel, E. K., McCollough, A. W., & Machizawa, M. G. (2005). Neural measures reveal individual differences in controlling access to working memory. *Nature*, 438(7067), 500–503.

Vokey, J. R., & Brooks, L. R. (1992). Salience of item knowledge in learning artificial grammars. *Journal of Experimental Psychology: Learning, Memory, and Cognition*, 18(2), 328–344.

von Fersen, L., Wynne, C. D. L., Delius, J. D., & Staddon, J. E. R. (1991). Transitive inference formation in pigeons. *Journal of Experimental Psychology: Animal Behavior Processes*, 17(3), 334–341.

Vonk, J. (2003). Gorilla (*Gorilla gorilla gorilla*) and orangutan (*Pongo abelii*) understanding of first- and second-order relations. *Animal Cognition,* 6(2), 77–86. doi: http://dx.doi.org/10.1007/s10071-003-0159-x.

Vosniadou, S., & Brewer, W. F. (1992). Mental models of the Earth: A study of conceptual change in childhood. *Cognitive Psychology,* 24, 535–585.

Waechter, R. L., Goel, V., Raymont, V., Kruger, F., & Grafman, J. (2013). Transitive inference reasoning is impaired by focal lesions in parietal cortex rather than rostrolateral prefrontal cortex. *Neuropsychologia,* 51(3), 464–471. doi: http://dx.doi.org/10.1016/j.neuropsychologia.2012.11.026.

Wagner, L., & Lakusta, L. (2009). Using language to navigate the infant mind. *Perspectives on Psychological Science,* 4(2), 177–184.

Waltz, J. A., Knowlton, B. J., Holyoak, K. J., Boone, K. B., Back-Madruga, C., McPherson, S., et al. (2004). Relational integration and executive function in Alzheimer's disease. *Neuropsychology,* 18(2), 296–305.

Waltz, J. A., Knowlton, B. J., Holyoak, K. J., Boone, K. B., Mishkin, F. S., Santos, M. de Menezes et al. (1999). A system for relational reasoning in human prefrontal cortex. *Psychological Science,* 10(2), 119–125.

Wason, P. C. (1968). Reasoning about a rule. *Quarterly Journal of Experimental Psychology,* 20, 273–281.

Waxman, S., Fu, X., Arunachalam, S., Leddon, E., Geraghty, K., & Song, H. J. (2013). Are nouns learned before verbs? Infants provide insight into a long-standing debate. *Child Development Perspectives,* 7(3), 155–159.

Wellman, H. M. (2011). Developing a theory of mind. In *The Wiley-Blackwell handbook of childhood cognitive development* (pp. 258–284): Oxford, UK: Wiley-Blackwell.

Wellman, H. M., Cross, D., & Bartsch, K. (1986). Infant search and object permanence: A meta-analysis of the A-not-B error. *Monographs of the Society for Research in Child Development,* 51(3), 1–51.

Wellman, H. M., Cross, D., & Watson, J. (2001). Meta-analysis of theory-of-mind development: The truth about false belief. *Child Development,* 72, 655–684.

Wendelken, C., Chung, D., & Bunge, S. A. (2012). Rostrolateral prefrontal cortex: Domain-general or domain-sensitive? *Human Brain Mapping,* 33(8), 1952–1963.

Wertheimer, M. (1945). *Productive thinking.* New York: Harper.

Wharton, C. M. et al. (2000). Toward neuroanatomical models of analogy: A positron emission tomography study of analogical mapping. *Cognitive Psychology,* 40(3), 173–197.

White, C. N., & Poldrack, R. A. (2013). Using fMRI to constrain theories of cognition. *Perspectives on Psychological Science*, 8(1), 79–83.

Wickelgren, W. A. (1979). Chunking and consolidation: A theoretical sythesis of semantic networks, configuring in conditioning, S-R versus cognitive learning, normal forgetting, the amnesic syndrome, and the hippocampal arousal system. *Psychological Review*, 86(1), 44–60.

Wilson, W. H., & Phillips, S. (2012). Systematicity, accessibility, and universal properties. In M. Thielscher & D. Zhang (Eds.), *AI 2012: Advances in Artificial Intelligence* (Vol. 7691, pp. 555–566). Springer Lecture Notes in Artificial Intelligence.

Wilson, W. H., Marcus, N., & Halford, G. S. (2001). Access to relational knowledge: A comparison of two models. In J. D. Moore & K. Stenning (Eds.), *Proceedings of the 23rd Annual Conference of the Cognitive Science Society* (pp. 1142–1147). Mahwah, NJ: Erlbaum.

Wilson, W. H., Street, D. J., & Halford, G. S. (1995). Solving proportional analogy problems using tensor product networks with random representations. In Y. Attiki-ouzel (Ed.), *Proceedings of the 1995 IEEE International Conference on Neural Networks* (pp. 2971–2975). IEEE.

Wilson, W. H., Halford, G. S., Gray, B., & Phillips, S. (2001). The STAR-2 model for mapping hierarchically structured analogs. In D. Gentner, K. Holyoak, & B. Kokinov (Eds.), *The analogical mind: Perspectives from cognitive science* (pp. 125–159). Cambridge, MA: MIT Press.

Wixted, J. T., & Mickes, L. (2013). On the relationship between fMRI and theories of cognition: The arrow points in both directions. *Perspectives on Psychological Science*, 8(1), 104–107.

Woodworth, R. S., & Sells, S. B. (1935). An atmosphere effect in formal syllogistic reasoning. *Journal of Experimental Psychology*, 18, 451–460.

Wynn, K. (1992). Addition and subtraction by human infants. *Nature*, 358, 749–750.

Wynn, K. (1995). Origins of numerical knowledge. *Mathematical Cognition*, 1(1), 35–60.

Wynne, C. D. L. (1995). Reinforcement accounts for transitive inference performance. *Animal Learning & Behavior*, 23(2), 207–217.

Xu, F., Carey, S., & Welch, J. (1999). Infants' ability to use object kind information for object individuation. *Cognition*, 70(2), 137–166.

Younger, B. A. (1985). The segregation of items into categories by ten-month-old-infants. *Child Development*, 56, 1574–1583.

Younger, B. A. (1993). Understanding category members as "the same sort of thing": Explicit categorization in ten-month-old infants. *Child Development*, 64, 309–320.

Younger, B. A., & Fearing, D. D. (1999). Parsing items into separate categories: Developmental change in infant categorization. *Child Development*, 70, 291–303.

Yuan, S., & Fisher, C. (2009). "Really? She blicked the baby?" Two-year-olds learn combinatorial facts about verbs by listening. *Psychological Science*, 20(5), 619–626.

Zelazo, P. D., Muller, U., Frye, D., & Marcovitch, S. (2003). The development of executive function in early childhood. *Monographs of the Society for Research in Child Development*, 68(3), Serial No. 274.

Zentall, T. R. (2000). Symbolic representation by pigeons. *Current Directions in Psychological Science*, 9(4), 118–123. doi:10.1111/1467-8721.00074.

Zielinski, T. A., Goodwin, G. P., & Halford, G. S. (2010). Complexity of categorical syllogisms: An integration of two metrics. *European Journal of Cognitive Psychology*, 22(3), 391–421.

Name Index

Subject Index

A not-B error, 158–159, 179–183, 185, 187, 276, 287
  neural correlates, 187
Abduction, 49
Abstraction, 42
ACCESS, 191
Accessibility, 55–56, 65–66, 71, 74, 78, 81, 138–139, 142, 149, 155, 160, 162, 164, 170, 174, 212, 215, 217, 225, 267, 287
ACME, 68, 287
Acquisition processes, 177, 194, 203, 206, 213, 228
Action-related prediction, 27, 164
ACT-R, 4, 27, 287
Adaptation, 27
Adolescents, 139
Affirmation of the consequent, 238
African Grey parrot, 150
Alzheimer's disease, 87
Analog, 287
Analogical mapping, 70
Analogical reasoning, 16, 26, 35, 49, 58, 67–70, 74–75, 86, 160, 162, 164, 174, 200, 202, 204–205, 214, 223–225, 287, 294
  base/source/target, 67, 294
  semantic similarity effects, 221
  unary relational, 138
Analogy. See Analogical reasoning
Analytic process, 2, 6

Analyzing cognitive complexity. See Cognitive complexity
Animacy, 196, 287
Animal cognition, 149. See also names of animals
Animal communication, 33
Animal navigation, 33
Anterior cingulate, 85
Ape reasoning, 81. See also Bonobo; Chimpanzee; Orangutan
APFC, 84–85, 87, 207, 287
Arity, 30, 53, 95, 140
Arrow. See Morphism
Artificial grammar, 146–147, 195, 198
Association, 11, 14, 25, 38–42, 65–66, 140, 167, 173, 197, 207, 214, 252
Associative operator, 127
Atmosphere heuristic, 126
Attachment heuristic, 234
Attention, 287
Attribute renaming, 72, 74
Attributes of relations, 72
Autoencoding, 34, 43, 212
Automaticity, 32
Availability in memory, 48
Awareness, 139, 164. See also Consciousness

BA, 287
BA10, 83–86, 182, 187, 266
BA11, 87